Labor Justice across the Americas

THE WORKING CLASS IN AMERICAN HISTORY

Editorial Advisors

James R. Barrett, Julie Greene, William P. Jones, Alice Kessler-Harris, and Nelson Lichtenstein

A list of books in the series appears at the end of this book.

Labor Justice across the Americas

EDITED BY LEON FINK AND
JUAN MANUEL PALACIO

**UNIVERSITY OF
ILLINOIS PRESS**
Urbana, Chicago, and Springfield

Library of Congress Cataloging-in-Publication Data
Names: Fink, Leon, 1948– editor. | Palacio, Juan Manuel, editor.
Title: Labor justice across the Americas / edited by Leon Fink and Juan
    Manuel Palacio.
Description: Urbana: University of Illinois Press, 2017.
Series: The working class in American history
Includes bibliographical references and index.
Identifiers: LCCN 2017031826| ISBN 9780252041501 (cloth : alk. paper) |
    ISBN 9780252083068 (pbk. : alk. paper)
Subjects: LCSH: Labor laws and legislation—America.
Classification: LCC KDZ432 .L33 2017 | DDC 344.701—dc23 LC record
    available at https://lccn.loc.gov/2017031826

Contents

Acknowledgments

The inception of this book is closely linked to the Latin American Studies Association. The first exchanges about this project took place at the XXX LASA Congress in San Francisco in May 2012, at the panel, "*La conformación de la justicia laboral en América Latina: México, Brasil y Argentina*," which was organized by Juan Manuel Palacio and included two of the volume's authors, William Suarez-Potts and Fernando Teixeira da Silva as panelists. The resulting debates inspired subsequent discussions of the project over the following years. Incentive to give this project its final form and complete the team of collaborators—widening the scope of the initial project to include the United States and Canada—came out of a 2013 "Mellon-LASA Seminar" Grant. Receiving this grant allowed the authors to hold two workshops that were decisive for the materialization of this book. The first occurred in the XXXII LASA congress in Chicago in May 2014, on the panel, "*La conformación de la justicia del trabajo en las Américas*," in which almost all of the collaborators of this book took part; the second occurred the same year at the University of California, Los Angeles, in a gathering genially hosted by Angela Vergara. In these successive meetings we discussed the projects and then the early drafts of what today comprise the chapters of this book. In the extended review process (including translation) required for the preparation of the volume, the editors are particularly appreciative of the penultimate literary examination of the essays by Frank Luce.

Labor Justice across the Americas

Introduction

Labor Justice across the Americas

JUAN MANUEL PALACIO

The creation of specialized labor courts proved a landmark moment in the development of the legal system in the Americas and composed a central chapter in the process of state formation that occurred across the first half of the twentieth century. Whether considered a tool of co-optation and control of the labor movement and social conflict, a prized means of engendering political loyalty through pro-labor tribunals, a key instrument to apply a legislative program of social reform, or a mechanism for increased interference of the state in industrial relations, labor justice generated a privileged space in the relationship between state and society during the twentieth century. Yet, although the formation of labor courts was a decisive chapter in workers' history, it has nonetheless received uneven attention from historians.

This book begins to fill this lacuna with an ambitious proposal: to understand *how, when, and why* these specialized courts took shape in the Americas in the twentieth century. These questions build on some key facts as well as some assumptions. We know, for instance, that over the course of only a few decades, most countries in the Americas established labor courts for the first time, and that these courts demonstrated notable similarities in terms of their antecedents, the final forms they took in each country, the rhetoric in which they were grounded, their design, and even their names.

The assumptions can be summed up in a single fundamental suspicion: there exist a number of circumstances or processes that explain the appearance of these new institutions throughout the continent and at a particular moment in time. These processes are complex and can be located at the intersection of diverse phenomena, including the rise of the "social question" at the end of the nineteenth century, growing labor unrest, and the development of new ideas and the emergence of a reformist movement that encouraged labor legislation; all of these factors generated a climate of ideas favorable to social law and state intervention in industrial relations.

The goal of this book thus is twofold. First, it attempts to find common patterns in the fundamental coincidence of the appearance of the labor courts, without falling into determinism or oversimplification, which would elide the particularities of national cases (including their assorted juridical and political traditions). Second, it recognizes the singular and, at the same time, contingent character of these processes in each national context; that is, it addresses the complex set of situations, political circumstances, intellectual currents, and actions and interactions of different actors, which collectively explain the concrete forms that these institutions took in each country.

Labor Justice in Historiography

The subject of this volume lies at the intersection of two strong historiographical traditions, either of which could claim it as their own: labor history and legal history. Nonetheless, until now, neither has fully embraced the topic, and thus it has remained something of an abandoned child, left at a crossroads with no parental field granting it much notice, except in passing.

Legal historians, for their part, have been far more focused on other areas (criminal history or the colonial legal system to name two) and, at least outside the United States and Canada, have largely neglected the twentieth century. It comes as little surprise, then, that they have not paid significant attention to the rise of labor legislation and justice, which has thus remained in the hands of lawyers interested in history or in the pages of old legal histories. There are a few notable exceptions to this rule, but even in these cases—works that have specifically studied social and labor legislation of the twentieth century—the place granted labor justice has, until now, been rather marginal.[1] And although legal history has explored (and rather extensively made use of) the enormous potentialities of judicial sources—as a privileged lens into social conflict and as a site of encounter and confrontation between state and subaltern discourses—very few studies have taken advantage of available labor court records.[2]

For their part, too few labor historians have pursued the hypothesis advanced by William Fortbath in 1991 that the law has always been a central part of workers' daily life and an inherent part of their identity as such.[3] Although in this case the exceptions are more numerous, it continues to be true that "legalist" approaches to labor history are in the minority.[4] Among the works that do address this subject, those that draw attention to the importance of the labor courts for the worker experience (and above all, underline the watershed that these tribunals represented) are all the more exceptional. Rarer still are the attempts to offer comparative or transnational examinations of labor law.[5]

Another more recent line of historiographical inquiry that could lay claim to the subject of this volume is the history of the modern state and the formation of bureaucratic elites, which has recently become a prolific topic of study in some parts of the Americas.[6] Concentrating on the last decades of the nineteenth century and the first decades of the twentieth, this historiography has focused on the growth and transformation of the state and, in particular, the role that "expert" elite bureaucrats (doctors, economists, lawyers, and high state functionaries) held in the process, as well as the contradictions and complexities that guided state action and public policy. Nevertheless, this literature has not paid significant attention to the creation of labor courts, even though they introduced a new category of "expert functionaries," which included labor judges, court staff and aids (secretaries, experts, labor doctors), inspectors, statisticians, and mediators, among others.

This book seeks to adopt this historiographical orphan, with the hypothesis that the history of labor justice in the Americas can illuminate many unexplored aspects of these and other historiographical inquiries. The creation of these courts constituted one of the culminating points of the social reform movement, which began during the final throes of the nineteenth century and expanded at the dawn of the twentieth. The courts proved to be a key instrument for both the effective application of new labor laws and the containment of social conflict, as well as an important component of transformations in the state in the twentieth century and of the obstacles encountered in the wake of those changes. Moreover, they constituted an important site of encounter—an arena of dispute—between the state, business owners, and workers during the last century. For all of these motives, the unprecedented exploration proposed in this book promises to illuminate new realms of legal history, labor history, and the history of the state in the Americas during the twentieth century. Likewise, the book's comparative approach—of analyzing national cases as a counterpoint to the global processes that shaped them—will contribute to recent advances in transnational history, which has already made a significant impact on labor history in the Americas.[7]

Labor Justice across the Americas

This book takes up the considerable challenge of walking a fine line, balancing analysis of the general processes and the specific cases that describe them, the context and the particularities that call them into question, and the structure of the backdrop and the actions of specific actors. In so doing, the process of the creation of labor courts in the Americas underlines a few points of intersection, reflected in the subsequent chapters.

The idea of creating a specific jurisdiction to contend with labor conflicts was rooted in a shared social context during the final decades of the nineteenth century: the rise of what has been vaguely labeled "the social question." This term alludes to the appearance of the social costs of industrial development in the most developed countries—and those related to the formation of export economies based on the exploitation of natural resources, in haciendas, plantations, and mines in Latin America—as well as the emergence of an organized workers' movement and union activity at the beginning of the twentieth century. As will become evident in the sub-sequent chapters, the appearance of the first labor laws in the Americas (and the first ventures to form specific institutions to apply those laws) was inextricable from the wave of strikes and social protests that erupted across the continent during the first years of the twentieth century.

Another common experience that traversed national lines was the formation of what might be called a "climate of ideas" that was favorable to social law. In effect, a context of social urgency allowed a series of more dated ideas to reemerge in public debates, in particular, regarding the exploitation of workers by capital and the need to limit or alleviate that exploitation via regulation. Nonetheless, this shared set of ideas did not imply a uniform ideology or philosophical alignment. Among the cham-pions of this debate across the Americas were a very heterogeneous group of social reformers (intellectuals, politicians, jurists, academics, religious and social leaders) that hailed from several backgrounds—Socialist, Catholic, Revolutionary Marxism, and Progressive Liberalism. In juridical language, these old ideas were now expressed in terms of the essential inequality inherent in labor relations and the need to cre-ate regulations that would protect the weaker party and reestablish the balance of power in the labor contract. In this way, labor law emerged in the Western world as an autonomous discipline.

In the development of this climate of ideas, and in its materialization as a con-crete legislative program, the actions of academic and intellectual groups linked to the political world (often directly, as government functionaries, diplomats, or par-liamentarians) were key. These actors promoted and helped to advance the social legislation program in each of their countries. They also created an international academic-political-diplomatic network, which took shape at the beginning of the twentieth century and made a more or less concerted effort to decisively influence the state action on the matter. Many of these individuals also played a key role in the creation and subsequent actions of the International Labor Organization, created in 1919 after the First World War.

Not surprisingly, the more or less coordinated efforts of this network of social reformers resulted in the appearance, across the continent, of similar laws and insti-tutions designed to study the labor situation, protect the most vulnerable, inspect workplaces, and address social conflict. Beyond specific laws and state institutions, many countries also formed more ambitious legislative projects, such as labor codes and constitutional reforms of a social character. Finally, most deemed it necessary to create a specific jurisdiction to address labor conflicts, although the format, reach, and institutional configurations of the new courts were varied.

A SHARED CHRONOLOGY

Another point of relative correlation was the chronology of this process. The final formation of the labor courts in the Americas occurred in almost all of the countries during the second third of the twentieth century, but all of the national cases analyzed here also exhibit a common earlier period, during the second and third decade of the century, when the first experiments with these courts took place. During this "early moment," which coincides with the emergence of the social question on the continent, most countries passed the first labor laws and created the first departments or state institutes of labor. These departments studied the social question (by collecting labor and economic data, for example) and inspected and regulated working conditions. During these years, the first conciliation and arbitration boards were founded in almost all of the countries. Politically, most of these changes occurred during liberal-conservative governments of a "progressive" color, although in several cases they occurred under democratic or republican regimes (United States, Canada, Bolivia, Argentina, Colombia, Costa Rica) and, in others, under military (Chile, Ecuador), authoritarian (Peru), or revolutionary (Mexico) governments.

A new global scenario shaped the second period: the Great Depression, World War II, the rise of interventionist states, and a renewed social question that emerged as a consequence of the growing concentration and organization of workers in industrial cities. This period witnessed a renovation and strengthening of all regulatory labor institutions: states passed broader laws that were more inclusive and created more state dependencies that were larger and had greater reach, amid a context in which states demonstrated a greater willingness for efficient regulation. During these years, the labor courts also adopted their definitive form and, for the most part, they acquired significant power and scope (with expanded jurisdictions and greater geographic coverage). In most cases, they professionalized and—with clear exceptions in the United States, Canada, and Mexico—acquired permanent status within the judiciary as a separate branch and at the same hierarchical level as civil or criminal courts. As in the earlier period, the national political contexts in which these changes occurred were not homogenous. They occurred during populist-corporatist regimes (Argentina, Brazil, Costa Rica, and to a certain extent, Peru) and revolutionary governments (Mexico), as well as during progressive military (Ecuador), "socialist" military (Bolivia), liberal progressive (Canada, United States, Colombia), and social-democratic (Chile) administrations.

After these foundational moments, which encompassed the entire first half of the twentieth century, the path of the courts was also varied. Although not all of the chapters in the book focus on this more contemporary period, we know that in some countries the new courts continued to consolidate and strengthen their role in the judicial system (as in Argentina, Bolivia, or Costa Rica), sometimes increasing it (as in the case of Brazil) and, in other cases, losing relevance (as in the United States, where they had been more of an exceptional institution created during the Depression and World War II). However, with the exception of Chile, where they were suppressed during Pinochet's dictatorship, labor courts became a lasting institution across the continent, surviving a number of challenges, including some that proved quite insidious during the neoliberal period at the end of the twentieth century.

QUESTIONS OF DESIGN: A MENU OF OPTIONS

Another commonality among the labor courts of the Americas was their design. These tribunals did not exhibit the same format in every country—in fact they were quite varied—but they all took form within a shared "menu of options" made available through the transnational experience of the era.

In effect, there was a common spirit or philosophy behind the new courts. They were designed to safeguard the substantive principles of labor law, which were geared toward counterbalancing the inequalities inherent in the labor contract by protecting the weaker party. Besides that founding and underlying assumption, the principles were elaborated through the concepts of the *nonwaiver* provision (no worker can give up a right granted by law), the presumption of continuity of the employment contract, the primacy of reality (in case of discrepancy between documents and facts, facts are to be privileged), *in dubbio pro operario* (in dubious cases, workers' claims have priority), and labor union autonomy.[8] Moreover, in most cases, these courts shared some common procedural principles, such as orality, propinquity, conciliation, and being gratuitous and expeditious. But to share these common traits did not signify a clear consensus over some important issues, like, for example, who (which actors and with what qualifications) would administer the courts, what type of conflicts (and what type of workers) would be heard, or whether rulings would become final or whether there existed the possibility of appeal to other courts or powers. Each country's reformers and legislators' answers to these questions shaped the different systems adopted across the Americas.

The first issue was whether the courts would be based on a conciliatory system (in which the final objective was either the conciliation of the parties or, alternatively, submitting the conflict to arbitration of peers) or a trial (in which the conflict was entrusted to the consideration and sanction of a judge). At first, most countries experimented with diverse forms of conciliation procedures, creating corporate or "classist" courts (generally tripartite, with representation from employers, workers, and the state), but only a few ultimately opted for this model (Mexico, Brazil, and the United States, although, in the latter case, the "Wagner boards" are ultimately subject to review by the courts). The other countries opted for a trial model, with courts at the charge of professional judges, either individual or collegiate. Still, some, like that of Argentina or Costa Rica, continued to use conciliatory procedures for the first stages of the process.

A second question faced by reformers was whether the courts would address collective actions (for example, demands for union recognition, the legality of strikes, or collective bargaining agreements), individual conflicts (disputes regarding the application of the labor law, e.g., worker's compensation lawsuits), or both. Here, we also observe considerable variety, with some countries reserving labor courts for collective bargaining conflicts (USA), others only for individual conflicts (Argentina), and others for both (Mexico, Chile, Costa Rica). Finally, a few countries opted to create a different court for each type of conflict (Canada and Brazil).

A third question was in which realm of the state the new courts would reside. The basic options were the executive branch, departments or ministries of labor (as occurred in the majority of countries at the beginning of this process and was ultimately the option selected by Mexico and the United States), or the judiciary, where the courts would become a new branch on an equal plane as the civil or criminal system. Several countries chose this second option from the beginning (Argentina, Colombia) while others chose it after first operating the courts from within the executive branch (Brazil, Chile).

The final major question centered on the workers whose claims would be heard: would these courts be available to all workers in the country, or only some? (And if so, to whom?) Although the majority of reformers proposed universal access, the essays in this book demonstrate that, in practice, many countries placed either de facto or de jure restrictions on this principle. Thus, for a considerable period of time, national labor laws applied only to industrial workers and not to rural agricultural workers (in most cases), to the private sector and not to public sector employees (United States, Mexico, Costa Rica), to unionized workers or others engaged in concerted activity and not to individual laborers (United States, Canada), to whites and not to indigenous workers (Bolivia), and to formal employees and not to domestic service or informal sector employees (as in the majority of countries, until recently).

ENEMIES AND OBSTACLES

Another common vein in this history is that the process of forming labor courts was neither quick nor simple in any country. On the contrary, all of the cases analyzed here show that efforts to establish these courts entailed overcoming various obstacles—obstacles that in some cases delayed the project and in other cases completely transformed their original design. The courts also had to endure attacks after their creation. These complications sometimes came from concrete actors (politicians, judges, business owners), other times from institutional systems, and occasionally from intangibles, like a nation's legal and political culture.

Among labor courts' most prominent enemies were employers (industrial, *hacienda* owners, miners) and their spokespersons, generally powerful lawyers from the establishment. As will become evident in the following chapters, these actors deployed diverse strategies: first, to delay or impede the approval of laws, and later, to block or obstruct the functioning of the new courts. Conservative politicians, who had a greater propensity to promote repressive policies toward workers' movements and unions, also created difficult hurdles for the process of legal reform. Less evident, but nonetheless powerful, were the different objections that arose from within the judicial system—as can be seen in the cases of Argentina, Brazil, and Mexico—or the overall resistance of the judicial branch to state intervention in labor conflicts—as seen in the United States. These were reflections of the views of a conservative judicial establishment that disputed the necessity of a special jurisdiction dedicated to the labor question and did not believe in the aptitude of the nonprofessional and corporative courts. Finally, although it would seem paradoxical, workers themselves sometimes rejected the creation of the new courts or distrusted the state's intervention in industrial relations, as can be seen in the Canadian and U.S. cases. These groups feared that state intervention would prove more damaging than helpful in their battles with the industrial sector.

The obstacles that stemmed from the institutional system were rooted in the constitutional design of most of the countries in the region (which were based on the French and U.S. models) and in two fundamental ideas in particular—federalism and the separation of powers. The first established that labor law fell to provincial jurisdiction—an obstacle to any effort to create a national system of labor regulation, as most reformers intended to do. The second put serious limits on the effectiveness of the new courts (e.g., their sanctioning power), particularly if the courts were housed in the executive branch.

Finally, a more intangible obstacle to the creation of labor courts was the political culture prevalent in some parts of the region—in particular in those countries (like the United States and Canada) that came from a liberal tradition that did not look fondly on the state's meddling in industrial relations. Unlike in most of the Latin American countries, this culture translated to a less benevolent vision of the state and its regulations that, as has been noted, meant that at times workers themselves voiced a preference for noninterference of the state.

REACH AND LIMITATIONS

This book only begins to touch on the courts' achievements after their founding—a topic that surely deserves its own volume and further attention and research. Nevertheless, the works included here permit us to make a few conclusions that show a varied trajectory with a few points of correlation.

First, these cases demonstrate a significant disparity between the good intentions behind the creation of the labor courts (and the other state offices created to regulate labor law) and their use in practice—a gap particularly notable during the first period of our chronology. Early courts had to confront every kind of impediment, from poor financing and limited personnel to legal and constitutional limitations (and judicial reversals) in the course of their operation; they had to navigate very effective procedural obfuscations put in place by employers' lawyers that limited their power of sanction. As a result, the new courts had a narrow territorial reach (there were few courts and they were located only in the largest cities and thus did not cover rural areas) and were not accessible to most workers. In some cases, they were also limited by law to hear only certain kinds of conflicts (for example, worker's compensation, in Bolivia, Costa Rica, and Chile), or serve only industrial and urban laborers (as in

Argentina, Brazil, and Bolivia) or only white workers, as was the case in the Andean countries. Other important roadblocks included resistance on the part of the judiciary to confirm sentences for labor court decisions (in particular if the courts were in the executive), something evident in cases of Mexico and Argentina. Some states also resisted a national system of applied labor law, as can be clearly seen in the Canadian case.

These cases also demonstrate that this disparity between intention and practice narrowed during the second period. A renewed sense of urgency, spurred by workers' demands during the Great Depression and wartime pressure on states to regulate industrial relations, generated a greater willingness on the part of governments to intervene in labor matters. Thus, the institutions charged with the task of imparting labor justice became better financed, were granted more (professional) personnel, and became more numerous, thus expanding across national territories. Legal barriers that once restricted the courts' ability to take action were also lifted, permitting them to reach a greater number of workers (notably, rural laborers). Hostility against the tribunals lessened, particularly within the judicial system, when the courts were moved from the executive branch to the judiciary. The geographic reach of the labor justice system also advanced considerably during these years, overcoming many of the obstacles that constitutional limitations once imposed (i.e., by creating provincial courts).

However, although it is true that this disparity between intentions and practice narrowed, the gap was never completely closed. The chapters in this volume that analyze this question and other existing work on the subject both suggest that many of the original juridical principles and intentions behind the labor courts were never realized—not merely because of challenges posed by powerful sectors, but often due to the courts' own performance. Issues like slow processes—due to a backlog of cases or bureaucratic inefficiencies—put the principle of expeditious trials at risk—a principle that was supposed to be a distinguishing trait of these courts. This sluggishness, alongside workers' urgency to find economic reparations for their demands, pushed plaintiffs to make settlements against their interests, for sums far smaller than those they demanded. The prevalence of these situations was such that, in several countries, some perceived the labor courts as a place for "justice at a discount." This betrayed the original spirit of conciliation, which far from being the central purpose of the judicial intervention, had become the currency of exchange for employers, in the face of an interminable trial.

In most countries, these and other deficiencies (analyzed in several chapters) did not stop workers from continuing to entrust the labor courts with their complaints against their employers, nor did it stop them from hoping for a just solution to their demands (or at least some sort of acceptable reparation). This is observable in the sustained (and in some cases growing) number of lawsuits presented to the courts through time—as is apparent in the cases of Brazil or Costa Rica analyzed in this book—and workers' untiring search for justice in those spaces today.

The Book

This volume begins with a chapter that is intended to serve as a guide for understanding the social context and intellectual debates that informed the creation of labor courts both in Europe and in the Americas. In grounding this history in an Atlantic-wide intellectual-historical narrative, Juan Manuel Palacio points to the common traditions that the countries in this study share. The chapter takes a comparative and transnational perspective rather than simply listing a number of parallel or coincidental events that occurred simultaneously across the region. For instance, the chapter describes the pioneering and coordinating network that came out of the International Labor Organization (ILO), established in Geneva in 1919. This network, to one degree or another, influenced legal scholarship and policy making in many of the countries discussed in this book. Similarly, other academic precursors and parallel endeavors, and their transnational encounters and exchanges, are detailed.

Chapter 1 also serves as a starting point for the subsequent discussions of each national case in the remaining chapters, which are grouped by region. These studies are not meant to be exhaustive; rather, they are intended to be representative of different geographic and human milieus (location, linguistic and ethnic configuration), as well as different cultural, political, and legal traditions. The chapters do not adhere to a common script, and although they each offer basic informative elements that reflect the overarching focus of the book (examining "how, when, and why" the labor courts were formed, or their basic design), the authors do so by paying attention to the particularities and unique contexts of their cases and by choosing what elements to emphasize and which key factors they consider most important to understanding the process of the creation of labor courts in their specific country context (e.g., some choose to emphasize political debates, others focus on the ethnic composition of the population, institutional evolution, or workers' and union movement).

In Chapter 2, Leon Fink analyzes the debate that arose in the United States around the prospect of creating a labor jurisdiction—something that never truly materialized. He shows how this debate became subsumed in another broader discussion of collective bargaining, the recognition of unions, and the role of the state in those relations. The chapter surveys the evolution of industrial relations in the United States from the end of the nineteenth century to the passage of the *National Labor Relations Act of 1935* and its amendment by the *Taft-Hartley Act of 1947*. The chapter examines why "the American Way" did not ultimately adhere to any of the models that the reformers had on hand (the arbitration system in Great Britain and Australasia, with different grades of state interference) but rather developed what the author calls a "juridically regulated system of collective laissez-faire" that was only modified during exceptional periods of severe economic crisis and world war.

In Chapter 3, Frank Luce describes labor laws and justice in Canada during the first half of the twentieth century as a system marked by fragmentation. In addition to having different labor tribunals for collective and individual suits and for public and private sector workers, and specific courts for the application of certain laws, each province also possessed its own judicial system, a product of the federalist structure of the Canadian constitution. Although such fragmentation is a formidable obstacle to a complete (or succinct) description of the history of labor courts in Canada, the chapter successively does both, taking collective bargaining conflicts and the case of the province of Ontario (and including a final section on individual suits) as a counterpoint to the process at the national level. The chapter thus describes how the system evolved from the first conciliation boards formed during the first decade of the twentieth century to the adoption of a modified *Wagner Act* model at the end of World War II, using the relationship between the union movement, the business sector, and the state as a key narrative.

Although Mexico shares geographic proximity with the United States and Canada, its experience was quite different. There, labor courts were the descendants of the 1910 Mexican Revolution and its contemporaneous ideology, expressed in its 1917 social constitution, the first of its kind in the Western World. In Chapter 4, William Suarez-Potts describes the formation of mechanisms to resolve collective conflicts and individual disputes, along with the establishment of administrative labor boards as alternatives to the civil judiciary, in connection with both international experiments and legislative programs and the revolutionary events of 1910–1917. Events through the 1920s, a period of marked social struggle and institutional development, are also summarized. The conclusion assesses the enactment of comprehensive federal labor legislation in 1931, which included the regulation of labor boards and their scope of activity among its aims.

In Chapter 5, Ronny Viales-Hurtado and David Díaz-Arias examine the evolution of labor institutions in Costa Rica over the long term, from the country's independence in 1821 until the present. After locating the distant origins of labor laws in early independence-era institutions and the civil code of the 1880s, the authors concentrate on the populist movement that gave way to the 1943 labor code and the creation of a system of labor justice in that country. The chapter thus analyzes the peculiar political context (the alliance between the Communist Party, the Church, and the workers) that made profound social reform possible during the government of Calderón Guardia. The final section analyzes the changes in said system from the Civil War in 1948 to the present.

In Chapter 6, Victor Uribe-Uran with Germán Palacio analyze the long history of the creation of the Colombian labor courts, from the first articulations of social laws in the middle of the nineteenth century until 1950. After locating the remote origins of these courts in the colonial period (in ecclesiastical, military courts, and commercial tribunals), the authors trace the country's first "labor laws" back to the compensation and "patriotic" pensions that independence and Civil War veterans fought for during the nineteenth century. The rest of the chapter analyzes how the conception of Colombia's protective labor institutions (including the courts) during the conservative and liberal governments from the 1920s to 1950 advanced as a steady counterpoint to the strikes and protests of organized workers who demanded new labor rights.

In Chapter 7, Rossana Barragán Romano addresses three major themes in her comparative study of the Andean nations (Peru, Ecuador, and Bolivia), all of which have large indigenous populations: the definition of "the worker" and the relationship between workers and indigenous populations, labor legislation adopted in each of the three countries, and the creation of labor courts and their operation, with special emphasis on Bolivia. The chapter traces the legal evolution of labor law in these three countries using two common analytical frames: first, by discussing the inclusion or exclusion of the majority indigenous population as beneficiaries of the new labor legislation; second, by examining the evolution of legislation and labor justice (labor courts, constitutional reforms) in these countries in light of the climate of ideas of social constitutionalism in the twentieth century, and, in particular, the actions taken by the ILO and its advisers in Latin America.

In Chapter 8, Juan Manuel Palacio analyzes the formation of labor courts in Argentina as a process inextricable from the political strategy and plans of Juan Domingo Perón, beginning the moment he rose to office as the secretary of labor in 1943. Nevertheless, the first part of the chapter delves into the decades preceding this event. It describes how social law doctrine began to gain adherents in academia and among intellectuals and political leaders at the beginning of the twentieth century, as well as the initial experiments with a labor jurisdiction that preceded the creation of the labor courts. The chapter then centers on the Peronist era (1943–1955) and analyzes the particularly contentious manner in which the new tribunals came into existence, amid extreme political polarization and strong resistance not only from employers, but also from politicians, provincial governments, and the judiciary.

In Chapter 9, Angela de Castro Gomez and Fernando Teixeira da Silva analyze the origins of labor justice in Brazil, beginning with the rise of Getúlio Vargas in national politics in 1930. The chapter first examines existing theories regarding the supposedly fascist origins of the institution in Brazil, and then propose that the courts' design drew from a more diverse array of inspirations, including Western judicial history and the corporatist state framework in Brazil. The chapter then details the evolution of the courts, beginning with their initial formation in 1941, tracing their survival amid attacks from diverse business and political fronts, and studying key aspects of their expansion and empowerment into the present day. Finally, by using available statistical data, the authors are able to evaluate the courts' performance since their founding and examine workers' increasing use of the courts as they became more evenly spread across the country.

In the final case study, Diego Ortúzar and Angela Vergara take a similar interest in investigating the ways in which labor courts functioned, this time in Chile. By using court data and a significant number of concrete trial records, the authors offer a vivid image of workers' experience as they made use of the new courts (or—in their words—how the workers "navigated" the new judicial system). From this perspective, the chapter describes the trajectory of the new labor courts in Chile, beginning with the first tripartite conciliation and arbitration boards in the 1920s, their transformation into professional courts in the judicial branch during the 1940s and 1950s, and, finally, their dissolution during the military government of Augusto Pinochet.

Finally, in his concluding commentary, Leon Fink assesses the state of "labor justice studies across the Americas" with an eye toward needed future work in the field. A few questions appear paramount: Did the developed systems of state mediation and arbitration of disputes and grievances prove, on balance, "progressive" or "regressive" for worker welfare and larger national democratic development? How, in general, did workers and their trade unions react to these quasi-legal institutions? What forces have defined either the success and evolution or failure and decline of the labor-justice project? Finally, can one speak of the diverse stratagems and variety of institutional forms described in these chapters under a common analytical umbrella or are they superficially comparable phenomena? In particular, does the concept of *corporatism* deserve renewed emphasis in our discussion of hemispheric-wide political economy?

Notes

1. Several of the scholars who have made labor law, specifically, a central theme of their work are collaborators in this volume. See Suarez-Potts, *The Making*; De Castro Gomes and Teixeira da Silva, *A Justiça do Trabalho*; Palacio, "Legislación" and "El grito"; Luce, "Rural Workers." Also see Fudge and Tucker, *Labour before*; Hunold Lara and Mendonça, *Direitos*; Grez, "Autonomía."

2. Beyond the cited collaborators on this project, recent Brazilian historiography has proved to be a relevant exception. An important nucleus of Brazilian scholars has been working with labor court records for some time. See, for example, Fortes, *Nos do Quarto*; Correa, *A tessitura*; Marques Mendes, *Clase Trabalhadora*; Varusa, *Trabalho e legislação*.

3. Forbath, *Law*.

4. Christopher Tomlins, *The State and the Unions*; Craven, "Canada." Among the Latin Americanists, see John French, *Drowning*; Meyers, *Mexican*; Drinot, *The Allure*; Bortz, *Revolution*; Middelbrook, *The Paradox*; De Castro Gomes, *Burguesia*; Rojas and Moncayo, *Luchas*; Lobato and Suriano, *La sociedad*.

5. A short list of recent, notable contributions to Americanist legal labor history, albeit all with a single-nation focus, includes Atleson, *Labor and the Wartime State*; Casebeer, *American Labor Struggles*; Gross, *Broken Promise*; Orren, *Belated Feudalism*; Tomlins, *The State and the Unions*; and Vinel, *The Employee*. A rare transnational exception is Stone, *Rethinking Comparative Labor Law*.

6. With origins in the social sciences (e.g., in Evans et al., *Bringing*; and, especially, Rueschemeyer and Skocpol, *States*; Skowronek, *Building*), this subject was picked up most recently in some Latin American historiographies. See Plotkin and Zimmermann, *Los saberes*; Campos Coelho, *As Profissoes*; Babb, *Managing*. A special thanks to Eduardo Zimmermann for these references.

7. Fink, *Workers*; Van Daele et al., *Essays*; Herrera and Herrera, *América Latina*; Friedman and Pérez-Perdomo, *Legal Culture*; Charle et al., *Transnational*; Rodgers, *Atlantic Crossings*.

8. Plá Rodríguez, *Principios*.

Bibliography

Atleson, James B. *Labor and the Wartime State: Labor Relations and Law during World War II*. Urbana: University of Illinois Press, 1998.

Babb, Sarah L. *Managing Mexico: Economists from Nationalism to Neoliberalism*. Princeton, N.J.: Princeton University Press, 2001.

Bortz, Jeffrey. *Revolution within the Revolution: Cotton Textile Workers and the Mexican Labor Regime, 1910–1923*. Stanford, Calif.: Stanford University Press, 2008.

Campos Coelho, Edmundo. *As Profissoes Imperiais. Medicina, Engenharia e Advocacia no Rio de Janeiro 1827–1930*. Rio de Janeiro: Editora Record, 1999.

Casebeer, Kenneth M., ed. *American Labor Struggles and Case Histories*. Durham, N.C.: Carolina Academic Press, 2011.

Charle, Christophe, Jürgen Schriewer, and Peter Wagner, eds. *Transnational Intellectual Networks: Forms of Academic Knowledge and the Search for Cultural Identities*. Frankfurt: Campus, 2004.

Corrêa, Larissa R. *A tessitura dos direitos: patrões e empregados na Justiça do Trabalho, 1953 a 1964*. São Paulo: LTr, 2011.

Craven, Paul. "Canada, 1670–1935: Symbolic and Instrumental Enforcement in Loyalist North America," in *Masters, Servants, and Magistrates in Britain and the Empire, 1562–1955*, ed. Douglas Hay and Paul Craven. Chapel Hill: University of North Carolina Press, 2004.

De Castro Gomes, Angela Maria. *Burguesia e Trabalho. Política e liegislaçao social no Brasil 1917–1937*. Rio de Janeiro: Editora Campus Ltda., 1979.

De Castro Gomes, Angela, and Fernando Teixeira da Silva, eds. *A Justiça do Trabalho e sua história: os direitos dos trabalhadores no Brasil*. Campinas: Editora da Unicamp, 2013.

Drinot, Paulo. *The Allure of Labor: Workers Race and the Making of the Peruvian State*. Durham, N.C.: Duke University Press, 2011.

Evans, Peter, Dietrich Rueschemeyer, and Theda Skocpol, eds. *Bringing the State Back In*. New York: Cambridge University Press, 1985.

Fink, Leon, ed. *Workers across the Americas. The Transnational Turn in Labor History*. Oxford: Oxford University Press, 2011.

Forbath, William E. *Law and the Shaping of the American Labor Movement*. Cambridge, Mass.: Harvard University Press, 1991.

Fortes, Alexandre. *Nós do Quarto Distrito. A classe trabalhadora porto-alegrense e a era Vargas*. Rio de Janeiro: EDUCS, 2004.

French, John D. *Drowning in Laws: Labor Law and Political Culture in Brazil*. Chapel Hill: University of North Carolina Press, 2004.

Friedman, Lawrence, and Rogelio Pérez-Perdomo. *Legal Culture in the Age of Globalization. Latin America and Europe*. Stanford, Calif.: Stanford University Press, 2003.

Fudge, Judy, and Eric Tucker. *Labour before the Law: The Regulation of Workers' Collective Action in Canada, 1900–1948*. Toronto: Oxford University Press Canada, 2001.

Grez, Sergio. "¿Autonomía o escudo protector? El movimiento obrero popular y los mecanismos de conciliación y arbitraje." *Historia* 35 (2002): 81–150.

Gross, James A. *Broken Promise: The Subversion of American Labor Relations Policy, 1947–1994*. Philadelphia: Temple University Press, 1996.

Herrera, Fabián, and Patricio Herrera, eds. *América Latina y la Organización Internacional del Trabajo. Redes, cooperación técnica e institucionalidad social, 1919–1950*. Michoacán: Instituto de Investigaciones Históricas, 2013.

Hunold Lara, Silvia, and Joseli Maria N. Mendonça, eds. *Direitos e justiça no Brasil: ensaios de história social*. Campinas: Editora da Unicamp, 2006.

Lobato, Mirta Zaida, and Juan Suriano, eds. *La sociedad del trabajo. Las instituciones laborales en la Argentina (1900–1955)*. Buenos Aires: Edhasa, 2013.

Luce, Frank. *Rural Workers and Labour Justice: The Estatuto do Trabalhador Rural in Brazil's Cacao Region, 1963 to 1973*. PhD diss., Osgoode Hall Law School of York University, 2009.

Marques Mendes, Alexandre. *Clase Trabalhadora e Justiça do Trabalho: experiencias, atitudes e expresoes do opérario do calçado*. PhD diss., Universidad Estadual Paulista, 2005.

Meyers, Frederic. *Mexican Industrial Relations from the Perspective of the Labor Court*. Los Angeles: Institute of Industrial Relations, University of California, 1979.

Middlebrook, Kevin J. *The Paradox of Revolution: Labor, the State, and Authoritarianism in Mexico*. Baltimore: Johns Hopkins University Press, 1995.

Orren, Karen. *Belated Feudalism: Labor, the Law, and Liberal Development in the United States*. New York: Cambridge University Press, 1991.

Palacio, Juan Manuel. "Legislación y justicia laboral en el populismo clásico latinoamericano: elementos para la construcción de una agenda de investigación comparada." *Mundos do Trabalho* 3:5 (Jan.–June 2011): 245–265.

———. "El grito en el cielo. La polémica gestación de los tribunales del trabajo en la Argentina." *Estudios Sociales* 48 (2015): 59–90.

Plá Rodríguez, Américo. *Principios de derecho del trabajo*. Buenos Aires: Depalma, 1978.

Plotkin, Mariano, and Eduardo Zimmermann, eds. *Los saberes del estado*. Buenos Aires: Edhasa, 2012.

Rodgers, Daniel T. *Atlantic Crossings: Social Politics in a Progressive Age*. Cambridge, Mass.: Harvard University Press, 1998.

Rojas, Fernando, and Víctor Manuel Moncayo. *Luchas obreras y política laboral en Colombia*. Bogotá: La Carreta, 1978.

Rueschemeyer, Dietrich, and Theda Skocpol, eds. *States, Social Knowledge and the Origins of Modern Social Policy*. Princeton, N.J.: Princeton University Press, 1996.

Skowronek, Stephen. *Building a New American State: The Expansion of National Administrative Capacities, 1877–1920*. New York: Cambridge University Press, 1982.

Stone, Katherine V. W., with Benjamin Aaron, eds. *Rethinking Comparative Labor Law: Bridging the Past and the Future*. Lake Mary, Fla.: Vandeplas publishing, 2007.

Suarez-Potts, William. *The Making of Law. The Supreme Court and Labor Legislation in Mexico, 1875–1931*. Stanford, Calif.: Stanford University Press, 2012.

Tomlins, Christopher. *The State and the Unions: Labor Relations, and the Organized Labor Movement in America, 1880–1960*. Cambridge: Cambridge University Press, 1985.

Van Daele, Jasmien, et al. *Essays on the International Labour Organization and Its Impact on the World during the Twentieth Century*. Bern: Peter Lang, 2010.

Varusa, Rinaldo J. *Trabalho e legislação: experiências de trabalhadores na Justiça do Trabalho (Jundiaí—SP, décadas de 40 a 60)*. PhD diss., Pontifícia Universidade Católica/Sao Paulo, 2002.

Vinel, Jean-Christian. *The Employee: A Political History*. Philadelphia: University of Pennsylvania Press, 2013.

CHAPTER 1

From Social Legislation to Labor Justice

The Common Background in the Americas

JUAN MANUEL PALACIO

During the first half of the twentieth century, one of the most important transformations in the contemporary legal history of the Western world took place: the emergence of social legislation and state regulation of the world of labor. This event occurred at the intersection of complex and diverse social, economic, and political processes: the emergence of the social question, the successive catastrophes of the First and Second World Wars, the capitalist crisis in 1930, the increased prominence of workers, the advent of new ideas and their circulation and "transplantation" in other latitudes, and the appearance of key actors and new national and international institutions. All of these factors contributed to the creation of a new "climate of ideas" that favored social law and heralded a prevailing sense of necessity for state intervention in labor relations.

A more-or-less parallel trajectory of events occurred on either side of the Atlantic. The passage of the first protective labor laws and state regulatory agencies were followed by efforts to draft labor codes, produce social constitutional reforms, and create specialized courts to enforce the law. This progression varied slightly across countries, but the many similarities, including their timing, institutions bearing similar names, and the prominence of similar actors, suggest a common pattern. This chapter attempts to serve as a guide or preliminary exploration of the transnational process by which labor law took form in the Americas and the role of specialized labor courts in that process.

The chapter first locates the roots (philosophical, conceptual) of the idea of labor law as an autonomous branch of law and trace its first institutional applications in Europe. Second, it reviews the parallel process of the development of labor law in the Americas: the initial appearance of laws and codes, the reformist moment during the first decades of the century, decisive social action in subsequent decades, and, finally, the emergence and evolution of specialized courts. Third, it analyzes how the circulation of ideas created international networks that were pivotal in the consolidation of labor law in the Western world during the early twentieth century.

The Rise of Labor Law in Europe

NEW IDEAS IN THE OLD WORLD

The idea that the worker or servant should be protected from exploitation is an age-old concept that can be traced back to Greek philosophy and the Bible. Nevertheless, it was only during the final decades of the nineteenth century, when the industrial revolution revealed its "social evils" and organized labor started to defy the new capitalist system, that labor regulation became a transformative legal project. It was then that new legislative efforts sought to apply standards of social and public law to labor relations in existing legal codes.

The revolutionaries of 1789 (and 1776–1787), the founders of European socialism, and the pioneers of Christian social thought all supported ideas such as the right to employment, limits on property rights, or the need for some state intervention to protect workers from employer exploitation. These ideas, which were revitalized when the so-called "social question" arose during the final decades of the nineteenth century, were expressed as criticisms of the liberal order, sanctioned in constitutions modeled on the Napoleonic Code of 1804. Critics charged that these legal systems were no longer suitable to the new social order. They contended that individualism, liberty, and property were not absolute values, and that the idea that the pursuit of individual interest resulted in collective welfare (the basis of laissez-faire) had been proven erroneous or, at least, should no longer guide the social and political order.

To further confront the standing liberal orthodox principles, reformers proposed alternatives. Arguing that the pursuit of individual interests was not conducive to the general welfare because it generated deficiencies and injustices, they proposed that freedom should be limited for the broader interest of society. For the same reasons, they argued that the right to private property, one of the most privileged forms of exercising freedom, should not be absolute but limited according to its social utility. Finally, as laissez-faire principles had enabled the powerful to engage in all types of abuse against the weakest members of society, it was necessary for the state to exercise some sort of supervision over these unequal relations.

The first labor reformers expressed these ideas by proposing that existing civil and private laws were insufficient to confront the new social reality. Thus, they advocated for a special legal framework that would address existing social problems and protect workers. This special law would consider employment relationships to be unlike other contracts (e.g., a lease). Given the unequal nature of the parties involved, employment contracts would henceforth not be modeled after a lease (which supposed an agreement among equals) but rather would be considered a dependent and subordinate relationship. Accepting that premise, the essential task of labor law was to regulate the relationship of subordination by protecting the weaker party. Under this framework, it was necessary to first protect the most vulnerable—women, children, the elderly—and then, more generally, to protect workers from job hazards, limit the number of working hours, secure weekly rest, prevent abuses in wage payments, compensate for work-related accidents and diseases, prevent unemployment and contract termination, and facilitate workers' organization and association. These became the central issues of labor law at the turn of the century.

Representatives of diverse ideologies (including Utopian Socialists, Catholics, Anarchists, Liberal Reformists, Revolutionary Marxists, and Positivists) mutually affirmed these ideas; differences surfaced only when it came time to devise solutions.[1] Socialists proposed a collectivist solution for property and argued for varying degrees of state intervention (e.g., Lasalle or Louis Blanc sought greater intervention, while others were more inclined to rely on private negotiations between unions and employers), Anarchists suggested a revolutionary stateless path, while countries in the *common law* tradition trusted in the system of "collective *laissez-faire.*" Meanwhile, the Church proposed Christian solidarity and the protection of the worker by the state, while also defending private property.

In effect, the so-called Social Doctrine of the Church also concurred with these proposals. Along with socialism, this powerful current of thought inspired social legislation in Europe at the end of the century. The reformist thought and action of nineteenth century Social Catholicism was properly summarized in its founding document, the *Rerum Novarum* encyclical (1891), authored by Pope Leo XIII.[2] The document conjured social Catholicism as a "third way" between socialism and liberalism but proposed insignificant differences when it came to solutions. It highlighted the uneven nature of the employment contract and the state's responsibility to protect the weaker party. It called for a fair wage, Sunday rest, reduced working hours, and limits on women's and children's labor. The encyclical also heralded Catholic workers' associations as a space of solidarity, deterrence, and conflict resolution.[3]

In the final decades of the nineteenth century, a number of jurists synthesized these ideas into treatises that became classic texts in labor law. Scholars disagree as to who authored the first texts that inspired labor law. South African trade unionist and labor law expert Bob Hepple argues that German scholars are the forefathers of the discipline in Europe. In particular, he has called Philipp Lotmar "the founder of labor law" and has emphasized the importance of Lotmar's disciple, Hugo Sinzheimer, who drafted the law of collective bargaining, a key piece of German labor legislation that was later included in the Weimar Constitution.[4]

However, when we consider Mediterranean Europe and its influence on the Americas, there are other jurists who appear to have had more impact. The Austrian lawyer Anton Menger, admired by Latin American socialists, serves as an example. In his texts, *The Civil Law and the Poor* (a critical study of the German Empire's Civil Code, published between 1879 and 1890) and *The Right to the Whole Produce of Labor* (1886), Menger argued that private law no longer reflected the changing forces at play in modern society, including the growing strength of labor vis-à-vis capital. He proposed that limitations on property rights would allow workers to fulfill their basic needs. He also proposed that the right to work should be added to the list of fundamental economic rights. Menger's work profoundly influenced Spanish labor reformers and, by extension, Latin American social law. His early works were translated into Spanish by Adolfo Posada, a jurist from the Oviedo School and a renowned essayist in the Spanish-speaking world. Posada was also one of the early drafters of the 1902 *Instituto de Trabajo* (Labor Institute), which served as a model for departments of labor in Argentina and in other countries.[5]

Another writer with considerable influence in both Spain and the Americas was the French jurist Leon Duguit (1859–1928) a professor at the University of Bordeaux. Working from another legal-ideological tradition, Duguit reached conclusions that were quite similar to those of his socialist colleagues. Duguit came from the tradition of Saint Simon and Comptean Positivism and argued that there were no "pre-social" subjective rights (as outlined in the Declaration of Rights of Man or the Napoleonic Code) but only obligations that were governed by "social function." Thus, he believed that the state should play a fundamental role in regulating the system, which rested on the social role played by each member in his or her respective community.[6]

THE INSTITUTIONAL PATH OF NEW IDEAS IN EUROPE AND THE RISE OF INTERNATIONAL LABOR LAW

Over time, these new ideas materialized into legislation. Beyond the actions of intellectuals, politicians, and social activists, this was largely a reflection of the efforts of workers and their increasingly numerous and powerful organizations and movements. Strikes in key sectors at the turn of the century, such as mining and transport, made a strong impact by empowering the European trade union movement while also pressuring the governing classes to address workers' demands. The legislative measures that were put in place sought to appease mobilized workers and avoid stoppages in sectors that were considered critical to the development of the industrial revolution.

Nevertheless, legislative change did not advance quickly. To the contrary, advances were made quite slowly and were wrought with indecision. Most of the legislation passed during these years did not reflect a predesigned legislative strategy but was actually more reactive in nature: congressional bodies responded to social challenges by conceiving of legislation as a preventive measure or as a way to "put out the fire."[7] The first labor laws protected the welfare of the most vulnerable workers (women and children) and sought to temper or address occupational hazards. Housing and sweatshops, child labor, excessive work hours, and wage vulnerability (instability, payments in kind), were some of the problems that required urgent attention. These legislative developments functioned under two basic models. The first one was based on the idea of self-help and "collective laissez-faire," (as was the case for Great Britain), and the second, prevalent in continental Europe, favored state regulation. Germany, a primary example, pioneered the development of social security.

In some European countries, labor offices and institutes were created alongside this new legislation. These offices shared common aims: to engage in the "scientific study" of labor issues, generate labor statistics, and circulate this information through publications. In some cases, these departments were created with the aim of instating controls and inspecting places of work. The pioneering French *Office du Travail*, created within the Ministry of Commerce in 1891, for example, focused on the technical study of labor and industry and advised state regulation and legislation. Its Belgian namesake, founded in 1894, generated scientific and statistical work but also held legislative duties (drafting laws) and executive powers (handling inspections and supervising the enforcement of laws and regulations). It also served as a model for the Spanish Labor Institute, inaugurated as *Instituto de Reformas Sociales* (Institute of Social Reform) in Madrid in 1904. In England, the Labor Department was created in 1893 out of a political and parliamentary effort to understand the labor issue through scientific study and statistics before enacting legislation. This institution, along with the offices of Trade and Statistics, were part of the Board of Trade, which was also responsible for intervening in disputes between companies and between workers and their employers. Similar institutions were created in other countries, including Germany's *Kommission für Arbeiter-Statistik* (1892) and the Office of Labor in Italy created in 1900 as part of the Ministry of Agriculture, Industry and Commerce.[8]

A movement promoting the internationalization of labor law built upon these national initiatives. Its advocates urged that it was essential that nations coordinate the enactment and application of labor legislation. This internationalist movement can be traced back to efforts among British socialists during the early nineteenth century, but it took concrete form decades later as intercontinental commerce and the movement of people and capital increased, making it important to elevate the advances in workers' rights achieved within major European countries to a more global stage.

Fourteen countries of the old continent met for the first time at the Berlin Conference of 1889 and agreed—though in a nonbinding arrangement—to adopt certain principles as international law, including restrictions on night labor for women and children, maximum daily working hours, weekly rest, and maternity leave, among others.[9] They also created, in 1900, the "International association for the legal protection of workers," with headquarters in Basel, which urged state intervention in labor matters and advocated for the creation of an International Labor Office, dedicated to the study and the provision of information regarding state protection of workers' rights. The organization later opened national offices in several countries and held conferences on specific aspects of social protection. These meetings occasionally produced (usually bilateral) international treaties, with the aim that workers in different countries would be assured the same protections.[10]

Another key player in this process was the international workers' movement. Several attempts to shape a unique international association failed during the first decade of the twentieth century, until 1913, when the International Federation of Trade Unions was founded in Zurich. The outbreak of World War I severely curtailed the federation's operation but members met again at the Berne Congress in 1919. This meeting, which also included socialist parties, passed a Labor Charter that was then read at the Versailles Peace Conference. The Charter advocated for state intervention to protect workers and for international labor legislation.[11] For its part, at their 1910 meeting at Copenhagen, the Second International members had proposed their own agenda: an eight-hour day, ban on night work for minors, thirty-six hours per week of leisure time, the abolition of wages in kind, guarantees to the right of association, and inspection of both industrial and agricultural workplaces in collaboration with workers' representatives.

The evolution of international law resumed after World War I, revived in President Woodrow Wilson's proposal to create a League of Nations, which took life on June 18, 1919, at the signing of the Treaty of Versailles. Part XIII of the treaty cited intervention in labor matters as urgent for lasting world peace, noting that if "the League of Nations is to establish universal peace, that peace can only be of such a nature founded on the basis of social justice."[12] To fulfill this purpose the Treaty created the International Labor Office (ILO) as a permanent office in the League and established an annual labor conference with the aim of developing the agenda laid out in the Treaty. This agenda, which is expressed in Article 427 as a declaration of fundamental principles, defined that labor should not be considered "a commodity or article of commerce" and provided a list of basic rights, in line with those already outlined in existing international law.[13] Finally, an Annex defined the location and date of the first conference, which was to be held in Washington between October and November 1919. From then on, the ILO annual conferences continued to advance the formation of international labor legislation transcending the ups and downs and even the breakdown of the institution that gave it life.[14]

The formalization of international labor law and the creation of a transnational institution for its promotion and implementation generated momentum for reform in postwar European constitutionalism. Inspired by important contemporary jurists like Mirkine Guetzevitch, who argued in favor of constitutionally protected social rights and the unification of an international program around worker's rights, a vast movement known as "social constitutionalism" arose. In the various countries in which it took place, the reformist process shared a common trait of introducing a series of limitations on individual rights into constitutional texts that were inspired in the collective interest (referred to as the "social control of individual liberty"). They also introduced limits to property rights, listed fundamental social rights, and proposed a new role for the state in guaranteeing these.

The Weimar Constitution of 1919 is often considered the first example of this trend in the Western legal world (according to Hepple it "raised labor law to levels thus far unforeseen in the world") but this contention—as we shall see—does not do justice to the 1917 Mexican constitution.[15] The Weimar Constitution contained a bill of social rights (which included, for example, the right to employment) and, although it guaranteed property rights, Article 153 noted, "its content and limits arise from the law." A subsequent article stated that "property obliges" and that "its use should be, at the same time, in service of the public interest." The constitution also included guarantees of freedom of association, established the foundation of social security, sanctioned collective agreements, and established the Boards and Labor Courts.[16] Other nations soon produced similar documents, Estonia (1920), Poland, and Yugoslavia (both in 1921) and, in the thirties, Russia (1936) and Ireland (1937). Finally, World War II revived social constitutionalism. Its best expression was the French constitution (1946), which offered the most complete list of workers' rights and social justice, guaranteeing the right to health, work, free association, social security, and collective agreements.[17]

THE FIRST LABOR COURTS

Alongside this new social legislation, European countries conceived of methods to address conflicts between capital and labor. This was a central issue. Once the need for protection and regulation of work had been defined, it was necessary to create agencies capable of enforcing the new sanctions. And while the legislation was considered "special" (i.e., not covered hitherto in existing codes and legal bodies) or, as some deemed it, "new law," it was essential to creating specialized courts. Much of this effort was grounded in criticisms waged by labor reformers against the ordinary courts. They regarded the existing venues as holding classist biases and lacking expertise in labor matters; they criticized that their high costs, delays, and incomprehensible formality made them inaccessible to the poor and illiterate. Taken together, these factors would severely limit the new legislation's effectiveness.

These arguments formed the foundation for the creation of special courts in Europe, which were founded more or less at the same time, (sometimes even before) the enactment of new labor laws. The first courts were conciliation and arbitration systems handled in courts with class representation that had existed in Europe since the early nineteenth century. Despite this format being common, the system varied considerably from one country to another. Most bodies included worker and employer representation and usually, although not always, a third member, representing the state. Participation was compulsory in some cases, and in others, was voluntary. The authority of decisions also varied: in some cases they were binding and final while in others they were open to appeal, in which case they could be heard in front of other authorities or before the ordinary courts. Finally, court decisions were usually limited to a specific conflict and decisions could not generate a precedent and be applied to other cases. In other cases, however, the decision had normative power (i.e., became law) and could be applied across the system.

The first European country to organize a conflict resolution system was France. The *Conseils de prud'hommes* were first used in 1806 in the city of Lyon, at the request of industrialists in the region.[18] The system then expanded nationwide, by law, in 1907. These courts used bipartisan representation without state intervention, were strictly non-professional (there were no magistrates or judges, only representatives from the two parties), and were limited to individual conflicts. Their resolutions could be appealed and heard before the ordinary courts. In 1893, Italy established its *Collegi di probiviri* (or councils of honored men) to resolve individual disputes in the industrial field. These councils created a conciliation office (*ufficio di conciliziano*) that was composed of worker and employer representatives and was chaired by an independent member who presided over practical, custom industrial disputes and collective agreements.

Germany created its specialized courts (*Arbeitsgerichte*) in 1926 (although there was a precedent in the oldest commercial courts that dated back to 1890 and applied to manual laborers). The courts heard all labor demands, except those of workers in the civil service, independent of whether they were collective or individual complaints. They were composed of a representative from the employers' associations and a union representative and were chaired by a professional judge. The system operated at local, state, and national levels (*Reichsarbeitsgericht*).[19] Finally, the British system, which became a model for U.S. and Canadian structures (and most *common law* systems), was based on trade union regulation. In this system, workers in each industry negotiated a collective agreement with their employers (on wages, working conditions, and so forth) through their trade union, which generally included methods of resolving disputes. These were also eventually resolved in conciliation and arbitration ad hoc boards, the decisions of which had to be respected by both parties. Thus, labor disputes were neither settled in the judiciary nor resolved through labor regulations applied by judges.

The Development of Labor Law and Institutions in the Americas

Contrary to what one might expect, in the Americas, social legislation and state institutions designed for the protection of labor did not emerge long after their counterparts in Europe; in fact, they were more-or-less contemporaneous, and, in some cases, American initiatives even predated their European counterparts. Three examples serve to clearly evidence this claim: early statistical bureaus in the United States established during the final decades of the nineteenth century; the first labor code drafted in Argentina in 1904; and the Mexican constitution of 1917.

First, early "labor departments" in some U.S. states (like the Bureaus of Labor and Statistics founded in Massachusetts in 1869, in Pennsylvania in 1872, and in Connecticut in 1873) as well as the federal Department of Labor, created in 1888, were dedicated to generating statistics, the scientific study of the labor question, and worksite inspections. They not only predated similar European institutions but often served as a model for offices created in the Old World.[20] Second, the 1904 Ley Nacional del Trabajo (National Labor Law) in Argentina, although ultimately rejected by Congress, exhibited notable doctrinal sophistication and a profound knowledge of the legal realities of the Western world (not only drawing from the European experience but also from the legislative systems of the United States and Oceania).[21] Taken as a model in other Latin American countries, the bill sought to address labor contracts and salaries, worker's compensation and accident insurance, the length of the workday and weekly rest, protective measures for women and children, and the creation of a National Labor Board (Junta Nacional del Trabajo), which was charged with the task of inspecting work conditions and engaging in conciliation and arbitration.[22] The third example is more widely recognized: the Mexican constitution of 1917 established the social function of property rights to land in Article 27, and a true legislative program of workers' protection in its monumental Article 123, which included the most complete list of workers' rights to that date. In granting constitutional status to those rights, the Mexican constitution predated and anticipated social constitutionalism. It was the most advanced labor legislation that the world had ever seen.[23] In fact, the text was one of the sources consulted by the Labor Commission of the Treaty of Versailles, which designed the original framework of the ILO.[24]

Recognizing these early American developments does not invalidate "transplant theories" nor deny that processes of borrowing and appropriation did exist. Likewise, it does not support the opposite thesis: that these ideas were originally American. In fact, it is well recognized that the most common trajectory of historical evolution in law has been one of "adapted borrowing": all legal systems are influenced by other traditions.[25] However, what is important to underline is that these antecedents and simultaneous developments clearly speak to the effectiveness and the speed with which ideas circulated and flowed bidirectionally across the Atlantic at the turn of the century. Printed in books, legal projects, and jurisprudence, and extended via the voices of academics, experts, politicians, diplomats, and the demands of trade unionists, these ideas traveled from shore to shore and across national borders. As a result, laws, practices, and similar institutions were being constructed amid contemporaneous processes of trial and error, in both parts of the world.[26]

Also coincident on both sides of the Atlantic was the rise of the social question and the impact that the development of workers' organizations and their increasing activity had in the birth of labor law and courts in the Americas. As some of the national cases addressed by this book demonstrate, strikes in the transport and industrial sectors of Canada and the United States and in key areas of the export economies of Latin America, such as mines or plantations, became a serious concern to elites and lawmakers across the Americas at the break of the twentieth century. And as we can clearly see in the cases of Chile or Colombia in this book, such worker pressure on the governing classes was fundamental to the passing of the first labor laws in the new continent, just as it happened more or less contemporarily in the old.

THE RISE OF "NEW LAW" IN THE AMERICAS

In the very first class on Labor Law given at the Law and Social Science School at the University of Buenos Aires in 1919, the renowned Argentine professor and politician Alfredo Palacios—the first Socialist representative to enter the Argentine Congress (in 1904) and the author of the first social laws in Argentina—informed his students that the course would be dedicated to "the study of the juridical renewal that is taking place across the world." He referred to the rise of labor law, which he would rename "new law."[27] A few years later, the esteemed Chilean jurist Moisés Poblete Troncoso, in his study on social law in America (written at the request of the ILO, which hired him for the task), echoed the sentiment: "a new law, which could be called 'Social Law or Labor Law' is in full formulation, fundamentally different from traditional forms of Law, because of its origins, its principles and its object," which was based "in new legal concepts, unconsidered in past decades and unknown to common law."[28]

What was "new law"? First, in countries with civil law systems, it consisted of a precise group of norms that were incorporated into common legislation. The content of these norms, as well as the sequence of their development in each country, more or less coincided. Before the 1930s, countries enacted legislation that mandated a weekly day of rest, worker's compensation, limited or regulated work for women and children, salary protection, maximum working day, regulation of work hazards and hygienic conditions, resolutions of labor conflicts, and social security, among others. And from the 1930s onward—although in some countries these reforms were made earlier—most countries enacted laws regarding the regulation of the work contract, collective agreements, the eight-hour workday, minimum wage, paid vacation leave, union organizations, labor courts, and agrarian labor, among others.

Despite having a different method of establishing labor norms, countries under a common law system, like the United States and (to some extent) Canada, exhibited a similar sequence of events. In these countries, the key laws related to the recognition of unions since the major mechanism of labor reform became collective negotiation by industry. Nevertheless, by 1920, a good number of U.S. and Canadian workers had acquired protection against work-related accidents, and various states had established minimum wage, a day of rest per week, and restrictions on night labor and on women's labor.

Some countries looked to go beyond issuing specific laws and sought to generate labor codes, although with different timing and degrees of success. These efforts aimed to unify new legislation within a single framework in order to set labor law apart while elevating it to the same level of other branches of codified law. Most labor codes had similar structures and content. All of them legislated on subjects related to "new law," and many created offices or labor departments and conciliation and arbitration boards, whether independent or as components of labor departments. Others, like Mexico's Federal Labor Law (*Ley Federal del Trabajo*) of 1931, the Chilean Code of the same year, and the Ecuadorian Code of 1938, included special regulations regarding agrarian work (while that of Bolivia in 1939 specifically excluded it). Several also established social security—for health, old age, unemployment, or incapacitation.[29] The process of codification continued into the 1940s and 1950s (in Central America, Colombia, and Canada). The most famous and monumental code was Brazil's *Consolidaçao das Leis de Trabalho* (or CLT), approved under Vargas in 1943. Some countries did not codify their labor laws during the first half of the twentieth century (Cuba, Perú, Uruguay, and Argentina, in addition to the United States)—in some cases, despite several efforts and extended debate on the proposed codes.

Finally, the Americas, like Europe, possessed their own examples of social constitutionalism. After the pioneer impulse of the Mexican constitution of 1917, there were other early cases. Among the principles that governed the new constitutional texts were the affirmation of work as a social right; the social function of property; and the duty of the state to protect the worker, regulate labor conditions, and guarantee a minimal social well being, among others. The constitutions of Peru (1919) and Chile (1925) recognized the freedom of association and established the need for state intervention on issues related to industrial safety and general organization, the minimum wage, work-related accidents, and social welfare. The Chilean constitution also limited property rights according to public utility.[30] These constitutions were, in some cases, the culmination of long processes of law-creation and preexistent labor codes. In others, they were the reverse: a point of departure. Such was the case with the Mexican constitution of 1917. The principles embodied in Article 123, reflective, in part, of earlier, revolutionary decrees and legislation, resulted in prolific labor legislation that finally coalesced in the emblematic law of 1931.[31]

After these early expressions, the constitutional reformist movement resumed with greater energy during the mid-1930s, beginning with the Brazilian constitution of 1934 and that of 1937, which established the "Estado Novo," and the Cuban and Paraguayan constitutions, both enacted in 1940.[32] In the postwar period, the process was again revived, inspired by the international declarations of social rights at the ILO Philadelphia Conference of 1944 and in the Declaration of Social Principles of America (*Declaración de principios sociales de América*) signed at the Chapultepec Conference in 1945. In this spirit, new constitutions were passed in Guatemala (1945), Ecuador and Brazil (1946), Venezuela, the Dominican Republic, and Nicaragua (1947) and Argentina (1949).

A NEW STATE BUREAUCRACY

Parallel to the creation of laws, codes, and constitutions, during the first half of the century American nations also created state offices to address the social question and enforce labor legislation. In their earliest versions, during the first decades of the century, these departments had, like their European counterparts, the function of "scientifically" studying the situation of workers, compiling statistics about labor conditions in factories and about workers' lives, and circulating that knowledge through publications. The offices also provided the state with legal and labor expert knowledge. In some cases, they were also assigned the task of inspecting working conditions and controlling the application of legislation; some were granted the capacity of issuing fines and penalties for violation of labor laws, and others were charged with the task of intervening in labor conflicts generally through their arbitration and conciliation boards. Official recognition of unions and of collective agreements between companies and workers were also tasks sometimes assigned to these institutions.

As we have seen, the first of these kinds of organizations were the Labor Bureaus that appeared in some U.S. states and Canadian provinces in the final decades of the nineteenth century.[33] In Latin America, early offices include the Labor Office (*Oficina del Trabajo*) in Chile—created in 1907 and reorganized as the Labor Bureau (*Dirección General del Trabajo*) in 1924—followed by the creation of the Labor Department (*Departamento del Trabajo*) in Mexico in 1911, which became the Labor Bureau (*Dirección de Trabajo*) within the Secretary of Industry, Commerce and Labor (*Secretaría de Industria, Comercio y Trabajo*) in 1917. Argentina's National Department of Labor was created by law in 1907 but was not active until 1912, whereas the São Paulo Labor Department in Brazil was founded in 1911. Later came the General Office of Labor (*Oficina General del Trabajo*) in Colombia (1923), the Labor Department in Bolivia (1926), and the Secretary of Labor and Social Welfare (*Secretaría de Trabajo y Previsión Social*) in Costa Rica (1928). The historiography on these institutions is still scarce, although the few studies available, including those presented in this volume, reveal that beyond their importance as state offices of information that provided relevant legal material to the state, their ability to control and enforce labor legislation was limited, due to small budgets and limited geographical reach. Their activities of inspection and sanctioning have largely been seen as restricted to tending to collective conflicts (strikes, union conflicts) and their actions limited to the major cities of each country, with scarce or no activity in rural areas.

As in the case with labor legislation, we can also define a second period in the evolution of state agencies charged with the task of applying the law, which followed the initial rise of these early institutions. By the 1930s, a growing concern over the labor question rooted in processes of industrialization in various countries, a significant concentration of workers in industrial and urban centers, and the effects of the global crisis on employment and on industrial and urban activity, compelled governments to elevate these offices' rank within state bureaucracy. Thus, some of these departments, which operated within other government dependencies, acquired autonomy, while others were converted into secretaries or ministries. In general, all of them underwent qualitative and quantitative structural transformations, gaining personnel, more functional power, a larger budget, and a greater territorial presence across national territory.

Thus, these offices did not merely change in name. In general, the new titles came with greater government intervention in the economy and society and, in particular, increased regulation of industrial relations. For example, in Mexico, the Labor Bureau of the Secretary of Industry became the autonomous Labor Department in 1932 and was transformed again into the Secretary of Labor (*Secretaría de Trabajo*) in 1940; in Chile, the Labor Department became the Ministry of Labor (*Ministerio de Trabajo*) in 1932, and the same change took place in Bolivia in 1937 and in Colombia in 1938. In Brazil, the Vargas administration inaugurated the Ministry of Labor in 1931; in Argentina, the government of the June Revolution of 1943 converted the Labor Department into the Secretary of Labor and Welfare (*Secretaría de Trabajo y Previsión*); and later, in 1949, the Perón administration turned it into a ministry. The United States founded the National Recovery Administration (created by the NIRA of 1933), which became a key office in the New Deal's large-scale state regulation of the economy and, in turn, considerably elevated the U.S. state apparatus' ability to intervene in labor relations.

LABOR COURTS

The development of labor law in the Americas also included the creation of systems of conflict resolution between workers and their employers. These were founded for many of the same reasons as they were in Europe. The Americas also exhibited a great variety of models, though there was considerable consistency. For example, almost all American nations experimented with systems of conciliation and arbitration that were similar to those in Europe; that is, they developed collegiate institutions with tripartite representation (of workers, patrons, and the state). These tribunals were based on a spirit of conciliation and peer arbitration.

But the American states not only used European models. In fact, we have considerable evidence that the tripartite conciliation boards put in place in Australia and New Zealand at the beginning of the twentieth century were just as well known by jurists and legislators in the Americas as their European counterparts. These models were taken into account when institutions were designed. Brazilian legislators, for example, learned of the Australian model long before 1930. Created in 1904, this model was cited in academic works and in the parliamentary debates that eventually led to the implementation of the Brazilian labor justice system, which was based in conciliation procedures.[34] In Argentina, Joaquín V. Gonzalez cited the same model when he presented the Labor Code of 1904 before Congress, noting that it was inspired by the European legal tradition and "the more perfect laws in the United States and the British colonies in Oceania." He added that in terms of arbitration, the Argentine plan followed the methods outlined by New Zealand law, "on which the legal experts of the most illustrious nations of Europe have bestowed much praise, and have also imitated what has been done there."[35]

These common antecedents gave way to considerable variations of this model across the Americas. The systems of conciliation and arbitration were often placed under the tutelage of the state offices previously listed (as was the case of the departments of labor in Argentina and Chile and the Office of Labor in Costa Rica, created in 1932) though they were sometimes independent (like the *Juntas de Conciliação e Jul-gamento* and the *Comissões Mistas de Conciliação* in Brazil). In other cases, they were ad hoc institutions created during a particular conflict with diverse formats and proce-dures established in collective agreements between the industry and the workers, as was the case in the prevailing systems in the United States and Canada.[36] Moreover, in some cases, these systems of arbitration evolved over time into distinct forms of labor courts (e.g., professional tribunals) and eventually disappeared, as was the case in Chile; in others, they remained the exclusive or predominant form of conflict resolution, placed either within the Executive Power (as in Mexico) or as a new court under the Judicial Power (as in Brazil). In other contexts, these tribunals persisted as an early administrative step before heading to trial, thus coexisting with the profes-sional labor tribunals of the justice system, as was the case in some of the Argentine provinces. Finally, in the United States and Canada, where the tribunals were created outside of the judicial and state system as private procedures of conflict resolution (*grievance procedures*) agreed to by both parties and included in collective bargaining agreements, they remained outside these environments, except in special cases— e.g., when no agreement was reached, when a collective bargaining agreement did not include a conflict resolution system, or when a national emergency demanded exceptional measures be taken place (for example, during the world wars).[37]

As occurred with legislation and with the labor departments, the system of labor justice also evolved from these more incipient forms toward a more perfected system with a more extensive (quantitative and qualitative) bureaucracy. In places where tripartite boards persisted, there was a proliferation of local, regional, and provincial organizations, and a nationalization of the system; in the case of professional courts, we can observe a greater number of technical personnel and judges and a greater jurisdictional reach and presence across national territory (e.g., in rural zones, where they previously had no legal jurisdiction, and so forth).

It is worth noting that these courts were consolidated only after extensive debate. Deliberations over labor courts were far more bitter and more animated than those that preceded the creation of labor laws and departments of labor. Indeed, the road to the establishment of labor courts was rather disputed everywhere; the courts' sup-porters had to confront every kind of resistance—from predictable conflicts with capi-talist sectors to less anticipated objections from the political and judicial sectors. It is worth citing a few examples. In the Mexican case, the early conciliation boards, which had existed in some states since the revolution and were constitutionally approved in 1917, were effectively disputed by employers and the local bourgeoisie until they were validated by a 1924 Supreme Court verdict that granted the courts' decisions legal power, and then by the *Ley Federal del Trabajo* of 1931, which ratified a national system of conciliation and arbitration, under the Executive Power.[38] In Brazil, the process took nearly fifteen years. Created by decree in 1932 and later upheld by the constitutions of 1934 and 1937, the Conciliation Boards were only implemented in

1940 as an administrative agency within the Ministry of Labor, although it would be another six years before they were confirmed as a new autonomous branch within the Judiciary.[39] Finally, the debates regarding voluntary or compulsory conciliation in the United States and Canada took the entire first half of the twentieth century. Although with opposite results, objections to both projects were similar in nature and based in large part on the fear of the encroachment of state power over private business and of the federal government on state autonomy.[40] Perhaps the best evidence of the strength and efficacy of resistance to the new courts is that, in most cases, they were not originally established through regular parliamentary procedures, which required debate and accord, but rather through executive decrees, either issued during a de facto regime (as was the case in Brazil and Argentina) or during a state of national emergency in which the government held special powers (as was the case in the United States, Canada, and Colombia).

ELEMENTS FOR A CHRONOLOGY OF LABOR REGULATION IN THE AMERICAS

A comparative look at the processes by which labor law in the Americas arose and matured suggests some common patterns. One of these is historical sequence. Without ignoring national particularities, we can say that, across the continent, there was a "first wave" of legislation and state intervention that took place during the first three decades of the twentieth century, a period of liberal-conservative governments and, in Latin America, of export growth based on strong liberal consensus. During this early stage, the first advocates of labor law ("liberal reformists"[41] like the Chilean Arturo Alessandri, the Colombian Rafael Uribe Uribe, or the Argentine Joaquín V. González; socialists like Alfredo Palacios; liberals like the Canadian Mackenzie King) took political and parliamentary action to promote the first labor laws (Sunday rest, work-related accidents, maximum working day, limitations on women's and children's work) amid a palpable threat of worker activism that manifested in strikes and social clashes across the region. From these efforts also arose the first labor departments, which were charged with the task of studying the labor question and, on occasion, with regulation and inspection. Labor jurisprudence also took form in civil courts "sensitive" to labor matters and in the first conciliation and arbitration boards, which were organized either within or outside the new labor departments. These boards, however, still had limited reach (e.g., in general, they did not apply labor law but only managed collective conflicts or were in charge of union recognition, and so forth).

During this initial period, state intervention was limited, both in terms of its intensity and its reach. Thus, although the labor departments made praiseworthy advances in statistical compilation and aided in the circulation of information (which ultimately informed the first laws), they had restricted regulatory capacity. In general, they did not possess the power to sanction, and conciliation was not always mandatory. Generally, these offices were also confined to large cities and did not reach rural areas. These limitations reflected the rather lukewarm effort on the part of conservative governments to apply the first labor laws or to commit to the reformist legislative agenda—which was accepted only as long as it remained a theoretical debate among a small group of intellectuals. Another reason for this "low intensity" intervention was that there were no courts that specifically addressed labor conflicts—or, as has been noted, there was a lack of power to sanction the existing arbitration systems. This meant that even labor laws with the most noble intentions were often sunk when they faced the civil courts, which, most of the time, were presided over by liberal judges who generally disliked the new social legislation.

The crisis of 1930 and the Great Depression that followed revived the "labor question" across the Americas, and in particular in those countries where industrialization had generated a greater concentration (and mobilization) of workers in large cities. This context was crucial to the emergence of a second wave of labor rights and state labor regulation in the Americas. The crisis of Western capitalism was not merely economic; it also compelled a profound revision in the liberal ideology upon which that system was based. Thus, the crisis revived preexisting ideas about the necessity for state intervention in labor relations. The grounds of the "social state" were born of this context and were characterized by more complete and efficient state intervention in economic life and industrial relations.

This second period was characterized by the renovation, reinforcement, and wider reach of labor regulating institutions. First, the laws multiplied exponentially and became more inclusive (e.g., they reached rural workers and indigenous populations). Several became emblematic, such as the *Wagner Act* for industrial workers in the United States or the Rural Worker Statute (*Estatuto del Peón Rural*) in Argentina. These years also represented a time in which movements toward the enactment of labor codes and social constitutions were revived. Second, state labor agencies (departments, secretaries or ministries of labor), were bestowed a higher rank, larger budgets and more extensive bureaucratic structures, real powers of sanction, and greater territorial extension through regional offices and delegations. Third, conflict resolution agencies that continued to act as administrative tribunals acquired new powers of sanction whereas others were converted into special tribunals within a new branch of the Judiciary, separate from civil and commercial courts. In countries where there was a strong federal tradition, like Canada and the United States, governments also passed laws with new national reach (including establishing a minimum wage, regulating work conditions, and so forth). They also created federal regulatory systems and national conflict resolution systems.

During this moment of expanding interventionism in labor regulation, the new (or renewed) labor tribunals were called to fulfill a fundamental role in the application of labor law. They were set to enforce laws that had been put in place at the beginning of the century and had been largely circumvented, as well as the new laws that had come out of the second wave of legislative development. Aside from their varying formulations (administrative institutions versus judicial courts; classist versus professional courts, conciliation or procedural justice) these courts projected a consistent rhetoric that emphasized the failure of ordinary tribunals to understand labor questions, the slowness and high costs of judicial procedures, the conservative tradition of civil judges, and the consequent necessity of applying labor law in special courts. This rhetoric was also sustained by the ILO, which, at the end of World War II, began to emphatically recommend that member countries organize specialized courts.[42] Thus labor courts, in their multiple forms, became a fundamental piece of the second wave of state-labor intervention across the Americas. These courts were charged with the task of effectively applying the new regulations in accordance with the spirit of "new law."

International Networks and the Circulation of Ideas in the Construction of Labor Law in the Americas

By the mid–twentieth century, labor law had become firmly rooted in the Americas. Important legislative advances, legal codes, new social constitutions, state institutions, and specialized tribunals all contributed to the trend. These developments spoke to the gradual conformation of a "climate of ideas" that was in favor of developing and applying social legislation, which, as we have seen, began to take shape at the beginning of the twentieth century. At the same time, these developments were the result of actions taken by specific strategic actors in each country (academics, congressmen, functionaries, trade unionists, and experts) who also created networks of exchange and circulated their ideas.

Previous sections considered the origins and the content of these ideas as well as the principal institutions that they advanced. The following section examines the channels by which these ideas circulated—by individuals, by way of written works and theses, and by news of novel legislation and institutions. Information circulated within each country, transatlantically, and bidirectionally, north and south, across the American continent.

THE ACADEMIC WORLD AND THE EMERGENCE OF THE FIELD OF LABOR LAW

Academia was a major site in which ideas about labor law developed and circulated. During the first decades of the twentieth century, a few key actors, who later became the leaders of labor reformism, began constructing what one could call a "field" of labor law within their respective countries. These men were specialists in social law, who had international ties or were immersed in diverse networks that exposed them to larger environments.

At the university level, these trends could be observed in the appearance of the first Labor Law courses, which were largely created as offshoots of Economics or Industrial Law. Specific research institutes or "seminars" (on social law, labor legislation, and so forth) also began to appear, often within the law schools at the most important universities in the region. For example, Chile hosted the first chair ("cátedra") and research program on social and labor-related subjects at the University of

Chile in the 1890s. These classes allowed students to attend lectures on the European juridical tradition and keep abreast of recent developments in social reform. The first major Chilean labor scholars, Moisés Poblete Troncoso and Francisco Walker Linares, studied there. Both men went on to make significant contributions as academics and professors and also served as Chilean representatives at the ILO and at the League of Nations.[43] A similar story could be told of scholars in Argentina during the early twentieth century. Alejandro Unsain and Leónidas Anastasi went on to become key participants in the advance of labor law at the university and at the state bureaucratic and legislative levels. Figures from academia were also instrumental in the development of labor law in North America. The Canadian William Lyon Mackenzie King graduated from Harvard, where he wrote theses on labor issues; he went on to become the first minister of labor in Canada.[44] The same can be said of John R. Commons, who took action in favor of labor law at the University of Wisconsin.

The first department chairs and university labor institutes became important channels by which information and news of global advancements in the field circulated (bibliographic and legislative, judicial, and institutional). These were also important avenues for the production of graduate theses, articles, and essays on labor law, which collectively contributed to a broader production of knowledge on the subject. They also hosted the first labor law journals, which had a decisive role in the circulation of information (about authors, books, treaties, and other journals, and through references and book reviews). These journals also validated the careers of labor law specialists, which was essential for their entry and permanence in the national academies of each country.

Moreover, these institutes and chairs also became incubators for new legislative initiatives and other state action, either on their own or at the request of state officials. These schools also trained a good number of the functionaries and experts who later went on to work in diverse state labor agencies (departments, ministries, as well as the conciliation boards). Finally, these academic spaces served as gateways to international conferences, visits, and exchanges, where members discussed academic works, theses and papers, and met foreign experts. Thus, these institutes often hosted European scholars, as occurred in 1910 when Adolfo Posada visited several South American countries, or when Leon Duguit visited Argentina in 1911 and Colombia in 1920 and 1921 to teach courses and deliver lectures.[45] From very early on, the academic world was key to the field of labor law, which acquired, on both sides of the Atlantic, an international dimension. Its members met and recognized themselves as part of a brotherhood that worked toward a truly global agenda.

OTHER SPACES

But the world of the academy was not the only environment in which these actors circulated. As members of elite families—as they most frequently were—these lawyers and jurists belonged to many other kinds of networks (social, political, religious) in which they shared their social ideology, professional knowledge, and convictions.

For example, *socialism* was a network unto itself. Both its cause and many of its founding fathers were closely connected to the labor reformers, regardless of their precise political affiliation or ideology; thus, socialism aided in the development of a labor law agenda without confronting these differences. In Europe, for example, the fight for labor law often served to unite socialists with social Catholics, Anarchists, and Positivists. A similar pattern developed in the Americas.

A good example of this can be seen in the case of the Argentine Socialist Alfredo Palacios. Palacios was an important political actor, one of the Socialist Party's founders in Argentina, and one of the most important *laboralistas* (labor reformers) in the country. He contributed to the advancement of labor law in a number of environments: in the academic field of labor law from his position at the University of Buenos Aires, as well as in the legal system, where he was the author of legislation in favor of Sunday rest and workers' compensation. Together with other socialists like Juan B. Justo, Palacios formed part of the commission that drafted the labor code of 1904, which took form during the conservative administration of President Roca and was authored by his minister of the interior, the liberal reformist Joaquín V. González. Situated at the intersection of these networks, Palacios was, moreover, a relevant actor in international socialism and had a great deal of personal and institutional contacts with his fellow socialists in other parts of the world.[46]

This socialist network was important in the creation of some state bureaucracies and was also relevant to the creation of the ILO. The first director of the regional office of the ILO for Latin America, Antonio Fabra Ribas, owed his appointment to the relationships he had established with French socialists at the beginning of the century. He developed particularly close ties with the first director of the ILO, Albert Thomas.[47]

Catholicism constituted another vast global network that facilitated the circulation of ideas and actions. This network was strongly revived with the publication of the *Rerum Novarum*. Indeed, in the late nineteenth century, the social work of some bishops on both sides of the Atlantic was widely known, as were their spaces of periodic exchange (Episcopal meetings, Eucharistic congresses, and so forth). For example, the social activism of Bishop von Ketteler and the Freiburg Union or that of Abbe Pottier in Belgium, found a parallel on the other side of the Atlantic, in the work of Bishop John Ireland and Baltimore Cardinal James Gibbons, both defenders of the Knights of Labor. At the parish level, the reformist work of the German entrepreneur Franz Brandt and his key role in the creation of associations of Catholic workers in that country (through the Social Courses and the People's Association for Catholic Germany), as well as Henri Lorin, who organized the French Social Weeks, were known and "replicated" in Latin America in the "Catholic circles" (organized by Father Grote in Argentina in 1891 and Bishop Holguin in Peru 1896) or the "social weeks" organized by Father Alberto Hurtado in Chile.[48]

Finally, *the international workers' movement* also functioned as another transnational network of exchange and mobilization among different labor organizations in Europe and the Americas. While workers did not form a singular or homogenous front, the different confederations and "internationals" that had been created since the end of the nineteenth century, and especially after the First World War, proved to be important networks of exchange. Much of labor's reformist agenda blossomed from their efforts and victories. As both multiplied, workers' demands generated the "transnational legal consciousness" that characterized the new social juridical thinking of the twentieth century.[49]

THE GREATER NETWORK: THE INTERNATIONAL LABOR ORGANIZATION

Among these channels of circulation, there was no organization that compared to the League of Nations and its specialized body, the International Labor Organization. The scale and resources, and their decisive roles in the construction of international labor law and the development of social legislation since their inception in the aftermath of World War I, were unparalleled. These organizations sometimes served to create new circuits or networks of relationships within nations and they occasionally became the springboard for international projects, giving fresh impetus to existing networks. Congresses and regular meetings were instrumental to establishing a framework of legitimacy; institutional membership in a larger organization dedicated to resolving labor problems generated a new level of international cooperation.[50]

The ILO's relationship with the Americas during its first decade of existence was actually quite lukewarm. The ILO's actions and interests were primarily focused on Europe, and by and large, the American nations returned the sense of indifference. There were several reasons for these mutual sentiments: the United States Congress's decision not to join the League of Nations (and to eventually join the ILO at a later date); the initial resistance of countries that had remained neutral during the war to join the organization, like Argentina; and the League's decision to leave Mexico out of the organization (and therefore, the ILO) at the Paris Peace talks, at the request of Britain and the United Sates.

As a result, the ILO had a meek early presence in the Americas. The United States, with its high levels of industrial development, hosted a regional ILO office in Washington, while Latin American nations were put under the care of a single regional office in Madrid. Latin American functionaries had a scarce presence in Geneva and, accordingly, there were few ILO correspondents in the Americas. This low-intensity relationship also took form amid rather weak participation by Latin American countries in the International Conferences. Representatives failed to show up, their attendance was often erratic, and their delegations were sometimes incomplete. Latin American countries also rarely ratified international labor conventions adopted by the organization, or they did so but with considerable delay.

This relationship changed considerably in 1931, when Mexico joined the ILO and Harold Butler began his term as director. He embarked on a mission to "de-europeanize" the institution and open it up to new horizons. This turn resulted in a higher number of regional correspondents (from only 2 in 1931 to 12 in 1944); a new project to organize regional conferences, beginning with one in Santiago de Chile in 1936; and the multiplication of missions and visits (first initiated when ILO director Albert Thomas visited the Southern Cone in 1925). A number of new nations also joined the ILO in this period, beginning with the United States, which joined in 1934, and continuing with Costa Rica in 1944 and Guatemala the next year, among others. This new global turn also prompted Latin American countries to ratify a greater number of the international conventions issued at the Conferences.

But the importance of the ILO for the development of labor law in the Americas was not limited to advances in international labor legislation, the conventions that it promoted, or the rhythm with which member countries incorporated its recommendations into their respective legal bodies. Its most decisive impact can be found in its role as a principle pathway for the circulation of ideas, information, literature, peoples, laws, and so forth, all of which became the building blocks of the "labor question" in the Americas.

What were these channels of circulation? First, the annual *International Labor Conference* (ILC), first held in Washington in 1919, served as a global forum for the debate of labor issues. Its plenary body produced and oversaw international labor standards. Additionally, its system of tripartite representation in each national delegation (a complete delegation consisted of at least two government delegates, one delegate representing the employers and one representing the workers, each of which could also be accompanied by a more or less significant number of advisors) made these summits a privileged meeting place in which specialists circulated ideas. Each conference ran for several weeks, allowing experts to cultivate relationships and form an international "brotherhood" of labor law. Regional conferences, which began with the 1936 Santiago meeting, focused on issues that particularly interested the countries of the Americas, which were subsequently brought up at the ILC. These were especially fruitful for cooperation and the creation of expert networks in the region, since a greater number of labor specialists and functionaries from institutes or ministries of labor from the Americas attended the regional conferences, as compared to the ILC. Regional meetings were held every four years and included the participation of Latin American countries as well as the United States, Canada, and the English-speaking Caribbean.

Second, *representatives* from the Americas at headquarters in Geneva and the organization's system of national *correspondents* fulfilled a key role, acting as points of connection between the organization's bureaucracy and the different state agencies in the various countries. They facilitated diplomatic and political relations with each government. As previously mentioned, early on there were not very many Latin Americans in Geneva. Those who were there were restricted to providing information regarding the countries of the continent to the organization (and vice versa). They were occasionally assigned specific tasks, like Poblete Troncoso's assignment in

1927 to prepare a volume about the state of social legislation on the continent.[51] The correspondents, meanwhile, served as "exterior functionaries" that acted as on-the-ground institutional informants in their respective countries. The ILO selected them among former public administration officials, intellectuals dedicated to the social cause, labor lawyers, and so forth, and the correspondents then generated periodic reports for the Organization. In that sense, they played a key role by drawing a picture of social problems and labor conditions in the Americas for Geneva. They also transmitted directives and recommendations, as well as policies, diplomacy, academic knowledge, and relationships between different actors on either side of the Atlantic.

Third, *technical visits and missions* were key to the local promotion of ILO labor standards, though the visits varied considerably in form and function. As mentioned, the first visit made to Latin America occurred in 1925 when ILO director Albert Thomas visited the countries of the Southern Cone. Although it was a diplomatic visit that functioned as a (rather late) debut or "discovery" tour, it facilitated the kind of personal contact that was crucial to the ILO's policy development in the region. After the tour, and as the ILO drew closer ties to the region, these kinds of visits multiplied. They were imbued with new purpose, even though they never acquired a systematic or homogenous format. While some visits remained diplomatic or political exercises, others were framed as "technical cooperation" missions: experts traveled to provide assistance on specific subjects or to help local governments legitimize their laws and political programs (e.g., by speaking before parliaments or union organizations), at their request.

In this way, maybe even more so than its legislative advocacy, declarations, and labor conventions, the most important function that the ILO fulfilled was to put a vast number of global actors involved in labor matters in contact with one another. This contributed in a decisive way to the establishment of a truly global "labor question" in the twentieth century. To the diverse individuals involved in the ILO (the annual Labor Conferences delegates, Geneva's bureaucrats, national correspondents, technical assistance experts, labor department officials from each country, and so forth) the organization served as a launching point for the international projection of local and regional networks. It generated a sentiment of mutual recognition and belonging among an international community that united around a common program.

• • •

The creation of social legislation and labor courts in the Americas occurred at the intersection of diverse and complex processes, with varied timing and nature. The social effects of industrial development, the consequences of wars and economic crises, workers' organization and struggle, revolution, and the development of new ideas and action among certain key actors in universities, politics, and the state, all contributed to create a climate of ideas in the Western world that favored state intervention in labor matters.

This process was not instantaneous. Rather, it gained favor over the course of the first half of the twentieth century at the hands of diverse historical circumstances and a group of varied but identifiable actors: social reformers, philanthropists, revolutionaries, the organized labor movement, priests, socialists of different stripes, political reformists, statesmen, and a "rebel" group of juridical scientists that fought for the independence of *new law* from existing legal canons. These actors made up the heterogeneous group of key players that pushed this story forward. Together with their activity in each country, these actors created a truly international brotherhood of labor reformers that connected both sides of the Atlantic and that, beyond their substantial differences (political, party, methodological) united around a set of ideas and common agenda. Thus, they contributed to the creation of a "transnational legal consciousness" that formed the base of the "globalization of the social" during the first half of the twentieth century.[52]

This program materialized across the Americas over the course of fifty years, in a gradual process that varied according to circumstances and the juridical-political tradition of each country. A comparative perspective allows us to visualize a common trajectory: labor law was born of lukewarm and cautious beginnings, and it evolved in a second wave, in which change was more decisive. The initial moment, in the first decades of the twentieth century, was one of experimentation with state intervention (the first laws and codes, labor departments, and arbitration tribunals were established) and occurred amid a context that was quite hostile to the reformist impulse, with strong resistance to state regulation. Nonetheless, although legal enforcement was rather weak, it was a prolific moment of intellectual development. The creation of the field of labor law in each country generated scientific data about the world of work, which, in turn, would later give life to reforms. The second moment of reform generated more decided state intervention. It coincided with the collapse of liberal ideology (upended by the crisis of 1930 and World War II) which generated a context more favorable to regulatory state action.

As the key institutions for the enforcement of the new laws, the labor courts serve as the climax of this story. It was not until these courts evolved from more limited and weak offices and became agencies with national reach, an effective presence, and sanctioning power across national territories, that labor law began to make a major impact on the American continent. It was not for nothing that these courts took so long to come to fruition—they did so only after overcoming enormous opposition in most countries. Resistance not only came from the ownership class, who did not want to lose their privileged position vis-à-vis their workers. The establishment of labor courts also posed critical constitutional questions, such as the reach (and limits) of state power in business-labor relations and in the judiciary and of federal intervention in provincial or state jurisdictions. It was thus not until the consolidation of the labor courts that labor law, and with it, the ideology of the twentieth century's labor reformers, took full form.

This conclusion is not meant to imply a uniform process throughout the continent. Much less does it intend to denote that the process was a lineal one evolving peacefully, without major obstacles or setbacks, to the perfect concretion of a predesigned project. The general overview offered in these pages rather represents an interpretative effort that needs to (and must) be put to the test through empirical case studies of the concrete actors behind, and circumstances under which, the formation of labor courts took shape in each country of the American continent.

Notes

1. In the introduction to his classic text on the formation of European labor law, Bob Hepple proposed five ideologies that informed labor law: the ideology of the market, of "self-help," of state intervention ("state-help"), of socialism, and of christianism. See Hepple, "Introduction," 27.

2. The encyclical was the result of at least a half-century of effort on the part of diverse actors in the Christian world who sought a papal definition on the social question, specifically in regard to the dangers of socialism. In particular, the efforts of Bishop Von Ketteler, who, together with his colleagues in the "Freiburg Union," advised Leo XIII on social issues and helped him write the encyclical. García de Fleury, *Introducción al estudio.* 44; Gargan, *Leo XIII.*

3. *Rerum Novarum.*

4. Hepple, "Introduction," 7–8. Moreover, Sinzheimer's period of exile in Holland during World War II was key to the development of labor law in that country and, indirectly, in England, through his disciple, Kahn-Freund.

5. Olaza Pallero, "La influencia." The original draft of the Institute in Buylla et al., *El Instituto del Trabajo.*

6. De Fazio, "La 'filosofía positiva'"; Zimmermann, "Un espíritu nuevo."

7. Ramm, "Epilogue."

8. Buylla et al., *El Instituto del Trabajo,* 264–272.

9. Ramm, "Epilogue," 279–80. It was there that, according to Alfredo Palacios, an "official state for the labor question" arose in Europe. Palacios, *El nuevo derecho,* 292.

10. Ibid., 293.

11. Ibid., 303–6. Ramm, "Epilogue," 281–282.

12. *El Tratado de Versalles,* 427.

13. Ibid., 443–444.

14. In fact, the renewed interest in the League of Nations—revived at the end of the 1980s after the collapse of the Soviet Union—rescued this "other aspect" of the League's mission, its technical organizations (including the ILO and the International Court of Justice), seeing them as a counterweight to the negative perception of the League. See Pedersen, "Back to the League."

15. Hepple, Introduction, 9.

16. Linares Quintana, "El derecho constitucional," 957.

17. Ibid. 958–962.

18. Ramm, "Workers' Participation," 270–272.

19. Ibid.

20. Buylla et al., *El Instituto del Trabajo*, 270–271. In Canada, the Bureau of Labour in Ontario was created in 1900.

21. The bill was presented before Congress by Minister González in a lengthy speech that, when printed, was 70 pages long. It was a true labor legal treatise of its era. Ministerio, *Proyecto de Ley*.

22. Ibid.

23. In effect, article 123 sanctioned the eight-hour workday, the prohibition of night work and child labor, mandatory weekend, the protection of women workers during maternity and pregnancy, minimum wage and its payment in currency, the participation of workers in company revenue, the right to education and housing, and the right to free association and to strike. It also established methods of conciliation and arbitration.

24. Herrera León, "México y la Organización," 341–342. The text was contributed by Samuel Gompers, president of the American Federation of Labor and a member of said commission.

25. Hepple, Introduction, 2.

26. The literature on the circulation of ideas, translations, and transplantations is as immense as legal historiography. See Duve, *Entanglements*; Sánchez Echevarría, *"Legal Transplants"*; Charle et al., *Transnational*.

27. Palacios, *El nuevo derecho*, 64. This book includes the course lectures given between 1919 and 1920, revised and annotated by the author.

28. Poblete Troncoso, *Evolución*, 155. Though published in 1942, this book includes a selection of previous work, including the report mentioned: *La legislación social en América Latina* (Ginebra, 1928–1929).

29. Ibid., 157.

30. Ibid., 119–120.

31. Besunsan, *La ley federal*.

32. Linares Quintana, "El derecho constitucional," 960–961.

33. Canada's Department of Labor was created in 1900 and transformed later into the Ministry of Labor in 1909.

34. Teixeira da Silva, "The Brazilian." In this model, labor justice was based on an obligatory system of conciliation and arbitration, which was at the hands of commissions with tripartite representation, presided over by a professional judge whose sentences had the force of law and were enforced by state authority.

35. Ministerio, *Proyecto de Ley*.

36. *Labour courts*.

37. So it was in the U.S. National Labor Relations Board and in the Wartime Labour Relations Board approved in 1944 in Canada. The Canadian system was similar to that of the United States although it differed on one significant point: in the United States the conflict resolution rules were established voluntarily (despite extensive debate over the years), while in Canada the system was compulsory, following the model of Australia and New Zealand.

38. Suarez-Potts, "The Mexican"; Middlebrook, *The Paradox*.

39. De Castro Gomes and Teixeira da Silva, *A Justiça do Trabalho*.

40. See the chapters by Leon Fink and Frank Luce in this volume. For an analysis of these resistances in the Argentine case, see Palacio, "El grito."

41. I am borrowing this phrase from Zimmermann, *Los liberales.*

42. For example, at the conferences in Geneva (1947) and San Francisco (1948) and in the third and fourth regional conferences of American nations (Mexico, 1946 and Montevideo, 1949). See *Labour courts,* 3. This publication is the ad hoc study on the state of the tribunals in the Americas that was prepared for the ILO in anticipation of the Montevideo meeting.

43. Yáñez Andrade, "La OIT."

44. See Frank Luce's contribution to this volume.

45. De Fazio, "La 'filosofía positiva,'" 75; Palacios, *El nuevo derecho,* 81. A detailed analysis of Duguit's visit to the University of Buenos Aires can be found in Zimmermann, "Un espíritu nuevo."

46. In his 1919 University of Buenos Aires course he said of Jean Jaurès: "[He] is the strongest figure of modern democracy. He was among us. I had the honor of being his friend, and I will always remember him with fondness." Palacios, *El nuevo derecho,* 101.

47. Fabra Rivas was an editor at "L'Humanité," the newspaper founded by Jean Jaurès, for some time. Yáñez Andrade, "La OIT," 35.

48. García de Fleury, *Introducción al estudio.*

49. I am borrowing this phrase from Duncan Kennedy, "Two Globalizations," 648.

50. Scholars have recently revisited the history of the ILO, a reflection of renewed interest in the circulation of ideas, construction of international networks, and formation of bureaucracies and "state knowledge." See Van Daele et al., *ILO Histories*; Lespinet-Moret and Viet, *L'Organisation*; Kott and Droux, *Globalizing Social Rights.* The literature on the organization's relationship with Latin America is scarce. See Herrera León and Herrera González, *América Latina.*

51. See note 28. Yáñez Andrade, "La OIT," 44–45.

52. Kennedy, "Two Globalizations," 648–651.

Bibliography

Bensusán, Graciela. *La ley federal del trabajo: una visión retrospectiva. Los intentos de reglamentación local del artículo 123 (1917–1929).* Mexico City: Fundación Friedrich Ebert, 1989.

Buylla, Adolfo, Adolfo Posada, and Luis Morote. *El Instituto del Trabajo.* Madrid: Establecimiento Tipográfico de Ricardo Fé, 1902.

Charle, Christophe, Jürgen Schriewer, and Peter Wagner, eds. *Transnational Intellectual Networks: Forms of Academic Knowledge and the Search for Cultural Identities.* Frankfurt: Campus, 2004.

De Castro Gomes, Angela, and Fernando Teixeira da Silva, eds. *A Justiça do Trabalho e sua Historia.* Sao Paulo: Unicamp, 2013.

De Fazio, Federico Leandro. "La 'filosofía positiva,' el derecho y las relaciones laborales en Argentina a principio del siglo XX." *Revista de Estudos Jurídicos UNESP* 15:22 (2011): 71–88.

Duve, Thomas, ed. *Entanglements in Legal History: Conceptual Approaches.* Frankfurt: Max Planck Institute for European Legal History, 2014.

El Tratado de Versalles de 1919 y sus antecedentes. Madrid: Publicaciones del Instituto Ibero-Americano de Derecho Comparado, 1920.

García de Fleury, María. *Introducción al estudio de la doctrina social de la Iglesia.* Caracas: Ediciones Trípode, 1994.

Gargan, Edward T., ed. *Leo XIII and the Modern World.* New York: Sheed and Ward, 1961.

Hepple, Bob. "Introduction." In *The Making of Labour Law in Europe. A Comparative Study of Nine Countries up to 1945*, ed. Bob Hepple. 1–30. London: Mansell, 1986.

Herrera León, Fabián. "México y la Organización Internacional del Trabajo: los orígenes de una relación, 1919–1931." *Foro Internacional* LI:2 (2011): 336–355.

Herrera León, Fabián, and Patricio Herrera González, eds. *América Latina y la Organización Internacional del Trabajo. Redes, cooperación técnica e institucionalidad social, 1919–1950.* Morelia: UMSNH, Instituto de Investigaciones Históricas, 2013.

Kennedy, Duncan. "Two Globalizations of Law and Legal Thought: 1850–1968." *Suffolk University Law Review* XXXVI: 3 (2003): 631–679.

Kott, Sandrine, and Joëlle Droux, eds. *Globalizing Social Rights: The International Labour Organization and Beyond.* New York: Palgrave, 2012.

Labour Courts in Latin America. Geneva/London/Washington, International Labor Office, 1949.

Lespinet-Moret, Isabelle, and Vincent Viet. *L'Organisation international du travail. Origine, développement, avenir.* Rennes: Presses Universitaires de Rennes, 2011.

Linares Quintana, Segundo V. "El derecho constitucional en la postguerra. El constitucionalismo social." *La ley* 41 (enero-marzo 1946): 952–967.

Middlebrook, Kevin J. *The Paradox of Revolution: Labor, the State, and Authoritarianism in Mexico.* Baltimore: Johns Hopkins University Press, 1995.

Ministerio del Interior. *Proyecto de Ley Nacional del Trabajo.* Buenos Aires: Compañía Sud-Americana de Billetes de Banco, 1904.

Olaza Pallero, Sandro. "La influencia de la legislación y doctrina española en el proyecto de ley nacional del trabajo de Joaquín V. González (1904)." *Revista de Historia del Derecho* 23 (2008): 229–255.

Palacio, Juan Manuel. "El grito en el cielo. La polémica gestación de los tribunales del trabajo en la Argentina." *Estudios Sociales* 48 (2015): 59–90.

Palacios, Alfredo L. *El nuevo derecho.* Buenos Aires: Claridad, 1960 [1920].

Pedersen, Susan. "Back to the League of Nations." *American Historical Review* 112:4 (2007): 1091–1117.

Poblete Troncoso, Moisés. *Evolución del Derecho Social en América.* Santiago: Editorial Nascimento, 1942.

Ramm, Thilo. "Epilogue: The New Ordering of Labour Law 1918–1945." In *The Making*, ed. Bob Hepple. 276–298. 1986.

———. "Workers' Participation, the Representation of Labour and Special Labour Courts." In *The Making*, ed. Bob Hepple. 242–276. 1986.

Rerum Novarum. In http://www.vatican.va/holy_father/leo_xiii/encyclicals/documents/hf_l -xiii_enc_15051891_rerum-novarum_sp.html (accessed April 7, 2017).

Sánchez Echevarría, Ada Inés. "*Legal Transplants*: una propuesta metodológica para el derecho comparado." In *La cultura jurídica latinoamericana y la circulación de ideas durante la primera mitad del siglo XX*, ed. Ezequiel Abásolo. 45–60. Buenos Aires: Instituto de Investigaciones de Historia del Derecho, 2014.

Suarez-Potts, William. "The Mexican Supreme Court and the Juntas de Conciliación y Arbitraje, 1917–1924: The Judicialisation of Labour Relations after the Revolution." *Journal of Latin American Studies* 41:4 (2009): 723–755.

Teixeira da Silva, Fernando. "The Brazilian and Italian Labor Courts: Comparative Notes." *IRSH* 55 (2010): 381–412.

Van Daele, Jasmien, et al., eds. *ILO Histories: Essays on the International Labour Organization and Its Impact on the World during the Twentieth Century.* Berna: Peter Lang, 2010.

Yáñez Andrade, Juan Carlos. "La OIT y la red sudamericana de corresponsales. El caso de Moisés Poblete, 1922–1946." In *América Latina*, ed. Herrera León and Herrera González. 45–53. 2013.

Zimmermann, Eduardo. *Los liberales reformistas. La cuestión social en la Argentina.* Buenos Aires: Sudamericana, 1995.

———. "'Un espíritu nuevo': la cuestión social y el Derecho en la Argentina (1890–1930)." *Revista de Indias* 73:257 (2013): 81–106.1.

PART I

The United States, Canada, and Mexico

CHAPTER 2

American Labor Justice and the Problem of Trade Union Legitimacy

LEON FINK

The fundamentals of U.S. industrial relations (IR), although long-standing, have not always been etched in stone. In a little-known aftermath to the Great Pullman Strike of 1894, e.g., railroad workers' leader Eugene V. Debs, while awaiting trial on charges of contempt and conspiracy (charges that would ultimately lead to a six-month sentence in a Woodstock, Illinois, jail), willingly testified before the U.S. Strike Commission, a government body convened by President Cleveland to seek post-Pullman remedies for industrial unrest.[1] What he and the inquiring commissioners concentrated on were the terms of a hypothetical system of compulsory arbitration, or political adjudication of industrial disputes.

The very obscurity of the terms under discussion offers testimony to the subsequent defeat and burial of these ideas on the American main stage. That there is no institutional court of resort for aggrieved parties (workers or employers) in workplace disputes, and that the state has no compelling interest in ensuring fair outcomes in labor-management disputes is taken for granted today. Indeed, by the end of World War II—and in a circumstance spurred by rising Cold War tensions and particularly fears of Communist labor influence in Europe—American labor leaders regularly trumpeted a homegrown model of "free and independent trade unionism." In addition to "freedom" from the taint of Communism, this effectively voluntarist model emphasized economic benefits via collective bargaining as the legitimate end (and limit) of the workers' movement and "independence" from the state and/or political parties as a guiding principle to achieve those ends.[2] Yet, as the Debs reference suggests, this is not the whole story, historically.

U.S. Labor Policy Menu, 1880s–World War I

All the world's industrial powers experienced a period of mass distress and unrest that broke out even before the extended depression of the 1890s. The result, across a wide variety of political regimes, was a near-universal proliferation of state-centered measures aimed variously at securing the public welfare and maintaining social control. In the course of their own confrontation with the most severe of capitalism's crises to that time, American policy makers—public officials, social investigators, and independent labor reformers, as well as union and business leaders—would locate themselves as never before in a larger, international spectrum of economic experimentation. This wider tableau of understanding is repeatedly apparent in congressional and other public debates and even more in a series of expert-led investigations of labor relations commissioned by Congress from the mid-1880s through World War I. And, while reaching out anecdotally to examples on the European Continent, turn-of-the-century American commentators tended, logically enough, to concentrate on English-speaking countries with a similar legal-political inheritance: the U.K., New Zealand, Australia, and (to a lesser degree) Canada.

In assaying the models embodied by their closest politico-cultural counterparts, American reformers were effectively beckoned by two competing strategic roads. One, which for simplicity's sake I will call the relatively antistatist "British road," looked to clear away state and especially court-sanctioned interference to allow organized workers to wrestle with employers on a more even playing field. In the U.K. (as in all her former colonies), modern industrial relations had first to overcome primitive master-and-servant and criminal conspiracy doctrines rooted in the common law that contradicted democratic norms. To this end, beginning with the 1906 *Labour Disputes Act*, British unions notably inoculated themselves from injunctions and other civil penalties in a regime of what Otto Kahn-Freund famously dubbed "collective laissez-faire"—permitting economic conflict between organized employers and workers—that largely lasted until the Thatcherite reforms of the 1980s.[3] The alternative path, which after both the Australian and New Zealand examples, we will label the "Australasian road," headed in the opposite direction toward a more statist regulation of labor-management relations and workplace standards most famously represented by the institution of compulsory arbitration. These arrangements also enjoyed an extended shelf life: though New Zealand bent toward a more market-driven system amid the pressures of "globalization" beginning in the mid-1980s, Australia has maintained a modified version of its arbitration system to this day.[4]

The United States, like Canada (as seen in Chapter 3), worked out something of an intermediary pathway or, perhaps more accurately, a veering back and forth, between the examples of the U.K. and Australia/New Zealand. Beginning in the late nineteenth century (or so-called Gilded Age), even American labor reformers themselves were pulled in both directions. Alas, their country arrived at neither destination. By the

1920s, and in further installments attendant to New Deal–era labor reforms (principally the *National Labor Relations Act* or NLRA of 1935) and their post–WW II aftermath (principally the *Taft-Hartley Act* of 1947), the United States achieved what might best be called a juridically regulated system of collective laissez-faire. What emerged was manifestly *not* the ideal that either American "statists" or "antistatists" had had in mind at the turn of the twentieth century. Just why, as we shall see, was a mixture of political structure, distinctive ideology, business intransigence, and perhaps no small measure of strategic blind spots among pro-labor advocates themselves. It goes almost without saying, moreover, that the end results in the United States diverged substantially from the state-suffused models common to Latin America (which had themselves taken some heed of the Australasian examples) and proved resistant even to the milder state oversight common to Canadian IR practices.

Rise and Fall of Compulsory Arbitration in U.S. Policy Thinking

As far back as the 1870s and continuing through the 1880s, the American labor movement imagined a positive role for government in buttressing workers' power and adjudicating major industrial disputes. Even as the commonly invoked term *arbitration* floated ambiguously as a signifier—here meaning *conciliation*, there meaning *collective bargaining*, and only occasionally specifying what later industrial economists would define as *compulsory arbitration*—there was no denying support for an active, interventionist state within the popular ideology of what historians have called *labor republicanism*.

Indeed, as witnessed by the special Senate Committee on the Relations between Labor and Capital commissioned in 1883, the concept generally reverberated in most favorable terms among otherwise quarreling labor leaders as well as among several of the inquiring legislators. It was perhaps not surprising that Robert Layton, general secretary of the broadly reform-minded Knights of Labor (KOL) would imagine where "a certain number of employees should meet an equal number of employers; they to select an umpire, whose decision should be final. Then let the men make their demands, and let the employers produce their books, and if it appears that they cannot afford to comply with the men's demands, that decision [of the umpire] will [be] made, and must be final."[5]

Positive reference to some sort of compulsory arbitration, moreover, was hardly limited to the politically inclined spirits of the Knights of Labor. As early as 1873, for example, the German socialist party document that had first impressed young cigar maker Sam Gompers with "the fundamental possibilities of the trade union" had pointed to "industrial arbitration courts and the simplification of judicial procedures" as key goals of the international workers' movement.[6] A decade later, W. H. Foster, a printer by trade who served as the first general secretary of the craft union federation that would shortly become the American Federation of Labor, did not sound much different from his Knights of Labor counterparts before the Senate Committee. When asked for a remedy to disputes over hours and wages, Foster pointed to a system of arbitration: "Instead of having it as now, when the one often refused to even acknowledge or discuss the question with the other, if they were required to submit the question to arbitration, or to meet on the same level before an impartial tribunal, there is no doubt but what the result would be more in our favor than it is now, when very often public opinion cannot hear our case."[7] Another Foster, this one Boston printers' leader Frank Foster (no relation), spelled out further the terms that, in principle, seemed reasonable to many in the organized skilled trades. Arbitration, he insisted, must be matched by full legal legitimation, and even encouragement, of organization among the workers themselves. "Experience among individuals and among classes," he suggested, "is the same in this respect as among peoples." "It is only the strong nations that arbitrate with each other. Very rarely a powerful nation arbitrates with a feeble one."[8]

Foster's analogy of workplace arbitration to the arena of international dispute resolution was probably instinctual, given the political backdrop of the times. Not that Foster and his contemporaries would necessarily remember much about specific, prior uses of this negotiating tool. Since the American Revolution (most notably the John Jay Treaty of 1794) and the War of 1812 (Treaty of Ghent), the United States had regularly resorted to arbitral forms to settle differences with Great Britain short of continuing war. Moreover, if Americans had sometimes dealt from weakness, late-nineteenth-century associations with the process likely centered on the post–Civil War Treaty of Washington, where the British swallowed humble pie in acceding to American claims stemming from the *Alabama* (and other Confederate destroyers built in British shipyards), the boundary of North Atlantic fisheries, and the northwest San Juan Island. The coming years would only witness more such "strong nation" resort to arbitration by the Americans—most famously, by pressing the judicial measure on the British in the case of Venezuelan land disputes in the late 1890s and again, before the Hague Court in 1904.[9] By the turn of the century, not only was arbitration regularly in the air as a preferred pathway to international peace, but some voices—perhaps most notably the Women's Christian Temperance Union (WCTU)—loudly made the connection, advocating for its use on both the international and domestic fronts.[10]

Foster's "strong nations" argument, however, would also serve as the very branch that other craft unionists would use to climb down from their original expressions of interest in arbitration. At the time of the Senate hearings in 1883, future AFL leaders like Gompers and carpenters' leader P. J. McGuire were already voicing their reservations about a doctrine that had generally united the cross-class labor reform community of the early Gilded Age. "I am in favor of arbitration when that can be accomplished," Gompers complained, "but [it] is only possible when the workingmen have, by the power of organization, demonstrated to the employers that they are the employers' equal."[11] Given later disparagement by the Gompers-led AFL of most state-sanctioned interventionism including arbitration, workers' compensation, and hours legislation as somehow "un-American," the initial circumspection of the movement regarding means and ends is noteworthy.[12] While reaching out simultaneously in multiple directions for a source of institutional stability and material support, the labor leadership took necessary note of what seemed the limits of both employer cooperation and American statecraft. As carpenters' leader McGuire, who had traveled to Great Britain and Germany two years before his testimony to the Senate Labor and Capital Committee, reported, "While the workers [there] do not perhaps have as much money, they are better off from a social standpoint and an economic standpoint and a sanitary standpoint and, upon the whole . . . enjoy life better than our workers do." Citing the Saturday half-holiday and shorter working hours prevailing among British workers, McGuire suggested "they come nearer to that which humanity generally desires, a contented existence." The United States, on the other hand, seemed caught up in its own digestive system. "This is a country," lamented McGuire, "that is intent chiefly on making money, getting wealth somehow, and our people care little for social comforts or public enjoyment if they are to be had at the expense of the money-making propensities."[13]

In such circumstances, the nearly autonomous national and local unions within the larger labor federation took a decidedly pragmatic, case-specific approach to arbitration systems. In Chicago, for example, the building trades hammered out a series of favorable settlements under the imprimatur of sympathetic federal judge Murray F. Tuley. In 1891, again, the city's carpenters secured a two-year agreement including the eight-hour day and compulsory arbitration through the duration of the Chicago World's Fair in 1893. Workplace-centered militancy as much as any cooperative spirit secured such beachheads; by 1899, the employers' Building Contractors' Council successfully locked out unionized workers, setting off years of further labor-management turmoil.[14]

Industrial unrest centered on the railroads—at once catalyzed by the Great Southwest Strike conducted by the Knights of Labor on the Gould line in 1886 and then reignited two years later by a joint walkout of railway brotherhoods against the Chicago, Burlington, & Quincy Railroad—first pushed serious talk of arbitration to the fore of national legislative consciousness. The principal proposal, originally offered in early spring 1886 by Democratic Congressmen John J. O'Neill (Missouri) and William H. Crain (Texas) as the *Arbitration Act* of 1888, envisioned only voluntary arbitration in future railroad disputes.[15] Yet, a strong undertow existed for more radical measures, including compulsory arbitration. West Virginia Democratic Representative Eustace Gibson, a Virginia-born former Confederate officer and presumably no partisan of federal power in the abstract, nevertheless demanded more than the Crain Bill offered. On the one hand, Gibson related, "skilled labor" had furtively combined in "an unarmed army for protection; and on the other hand we have organized capital, with its paid attorneys in every Legislative Assembly that meets in this land—whether it be National or whether it be State—passing through the legislative halls and leaving their slime on every act of legislation that is passed."

The remedy, as attested to by growing evidence both at home and abroad, was obvious. Citing the constitution's interstate commerce clause, which seemingly invited regulation of railroad traffic and rates, Gibson asked, "So why not wages and hours?" Gibson followed with a series of further rhetorical questions: "Why do we want national legislation on this subject? Is it true that questions of supply and demand will not regulate themselves? Is it true that labor is weak and unable to compete against the power of money? Is it true that the money-power has acquired a hold upon the legislation of this country which it requires the masses of people by their votes at the ballot-box to break? If it be true then we must step in and legislate."[16]

Sharing Gibson's assumptions, Kansas Republican John A. Anderson went one step farther. Relying on both the interstate commerce and the general welfare clause (and thus the power to compel any corporation with a public charter to perform its duty), Anderson sought a permanent investigatory commission over railroad disputes, whose "voluntary" recommendations, if rejected by the parties, would be examined by the courts and transformed into a "compulsory" settlement. In a characteristically partisan explanation, Anderson insisted that principles on this pivotal matter divided on party lines: "The Democratic doctrine is that of supreme State rights . . . under the strictest construction of the Constitution. . . . The Republican doctrine is that of a Government strong enough and wise enough to protect its people, no matter what may be the form of attack, nor where."[17]

Though Anderson surely exaggerated mainstream Republican commitment to a compulsory arbitration bill, his assessment of the antistatist presumptions among most Democrats—and especially those most closely identified with the craft unions— was not inaccurate. A portent of battle lines to come was signaled by the position on the Crain Bill of Martin Foran (D-Ohio), president of the Coopers International Union. Foran opposed the conciliation bill not because it was too weak but because it was too strong. Once Congress started meddling in industrial relations, even by mere investigatory process, he worried, where would it end? "May not some future Congress," he conjectured, "pass laws making it a felony . . . for employees to interfere with the commerce of such roads or the transmission of the mails by striking?" As a potential "entering wedge" to crush organized labor, such would-be government assistance must be opposed. Not by legislation, Foran insisted, but only "through organization that labor will work out its freedom . . . and exact from capital . . . its just reward."[18]

Foran's coolness, moreover, was just the tip of an iceberg of opposition by the soon-to-be dominant AFL toward the entire concept of arbitration. From early on, Samuel Gompers himself led the AFL defiance of the reformers' interventionist efforts. Already by the time of the Homestead Strike in 1892, when a friendly Ohio legislator had asked for his bill-drafting help, Gompers and his tight leadership circle had sharpened a questioning skepticism into unalterable opposition to compulsory arbitration.[19]

Already dodging hostile judicial verdicts, the idea of putting any more power in the hands of the federal government had by then proved anathema to the AFL high command. As P. J. McGuire chided an arbitration advocate at the federation's national convention in December 1892, arbitration "smacked of the Elizabethan age. If the Government makes arbitration, why should it not also regulate wages and the hours of labor? The powers that now direct the militia against strikers would then use the Board of Compulsory Arbitration."[20]

Reiterated as the official AFL position in 1900, opposition to any and all compulsory arbitration became a principle from which it never subsequently deviated.[21] That year, Gompers went so far in an address to the National Civic Federation Conference to equate any settlement imposed on labor by arbitration with a "demoralized, degraded, and debased manhood." It was no less than "a negation of liberty and a return to serfdom."[22]

> In the end, therefore, the Crain Bill of 1886 galvanized no major working-class constituency. Even as the AFL was drawing an increasingly hard line against the incursion of state authority on union autonomy, the more politically oriented Knights of Labor pointedly remained on the sidelines. Unlike proposals for land or currency reform, the legislated eight-hour day, or government ownership of the railroads, telephone, and telegraph—which all received enthusiastic endorsement in the course of the Knights' national assembly in June 1886—the arbitration issue did not command the delegates' attention, one way or the other.[23]

On the domestic political front, likely the most powerful voice for arbitration in industrial affairs was the Civic Federation of Chicago (CFC), a body that gave way to the National Civic Federation in 1900. Linking capitalists like Chicago banker and future secretary of the treasury Lyman Gage and flour king Charles A. Pillsbury, politicians led by Mark Hanna, labor leaders including Gompers and Mitchell, and clergymen like Washington Gladden and Father John A. Ryan with reformer/social scientists Carroll D. Wright, Jane Addams, Ralph Easley, Henry Carter Adams, Henry Demarest Lloyd, and Edward Bemis, the Civic Federation presented a social bloc of considerable potential significance. Tellingly, in accord with both a national and transnational intellectual mood, the Federation's gaze fell early and heavily on the subject of compulsory arbitration. Only months after the collapse of the 1894 Pullman strike, Gage convened a conference in Chicago to build support for national legislation on the subject. The spirit in the room was reflected in business editor James D. Weeks's attack on the principles of traditional political economy as a "gospel of grab . . . not in accordance with our civilization."[24]

Citing the commerce clause of the constitution, Representative James A. Tawney, Republican of Minnesota and a former machinist, offered perhaps the most developed rationale for compulsory adjustment of "such controversies as impede or obstruct . . . our commerce between the states." Tawney neatly contrasted the treatment of the nation's two main "instrumentalities" of commerce: water and rail. In the case of the former, as he accurately cited maritime law stretching back a century, "the medicine in the chest, the license to the engineer, the commission to the captain are all governed by federal statute; even the machinery on the vessel, including the boilers, cannot be used until thoroughly inspected, tested and its safety certified to by a duly authorized government inspector." What was more, he counseled his listeners, Congress had also brought the instrumentality of rail within its regulatory gaze with the *Interstate Commerce Act* of 1887. Now, urged Tawney, it was time to go farther. "The right of the employees of railroad companies to go out on strike is not denied, but the necessity for the exercise of the right should be removed by giving to either party to the controversy an adequate, peaceable remedy."[25]

Generally in line with the logic of the Civic Federaton, the 1894 U.S. Strike Commission tried again to raise the banner of compulsory arbitration.[26] Given the unequal power relations in which they found themselves, writer-activist Demarest Lloyd testified to the commission, industrial workers had no chance to cope on their own against obdurate employers: "The attitude of the employer amounts simply to this: Reason shall not arbitrate between us, because there is a Judge sitting on your case who always decides in my favour, if he has time enough—Judge Hunger."[27]

Led by their chairman, Carroll Wright, the commissioners attempted to move the American system toward an accommodation with foreign examples of state engagement. As an issue effecting "quasi-public corporations," asserted their final report, railroad regulation—including questions of compulsory arbitration as well as government ownership—"is one of expediency and not of [inherent] power." Applauding a move away from class strife and toward the institutionalization of the "rights of labor" within "conservative" trade unions, the commission noted that "capital abroad prefers to deal with these unions rather than with individuals or mobs, and from their joint efforts in good faith at conciliation and arbitration much good and many peaceful days have resulted."[28] Building on what it claimed was now a common agreement among both workers and employers internationally in favor of peaceful collective bargaining, the commission sought self-consciously to advance "harmonious relations of equal standing and responsibility before the law."[29] Leaving aside larger questions of industrial governance, the commission's report urged strong intervention in future railroad disputes by a permanent strike commission empowered, like the Interstate Commerce Commission with respect to freight rates, to resolve disputes by decisions enforceable through the courts. In any particular "controversy," both the affected union and employer would have a right to select a representative as a temporary member of the commission, but each side would be subject to governmental discipline: employers could not discharge workers for union membership, unions could not "intimidate" nonstriking workers in the course of the dispute.[30]

The commissioners were clearly eager to identify their recommendations as a basic rebalancing of the national scales of social justice. While acknowledging that the "growth in corporate power and wealth has been the marvel of the past fifty years," they expressed the hope that the next half-century would witness "the advancement of labor to a position of like power and responsibility." The key to their proposal—like the plans developed in New Zealand and Australia—was institutionalization of the labor movement through a combination of incorporation of trade unions, collective bargaining, and compulsory arbitration. As the commission concluded, "Since nations have grown to the wisdom of avoiding disputes by conciliation, and even of settling them by arbitration, why should capital and labor in their dependence upon each other persist in cutting each other's throats as a settlement of differences?"[31] The point was to set limits to collective protest while legitimating and normalizing the presence of trade unions within the industrial order.

Encountering repeated skepticism from most of their trade union witnesses (who for almost a decade now had rejected the arbitration option), the commissioners bent over backward to recruit at least a few working-class representatives—and Eugene Debs in particular—to support their proposal. But Debs's qualified and provisional conversion to compulsory arbitration demanded no giant leap from the ARU leader; he had skillfully deployed Minnesota's state arbitration statute to win recognition from the Great Northern Railroad in 1893. Moreover, even amid the hostilities of the Pullman strike and boycott, Debs had twice offered to submit the issues to arbitration.[32]

The unequivocal recommendation of the Pullman commission may have been the nation's best, if not its last, chance for a fundamental shift in industrial social policy. Despite the commission's own considerable intellectual heft, however, neither President Cleveland and his party nor prevailing elements of the organized business or labor community made the recommendations their own. The closest turn-of-the-century reformers got to a serious role for government action in industrial disputes was the *Erdman Act* of 1898, which, mandating only mediation and voluntary arbitration on the railways, was not concretely applied until 1906. The Anthracite Coal Commission, established by President Roosevelt following his settlement of a strike during the harrowing winter of 1902, pushed for a strengthening of Erdman—including a penalty for whichever party initiated a strike or lockout without first resorting to the machinery of arbitration—but this appeal, too, was lost on Congress. The sole legacy of Pullman-era energies were a series of federal railroad acts limited to the running trades and aimed at averting any further catastrophic work stoppage by way of conciliation, investigation, or, at most, voluntary arbitration.[33]

IR Intellectuals and the Search for Industrial Democracy

Despite the continuing odds against a regulated industrial relations system, public discussion of the subject was kept alive by the new generation of institutional economists who had gained a foothold in the universities in the 1890s. These university-based reformers, already in evidence in the deliberations of the Civic Federation and

1894 Strike Commission, first seized a national platform amid the deliberations of the United States Industrial Commission (USIC), a four-year investigation (1899–1902) of American economic institutions instigated by President McKinley. With a tripartite structure of business, labor, and congressional representatives, the nineteen-member USIC fairly took the measure of its times. Though both USIC secretary E. Dana Durand, a Stanford economist, and staff investigator John R. Commons initially assembled comprehensive and generally positive reports on arbitration procedures abroad, the commissioners, after hearing sustained opposition from both business and labor representatives, quickly dropped arbitration and other strong-state interventions from their policy playbook.[34]

Without a labor or political champion (Mark Hanna died in early 1904), arbitration largely fell out of the national progressive toolkit in precisely the years of most fertile reform agitation on most other subjects. In its place, for the most part, continued an ongoing war between hardline "open-shop" employers on one side and "closed shop" trade unionists on the other. In the long run, the stalemate surely worked to the distinct disadvantage of the labor forces. Not only would the unionists search in vain for the elixir that would put the United States on the British road of collective laisssez-faire, but the open-versus-closed-shop debate lent employers an important ideological edge as champions of "voluntary" individual rights against "compulsory" union membership.

As one of the idea's foremost advocates, Jane Addams also sensed when the air was leaving the arbitration bag. In Pullman's aftermath, Illinois had established a State Board of Conciliation and Arbitration, but to Addams's regret its voluntary apparatus went largely unused. In 1896, for example, Chicago clothing manufacturers determined to break the cutters' union, precipitating a strike. In the pages of the *Hull-House Bulletin*, Addams chided the owners for their disavowal of the "fundamental principle of representation, upon which our entire government is founded," as well as for a basic "lack of discipline." Still appealing for arbitration, she counseled the parties, "Trained and responsible people do not try to settle their difficulties by fighting."[35] The ensuing decade sapped her hopes. "There is no doubt," she wrote after the city's bitter teamster strike in 1905, "but that ideas and words which at one time fill a community with enthusiasm may, after a few years, cease to be a moving force, apparently from no other reason than that they are spent and no longer fit into the temper of the hour. Such a fate has evidently befallen the word 'arbitration,' at least in Chicago, as it is applied to industrial struggles."[36] Without legislative advance on the issue, what was left on the edges of the industrial scene was a select series of local experiments in employer/union cooperation (sometimes including voluntary arbitration machinery) as well as the continuing reports of a phalanx of social scientists and reform thinkers still looking at various international alternatives.

The most prominent of such experiments occurred in garment manufacturing. Following upheavals and militant strikes among a semiskilled, largely immigrant and female labor force, two new industrywide unions—the International Ladies' Garment Workers' Union and the Amalgamated Clothing Workers (ACW)—gained a foothold, respectively, in the women's and men's clothing industry on the basis of mediated settlements that institutionalized arbitration in the settlement of industrial disputes. It was no accident that such agreements were reached within a relatively homogeneous surrounding of large, Jewish-owned firms at once susceptible to community pressures and capable of imposing a floor of work-based standards under all competitors.

In New York City, progressive Boston attorney (and future Supreme Court justice) Louis Brandeis negotiated the industry's first "Protocol of Peace" following the cloak-makers' Great Revolt in July 1910. As a tripartite agreement between labor, manage-ment, and the public, the protocols—quickly established across the needle trades—promised both industrial peace (secured through a no-strike, no-lockout pledge from the parties and binding arbitration for future grievances) and labor rights, the latter vouchsafed by a union-management committee on working conditions and a "pref-erential" union shop.[37]

A similar logic prevailed in Chicago. Following a walkout of 40,000 workers at Hart, Schaffner, and Marx settled by arbitration in 1911, Sidney Hillman and fellow strike leader (and future spouse) Bessie Abramowitz led a rebellion against the cor-rupt leadership of the United Garment Workers and chartered the ACW in 1914 with a combined commitment to industrial unionism, scientific efficiency, and coopera-tive adjudication of disputes. That same year, a model ACW settlement was signed with the garment giant Sonneborn in Baltimore; there, German Jewish attorney and reformer Judge Jacob Moses arbitrated an agreement that included pensions, safety measures, and a new medical unit as well as union recognition. In return, the union would discipline its members, forsaking wildcat strikes in favor of arbitration to estab-lish "joint control" of the industry.[38]

The logic of "industrial democracy," to cite a favorite phrase of Brandeis, developed in the special circumstances of the big-city garment districts as in no other places. Both a flexible labor leadership—for example, willing to accept a "preferential shop" over the unions' preferred "closed shop"—and "moderate" owners (like Lincoln A. Filene, Meyer Bloomfield, and bankers Jacob Schiff and Louis Marshall) worried about low-wage competitors coming to terms around the long-term health of the industry as well as worker welfare. Unlike most other industrial conflicts, the big-city garment strikes attracted numerous middle-class supporters, determined to find a pathway to long-term labor peace. Moreover, the very fact that the "manliness" of the work-ers was not at stake in an industry dominated by women semiskilled operatives may have heightened cooperation among the parties. As discovered elsewhere, arbitration appealed particularly to a labor force not confident of its own combative strength. Here, then, according to Brandeis's vision, was an arena where the raw inequalities of industrial capitalism could be softened by countervailing power in the hands of work-ers as well as management.[39] Organized garment workers could thus look back with pride on several years of stable employment and rising wages. Even in this selective sphere, however, as post–World War I conflicts flared up over union bureaucratization and lack of democracy as well as between labor and management, "protocolism" proved no sure guarantor of social harmony.[40] In the United States, room for even a trial run for arbitration was thus most narrowly confined.

Even before his arbitration experience, however, Brandeis had recognized the need for a dramatic breakthrough from the legal constraints defining American labor relations. Preparing to teach a course on business law just as the Homestead Strike of 1892 erupted, Brandeis later explained how the conflict had first upset his conventionally sanguine assumptions about the capacity of the legal system to offer equal protections to all: "I saw at once that the common law, built up under simpler conditions of living, gave an inadequate basis for the adjustment of the complex relations of the modern factory system. I threw away my notes and approached my theme from new angles."[41]

How to trump the common law and its bias toward the employer's property rights became a central strategic preoccupation not only of legal reformers like Brandeis but a host of progressive scholars, not to mention the stewards of the labor movement itself.[42] As we have seen, the garment protocols, like the progressive economists' industrial commissions, tried to substitute an alternative legal authority for that of the civil courts. Their concern was not misplaced. After 1880, employers customarily sought injunctive relief and subsequent suits for damages in the case of strikes or boycotts; indeed, from 1880 to 1931, 1800 injunctions would be issued in U.S. courts against strikes alone.[43] The dominant legal voice echoed in two opinions from the bench only a few months before the Pullman conflict of 1894. In the first, Circuit Court Judge William Howard Taft, disallowing strikes and boycotts to enforce the closed shop, ruled that the constitutional provision of the conservative Brotherhood of Engineers requiring members to act in solidarity with brothers on strike "make[s] the whole brotherhood a criminal conspiracy against the laws of their country." In the second, a Wisconsin federal court similarly compared striking railroad workers to surgeons suspending work in the middle of an operation: "It is idle to talk of a peaceable strike. None has ever occurred."[44]

A crucial division nevertheless erupted among those who would uphold trade union rights. Brandeis and university-based policy intellectuals like John R. Commons generally leaned toward a variety of "statist" interventions. Tripartite investigatory commissions, conciliation, and arbitration panels, obligatory incorporation of unions, as well as minimum wage and maximum hours legislation were generally all part of a mix of interventions into the private marketplace, consistently pushed by progressive labor reformers and regularly recommended in high-level forums convened after major industrial conflicts and meant to set an agenda for national ameliorative action.

The mainline AFL (i.e., excepting the garment unions and railroad brotherhoods) tended to rebuff all such initiatives in favor of a determined pursuit of what we have identified as the path of collective laissez-faire. Aversion to even the most enabling of governmental regulation was on display in the 1912–1915 Commission on Industrial Relations (CIR), originally appointed by President William Howard Taft to recommend solutions to "a state of industrial war." Three years of exhaustive investigations overseen by a tripartite panel of business, labor, and public representatives—all sympathetic in principle to a role for organized labor in the body politic—produced in the end a policy stalemate between the allies of the commission's chair, radical attorney and AFL confidant Frank Walsh, and those of its most distinguished public member, Professor Commons, as aided by Wisconsin legislative librarian Charles McCarthy.[45] Commons's proposals included calls for minimum wage regulation and other worker safety and welfare measures combined with a proposal for the institutionalization of Wisconsin-style industrial commissions. If self-consciously less "compulsory" than New Zealand arbitration's system, the commission model nevertheless anticipated a permanent investigatory role for government in labor-management disputes. The idea was abhorrent to the Walsh-led trade union bloc.[46] With more sharply anticapitalist language, Walsh and the labor commissioners called for stringent inheritance taxes, nationalization of utilities and no restrictions on the right to strike, but they warned against German-style "bureaucratic paternalism" and "ponderous legal machinery" that would subject business and workers equally to "the whim or caprice of an army of officials, deputies, and Governmental employees."[47]

Again and again, pro-labor legal strategists looked for a single legislative remedy, like Britain's *Trade Disputes Act*, that would legitimize the unions' normal behavior—i.e., accepting a role for disciplined, collective action in industrial conflicts, including the inoculation of labor strikes from civil prosecution for damages. Alas, they never found the cure. The closest they got by World War I were Sections 6 and 20 of the *Clayton Antitrust Act* of 1914, exempting unions from antitrust provisions of the *Sherman Act* (that had been used against the Pullman strikers) and famously declaring that "the labor of a human being is not a commodity or article of commerce."[48]

By themselves, however, such doctrinal changes in statutory law—what Gompers at the time christened as "labor's Magna Carta"—could never shut the door to the coercion available to employers (and sympathetic justices) via case law. In part, American courts (with the power of judicial review), unlike their British counterparts, owed no constitutional deference to legislative mandate. In this particular arena, for example, whereas British legislation as early as 1875 had "statutorily specified strike offenses," American laws, notes historian David Brody, through the *Clayton Act* and beyond, "never overrode the authority of the courts to decide what 'intimidation' [of nonstrikers] meant." With its intentionally vague and open-ended definitions of what in the end constituted lawful acts, Clayton opened a hole that justices could ride a carriage through.[49] Generally impressed with American progressive thinking on social welfare issues while touring the United States in 1914, the great Australian jurist H. B. Higgins expressed a mixture of admiration and sympathy for the political position of his hosts (who included Brandeis, Felix Frankfurter, and National Consumers' League leader, Josephine Goldmark). "It is to America," he wrote Frankfurter, "that we must look for the humanizing of our civilization . . . and yet you are horribly shackled by your constitution."[50]

In the end, when the "legal machinery" of the state arrived only two years after release of the CIR Report, it was packaged in irony. With U.S. entry into World War I, two old labor-management foes and equally fierce advocates of the industrial "free contract"—William Howard Taft and Frank Walsh—became cochairs of the War Labor Conference Board, which quickly morphed into the more administrative National War Labor Board (NWLB). The NWLB presided over a joint no-strike–no-lockout pledge by leading employers as well as the AFL. In addition to a guarantee of the right to organize (without coercive methods), the wartime federal government would also impose an eight-hour workday as the industrial norm. Finally, and most dramatically, the NWLB inserted itself as a powerful broker of industrial disputes; its offers to arbitrate were voluntary but—freighted with the authority of the "national interest"—once accepted by the parties, its judgments were enforceable under law. Despite the efforts of Walsh to extend the life of the wartime board, the edifice of government-backed industrial relations quickly came asunder in the face of employer opposition. Within months of the armistice, the war labor agencies had collapsed."[51] In retrospect, it was obvious that "wartime fervor" more than "progressive ideals" had accounted for the experiment in expanded government that included the NWLB.[52]

Unable to buck the courts and equally unable to generate any alternative state-centered authority, the American labor movement limped into the 1920s as a weak counterpart to corporate control of the economy and the workplace. Determined to defend its own organizational autonomy and strategic room to maneuver from governmental interference, the AFL struggled in vain until the 1930s to construct a British road on American industrial soil.

The Great Depression and Rise of State Intervention

Within the extended legal paradigm of American voluntarism—or privately negotiated labor-management relations—the years 1937–1947 marked a brief "honeymoon decade" when the federal government and the administration of labor law *did* tilt decisively toward the recognition and protection of labor unions. Building off language originally voiced (albeit undeveloped in practice) in Section 7A of the early New Deal's *National Industrial Recovery Act* of 1933, the *National Labor Relations Act* of 1935 (upheld by the Supreme Court in 1937), as historian James A. Gross summarizes, "intentionally favored collective bargaining." The NLRA (better known as the *Wagner Act* after its principal congressional sponsor) identified unions at once with the basic building blocks of democracy and as a necessary prod on business to lift wages and thus restore a Depression-deflated consumer economy. Both formally (through an extended list of prohibitions of employer antiunionist techniques) and informally (via the semiautonomous authority of generally pro-union administrative law judges), the state effectively acted as the unions' (and especially the newly minted Congress of Industrial Organizations [CIO]) key ally in facilitating legal recognition and uncoerced bargaining across America's heavy industries. Regionally centered labor boards, framed by the logic of their enabling legislation, would henceforth act as the court of at least first resort (even as decisions could ultimately be appealed to civil jurisdiction) in the case of labor disputes. Reflecting the impetus behind the new law, Senator Robert Wagner declared, "[The] struggle for a voice in industry through the process of collective bargaining is at the heart of the struggle for the preservation of political as well as economic democracy in America."[53]

The same spirit, although now in enhanced bureaucratic form, prevailed throughout the WWII years in the form of the National War Labor Board. Picking up on the friendly labor-government relations of the late thirties, the war years institutionalized the peace pact in the form of price controls, a no-strike pledge, union dues checkoff, and ultimate compulsory arbitration in the case of industrial disputes. Drawing on tripartite representation (labor, business, and the government) rooted in often-frustrated progressive-era principles, the new Labor Board of 1942–1945 granted government more authority than it had ever previously exercised in industrial affairs. As historian Ronald Schatz summarizes:

> They could issue edicts to employers and unions regarding hours of work, working conditions, union membership policies, workers' grievances, and virtually every other aspect of union-management relations. In October 1942, the president gave the Board control of wage rates at every company, whether unionized or not. As the responsibilities increased, the National War Labor Board set up thirteen regional boards for each section of the country and its territories and, later in the war, eighteen additional boards for industries deemed essential to war production. The thirty-one auxiliary boards handled the vast majority of the cases, while the national board became the industrial equivalent of the U.S. Supreme Court.[54]

In exchange for their commitment to the war effort via a binding no-strike pledge, unions received a heretofore unknown security guarantee in a "maintenance-of-membership" formula that tied the organized worker (and his/her dues) to the union through the life of the contract. Overall, a steelworkers' union accountant thus remembered the membership boon of wartime labor administrative policy as "manna from heaven."[55] Here was a moment, in short, when the federal government had seemingly placed its full stamp of approval on both the legitimacy and significance of the trade union presence in the industrial workplace.

Alas (and as in the case of World War I), the warm embrace of organized labor by the administrative state did not long survive the war years. The thinness of NLRB protections (let alone preference) for collective versus individual bargaining arrangements was quickly apparent in the conservative "adjustments" of the law institutionalized by the Taft-Hartley Amendments of 1947. Whereas the *Wagner Act* had sought to promote a union presence within industry, the business counterresponse reflected in Taft-Hartley emphasized the right of the *individual worker* to choose the terms of his/her employment, union or no-union. To this end, the new legislation asserted an employers' right of "free speech" (i.e., communication with employees during union drives) while also elaborating a new list of union "unfair labor practices" aimed at stopping union "coercion" or "restraint" of individual employees or employers. In addition, in the name of the "free flow of commerce," it curtailed a host of practices that had once enhanced the effectiveness of union collective action: e.g., mass picketing, secondary boycott, and foremen's unions. Finally, and most famously, Taft-Hartley's Sec. 14B also struck at the organizational base of union security by permitting individual states to outlaw the "closed" *union shop*. In such "right-to-work" jurisdictions, unions could no longer negotiate contracts that required union membership (or at least the payment of union dues) as a criterion of employment. Without exaggeration, George Taylor, former head of the WW II War Labor Board, called the Taft-Hartley measures a "positive program to develop union insecurity."[56] With the dispersal of the circumstances (depression and war), which had made for a special accommodation to organized labor, the letter of the *Wagner Act*, as amended, was increasingly turned to conservative policy ends. Historian Howell John Harris thus estimates that by 1950, "businessmen were once again in the saddle."[57] And, in the long run, notes historian Colin Gordon, "federal labor policy would prove as capricious as its private counterparts":

> [W]itness the candid effort to "zap labor" by administration after administration in the 1970s and 1980s and the unwillingness of the postwar NLRB to constrain antiunion employers or protect workers' rights with any sincerity. The Wagner Act was not a work of philosophy but a means to an end: an economic order characterized by industrial peace, competitive stability, and adequate consumption. In the postwar world, the same goals demanded quite different strategies and priorities.[58]

One little-known and ultimately inconsequential sidebar to post–WW II labor law discussion in the United States is worth mentioning precisely for its juxtaposition to the Latin American trajectories discussed elsewhere in this volume. A plan for a system of American "labor courts" that would relieve the "flood" of labor cases in the courts, oversee decisions of the NLRB, and provide a distinct and sovereign space for the resolution of disputes (albeit with decisions ultimately appealable to the federal courts) was, in fact, introduced in the same Republican Congress that enacted the *Taft-Hartley Act* in 1947. Noticeably, however, the proposal lacked the policy priority—let alone the imprimatur of executive authority or popular support—generated in other countries. Proposed by Republican Senators H. Alexander Smith of New Jersey and Homer Ferguson of Michigan as a further hedge against union power by forces inherently suspicious of the motives of NLRB bureaucrats, the measure was quickly swallowed and buried after two months of hearings in the Joint Committee on Labor-Management Relations. Rejected from the outset both by labor-liberals and business conservatives, the basic concept rang not only unnecessary but downright "un-American." With characteristic dispatch, Montana's labor commissioner called the idea "totalitarian": "It is evident here that the proposers of this plan have not read their history or have conveniently chosen to forget it. Both the controlling dictatorships of Germany and Italy proposed and placed in operation such a plan."[59]

Concluding Remarks

If a stronger state-based system of dispute resolution—an option repeatedly raised on the U.S. public agenda at least from 1880 to 1920—would have simultaneously served the cause of worker welfare while still being eminently compatible with a capitalist-centered industrial economy, why did it not get established? I would point to three main culprits. First, the effective recognition of trade unionism as a natural part of the industrial system, as required in any arbitration system, remained anathema to the most dynamic of American business lobbies in this era. Although, as we have seen, major industrialists like Carnegie and Rockefeller and financiers like Morgan gave at least momentary consideration to such alternatives, particularly through the entreaties of the National Civic Federation, Main Street employers looked in a decidedly different direction. Both the National Association of Manufacturers (at least post-1903) and the U.S. Chamber of Commerce (established in 1912) took a hard line against enforced collective bargaining and any state-led coordination of the economy. In crusading for the open shop, autonomy-minded employers thus counterposed the very principle of "personal liberty" to union discipline.[60] With no space for ideological reconciliation, the only "give" available would be through the courts or brute industrial warfare. Following World War II, of course, business was forced to reckon with the much-expanded influence of organized labor in industry. Yet, by a determined, virtually unceasing attack on unions as "monopolies" and threats to individual freedom, a combination of old and newer business lobbies decisively regained the political-ideological offensive.[61] Politically, we have identified no shortage of articulate advocacy for an interventionist state, seemingly stronger among Republican than Democratic legislators. Yet, no single event or individual could catalyze these disparate elements into a positive reaction. The one political power broker, with sympathetic ties to labor as well as to a national bloc of manufacturers with an interest in tariff protection, was probably Mark Hanna, and he passed from the scene too early to see any such event through. Otherwise, even when they invoked arbitration (as did President Theodore Roosevelt after the anthracite strike) and Wilson during World War I on a de facto basis, the nation's political leadership never embraced the concept in any convincing way.

Nor could the state effectively intrude upon labor-management relations without the consent, let alone active support, of at least a sizable part of the labor movement. Third-party intervention, to be sure, never fully replicates what an organized body of workers wants for itself; nevertheless, both the isolated examples in the United States and the record in Australasia indicate that much can be gained by public leverage in the larger bargaining process. Since the 1890s, however, the forces within U.S. organized labor cleaved to a collective version of "personal liberty" or group autonomy in rejecting the dilution of industrial authority implicit in arbitration award. Part hardheaded pragmatism, part macho braggadocio, the AFL (and subsequent AFLCIO) attitude simply failed to reckon with how fragmentary, how limited was its own reach over the American workforce. To be sure, such attitudes began to change in the 1930s–1940s, particularly with the coming of the CIO. Yet, even then, without a preferential legal option for union recognition (which was effectively accomplished in arbitration regimes but not under the officially "neutral" aegis of the NLRB and the civil courts), the pro-labor tide proved eminently reversible amid a conservative Republican and pro-business political resurgence. The result is one of the lowest recorded union-density rates in the developed world.[62]

Finally, as a cross-class model, a nationally sanctioned arbitration system required a core of professional-class advocates or public intellectuals to turn the idea into a public priority high enough to command attention from the political and industrial actors themselves. In Australasia and most Latin American countries (as we'll see in the following chapters), the effective ramrod came from labor-sympathetic lawyers, writers, and journalists in alliance with select trade union and government figures. That same social formation existed in the United States in the amorphous circles of reform we call the "Progressives" and then the "New Dealers." Powerful labor-reform voices like Jane Addams, Henry Demarest Lloyd, Louis Brandeis, John R. Commons, Senator Robert Wagner, and Frances Perkins tried but failed to find an institutional alternative to class conflict and class subjugation in the form of state mechanisms of investigation, conciliation, arbitration, or official government support for union recognition and collective bargaining. For all their energy and good will, however, these American progressives only rarely found a vehicle to translate the message of their speeches and writings, commissions, and ultimately even legislative accomplishments, into determinative public policy.

Notes

1. Buder, 187; Salvatore, 20–38.
2. Millen, 5–6.
3. Wedderburn, "Otto Kahn-Freund and British Labour Law," in Wedderburn et al., 40.
4. In New Zealand, compulsory arbitration was abolished (under a Labour government) in the private sector in 1984 and the public sector four years later. By 1991, the *Employment Contract Act* had also abolished compulsory trade union membership and minimum wage awards that buttressed the entire system. Melanie Nolan and Pat Walsh, "Labour's Leg-Iron? Assessing a Century of Trade Unionism under the Arbitration System," in Walsh, 9–37, appendixes 199–204; Anderson and Quinlan, 125–127; Howell, 8.

5. Robert Layton testimony, *Report...Labor and Capital*, 23.

6. "Samuel Gompers Introduction to Socialist Thought, 1: 22, SGP; A Translation of a Pamphlet by Carl Hillmann," 1:37, SGP.

7. *Report...Labor and Capital*, 1177.

8. Ibid., 85.

9. Bailey, 77, 155, 207, 384, 440–441, 502.

10. Tyrrell, 178.

11. Samuel Gompers Papers (SGP), 1: 349.

12. For a recent qualification and partial defense of the early AFL's "anti-government" message as well as vigorous discussion thereon, see Cobble.

13. McGuire testimony, *Report...Labor and Capital*, 1: 339.

14. Westhoff, 137–138; Cohen, 108–111, 123–139.

15. 25 Stat. 501. For the most thorough treatment of these events, see Eggert, 54–107.

16. Cong. Rec., House, 49th Cong, 1st sess., vol. 17, pt. 3, April 1, 1886, 3008–3010.

17. Ibid., 3017–3018.

18. Ibid., 3034. Foran, of course, was all too prescient in citing the federal mails as a potential source of government repression of railway strike activity—exactly what happened amid the Pullman Boycott of 1894 (though the *Crain Act* had nothing to do with state intervention in that case).

19. Gompers to George Iden, July 15, 1892, SGP, 3: 192.

20. McGuire, AFL Convention, 1892, SGP, 3: 258–259.

21. Witte, 9–10.

22. Gompers Address to National Civic Federation Conference on Industrial Arbitration, December 17, 1900, SGP, 5: 300.

23. *John Swinton's Paper*, June 6, June 13, 1886.

24. Civic Federation of Chicago, 50.

25. Ibid., 31.

26. Kaltenborn, 37.

27. Westhoff, 152.

28. U.S. Strike Commission, 1894, xlvii.

29. Ibid., xlviii.

30. Ibid., lii–liv.

31. Ibid., xlvi–xlvii.

32. Salvatore, 134, 136. Unsurprisingly, therefore, Debs publicly applauded the recommendations of the Strike Commission. Lindsey, 357–358.

33. Witte, 17.

34. Wunderlin Jr., 27–45, 64–68, offers the definitive account of USIC operations. Washington, D.C.: Woodrow Wilson Center Press, 1993, 230–231.

35. "Industrial Arbitration" [reference courtesy of Shana Bernstein]; Addams, *Twenty Years at Hull House*, 128–129.

36. Addams, *Newer Ideals of Peace*, 133.

37. Greenwald, 14, 57, 68, 73–74.

38. Argersinger, 43–44, 122.

39. Strum, 27, 34.

40. Greenwald, 214–222.

41. Brandeis, as quoted in Strum, 24–25.

42. On the unions' repeated attempts to secure legislative relief from injunctions, see Fink, "Labor, Liberty, and the Law," 155–156.

43. Millis and Montgomery, 505–506, 630–631.

44. Dubofsky, 163, 165.

45. Interacting with its internal policy differences, the commission was riveted by a series of personal and political conflicts, narrated previously in Fink, *Progressive Intellectuals*, 80–113.

46. U.S. Commission on Industrial Relations, 1916, 310–404.

47. Fink, *Progressive Intellectuals*, 105.

48. *Clayton Antitrust Act*, Sec. 6, (codified at 15 U.S.C. § 17).

49. Jones, 214; Brody, 227–228. Yet, even the more politically effective *Norris-LaGuardia Act* (1932) and *Wagner Act* (1935)—that buttressed labor's legitimacy in later years—never escaped; according to Brody, the core ideological and legal confinement of collective worker behavior was embedded in an "insurmountable case law." As Brody demonstrates, despite the legislative presumption under the *Norris-LaGuardia Anti-Injunction Act* (1932) and the *Wagner Act* (1935) that organized workers could best exercise "actual freedom of contract," core legal doctrines of individual property rights, subsequently confirmed and underlined by the *Taft-Hartley Act* (1947), privileged the rights of nonassociation as well as the employer's right to at-will decisions of hiring and firing, 236–244, quotations, 237, 241.

50. Lake, 172–188, quotation 174.

51. McCartin, 90, quotation 175.

52. Karl, 43.

53. Gross, 1.

54. Schatz, 40.

55. Lichtenstein, 80.

56. Gross, 2–4, 9.

57. Harris, 203.

58. Gordon, 302–303.

59. Hearings before the Joint Committee, 1948.

60. Jacoby, 173–200, esp. 178–179; Martin, 174, 181; Steigerwalt, 114.

61. Fones-Wolf, 257–290.

62. At 10.8 percent, the United States ranked at the bottom of reported OECD countries for union density—behind Mexico as well as Europe and Australasia, in 2013, http://stats.oecd.org/Index.aspx?DataSetCode=UN_DEN (accessed Nov. 20, 2015).

Bibliography

Addams, Jane. *Twenty Years at Hull House.* Boston: Bedford, 1999 [1910].

Addams, Lane. *Newer Ideals of Peace.* New York: Macmillan, 1907.

Anderson, Gordon, and Quinlan Michael. "The Changing Role of the State: Regulating Work in Australia and New Zealand, 1788–2007." *Labour History* 95 (November 2008): 111–132.

Argersinger, Jo Ann E. *Making the Amalgamated: Gender, Ethnicity, and Class in the Baltimore Clothing Industry, 1899–1939.* Baltimore: Johns Hopkins University Press, 1999.

Bailey, Thomas A. *A Diplomatic History of the American People.* New York: Appleton-Century-Crofts, 1969.

Brody, David. "Free Labor, Law, and American Trade Unionism." In *Terms of Labor: Slavery, Serfdom, and Free Labor*, ed. Stanley Engerman. 213–244. Stanford, Calif.: Stanford University Press, 1999.

Buder, Stanley. *Pullman: An Experiment in Industrial Order and Community Planning.* New York: Oxford University Press, 1967.

Civic Federation of Chicago. *Report on Congress on Industrial Conciliation and Arbitration.* Chicago, November 13–14, 1894. Chicago: Wm. C. Hollister and Bro., 1894.

Cobble, Dorothy Sue. "Pure and Simple Radicalism: Putting the Progressive Era AFL in Its Time," with responses by Melvyn Dubofsky, Andrew Wender Cohen, Donna T. Haverty-Stacke, and Julie Greene. *Labor: Studies in Working-Class History of the Americas* 10 (Winter 2013): 89–116.

Cohen, Andrew Wender. *The Racketeer's Progress: Chicago and the Struggle for the Modern American Economy, 1900–1940.* New York: Cambridge University Press, 2004.

Dubofsky, Melvyn. "The Federal Judiciary, Free Labor, and Equal Rights." In *The Pullman Strike and the Crisis of the 1890s*, ed. Richard Schneirov, Shelton Stromquist, and Nick Salvatore. Urbana: University of Illinois Press, 1999.

Eggert, Gerald G. *Railroad Labor Disputes: The Beginnings of Federal Strike Policy.* Ann Arbor: University of Michigan Press, 1967.

Fink, Leon. "Labor, Liberty, and the Law: Trade Unionism and the Problem of the American Constitutional Order." In *In Search of the Working Class: Essays in American Labor History and Political Culture*, ed. Fink. 144–171. Urbana: University of Illinois Press, 1994.

———. *Progressive Intellectuals and the Dilemmas of Intellectual Commitment.* Cambridge, Mass.: Harvard University Press, 1997.

Fones-Wolf, Elizabeth A. *Selling Free Enterprise: The Business Assault on Labor and Liberalism, 1945–60.* Urbana: University of Illinois Press, 1994.

Gordon, Colin. *New Deals: Business, Labor, and Politics in America, 1920–1935.* New York: Cambridge University Press, 1994.

Greenwald, Richard A. *The Triangle Fire, the Protocols of Peace, and Industrial Democracy in Progressive Era New York.* Philadelphia: Temple University Press, 2005.

Gross, James A. *Broken Promise: The Subversion of U.S. Labor Relations Policy, 1947–1994.* Philadelphia: Temple University Press, 1995.

Harris, Howell John. *The Right to Manage: Industrial Relations Policies of American Business in the 1940s.* Madison: University of Wisconsin Press, 1982.

Hearings before the Joint Committee on Labor-Management Relations, 80th Congress of the U.S. 2d session on the Operation of the Labor-Management Relations Act, 1947, Pts 1 and 2, 1948, 1218–1220.

Howell, Chris. *Trade Unions and the State: The Construction of Industrial Relations Institutions in Britain, 1890–2000.* Princeton, N.J.: Princeton University Press, 2005.

"Industrial Arbitration." *Hull-House Bulletin* 1 (April 1896).

Jacoby, Sanford M. "American Exceptionalism Revisited: The Importance of Management." In *Masters to Managers: Historical and Comparative Perspectives on American Employers*, ed. Jacoby. New York: Columbia University Press, 1991.

John Swinton's Paper, New York City. 1886.

Jones, Dallas L. "The Enigma of the Clayton Act," *Industrial and Labor Relations Review* 10 (January 1957): 201–221.

Kaltenborn, Howard S. *Governmental Adjustment of Labor Disputes.* Chicago: Foundation Press, 1933.

Karl, Barry D. *The Uneasy State: The United States from 1915 to 1945.* Chicago: University of Chicago Press, 1983.

Kaufman, Stuart B., ed. *The Samuel Gompers Papers* (SGP), vol. 1, *The Making of a Union Leader, 1850–86.* Urbana: University of Illinois Press, 1986, 287–288.

Kaufman, Stuart Bruce, ed. *The Samuel Gompers Papers* (SGP). Urbana: University of Illinois Press, 1986–2013.

Lake, Marilyn. "'This Great America': H. B. Higgins and Transnational Progressivism." *Australian Historical Studies* 44, 2 (2013): 172–188.

Lichtenstein, Nelson. *Labor's War at Home: The CIO in World War II.* Cambridge: Cambridge University Press, 1987 [1982].

Lindsey, Almont. *The Pullman Strike: The Story of a Unique Experiment and of a Great Labor Upheaval.* Chicago: University of Chicago Press, 1942.

Martin, Cathie Jo. "Sectional Parties, Divided Business." *Studies in American Political Development* 20 (Fall 2006): 160–184.

McCartin, Joseph A. *Labor's Great War: The Struggle for Industrial Democracy and the Origins of Modern American Labor Relations, 1912–1921.* Chapel Hill: University of North Carolina Press, 1997.

Millen, Bruce H. *The Political Role of Labor in Developing Countries.* Washington, D.C.: Brookings Inst., 1963.

Millis, Harry A., and Royal E. Montgomery. *Organized Labor.* New York: McGraw-Hill, 1945.

Papke, David Ray. *The Pullman Case: The Clash of Labor and Capital in Industrial America.* Lawrence: University Press of Kansas, 1999.

Salvatore, Nick. *Eugene V. Debs: Citizen and Socialist.* Urbana: University of Illinois Press, 2007.

Schatz, Ronald W. "'Industrial Peace through Arbitration': George Taylor and the Genius of the War Labor Board," *Labor: Studies in Working-Class History of the Americas* 11 (Winter 2014): 39–62.

Steigerwalt, Albert K. *The National Association of Manufacturers, 1895–1914: A Study in Business Leadership.* Grand Rapids: Bureau of Business Research, University of Michigan, 1964.

Strum, Philippa. *Brandeis: Beyond Progressivism.* Lawrence: University Press of Kansas, 1993.

Tyrrell, Ian. *Woman's World/Woman's Empire: The Woman's Christian Temperance Union in International Perspective, 1880–1930.* Chapel Hill: University of North Carolina Press, 1991.

U.S. Commission on Industrial Relations. Final report of the Commission on Industrial Relations, including the report of Basil M. Manly, director of research and investigation, and the individual reports and statements of the several commissioners (1916), http://archive.org/details/finalreportofcom00unitiala (accessed April 4, 2017).

U.S. Senate, *Report of the Committee of the Senate upon the Relations between Labor and Capital. Vol. 1.* Washington, D.C.: GPO, 1885.

U.S. Strike Commission, *Report on the Chicago Strike of June–July, 1894*, "Conclusions and Recommendations," xlvii, http://books.google.com/books?id=KUopAAAAYAAJ&printsec

=frontcover&source=gbs_ge_summary_r&cad=0#v=onepage&q&f=false (accessed April 4, 2017).

Walsh, Pat, ed. *Trade Unions, Work and Society: The Centenary of the Arbitration System.* Palmerston North, N.Z.: Dunmore Press, 1994.

Wedderburn, Lord, Roy Lewis, and Jon Clark, eds. *Labour Law and Industrial Relations: Building on Kahn-Freund.* Oxford: Clarendon Press, 1983.

Westhoff, Laura M. *A Fatal Drifting Apart: Democratic Social Knowledge and Chicago Reform.* Columbus: Ohio State University Press, 2007.

Witte, Edwin E. *Historical Survey of Labor Arbitration.* Philadelphia: University of Pennsylvania Press, 1952.

Wunderlin, Clarence E., Jr. *Visions of a New Industrial Order: Social Science and Labor Theory in America's Progressive Era.* New York: Columbia University Press, 1992.

CHAPTER 3

Labor Justice in Canada

Mackenzie King and Collective Labor Rights

FRANK LUCE

Introduction: A Fragmented System

Labor justice in Canada is a fragmented system in several ways: first, it is bifurcated into distinct institutions for individual labor rights and collective labor rights; second, private sector workers and public sector workers are covered by separate legal regimes; third, different labor rights are adjudicated in different legal forums; finally, each political jurisdiction within the Canadian federation has a different labor justice system.[1]

This chapter provides an analysis of how this fragmentation resulted from a historical process of legal and social change. I argue that the historical process was driven by a conflict between organized labor's search for collective bargaining and employers' determination to advance management rights, assisted by police intervention in times of industrial disputes. For their part, politicians at times sought to mediate industrial disputes resulting from this conflict and at other times accommodated the growing strength of organized labor through legal change. Fragmentation resulted when governments took a minimalist approach, legislating collective and individual labor rights on a piecemeal basis, according to changing social circumstances.

This piecemeal approach reflected the historical reluctance of Canadian state actors to interfere in industrial relations except as deemed necessary to maintain social order, when police intervention proved inadequate. While corporatist solutions appealed to certain politicians in the French-language Province of Quebec, their counterparts in English Canada instead preferred the "British road" in which, as we saw in Chapter 2, "collective laissez-faire" was the dominant approach, while rejecting the "Australasian road" of compulsory arbitration. In later years, the trade union movement successfully cajoled these politicians into accepting the road followed in the United States of America, a more interventionist solution, which fell far short of the "state-suffused models" found elsewhere in the Americas, including the corporatist road of Mexico (see Chapter 4) and Brazil (see Chapter 9).

Canada is a constitutional monarchy with a written constitution, which was originally enacted by the British parliament in 1867; for historical reasons, the constitution is federalist, with a prescribed division of powers between the federal government and its provincial counterparts. Since labor rights were deemed to be primarily within provincial jurisdiction, the historical process under analysis was different in each of the various political jurisdictions, albeit with certain characteristics in common: each of the different processes involved a dialectic between the federal and provincial levels of government; each process resulted in the creation of two similar core institutions for collective labor rights, that is, a labor board and grievance arbitration, in the manner of parallel institutions found in the United States. As for individual labor rights, each jurisdiction established distinct legal regimes for different labor rights.

A practical effect of the constitutional division of powers is that space is not available within a single chapter for a detailed analysis of the historical process in each political jurisdiction. Instead, the chapter uses the province of Ontario as a case study; the choice is justified by the economic, political, and legal weight of Ontario within the federation, at least among the common law provinces (Quebec is a civil law jurisdiction).

Another practical limitation to this study is that the available space does not allow for a detailed analysis of both collective and individual labor rights, or for both the private sector and the public sector. Instead, the chapter is focused on the two core institutions for collective labor rights in Ontario, that is, the Ontario Labour Relations Board and a semiprivate cohort of grievance arbitrators. With this focus in mind, one political figure stands out as central to the process of legal change over the course of the entire first half of the twentieth century, William Lyon Mackenzie King, a Canadian politician whose contribution to the process was influenced by his experience as an industrial consultant in the United States.

The chapter begins with Mackenzie King's life story and then turns its focus onto the historical process under study, following the historical narrative that led to the creation of Ontario's two core institutions. The chapter divides this historical narrative into six corresponding stages or topics: compulsory conciliation, company unionism, industrial organizing, War Measures and labor peace, labor court or "Wagner board," and finally the "postwar compromise." The chapter then takes up a distinct but parallel historical narrative to analyze the making of Ontario's labor justice system for individual labor rights; this is followed by an overview of the public sector. The chapter concludes with comments on how the labor justice system has evolved in the decades since the postwar compromise.

William Lyon Mackenzie King: A Life Story

Among the political figures who gave Canada's labor justice system its legal form, William Lyon Mackenzie King is dominant; he did not, however, make labor justice history as he pleased, but rather he made it in relation to the circumstances he encountered.[2]

King was born in 1874 in the city of Berlin (now Kitchener), Ontario. His father was a lawyer and his mother was the daughter of William Lyon Mackenzie, the first mayor of Toronto and the leader of the Upper Canada Rebellion in 1837, a seminal event in the evolution of liberalism in Canadian history. King was a graduate of the University of Toronto, with an MA and an LLB, and later of Harvard University, with a second MA and a PhD. He was a pioneer in the academic field of industrial relations; his MA thesis in 1897 was about the International Typographical Union (ITU), an affiliate of the American Federation of Labor (AFL),[3] and his doctoral dissertation in 1909 was entitled "Oriental Immigration to Canada," with its primary focus on the labor market.

King's political philosophy was shaped by the "new political economy" of Arnold Toynbee. For a brief period he resided with Jane Addams at Hull House in Chicago, a social settlement project inspired by Toynbee's movement. As we saw in Chapter 2, Addams was a leading voice for labor reform in the United States; like Addams, King accepted the idea of trade union legitimacy and rejected both socialism and laissez-faire capitalism. While Addams engaged directly with marginalized social classes, King soon discovered that his vocation was in politics, and in entering the political arena he brought a renewed form of liberalism to his chosen vehicle, the Liberal Party of Canada. As a senior civil servant and as a politician, King actively resisted the compulsory arbitration concept for which, as we saw in Chapter 2, Addams was a leading advocate.

King entered the federal civil service as Canada's first Deputy Minister of Labour in 1900; after being elected to parliament in 1908, in 1909 he became the first full-fledged Minster of Labour in the Liberal Party government of Sir Wilfred Laurier. He was defeated in the general election of 1911, along with the government; in 1919, he replaced Laurier as party leader and was elected Prime Minister in 1921; he was defeated in parliament in 1926 but resumed his post as Prime Minister in a general election held a few months later; he was again defeated in a general election in 1930; he returned to power in the general election of 1935, remained as Prime Minister until his retirement in 1948, and died two years later.[4]

Compulsory Conciliation

Prior to the start of the twentieth century, federal involvement in labor rights was limited to its criminal law power. In the wake of a printers' strike in Ontario, led by the ITU, in 1872 the Conservative Party government of Sir John A. Macdonald enacted *The Trade Unions Act*, in which a *trade union* was declared not to constitute a criminal conspiracy, an enactment that entered history as "the statutory legalization of trade unions."[5] The usage of the term *trade union* in the statute was in reference to the form of unionism then prevalent in Canada, when workers organized according to their craft, skills or trade; in more current usage, the term includes the industrial form of unionism in which workers organize according to their common employer.

With trade unions effectively declared lawful, the federal government turned its attention to industrial disputes, first using the criminal law and then conciliation. In companion legislation to *The Trade Unions Act*, Macdonald used the criminal power to regulate union conduct during a labor dispute. Although strikes were lawful per se, the *Criminal Law Amendment Act* of 1872 created a series of criminal offenses specifically directed toward strike-related misconduct.[6] In 1876, a Liberal government enacted *The Breaches of Contract Act*, which repealed the criminal sanctions for breach of an employment contract, set out in federal *Master and Servant* legislation, on the basis that employment was a matter within provincial jurisdiction. In the same statute, however, the government introduced criminal sanctions for breaches of contract caused by a railway dispute.[7]

Federal concern over labor disputes led Macdonald to appoint the Royal Commission on the Relations of Labor and Capital in Canada in 1886. The Royal Commission, "after reviewing some startling evidence on working conditions in Canada," and after studying initiatives taken in other common law jurisdictions, in 1889 recommended an institutionalized federal system of conciliation to deal with labor disputes across the country, instead of the existing practice of having ad hoc federal conciliators intervene on a voluntary basis.[8] The Royal Commissioner acknowledged that its institutional proposal may intrude on provincial jurisdiction, giving the Liberal government of Sir Wilfred Laurier enough reason to limit itself to a voluntary system. The Liberals assigned their favorite conciliator, Roger Clute, a lawyer from Belleville, Ontario, to draft the *Conciliation Act* of 1900, which did little more than legitimate the existing practice. Conciliation remained strictly voluntary, invoked only at the invitation of the disputing parties, thus mirroring the contemporaneous practice in Great Britain, and rejecting the compulsory arbitration concept that Addams promoted in the United States (see Chapter 2), despite its positive acceptance in New Zealand in 1894 and in Australia a decade later.[9]

The *Conciliation Act* mandated the creation of a labor department, to be administered by Postmaster-General Sir William Mulock. Mulock appointed King to head the department as a Deputy Minister, while calling himself Minister of Labor, even though there was not yet a federal ministry in existence.[10]

As Deputy Minister, King immersed himself in the dynamic field of labor relations. He drafted *The Railway Labour Disputes Act*, a statute that was enacted in 1903 and then merged with the *Conciliation Act* in 1906 into the *Conciliation and Labour Act*. For a labor dispute within the rail industry, the Minister of Labour could appoint an ad hoc Committee of Conciliation, Mediation and Investigation at the request of either party to the dispute, or on his own initiative. The Committee's structure would be tripartite, in the sense that each party would first appoint a representative and then the minister would appoint a neutral chair, allowing the Committee to be relatively autonomous from government.

King soon earned himself a positive reputation as a conciliator due to his success in the mining industry, at a time when two rival unions from the United States were actively organizing along industrial lines in Western Canada: the United Mineworkers (UMW), an affiliate of the AFL, and a more radical union then known as the Western Federation of Miners, later known as the International Union of Mine, Mill and Smelter Workers (Mine-Mill). In this organizing campaign, union recognition was the key strategic issue, serving both to force management to bargain collectively and to exclude the rival union from the workplace. King found success with a compromise model in which management would agree to recognize a workplace committee, rather than the union, while at the same time agreeing not to discriminate against union supporters.

In November 1906, King used his nonunion model to settle a strike at the Galt coal mine in Lethbridge, a city located on the Alberta-Saskatchewan border. Upon arriving on the scene as the federal conciliator, he critiqued the UMW's demand for union recognition as "arbitrary and objectionable," and he threatened to place public blame on UMW for putting the lives of prairie wheat farmers at risk for lack of coal to heat their homes during the frigid prairie winter. Rather than put its reputation at risk, the UMW acquiesced to a nonunion representation model.[11]

Convinced in the ability of conciliation to prevent a labor dispute, upon returning to Ottawa, King set about to institutionalize the practice at the federal level. With the *Conciliation and Labour Act* still in force, King supplemented its provisions through the enactment of the *Industrial Disputes Investigation Act* (IDIA) in 1907. The main effect of the IDIA was to make conciliation compulsory, in the sense that a strike or lock-out would be unlawful unless the parties first exhausted the conciliation procedure. Administered by a registrar within the labor department, conciliation would hence-forth involve a two-step process: first the minister would appoint a conciliation officer, at the request of either party; then, in the absence of a settlement, the registrar would appoint a tripartite Board of Conciliation and Investigation whose recommendations could then be publicized. Whether or not King so intended, for trade unions an effect of this two-step process was to create inordinate delay, making a recognition strike in particular less likely to succeed.

With the institutionalization of conciliation at the federal level, King attempted to exclude the courts from interfering in the process through the introduction of a privative clause, pursuant to which a court may not invalidate conciliation proceed-ings for any "technical irregularity." For organized labor, excluding the courts from labor matters was a welcome measure for reasons that included historical animosity, perceived class bias, an aversion to legal formalism, and a lack of expertise.[12] However, privative clauses soon proved of limited effect, leading Bora Laskin to conclude that "privative clauses have had no apparent effect on the courts' reviewing power."[13]

King's renown in the field led to his appointment as minister in 1909, but in 1911 the Laurier government, along with King, went down to defeat. In 1914, the Conservative government led Canada into a "total war" effort on behalf of the British Empire. The government used its emergency power under the constitution to enact the *War Measures Act* in 1914, allowing the government to rule by decree. Among the emergency measures decreed was the expansion of the federal jurisdiction over the economy to include any industry engaged in war production, with the effect that the reach of King's IDIA was expanded accordingly. For a brief period leading up to the end of the war, the government went even further and decreed that the recommendations of a Board of Conciliation and Investigation were binding, in a short-lived experiment with compulsory binding arbitration.[14]

King, the Father of Company Unionism

King used the period of the Great War (1914 to 1918) to launch a new career as an industrial relations consultant. His career began to take shape in 1914 when John D. Rockefeller Jr. invited him to be the Director of Industrial Relations for the charitable Rockefeller Foundation and to advise him on labor matters, at a time when Rockefeller was preoccupied with an ongoing recognition strike by the UMW in Colorado. After seventeen UMW supporters were killed in the infamous "Ludlow massacre," Rockefeller asked King to find a resolution that did not involve imposing union recognition on local management. King devised the so-called "Rockefeller Plan," a sophisticated version of his nonunion workplace committee model. When the UMW abandoned the strike, King was able to legitimate his plan through a management-supervised workplace ballot, earning himself a reputation as "the father of company unionism on this continent."[15] In this context, company unionism implied direct dealings between management and a committee of workers, rather than through a union, a model that management easily dominated, with the added advantage that the existence of a company union blunted the threat of unionization. Thanks in part to King's work as a labor consultant, company unionism spread throughout the United States until it was effectively outlawed by the *Wagner Act* in 1935.[16]

In Canada, in response to a wave of labor unrest in the postwar period, the federal government (then a Conservative-led coalition) appointed Judge Thomas G. Mathers, from the Manitoba Court of Appeal, to head a Royal Commission on Industrial Relations (the Mathers Commission). With industrial organizing on the agenda of organized labor, the mandate of the Mathers Commission included a study of the Rockefeller Plan and a study of Whitley Councils, a form of nonunion representation, through a Joint Industrial Council, that had been introduced in Great Britain during the war. In his final report, Mathers recommended that the federal government "establish a bureau for promoting industrial councils." The federal Ministry of Labor responded first by organizing a National Industrial Conference, in a futile attempt to forge a consensus, and then by allocating ministry resources toward the promotion of the Joint Industrial Council model, with some degree of success. In the private sector, many workplaces introduced a company union model, while both the federal and Ontario governments later established an industrial council model for their own civil servants.[17]

Industrial Organizing

With King back in politics as Prime Minister after December 1921, the key federal labor policies of conciliation and company unionism were challenged by an upsurge in union organizing along the lines of industrial unionism.

The first major challenge to King's conciliation policy came not from the unions but from the courts. In January 1925 the Judicial Committee of the Privy Council (JCPC) in Great Britain ruled that the IDIA was an unconstitutional encroachment on provincial powers, even though it applied only to labor disputes in specified sectors of strategic importance to the national economy.[18] With industrial disputes of increasing concern in Canada, King circumvented the effect of this ruling by amending the IDIA so its reach was limited to sectors that the JCPC agreed were within federal jurisdiction, and he invited the provinces to delegate their authority over labor disputes within the province to the federal government. One by one the provinces agreed, with Ontario and Quebec finally coming on board in 1932, leaving behind only the province of Prince Edward Island.[19]

King was again out of office from 1930 to 1935, at a time when the move toward industrial organizing accelerated, in response to the crash of 1929 and the Great Depression. King was still out of office in July 1935 when the *Wagner Act* was enacted in the United States, facilitating industrial organizing and promising organized labor a New Deal, as we saw in Chapter 2.[20] Industrial unions were now able to replace the recognition strike with a legal path to recognition, which imposed compulsory collective bargaining on management and protected unions and their supporters against unfair labor practices, all of which was under the administration of a board with expertise in labor matters: the National Labor Relations Board, or a "Wagner board," as it became known in Canada. With King back in power, his Liberal government remained opposed to similar legislation for Canada.

One of the stumbling blocks along the path toward a *Wagner Act* for Canada was the historical opposition of the AFL to state intervention, as we saw in Chapter 2, while AFL-affiliated craft unions in Canada were nervous about the *Wagner Act*'s bias in favor of the industrial form of unionism. In the United States, the UMW led the fight for industrial unionism within the AFL, and in 1938 it formed a rival central labor body known as the Congress of Industrial Organizations (CIO), with the United Auto Workers (UAW) and the Steel Workers Organizing Committee, later known as the United Steel Workers (USW), as affiliates. This had a spillover effect into Canada when the CIO unions began to organize in the auto, steel, and other sectors, leading to a split along similar lines in 1940, with the craft unions remaining in the Trades and Labour Council (TLC) and the industrial unions forming the Canadian Congress of Labour (CCL).

Organized labor was also split along political lines. While King and his Liberal party maintained a political base within the TLC, two anticapitalist parties enjoyed growing support within the labor movement. The first of these was the Cooperative Commonwealth Federation (CCF), a social-democratic party formed in 1932 by a coalition of labor politicians, social justice advocates, and religious leaders from the Social Gospel movement. Within a decade of its formation, the CCF had become the dominant political force within the CCL and a significant rival to the Liberals in electoral politics both federally and in Ontario. The second was the Communist Party of Canada (CPC), a Bolshevik party formed in May 1921. The CPC never matched the CCF's electoral strength, but it rivaled the CCF within the leadership of the CCL and the Liberals within the TLC. Moreover, the CPC had a positive record of industrial organizing, through a campaign led by the Workers Unity League (WUL) from 1930 to 1935, leading many trained CPC organizers to work on CIO campaigns.[21]

The CIO-affiliated unions raised the demand for a Wagner board in Canada to eliminate the need for a recognition strike. They brought the issue to a head in Ontario in April 1937 when the UAW engaged in a sit-down recognition strike at the General Motors plant in Oshawa. The strike was led by Charlie Millard, the local union president, with the result that local management agreed to voluntary recognition. The strike gave rise to a feud within the Liberal Party between King, who had no problem with voluntary recognition, and the Liberal premier of Ontario, Mitchell Hepburn, who recruited a posse of strikebreakers, popularly known as "Hepburn's Hussars" or "Sons-of-Mitches."

War Measures and Labor Peace

In September 1939, the King government declared war on Germany and its allies. Invoking the *War Measures Act*, his government ruled by decree and expanded federal powers to include industries involved in war production. King issued a nonbinding declaration of labor principles, declaring that "workers should be free to organize in trade unions" and "employees, through the officers of their trade union . . . should be free to negotiate with employers . . . with a view to the conclusion of a collective agreement."[22]

To support the war effort, King called on workers and unions to accept voluntary wage controls. With a booming war economy, however, workers whose wages had been rolled back during the depression and were now being eroded by wartime inflation, were reluctant to accept wage controls. Instead of voluntary controls, King introduced the "Wartime Wages and Cost of Living Bonus Order" in October 1941.[23] A National War Labour Board, chaired by the federal Minister of Labor, was created to control wages, with a subordinate regional board in each province.

Labor leaders found it anomalous that wage controls were compulsory and union recognition voluntary. To make matters worse, the government complicated a union's ability to conduct a recognition strike by adding a third step to the existing two-step conciliation process. That is, in between a conciliation officer and a conciliation board, the minister was given the option of appointing an Industrial Disputes Inquiry Commission.[24] Worse yet, a fourth step was added later, requiring the union to conduct a government-supervised strike vote, following the report of the conciliation board.[25] The only benefit to labor was that the minister gained the authority to order reinstatement of a worker fired for union activity.[26]

A recognition strike in the mining sector put the government's declared labor principles to the test. In 1941, Mine-Mill, then a CCL affiliate, organized workers at five gold mining companies in Kirkland Lake, Ontario.[27] Mine-Mill's support among the workers was undisputed, but management of each of the five companies refused to meet with union representatives. Mine-Mill applied for conciliation, and when conciliation failed, the minister appointed a Commissioner in the person of Humphrey Mitchell, a ministry bureaucrat whose background was with the TLC.

Mitchell was born in England in 1894, served in the Royal Navy during the Great War, and then settled in Hamilton, Ontario, after the war, where he worked as a land surveyor with Hamilton Hydro. He became active in his craft union, and later served as president, and then secretary, of the Hamilton and District Trades and Labor Council, and later still as chair of the Ontario executive of the TLC. In 1931, he was elected to federal parliament under the banner of the Independent Labour Party, but when his party dissolved itself to join the CCF, Mitchell opted instead to support King's Liberal Party. In the 1935 general election, King was restored to power but Mitchell was opposed by the CCF and as a result was defeated by a Conservative. King rewarded Mitchell with an appointment to the federal labor ministry.

As Commissioner, Mitchell urged the union to accept a company union model. Mine-Mill instead moved toward a legal strike; the next step was for the minister to appoint a conciliation board, whose members were autonomous from government, and which unanimously recommended that management accept voluntary recognition. The union then conducted a supervised strike vote, only to have the minister step in to personally advocate for the company union model. By then the process had been delayed until winter, and Mine-Mill was forced out on strike in November 1941. Adding insult to injury, with Mine-Mill still on the picket line, King appointed Mitchell as his new Minister of Labor, in December 1941. After a cold winter on the picket line, Mine-Mill abandoned the strike in February 1942.

Although Mine-Mill lost the strike, King's support within organized labor was rapidly eroding. For the CCL, Kirkland Lake was a "battle for union recognition and for the very existence of a labor movement in Canada," and at its 1942 convention it endorsed the CCF as the "political arm of labor." For their part, the TLC leadership experienced a change of heart and endorsed the demand for a *Wagner Act* in Canada.[28]

With the CCL firmly within the political camp of the CCF, the USW took up the struggle against wage controls under the leadership of Charlie Millard, who had moved from the auto sector to become National Director of the USW, while at the same time serving on the provincial executive of the CCF.[29]

Steelworker wages were relatively low and they varied from province to province, while the booming steel industry remained within provincial jurisdiction, despite its contribution to the war economy. Millard's goal was to achieve an industrywide agreement with a uniform base rate across the country, while his strategy was to have the National War Labour Board declare steel a war industry and set a national wage. When his CCF colleagues in parliament conveyed his threat of a national strike in the steel sector against wage controls, King responded with the appointment of a Royal Commission, which in December 1942 recommended against Millard's position. Ignoring the conciliation requirement, the union then launched a national strike.

According to Laurel Sefton MacDowell, "the labor movement and the [King] government were completely at odds over the related issues of collective bargaining and wage controls," forcing King to rethink his labor strategy.[30] When Mitchell advocated for a hard line against the strike, King decided to bypass his minister and conciliate a settlement, since he agreed that steel wages were too low.[31] However, he reached an agreement with Millard that had implications reaching far beyond the steel industry: the National War Labour Board was reconstituted as a tripartite board, autonomous from government; Mitchell was replaced as chair by Judge Charles McTague of the Ontario Court of Appeal, with a management lawyer from McTague's former law firm and J. L. (Jacob) Cohen as management and labor representatives. Representing the labor movement, Cohen was a Toronto lawyer with the rare quality of having the respect of union leaders from both CCL and TLC, and the leadership of both CCF and CPC.[32]

Pursuant to his agreement with Millard, King referred the strike issues to the reconstituted board for determination, while Millard worked to end the strike. After the strikers returned to work, however, the McTague board issued a unanimous award in which the steel sector remained within provincial jurisdiction, with some limited improvement in wages. In agreeing to this unanimous award, we can speculate that Cohen was outvoted by the other board members and likely settled for the best deal available. In any event, Millard felt justifiably betrayed because he thought that he and King had an agreement.

From a Labor Court to a Wagner Board

Further to his agreement with Millard, King also mandated the McTague board to inquire broadly into "wartime labor relations and wage conditions," allowing Cohen to engage in a broader strategy of support for a Wagner board. In January 1943, he broke with the McTague board's culture of unanimity and sent King his minority report in which he called for a Wagner board, a report which King kept private for the time being.

Cohen also embroiled himself in a parallel development at the provincial level in Ontario where, after the Kirkland Lake strike, Hepburn felt threatened by the rising popularity of the CCF. In an effort to put the General Motors strike behind him, Hepburn sent his labor minister, Peter Heenan, to speak to the CCL convention in 1942, with a promise that a provincial *Wagner Act* would soon be forthcoming.

As a locomotive engineer in Kenora, Heenan had been active in his craft union and within his local TLC. In 1919, he turned to provincial politics, was elected under the banner of the Independent Labour Party, and was instrumental in negotiating with the United Farmers of Ontario to form a coalition government. In 1926, he switched to federal politics and was elected under the banner of the Liberal Party, serving as King's Minister of Labor from 1926 to 1930. In 1934, he switched back to provincial politics, still with the Liberal party, and served as Hepburn's labor minister in 1938, and again from May 1941 to August 1943.

Assigned the task of drafting labor legislation, Heenan hired Cohen to produce a proposal for internal review and public debate. As expected, Cohen proposed a Wagner board for Ontario, but when Ontario's *Collective Bargaining Act* was enacted in April 1943, Ontario ended up with a labor court instead of a Wagner board. How this surprise result came about is a matter of speculation. As an academic commentator, Bora Laskin (later Chief Justice of the Supreme Court of Canada) welcomed the legislation as "the first attempt in Canada to enforce on employers in positive terms a duty to bargain collectively," but he expressed surprise that the administration of the legislation was entrusted to judges of the High Court, a result that he thought was "unique" and "of wider interest."[33] As Laskin pointed out, Heenan's draft legislation went through public hearings before a legislative Select Committee that lasted twelve days and heard from ninety-two witnesses, none of whom suggested that the legislation be administered other than by the ministry or by a Wagner board. However, when the Select Committee submitted its final report, its draft bill contained provisions for a labor court.[34] The government's change of heart is likely attributable to lobbying behind closed doors by lawyers for the auto industry.[35]

Ontario's Labour Court was a division of the Ontario High Court of Justice, whose judges were lifetime appointees of the federal government. Although a few judges had sat as chairs of conciliation boards, they only sat as labor judges on a two-week rotation, with little chance to develop any expertise. Union leaders were further alienated by the formality of the pleadings, the formal rules of evidence, and the judge's over-reliance on technicalities, while crucial labor issues, such as the configuration of the appropriate bargaining unit, were more amenable to policy and expertise than to formal proof.[36] More than any other single factor, the frequent certification of company unions caused the Labour Court to be discredited within its first months of operation.[37]

With the war economy under federal jurisdiction, the Ontario legislation had a very limited reach, while the goal of the labor movement was a uniform legal regime at the federal level. Unions hoped that a uniform system would lead to uniform agreements in various sectors, as we saw in the case of steel. In support of this goal, Cohen continued to fight for a Wagner board from the privileged position of his membership on the McTague board.

While Cohen's minority report remained on King's desk, he and McTague remained at odds within the board, as McTague opposed a Wagner board and delayed forwarding his own majority report to King until August 1943. King then sat on both the majority and minority reports, prompting Cohen to embarrass King in public over the issue and leading McTague to demand Cohen's resignation. Refusing McTague's demand, Cohen instead launched a public campaign: he addressed the delegates to a TLC convention on the topic, urging the TLC to mobilize in favor of a Wagner board; he then delivered a similar message to the CCL convention a few weeks later, prompting King finally to dismiss him from the board in September 1943. In November, King had Mitchell convene a Conference of Labor Ministers to discuss wartime labor legislation, and finally on February 17, 1944, King decreed into law the *Wartime Labour Relations Regulations*, known as PC 1003.

PC 1003 gave Canadian unions their first Wagner board, known as the Wartime Labour Relations Board. The function of this wartime board was to determine what would be an appropriate bargaining unit and to certify a bargaining agent that showed majority support within the unit, including a company union. Certification required management to recognize the union and to bargain in good faith, although there was no obligation to reach a collective agreement, leaving the union with the strike option. Although the Wartime board was available to administer the process, a violation of the decree, generally known as an unfair labor practice, was punishable only as a quasi-criminal offense, with prosecution requiring the prior consent of the board.

Once a collective agreement was reached, however, PC 1003 imposed a system of rights adjudication, one that was later institutionalized as grievance arbitration. Prior to PC 1003, grievance arbitration was well known as a means of settling workplace disputes, especially in the garment industry, as we saw in Chapter 2. In effect, however, grievance arbitration decisions were not binding on the parties since the legal regime provided no enforcement mechanism; instead a union could take strike action to enforce a decision, although in Canada, unlike in the United States, a strike was lawful only after conciliation. PC 1003 removed the possibility of any strike being lawful during the term of a collective agreement, again unlike in the United States, requiring that the agreement contain "a procedure for final settlement, *without stoppage of work* [emphasis added], of differences concerning its interpretation or violation." The legal form of this procedure was left for the workplace parties to bargain, and in practice unions bargained a grievance system, with arbitration as a final step, either with a tripartite board or a single arbitrator. The same judges who often chaired conciliation boards were often chosen to chair arbitration boards, and if the parties failed to agree on a choice, the labor minister would appoint an arbitrator, often from among these same judges. After a few decades of controversy over the role of judges as arbitrators, the ministry assisted in the development of a semiprivate cohort of professional labor arbitrators.

With strikes unlawful during the term of a collective agreement, PC 1003 provided further that a strike was lawful only after fourteen days from the date of the report of a conciliation board. However, if the conciliation officer recommended that a conciliation board *not* be appointed, and the minister was in agreement, the fourteen-day period ran from the date the minister issued a "no-board" report. The request for a no-board report became a hallmark of collective bargaining in Ontario.

Prior to the PC 1003 decree, Ontario's Liberals were defeated in a general election and replaced by a Conservative government, with the CCF as the official opposition. With some industries under partly federal and partly provincial jurisdiction, the new government agreed to incorporate the provisions of PC 1003 into provincial jurisdiction, and the federal government delegated the administration of the federal regulation to an Ontario Wagner board known as the Ontario Labour Relations Board (OLRB), although for the sake of uniformity, OLRB decisions could be appealed to the Wartime board. Ontario's *Collective Bargaining Act* of 1943 was replaced by *The Labour Relations Board Act, 1944*, and Ontario's much maligned Labour Court was abolished. The OLRB could receive whatever evidence it deemed "fit and proper whether admissible as evidence in a court of law or not," and a strong privative clause provided that OLRB decisions could not "be questioned, reviewed, restrained or removed . . . by any court."

A Postwar Compromise

Canada's war in Europe ended in May 1945 and a general election was held a month later. King maintained power, with some assistance from the CPC, but the transition back to a peacetime economy took six years, with federal government ceding its wartime jurisdiction piecemeal. As a preliminary step toward replacing PC 1003, King had Mitchell convene another federal-provincial conference of labor ministers in October 1946, again seeking a consensus. On the constitutional issue, according to F. R. Scott, the stakeholders remained divided, with the unions still wanting uniformity, while "the preference for provincial jurisdiction reflected the prevailing employers' viewpoint," and King's government "gave no strong leadership for a national labour policy."[38]

With uniformity still at issue, and with the Wagner board issue apparently settled, organized labor turned its attention from union recognition to union security, agitating for organizational and financial security, either through the political process or through collective bargaining. The fight for union security was taken on by the UAW in 1945, with a lawful strike at the Ford Motors plant in Windsor, Ontario, a union and a city in which Liberals and the CPC were strategically allied.

The Ford plant had been placed under federal jurisdiction at the start of the war, and in 1941 Ford agreed to a representation vote conducted by the federal ministry, which led to voluntary recognition for the UAW. The bargaining relationship remained troubled throughout the war, and at war's end it remained uncertain when Ford's labor troubles would revert to provincial jurisdiction. When the union relied on some unlawful tactics to accelerate the 1945 strike, the provincial Conservative government called for a forceful intervention on the side of management; at the federal level, Mitchell claimed neutrality as he convened the parties to seek a conciliated settlement, although he personally was opposed to the union's demands and refused to legislate any form of union security. After a standoff that lasted ninety-nine days, a Liberal cabinet minister from the Windsor area, Paul Martin Senior, brokered a settlement in which the parties agreed to end the strike by referring the union security issue to arbitration, with Judge Ivan Rand of the Supreme Court of Canada sitting alone as an interest arbitrator.

The UAW demanded union security in a form that Ford's management had already agreed to in the United States, that is, a "union shop," one in which all workers within the bargaining unit would be union members, with a "dues checkoff" in which union dues would be deducted from their wages and remitted to the union. In January 1946, Rand rejected the Ford United States solution and instead imposed a compromise known as the "Rand formula" in which union membership was voluntary but with a dues checkoff for all members of the bargaining unit, whether union members or not. In the absence of any legislated union security provision, including the individual-ism of the Taft-Hartley Amendments in the United States (see Chapter 2), the Rand formula spread throughout the province through the collective bargaining process.[39]

In January 1948, King announced his intention to retire, but before leaving office he negotiated an understanding with the provinces that involved a reciprocal delegation of authority: King would replace PC 1003 with a federal labor code, while the provinces would delegate their jurisdiction in part to the federal government. This initiated a process of further negotiation among governments, employers, and unions. With these negotiations still in progress, and without knowing their final outcome, in April Ontario's Conservative government enacted *The Labour Relations Act, 1948* as enabling legislation, the effect of which was to adopt the contents of the federal labor code by reference and delegate aspects of its administration back to the federal government. The Conservatives agreed to reconstitute the OLRB to consist of a chair and four members, with its decisions protected by two privative clauses but still subject to an appeal to a federal board. In June 1948, the Ontario enabling legislation was followed by a federal labor code, *The Industrial Relations and Disputes Investigation Act*, replacing PC 1003 and other wartime labor measures. This federal code prohibited the certification of "an employer dominated organization," with the legislative purpose of finally put-ting an end to the company unionism with which King's name was long associated. The administration of the federal code was divided between the federal and provincial governments, with the federal government constituting a new tripartite Wagner board known as the Canada Labour Relations Board (CLRB).

When the issue of uniformity was still under debate, in 1947 the government of the province of Nova Scotia had referred the reciprocal delegation proposal to the Supreme Court of Canada for a ruling on its constitutional viability. Two years after the recipro-cal arrangement with Ontario, in 1950 a panel of seven judges, including Judge Rand, ruled that reciprocal delegation was unconstitutional, thereby frustrating organized labor's search for uniformity.[40] Reacting to the court ruling, Ontario's Conservative government enacted *The Ontario Labour Relations Act, 1950*, in a form similar to the 1948 federal code, with the final result that jurisdiction over labor rights remained divided within the Canadian federation, albeit in a manner different from that which the Taft-Hartley Amendments had introduced in the United States.

We have seen that the fragmented character of Canada's labor justice system resulted from a historical process in which compromise was a distinguishing feature, with organized labor seeking a uniform system of legal protection for collective bargaining, employers seeking to protect management rights, and governments seeking to avoid the economic disruption caused by industrial disputes. For some authors, the historical narrative ended in the period immediately after the Second World War, with a "postwar compromise" or "historic compromise," within which trade unions and management accepting a compromised form of industrial legality. For the labor movement, however, the process never ended as its goal was to achieve collective bargaining for the entire workforce. The compromise gave organized labor the degree of organizational and financial security that its leaders felt they required to achieve this goal, but the overall majority of the workforce remained nonunion, for reasons that are beyond the scope of this chapter to explain.

Individual Labor Rights

In the logic of the postwar compromise, the core institutions of labor justice were programmatic in the sense that organized labor's ambition was to unionize the entire Canadian workforce. In practice, only a minority of the workforce became unionized and union strength was concentrated in major industries and later in the public sector. However, organized labor also acted politically to improve individual labor rights, and as unions succeeded in improving wages and working conditions through collective bargaining, the expectations of nonunion workers grew accordingly. There are significant areas of overlap between unionized and nonunion sectors, but as a general proposition the individual labor rights of unionized workers are enforceable only by their union through grievance arbitration, while nonunion workers must rely on their own resources to confront a more fragmented enforcement system.

The fragmentation of the labor justice system for individual labor rights in Ontario is attributable to the historical reluctance of governments of various political stripes to confront management rights at the workplace level, instead of relying on a variety of relatively ineffective enforcement mechanisms that required the expenditure of considerable state resources, which governments failed to allocate. Rather than encourage worker self-help through unionization, Ontario governments introduced individual labor rights on a piecemeal basis that for most workers were virtually unenforceable.

Primary responsibility for the enforcement of individual labor rights remains with the province's labor ministry. As did its federal counterpart, Ontario's labor ministry evolved in a piecemeal fashion. A decade after the federal government declared trade unions to be lawful in 1872, the government of Ontario ventured into the field of industrial relations when it established a Bureau of Industries within the Department (as a ministry was then known in Ontario) of the Commissioner of Agriculture. A year after the report of the federal Royal Commission on the Relations of Labor and Capital in 1889, the Bureau shifted its focus from industry to labor, was renamed the Bureau of Labour and transferred to the Department of Public Works. In 1916, the Bureau became the Trades and Labour Branch of Public Works until 1919 when a Department or Ministry of Labour was finally created, on the eve of a general election, and a decade later than its federal counterpart. The general election resulted in the defeat of a Conservative government and, in a deal brokered by Peter Heenan, his Independent Labour Party (ILP) joined forces with the United Farmers of Ontario, a rural protest party, to form a coalition government; Walter Ritchie Rollo, a labor leader from the Hamilton Trades and Labour Council, was appointed the province's first Minister of Labor.

Prior to Rollo's appointment, individual labor rights were fairly minimal while, as the Royal Commission revealed, working conditions were rather harsh. Beginning with the *Ontario Factories Act* in 1884, women and children enjoyed some basic protections in factory work, while occupational health and safety conditions were minimally regulated in a few other sectors. Concern over industrial accidents led to a major breakthrough in 1915 with the enactment of a no-fault insurance scheme for workers, which at the same time limited employer liability. The scheme was financed by a compulsory levy on employers and it was administered by an autonomous board, then known as the Workmen's [sic] Compensation Board, with unionized and non-union workplaces subject to the same system, a modified version of which remains in force.

If labor rights were minimal prior to Rollo's appointment, they improved only marginally during his term of office. Canada was a signatory to the Treaty of Versailles in 1919, and therefore morally bound to implement the Labor Section of the Treaty, which was assigned to the International Labor Organization to administer. Although the Mathers commission endorsed the ILO's founding principles, employment was a matter of provincial responsibility; for his part, Rollo limited himself to a minimal response, in a manner consistent with the paternalism of the *Ontario Factories Act*. His only noteworthy contribution was to introduce a *Minimum Wage Act* in 1920 that applied only to women. Rather than assigning its administration to his own ministry, Rollo created the Ontario Minimum Wage Board, which acted autonomously and in a manner welcomed by management because "it respected business values and set [women's] wage rates to accommodate business needs."[41] The board proceeded cautiously on an industry-by-industry basis, and consequently its reach extended only to a few industries. The board also proved reluctant to enforce its own standards, responding cautiously to complaints from an individual woman and refusing to prosecute offending employers.

During the Great Depression, the threat of social turmoil pushed the Liberal government of Mitchell Hepburn to act in 1935 with the enactment of the *Industrial Standards Act*, legislation intended to act as an alternative to collective bargaining through voluntary industrial councils that would be established voluntarily on a sectoral basis, an approach that was never implemented.[42] With Hepburn still Premier, in 1937 his government enacted a new *Minimum Wage Act*, which created a new autonomous board, the Industry and Labour Board, with authority to set minimum wages sector by sector for both men as well as women. This board was no more effective than its predecessor and in fact set no male minimum wages whatsoever.[43]

As the Second World War drew to a close, in 1944 Ontario's Conservative government enacted the *Hours of Work and Vacations with Pay Act* to establish an eight-hour workday, with a six-day week, and one week of paid vacation per year, labor rights that would be administered directly by the ministry.

Another significant breakthrough was achieved when a social movement coalesced in the postwar period, based on the principles contained in the Universal Declaration of Human Rights. In this movement, organized labor formed a coalition with leaders from Ontario's Black and Jewish communities to campaign for state protection of human rights, including a prohibition against racial discrimination in employment for both unionized and nonunion sectors. The Conservative government first responded in 1952 with the enactment of the *Fair Remuneration to Female Employees Act*, providing equal pay for men and women, and then after a ten-year human rights campaign, the government finally enacted the *Ontario Human Rights Code* in 1962. The administration of the Code was assigned to an autonomous Human Rights Commission, with controlled access to an independent human rights tribunal for purposes of adjudication.[44]

With the issue of employment-related discrimination allocated to a human rights commission, the Conservative government then established a comprehensive scheme for adjudicating a legislated set of minimum employment standards, through the enactment of the *Employment Standards Act (ESA)* in 1968. Although replete with exclusions and exceptions, the purpose of the ESA was to establish minimum standards for unionized and nonunion sectors that could be exceeded by employers or improved upon through individual or collective bargaining. The ministry provided a team of Employment Standards Officers to respond to individual complaints, with the authority to order violators to provide compensation; these orders could in turn be appealed to an independent tribunal, a function that was later assigned to the OLRB.

A decade later, in response to an extensive campaign by the trade union movement, the Conservative government enacted the *Occupation Health and Safety Act* of 1978, introducing a comprehensive scheme for workplace safety in both unionized and nonunion sectors. The ministry's cohort of Health and Safety Inspectors has authority to issue compliance orders and to initiate prosecution. At the workplace level, individual workers were empowered to refuse unsafe work, subject to the order of an inspector, which orders could be appealed to an independent tribunal, a function that again was later assigned to the OLRB.

In recent years, the courts have interpreted privative clauses in a manner that narrows the overlap in enforcement procedures between unionized and nonunion sectors, assigning exclusive jurisdiction to grievance arbitrators and the OLRB in various circumstances. Among the effects of this exclusivity is that while individual workers can seek damages for wrongful dismissal through the civil justice system, unionized workers have access exclusively to the grievance arbitration system, where, besides damages, they can seek reinstatement.

The Public Sector

Since Canada is a constitutional monarchy, public service workers are said to be Crown employees and as such are excluded from the general regime of labor legislation. This category includes employees of the federal government, provincial governments, and Crown corporations, but teachers, healthcare workers, and municipal workers are in separate categories, each of which has a distinct regime, with some areas of overlap, while municipal workers are covered by the regime of general application. Unionized public sector workers who are deemed to be essential do not have the right to strike; instead their collective agreements are subject to compulsory binding arbitration, imposed by interest arbitrators who exercise a normative power and are generally chosen from the cohort of grievance arbitrators.

One of the key differences between the union movement in Canada and in the United States is that the majority of public sector workers in Canada are unionized, while public sector workers in the United States are generally nonunion. However, unionization came late to Canada's Crown employees. In the federal sector, Crown employees had begun to organize as early as 1889 when the Railway Mail Clerks' Association held its first convention. As the federal public service expanded, public servants formed two voluntary associations, the Civil Service Federation of Canada and the Civil Service Association of Canada, which eventually merged in 1966 to form the Public Service Alliance of Canada (PSAC), a union that includes the majority of federal Crown employees; postal workers and others formed their own unions in a similar time period.

Rather than allowing its employees to unionize, the federal government adopted an industrial council model in 1944, while the voluntary associations continued to push informally for collective bargaining and then campaigned for enabling legislation during the 1963 general election. In 1967, the Liberal government enacted the *Public Service Staff Relations Act*, which Harry Arthurs described as "profoundly significant." According to Arthurs, the *Act* "establishes for employees of the Canadian federal government a regime of collective bargaining which in all essential respects parallels that prevailing in the private sector."[45]

A parallel process played out in the province of Ontario. The Civil Service Association of Ontario was formed in 1911 as a cooperative social club, until in 1944 the government designated the Association to represent provincial Crown employees on a Joint Advisory Council. By 1956, the Association was functioning more like a trade union than a social club, later changing its name to the Ontario Public Service Employees Union (OPSEU). In 1972, the government enacted the *Crown Employees Collective Bargaining Act*, the effect of which was similar to that of its federal counterpart legislation, although collective labor rights were initially more restrictive than those of the federal legislation.

Union organizing left governments at both the federal and provincial levels with little choice but to accede to public sector workers' demands for collective bargaining; as Arthurs wrote: "[T]he choice is not between collective bargaining and unilateral control by a sovereign employer. Rather, it is between orderly collective bargaining and chaotic, extralegal conflict."[46]

Conclusion: Still a Fragmented System

Since 1950, Ontario's core institutions have evolved significantly, as the relative strength of organized labor has ebbed and flowed and governments of different political perspectives have come and gone. The OLRB has gained extensive remedial powers and its jurisdiction has expanded into areas that include employment standards and occupational health and safety. Grievance arbitration has been institutionalized into a semiprivate cohort of private lawyers and academics who in turn have taken on the complex task of interest arbitration. The courts now more readily defer to the expertise of the OLRB and arbitrators in labor matters, accepting the exclusivity of their jurisdiction, which for grievance arbitrators has expanded to encompass all matters within the ambit of a collective agreement. The judges enforce the orders of the OLRB and grievance arbitrators in the same manner that they enforce court orders.

Nonunion workers are often perplexed by the complexity of the fragmented system that they must access to enforce even their minimum rights, while the growth of precarious work in the current neoliberal economy serves to exclude many workers from access to even these minimums.

Public sector workers are now a majority within the ranks of organized labor as the implementation of the *Wagner Act* model in Canada, even without the Taft-Hartley Amendments, has not resulted in effective access to collective bargaining for most workers in the private sector. The unionization of Canada's public sector workers, including teachers and healthcare workers, has changed the face of organized labor as women are more present and racialized workers are more visible. Despite these welcome changes, with the vast majority of the current workforce still unorganized, it is clear that the promise of the postwar compromise has not been met.

Notes

My thanks to Paul Craven, Ian Anderson, the two editors of this volume, and my fellow authors, for their insightful comments on earlier drafts of this chapter. The errors, if any, are solely my own.

1. Fudge and Tucker, "Pluralism or Fragmentation?"

2. Marx, "Eighteenth Brumaire," 97.

3. King, "International Typographical Union."

4. King's life and career has been the subject of frequent study. For example, see Craven, *Impartial Umpire*; Dawson, *William Lyon Mackenzie King*; Ferns and Ostrey, *Age of Mackenzie King*; McGregor, *Fall and Rise of Mackenzie King*; Scheinberg, "Rockefeller and King"; Whitaker, "The Liberal Corporatist Ideas"; Craven, "King and Context."

5. Tucker, "That Indefinite Area of Toleration," 41; and see Craven, "Workers' Conspiracies."

6. *Criminal Law Amendment Act* of 1872; but see Finkleman, "The Law of Picketing," and Tucker, "That Indefinite Area of Toleration."

7. Craven, "Canada, 1670–1935," 202–203.

8. Scott, "Federal Jurisdiction," 155.

9. Atherton, "British Columbia Origins," 104.

10. Webber, "Compelling Compromise," 27.

11. Baker, "Miners and the Mediator," 89; Craven, *Impartial Umpire*, 267.

12. Fudge and Tucker, *Labour before the Law*; Fudge and Tucker, "Forging Responsible Unions"; Laskin, "Labour Injunction in Canada."

13. Laskin, "Certiorari to Labour Boards," 992.

14. PC 1743 (July 11, 1918); PC 2525 (October 11, 1918); Webber, "Malaise of Compulsory Conciliation," 65, n. 17.

15. Millar, "Shapes of Power," 140.

16. Taras, "Why Nonunion Representation"; Scheinberg, "Rockefeller and King."

17. Kealey, "1919"; Taras, "Why Nonunion Representation," 766; McGregor, *Fall and Rise*, 210; Arthurs, "Collective Bargaining."

18. *Toronto Electrical Commissioners v. Snider*; Scott, "Federal Jurisdiction."

19. *An Act to Amend the IDIA*; Scott, "Federal Jurisdiction," 159.

20. *National Labor Relations Act*.

21. Endicott, *Raising the Workers' Flag*.

22. PC 2685 of June 1940, as quoted in Lang, "Lion in a Den of Daniels," 33.

23. PC 8253 of October 1941.

24. PC 4020 of June 1941.

25. PC 7307 of September 1941; Webber, "Malaise of Compulsory Conciliation," 68.

26. PC 4020 of June 6, 1941, Article 5; *Labour Relations Board Act*, Schedule B.

27. Lang, "Lion in a Den of Daniels," 23.

28. Ibid., 36; Millar, "Shapes of Power," 81.

29. MacDowell, "1943 Steel Strike," 74.

30. MacDowell, "Formation of the Canadian Industrial Relations System," 189.

31. MacDowell, "1943 Steel Strike," 73.

32. MacDowell, *Renegade Lawyer*, 122–138.

33. Laskin, "Collective Bargaining in Ontario," 684.

34. Ibid., 685, n. 8.

35. Millar, "Shapes of Power," 91.

36. Fudge and Tucker, *Labour before the Law*.

37. Millar, "Shapes of Power," 136.

38. Scott, "Federal Jurisdiction," 160.

39. Kaplan, *Ford Motor Company* (Rand).

40. *Attorney General of Nova Scotia v. Attorney General of Canada.*

41. McCallum, "Keeping Women in Their Place," 41; Russell, "A Fair or a Minimum Wage?" 70–71.

42. Klee, "Fighting the Sweatshop."

43. Thomas, "Setting the Minimum."

44. Luce and Schucher, "Right to Discriminate."

45. Arthurs, "Collective Bargaining," 971.

46. Ibid., 1000.

Bibliography

Arthurs, Harry W. "Collective Bargaining in the Public Service of Canada: Bold Experiment or Act of Folly?" *Michigan Law Review* 67.5 (1969): 971–1000.

Atherton, Jay. "The British Columbia Origins of the Federal Department of Labour." *BC Studies* 32 (Winter 1976–1977): 93–105.

Baker, William M. "The Miners and the Mediator: The 1906 Lethbridge Strike and Mackenzie King." *Labour/Le Travailleur* 11 (1983), 89–117.

Craven, Paul. "King and Context: A Reply to Whitaker." *Labour/Le Travailleur* (1979): 165–186.

———. *"An Impartial Umpire": Industrial Relations and the Canadian State 1900–1911.* Toronto: University of Toronto Press, 1980.

———. "Workers' Conspiracies in Toronto, 1854–72." *Labour/Le Travail* 14 (Fall 1984): 49–70.

———. "Canada, 1670–1935: Symbolic and Instrumental Enforcement in Loyalist North America," in Douglas Hay and Paul Craven, eds., *Masters, Servants, and Magistrates in Britain & the Empire, 1562–1955.* Chapel Hill: University of North Carolina Press, 2004.

Dawson, R. MacGregor. *William Lyon Mackenzie King: A Political Biography.* Toronto: University of Toronto Press, 1958.

Endicott, Stephen L. *Raising the Workers' Flag: The Workers Unity League of Canada, 1930–1936.* Toronto: University of Toronto Press, 2012.

Ferns, H. S., and B. Ostrey. *The Age of Mackenzie King: The Rise of the Leader.* London: William Heinemann Ltd., 1955.

Finkelman, Jacob. "The Law of Picketing in Canada." *University of Toronto Law Journal* 2 (1936–1937): 67–102, 344–360.

Fudge, Judy, and Eric Tucker. "Forging Responsible Unions: Metal Workers and the Rise of the Labour Injunction in Canada." *Labour/Le Travail* 37 (1996): 81–120.

———. "Pluralism or Fragmentation? The Twentieth Century Employment Law Regime in Canada." *Labour/Le Travail* 46 (Fall 2000): 251–306.

———. *Labour before the Law: The Regulation of Workers' Collective Action in Canada, 1900–1948.* Toronto: Oxford University Press Canada, 2001.

Kaplan, William. *Canadian Maverick: The Life and Times of Ivan C. Rand.* Toronto: University of Toronto Press, 2009.

Kealey, Gregory S. "1919: The Canadian Labour Revolt." *Labour/Le Travail* 13 (Spring 1984): 11–44.

King, William Lyon Mackenzie. "The International Typographical Union." MA thesis, University of Toronto, 1897.

Klee, Marcus, "Fighting the Sweatshop in Depression Ontario: Capital, Labour and the Industrial Standards Act." *Labour/Le Travail* 45 (2000): 13–51.

Lang, John B. "A Lion in a Den of Daniels: A History of the International Union of Mine Mill and Smelter Workers in Sudbury, Ontario, 1942–1962." MA thesis, University of Guelph, 1970.

Laskin, Bora. "The Labour Injunction in Canada: A Caveat." *Canadian Bar Review* XV (1937): 270–284.

———. "Collective Bargaining in Ontario: A New Legislative Approach." *Canadian Bar Review* XXI (1943): 684–706.

———. "Certiorari to Labour Boards: The Apparent Futility of Privative Clauses." *Canadian Bar Review* XXX (1952): 987–1003.

Luce, Frank, and Karen Schucher. "The Right to Discriminate: Kenneth Bell versus Carl McKay and the Ontario Human Rights Commission," in Eric Tucker, James Muir, and Bruce Ziff, eds., *Property on Trial*. Toronto: Irwin Law, 2012.

MacDowell, Laurel Sefton. "The Formation of the Canadian Industrial Relations System during World War Two." *Labour/Le Travailleur* (1978): 175–196.

———. "The 1943 Steel Strike against Wartime Wage Controls." *Labour/Le Travailleur* 10 (1982): 65–85.

———. *Renegade Lawyer: The Life of J. L. Cohen*. Toronto: University of Toronto Press, 2001.

Marx, Karl. "The Eighteenth Brumaire of Louis Bonaparte," in *Karl Marx and Frederick Engels Selected Works*. Moscow: Progress Publishers, 1968.

McCallum, Margaret E. "Keeping Women in Their Place: The Minimum Wage in Canada, 1910–25." *Labour/Le Travail* 17 (1986): 29–56.

McGregor, F. A. *The Fall and Rise of Mackenzie King: 1911–1919*. Toronto: Macmillan of Canada, 1962.

Millar, Frederick David. "Shapes of Power: Labour Relations Board, 1944 to 1950." PhD dissertation, York University, 1980.

Russel, Bob. "A Fair or a Minimum Wage? Women Workers, the State, and the Origins of Wage Regulation in Western Canada." *Labour/Le Travail* 28 (Fall 1991): 59–88.

Scheinberg, Stephen. "Rockefeller and King: The Capitalist and the Reformer," in John English and J. O. Stubbs, eds., *Mackenzie King: Widening the Debate*. Toronto: Macmillan, 1977.

Scott, F. R. "Federal Jurisdiction over Labour Relations—A New Look." *McGill Law Journal* 6, n3 (1960): 154–167.

Taras, Daphne Gottlieb. "Why Nonunion Representation Is Legal in Canada." *Relations Industrielles/Industrial Relations* 52, 4 (1997): 763–786.

Thomas, Mark. "Setting the Minimum: Ontario's Employment Standards in the Postwar Years, 1944–1968." *Labour/Le Travail* 54 (2004): 49–82.

Tucker, Eric. "'That Indefinite Area of Toleration': Criminal Conspiracy and Trade Unions in Ontario, 1837–77." *Labour/Le Travail* 27 (1991): 15–54.

Webber, Jeremy. "The Malaise of Compulsory Conciliation: Strike Prevention in Canada during World War II." *Labour/Le Travail* 15 (1985): 57–88.

———. "Compelling Compromise: Canada Chooses Conciliation over Arbitration 1900–1907." *Labour/Le Travail* 28 (1991): 15–57.

Whitaker, Reginald. "The Liberal Corporatist Ideas of Mackenzie King." *Labour/Le Travailleur* (1977): 137–169.

STATUTES

The Trade Unions Act (1872) 35 Victoria c. 30
An Act to Amend the Criminal Law Relating to Violence, Threats and Molestation (1872) 35 Victoria
    c. 31
The Breaches of Contract Act (1877) 40 Victoria c. 35
Ontario Factories Act (1884) 47 Victoria c. 39
The Conciliation Act (1900) 63–64 Victoria c. 24
The Railway Labour Disputes Act (1903) 3 Edward VII c. 55
Conciliation and Labour Act R.S. (1906) c. 96
The Industrial Disputes Investigation Act (1907) 6–7 Edward VII c. 20
War Measures Act (1914) 5 George V, c. 2
Minimum Wage Act (1920) S.O. c. 277
An Act to Amend the Industrial Disputes Investigation Act, 1907 (1925) 15–16 George V c. 14
National Labor Relations Act of 1935 (29 U.S.C.A. § 151 et seq) (the *Wagner Act*)
Industrial Standards Act (1937) S.O. c. 90
The Collective Bargaining Act, 1943 S.O. c. 4
The Labour Relations Board Act (1944) S.O. c. 29
Hours of Work and Vacations with Pay Act (1944) S.O. c. 26
The Industrial Relations and Disputes Investigation Act (1948) 11–12 George VI c. 54
The Labour Relations Act, 1948 S.O. c. 51
The Labour Relations Act, 1950 S.O. c. 34
Fair Remuneration to Female Employees Act (1952) S.O. c. 104
Ontario Human Rights Code (1962) S.O. c. 93
Employment Standards Act (1966) S.O. c. 41
Collective Bargaining in the Public Service Act (1966–1967) S.C. c. 72
Crown Employees Collective Bargaining Act (1972) S.O. c. 67
Occupation Health and Safety Act (1978) S.O. c. 83

DECISIONS

Toronto Electrical Commissioners v. Snider (1925) A.C. 396
*Ford Motor Company of Canada Limited and The International Union United Automobile, Aircraft and
    Agricultural Implement Workers of America (U.A.W.–C.I.O.)*, arbitration award of Mr. Justice
    Rand, January 29, 1946
Attorney General of Nova Scotia v. Attorney General of Canada (1951) S.C.R. 31

CHAPTER 4

The Ambiguity of Labor Justice in Mexico, 1907–1931

WILLIAM SUAREZ-POTTS

Introduction

On January 4, 1907, Mexico's president, Porfirio Díaz, must have thought that he had resolved a difficult labor conflict in the nation's textile industry when he pronounced his arbitral award to settle an employer-driven lockout in this economic sector. Since the fall of 1906, manufacturers in one state, Puebla, had imposed new factory regulations and locked out workers who had begun to strike for higher wages, better working conditions, and the recognition of their association. In December, their counterparts in Veracruz joined the lockout. Workers and their organization petitioned the president to intervene in the conflict. The industrialists were initially reluctant to consent to state mediation but finally relented, agreeing to the president's arbitration.[1]

The arbitral award favored employers. Indeed, its proclamation provoked a violent reaction among workers in Río Blanco, one of the company towns near Orizaba, Veracruz. Workers attacked and burned a reputed company store, in a riotous uprising that caught authorities off guard. The federal government had to send troops to Orizaba and the surrounding area to restore order. The soldiers killed scores of workers, and the army detained and incarcerated more. The local political prefect was removed from his position, the state governor compromised. Both had promoted a policy of mediation. This was not the resolution of a labor conflict envisioned by the government and industrialists.

Mexican industrial and government elites thus faced the social question: how to deal with the emerging working class, which throughout the Atlantic world (including continental Europe, the United States, Canada, Britain, and its settler colonies of Australia and New Zealand) was seemingly threatening social orders undergoing economic and social changes resulting from the first and second industrial revolutions. Mexican periodicals had begun to comment about strikes in Europe and the United States, the growth of socialist parties and movements, and urban problems attendant with the expansion of industries. The semiofficial newspaper of the Porfirian government, *El Imparcial*, expressing bewilderment at the uprising in Río Blanco, opined that Mexico had now faced the *cuestión obrera*, like many European countries.[2]

The violent suppression of workers' resistance to an unpopular resolution of an employer lockout, which in turn had been implemented to break a bourgeoning labor movement, followed an earlier violent confrontation between mineworkers and an American employer in Cananea, near the U.S. border, in June 1906, and overlapped with railroad workers' organizing efforts. But economic recession soon weakened the labor movement, apart from any state repression, although the social question remained pending (violent suppression hardly could have seemed a suitable answer to anybody) when Díaz and his inner circle began to consider a different kind of crisis. The looming presidential election of 1910 revived the question of whether Díaz again would stand for reelection. Almost 80, it was doubtful he could survive another presidential term. The strongest challenger to Díaz in the elections proved to be Francisco Madero, who in his campaign made credible overtures to workers. If labor had been contained by 1909–1910, workers still enthusiastically rallied around Madero.

The Porfirian political machine ensured the victory of the incumbent president, who had his challenger jailed. Madero escaped, crossed the border into the United States, and pronounced a revolution to overthrow the Porfirian dictatorship, to begin in November 1910. People around Mexico, including workers in a few areas, rose up. The army mostly put them down. But the revolution could not be quashed altogether— it was too dispersed—and as it spread, it was peasants, not industrial workers, who were crucial in the mobilization of armed opposition to the Porfirian *ancien regime* that had endured since 1877. Díaz resigned in May 1911, an interim president and cabinet replaced him and his ministers, and Madero ran again for president. This time he won—officially, too.

The Mexican Revolution had begun. It did not end, arguably, until the late 1930s, although pitched battles between different forces diminished after 1915. In the midst of revolutionary struggles, workers asserted themselves and contributed to subsequent political and social-economic arrangements. The revolution, however, was never proletarian, albeit one that resulted in the first social constitution—a fundamental, national charter incorporating social legislation, including a section on workers' rights. At the same time, however much this result amounted to major achievements for Mexican workers, it is also remarkable how much the constitution's stipulated workers' rights have resembled those of other labor laws across the Americas.

The affirmation of labor rights in the constitution of 1917, contained in thirty paragraphs or *fracciones* in Article 123, did not lead to immediate implementation. And the paragraphs requiring that boards of conciliation and arbitration (*juntas de concili-ación y arbitraje*) should resolve all labor conflicts produced political and legal friction throughout the 1920s. Only in 1931 was comprehensive federal (i.e., national) labor legislation adopted that elaborated the basis for a system of industrial relations in which the labor boards as administrative tribunals were made the indisputable, central mechanism for resolving employment disputes. This chronology of the formation of a system of labor justice approximates that of several other American nations, even as none of them underwent a revolution similar to Mexico's. Moreover, as in Canada, the United States, or Argentina, to name three nations, a federal, constitutional order conditioned the evolution of labor legislation and the organization of special tribunals, although how and to what degree federal questions influenced the institutionalization of labor justice varied from nation to nation. In Mexico, the politically contentious implementation of Article 123 initially had to proceed piecemeal, as each state was responsible for enacting labor legislation in accord with the constitutional article's dictates. And while Article 123 clearly expressed basic principles of social legisla-tion, the consolidation of arrangements with corporatist elements came later—not until 1948. In this regard, one might compare Mexico's evolving industrial relations system, including its boards, with that of Brazil's, where its labor charter of 1943 has been termed corporatist, but where broader intellectual currents along with changing domestic circumstances also contributed to its form and practical significance.[3]

This chapter reviews the establishment of the boards of conciliation and arbitra-tion in Mexico, as the principal forums of first instance adjudication for industrial disputes. In Mexico, the context was the nation's revolution, however delimited or defined, but in any event covering the period from about 1910 to the 1930s. Nonethe-less, the larger contexts of economic change, the emergence of a corresponding work-ing class, and a shared intellectual and legal tradition with other nations on both sides of the Atlantic Ocean (and the far side of the Pacific Ocean) were also relevant for the development of these boards and the labor law that contributed to their structure, nature, and decision making. Accordingly, the first section of the chapter discusses further the social question, and early, transnational articulations of reformist, legal doctrine that assumed the form of social legislation. The second section turns to the revolutionary situation existing in Mexico in the first decades of the twentieth cen-tury, the political and juridical inadequacies of the time (for workers), and early state mechanisms to resolve labor conflict. Section three discusses the mandate of Article 123, requiring that conciliation and arbitration boards resolve all labor disputes. Sec-tion four discusses the evolution of such boards in the 1920s, in connection with the various political and judicial factors affecting their operation in this decade. Section five notes briefly the enactment of comprehensive, federal labor legislation in 1931 that ratified the nature and operation of the boards. The conclusion considers their significance for workers, unions, and the state thereafter.

Social Legislation

The term *social question* was used in Mexico in the 1840s, but its invocation by the century's end specifically referred to *social problems*—and industrial conflicts—associated with the new working class, in Europe or the United States. By the 1890s, there had appeared a few essays in the nation's major law journals (either by Mexican lawyers or Europeans) discussing critiques of liberal-legal doctrine, in addition to proposed remedies for said problems—namely, social legislation.

In a few words, what proponents of social legislation criticized was the notion that a contractual regime fairly governed employment relations. Critics questioned whether parties to an employment contract could negotiate its terms on the basis of equality. They underscored the obvious discrepancies in power, which raised the issue of whether the worker agreed to the contract voluntarily. Further, reformers observed that social problems, such as illnesses or crime, stemmed from the penury of workers, their long hours of work, occupational accidents, or idleness caused by unemployment. Strikes that further harmed workers' lives as well as production, while threatening the political and social order, were attributed to low wages, which workers, negotiating individually, could not raise.

This pessimistic analysis by mostly European law reformers was coupled with proposals for collective solutions: social legislation that would assign employers a larger burden of the social costs of production and direct the state to intervene in labor conflicts and the economy. The right to strike typically was treated ambivalently; the articles published in Mexico were written by political economists or lawyers who sympathized with laborers, not by revolutionaries or workers. The lawyers proposed reform as an alternative to revolution or social dissolution.[4] It is noteworthy that critiques of laissez-faire liberalism that proposed social legislation were reprinted in Mexico in the journals of the political and legal elite, not in radical broadsheets. Indeed, the Ministry of Development (Secretaría de Fomento) began publishing a translated version of Paul Pic's major treatise on labor legislation early in the new century.[5] And *El Imparcial* covered the growing labor movement in the textile industry, not altogether unsympathetically, while mentioning in some articles foreign experiments to resolve employment disputes that were alternatives to the established judiciary. Even after the debacle of 1906–1907, the newspaper imagined the beginnings of a new order in industrial relations, in some respects similar to contemporary institutional arrangements in Western Europe.[6]

Justice

That the Porfirian state had killed workers struggling merely for a modestly better living against foreign-owned companies was a point not lost on most Mexicans able to follow the news. Mexico's liberal constitution of 1857 guaranteed freedom of labor and the right to associate. The president himself had confirmed these rights, and one important cabinet minister in a speech to workers had also reaffirmed their right to strike peacefully.[7] At the same time, the regime deemed many strikes potentially subversive and persecuted the PLM (the Partido Liberal Mexicano or Mexican Liberal Party), which it suspected was behind much of the labor turmoil. The PLM was a presence in some strike movements and committed to overthrowing the state, and while its leadership was anarchist, its public proclamations as of 1906, which put forward a labor agenda, were ideologically liberal. Government officials did marginalize it, while leaders of the main labor organization in the textile industry chose to collaborate with the state, claiming their rights under the constitution as Mexican citizens. For their part, Díaz, the governors of two states, Puebla and Veracruz, and political prefects near the factory towns had all become involved in mediating and arbitrating labor disputes in an ad hoc, informal manner. This was a continuation of the practice of earlier public authorities.[8] But after Río Blanco, it was failing. In 1906–1907, the inner circle of the Porfirian elite (the *científicos*) considered drafting repressive labor legislation.[9] Meanwhile, in 1904 and 1906, the governors of the states of Mexico and Nuevo León promulgated workers' compensation legislation.[10] Social legislation of one kind or another was afoot, while labor leaders pressed for maximum realization of the liberal promise of the constitution.

Labor justice might have been addressed more comprehensively by the nation's law courts. Employment matters framed as contractual disputes, for example, could be presented to a court. And employers, such as large landholders, did file complaints with local authorities against their workers who had quit their jobs, normally alleging that the worker was in debt to the employer or had not completed his employment term. Local authorities, in some states under a peonage statute, did jail such workers, who sometimes were able to appeal to the federal judiciary pursuant to the *juicio de amparo*. This was a civil action used to obtain individual, injunctive relief in the federal courts against state and local authorities by petitioners alleging violations of their constitutional rights—such as the right to free labor or the right not to be imprisoned for a civil debt.[11] The *amparo* action was utilized extensively by individuals of different social classes during the Porfirian era, including, even if only occasionally, debt peons or agricultural workers.[12] Supreme Court judges, in their cases, ruled repeatedly against local authorities who had violated complainant-workers' right of free labor. But the Court generally was silent regarding concerted actions and industrial disputes.[13] The judiciary, liberal or bourgeois, was not hospitable to the new working class.

After the revolution broke out and Díaz resigned, the national congress approved legislation establishing a labor department. The interim president, Francisco León de la Barra, endorsed it. He, like others of the political elite, believed there was a need for such a department (and he had observed similar agencies in operation in Buenos Aires and Belgium, while on diplomatic missions there). The department began to operate in 1912, approximately coincident with the inauguration of Madero. Its first director, Antonio Ramos Pedrueza, a socialist and lawyer, had also held governmental positions in the Porfirian regime, including that of a deputy in the lower house of Congress. The new labor department was charged with collecting statistics related to working conditions and copies of labor legislation passed in Europe and elsewhere; if the relevant parties consented, it could also mediate work stoppages.[14]

Frequent and recurring strikes in mining, transport, and textile manufacturing accompanied the revolution and change in governments, and the resurgent labor movement proved an important part of the revolutionary process. Madero's administration encountered a turbulent situation in the textile industry. The labor department stepped in, along with the cabinet level secretaries of finance and the interior, to mediate an industrywide contract setting a comprehensive, higher wage level. In July 1912, such a broad collective agreement formulating a wage and hour schedule was reached. The workers' committee that had participated indirectly in the negotiations for the agreement accepted its premises and framework, although the employer representative insisted on separate meetings with the government officials. The agreement, moreover, depended on the voluntary compliance of employers. To induce their cooperation, Madero's administration lobbied for an amendment to a tax law in Congress; if a firm complied with the agreement, its tax rate was lowered. Congress voted for the tax amendment—it was the only substantial labor bill it approved in this period. Thereafter, workers' groups in the industry used the new wage rates as a benchmark. Employers' compliance, despite the fiscal subsidy, was sporadic.

Madero had to address other challenges at the same time: a peasant insurgency near Mexico City (the Zapatistas) and rebels in the north dissatisfied with the turn in the revolution. More perilous was the gathering movement on the right to depose him, comprised of adherents of the Porfirian regime, including army officers, as well as large landholders, foreign capitalists, and their diplomatic representatives, disgusted with Madero's tolerance of democratic, popular mobilization. In February 1913, a coup attempt became a destructive street battle in Mexico City. One general, Victoriano Huerta, with the encouragement of the diplomatic corps and particularly the American ambassador, betrayed Madero, joined the coup leaders, seized executive power, and arranged the murder of the president and vice president.[15]

Meanwhile, in 1912–1913, Congress debated several bills of social legislation, and the labor department continued with its operations of collecting copies of foreign labor statutes and mediating industrial disputes.[16] Huerta, as the new de facto chief executive, supported the agency's activities and initially tolerated workers' organization. He was preoccupied with the Constitutionalist revolution declared against him in northern Mexico and the interminable peasant insurgency in the south. But the more radical wings of the labor movement were anti-Huertista and potentially destabilizing. Huerta ultimately repressed the anarchist-leaning COM (Casa del Obrero Mundial or House of the World Worker). Congress was also closed, but in the summer of 1914, the Constitutionalists, led by Venustiano Carranza defeated Huerta.

In the fall of 1914, the revolutionary war might have ended. A multiclass coalition of disparate forces had demolished the state apparatus of the old regime, under the banner of the 1857 constitution. But the triumphant coalition fragmented, and civil war ensued between revolutionary factions. The Constitutionalists, who were generally more middle- or upper-class in background and orientation than their mostly rural-based opponents (whether Zapatistas or Francisco Villa's army), proved better strategists, both politically and militarily, and they wooed the working-class movement.

Among Carranza's close civilian advisers were the *renovadores* (renovators), who had endorsed social legislation in the XXVIth Congress that Huerta finally disbanded.[17] Carranza himself began advocating for social legislation, as did a number of leading generals in his coalition, including Alvaro Obregón and, in Yucatán, Salvador Alvarado. The Constitutionalists recognized the social motives of the violent, ongoing struggle (and, specifically, of their agrarian, revolutionary adversaries): the drive to end the gross oppression and exploitation of the majority of Mexicans, both rural and urban, and to realize a substantial degree of justice. In any event, Carranza proclaimed the immediate need for social legislation, in December 1914, and a month later his civilian advisers began to draft such bills (derived from earlier ones debated in the XXVIth Congress). Meanwhile, Carranza's generals issued pro-labor decrees in zones under their control. Obregón also encouraged Carranza to agree to an alliance with the COM. In the state of Veracruz, workers continued to organize and expand their influence. The governor started to pass labor legislation, too. And, in Yucatán, General Alvarado initiated his socialist project as military commander of the region and state governor. The centerpiece of the project was an industrial relations system with state mediation and arbitration, structured through boards of conciliation and a tribunal of arbitration, modeled in part on New Zealand's system.[18] Together, they would resolve all individual and collective conflicts arising in production in this overwhelmingly agricultural state that had been dominated by large, exploitive, and oppressive plantations.

By the summer of 1916, Carranza was sufficiently confident of prevailing in the civil war to contemplate convening a special congress to amend the liberal constitution and legitimize his power to become the next duly elected president. The new or reformed constitution, however, would have to contain social legislation—both agrarian and labor provisions—in order to satisfy his military, popular, and labor constituencies. It was a complicated political game. In mid-summer 1916, Carranza called out the military to repress a general strike in Mexico City and then attempted to prosecute strike leaders under an antisedition statute. Other Constitutionalists largely frustrated him. Carranza had earlier disbanded the military brigades formed by the COM, and now he suppressed the organization. But the labor militants remained active. And, in Veracruz and Yucatán, the governors were tied closely to a mobilized working class (both rural and urban).

Article 123

The complex labor politics of the victorious revolutionaries contributed to the peculiar gyrations at the constitutional congress: when Carranza spoke at its inauguration on December 1, 1916, his draft charter omitted social legislation, whose incorporation into the constitution purportedly was one of the reasons for holding the convention. Carranza contended that the power to legislate labor laws should be placed in the federal legislature, and that enactment of specific statutes, concededly necessary, should be deferred to a date when it eventually met. Once the constitutional delegates began to discuss the issue of labor rights, however, the majority concurred that much more had to be added to the draft. At this point, the lawyer and *renovador* José Natividad Macías, who had coauthored Carranza's draft constitution, with a few others, some also *renovadores*, preempted the discussion. Macías argued that he had always promoted social legislation. He read to the convention the labor bills that he had helped write earlier, emphasizing a vision of state-sponsored organs that could resolve and regulate labor conflict, in conjunction with unions that would be parties to collective contracts with their employers.[19]

It was a tour de force clearly predicated on principles of social legislation then current in the Western world. The imagined state institutions would mediate or arbitrate labor conflicts, obviating the need for the strike, which Macías acknowledged was a social right (*derecho social*). These state bodies also would set equitable wage levels, as immiserating wages had been the main cause for strikes. Their establishment would be complemented by the replacement of the contract between the individual worker and employer with one between the union, representing all workers, and the firm. The union, collective agreement, and state conciliation agency would become the bases for a new, just, industrial order.

Macías largely persuaded the constitutional delegates that labor rights differed from individual rights—the former was social legislation—and that such rights should be enumerated in a separate section of the constitution, if they were to be incorporated in it. He, with other delegates and the head of the labor department, then formed a special ad hoc committee, with the convention's consent, to draft a special section of labor rights. The single contemporaneous account by one of the participants, Pastor Rouaix, at the time minister of development, recounts that Macías played an influential role in its drafting. The outcome was Article 123, which more radical delegates, including Francisco Múgica, modified to strengthen the right to strike in particular.[20]

Article 123 flatly directed that boards of conciliation and arbitration should resolve all labor conflicts.[21] It did not detail their nature, other than they were to be tripartite organs, comprised of an equal number of employer and labor representatives and one government official. That is, the delegates contemplated that they would not be tribunals within the judicial branch of government. During the convention, the few working-class delegates, along with others, expressed strong animosity for civil law courts: judges were unsympathetic to workers' claims and legal procedures were slow and expensive. An alternative system of dispute resolution was necessary for workers.

The text of Article 123 left pending the actual labor justice system to be established. Delegates had proposed at least two types of alternative-dispute institutions. One group advocated for Yucatán's revolutionary labor tribunals, which were empowered to decide cases as courts, that is, with final, binding rulings (albeit without being part of the judiciary). The Yucatán delegate, Héctor Victoria, in insisting that the states must have the authority to legislate in labor matters rather than the federal government, seemingly even suggested that labor tribunals should have this power.[22] Another proposal, articulated by Veracruz's delegates, envisioned boards as mediating bodies that would resolve collective conflicts, perhaps without issuing binding decisions. Related to the question about how obligatory such decisions should be, was the extent of the boards' jurisdiction: should they take cognizance of individual disputes or collective conflicts, or both?

Article 123 was certainly a seminal achievement in constitutional law and the establishment of a system of labor justice: the constitution of 1917 arguably was the first to incorporate social legislation.[23] In connection with this symbolic achievement, Macías and Carranza had prevailed on an important point: Article 123 was to be largely hortatory, not self-executing.[24] It was, as Macías had argued, distinct from nineteenth century liberal, individual rights guaranteed in another section of the constitutional text. Article 123 encompassed social legislation—which required a legislature to enact. Macías and Carranza had also compromised with their convention counterparts who wanted the states not the federal congress to legislate over labor matters (for representatives from states that already had social legislation, such as Veracruz and Yucatán, it was a way to protect their accomplishments). Victoria's pronouncements in favor of the states reflected the predominant sentiment at the convention. The power to enact labor legislation, including the establishment of conciliation and arbitration boards, was consequently delegated to state legislatures and only to Congress for the federal district and territories. Importantly, this meant that there would be multiple labor statutes and different bodies charged with the regulation of industrial relations—and that any intervention by the federal government in industrial situations that affected the entire nation would be suspect constitutionally. As in Canada, the United States, or Argentina, political and federal issues became intertwined with labor relations.

The Boards of Conciliation and Arbitration, 1917–1931

Administrative labor boards, mandated by Article 123, thus were established unevenly across Mexico after the effective date of the new constitution, May 1917. Government officials, if they aimed to collaborate with labor, furthered the formation of administrative boards and, in the course of the 1920s, came to realize the potential of regulating industrial relations through them. For political leaders, keen on solidifying state power after its near dissolution during the years of revolutionary civil war, administrative labor boards presented one way to extend governmental authority both into industry and among a segment of the population, while for union leaders such boards held out the opportunity of leveraging their limited negotiating power in the labor market vis-á-vis employers. But capital, and, significantly, federal judges, including many of the justices of the Supreme Court, viewed such boards with hostility, if not for the same reasons.

Whether a particular state legislature passed legislation to establish labor boards, in accord with Article 123, depended on the strength of the local union movement, the effectiveness of resistance by employers, and how politicians in the executive and legislative branches perceived such social legislation. The first state to enact a labor statute was Veracruz, which, as noted, already had in effect legislation before the signing of the new constitution. Its 1918 statute became the model for most subsequent laws and labor boards; among other things, it set up a system of municipal boards of conciliation and a central board to arbitrate all labor disputes. The boards were defined as administrative authorities with a tripartite membership of government, labor, and business representatives. Some states, however, did not pass legislation, or enacted laws only establishing administrative boards, without corresponding, substantive statutes, such as, importantly, the jurisdictions of the state of Mexico and the federal district, the location of Mexico City.[25] Where established, even before the constitution's effective date, the boards began to operate, but frequently only haphazardly.

There is insuffficient historical research on the makeup of the labor boards between 1917 and 1931. In some states, archives of the early boards were destroyed or are not readily accessible.[26] Hence it is impossible, both because of the nature of their operation and the related question of the historical record, to generalize across the country about the first labor boards, other than to suggest that they conformed as much to local political forces as to national and constitutional norms. Contemporaneous scholars and newspapers remarked that they tended to side with workers and unions.[27] This elementary observation, however, is complicated as the decade of the 1920s progresses, because of pervasive interunion rivalries, which governments and employers frequently exacerbated. And throughout most of the 1920s, the state of Nuevo León presents a partial qualification of this generalization while still reflecting the politicization of labor relations and the manipulation of interunion conflict. This is largely because of the successful strategy of Monterrey's powerful industrialists, who fostered company unions who, in turn, dominated the local labor board.[28]

In the region around Orizaba, unions continued to increase their influence, even placing their members in municipal government; in turn, municipal officials controlled the local conciliation boards along with union representatives. The large textile firms, once predominant in these company towns, lost before them.[29] Veracruz's central state board also sympathized with workers, while state governors aligned with unions.[30] The situation for employers was little better in Yucatán, where progressive governments expressed socialist principles.[31] Similar tendencies, although not so pronounced as in these states, were evident elsewhere, too, as a new labor confederation, the CROM (Confederación Regional Obrera Mexicana, Regional Confederation of Mexican Workers), undertook alliances with government officials (municipal council members, mayors, governors, and Presidents Obregón and Plutarco Elías Calles).[32]

The CROM argued for "multiple action" as opposed to "direct action"—a strategy of engaging in politics, negotiating with state and employer counterparts, lobbying for (and drafting) labor laws, and participating in labor board proceedings.[33] On a number of boards at the state or municipal level, such as in Veracruz or Mexico City, the CROM came to exert substantial influence in the 1920s. Infamous for being corrupt or compromising with employers and governments, it nonetheless became a key proponent of the elaboration of labor law and administrative boards.[34] In 1919, Obregón, as presidential candidate, entered into a secret pact with the CROM. It was never fulfilled, partly because Obregón was unable to persuade federal legislators to pass its provisions and partly because their partnership soured, but the CROM partially staffed the federal labor department during his presidency (1920–1924). Calles was even closer to the CROM leadership while president (1924–1928). When Obregón designated him the presidential successor, in late 1923, nearly half of the army revolted, with the support of some conservatives, business elements, and disaffected labor groups. CROM allegiance was an important component of Obregón and Calles's victory against the military rebels.[35] After the rebellion, with the inauguration of Calles, the CROM's rejuvenated position in high, government circles was patent: the new secretary of industry, commerce, and labor (SICT, Secretaría de Industria, Comercio y Trabajo) was the general secretary of the CROM, Luis N. Morones. CROM leaders continued to control important positions in the federal labor department and on the federal district's labor board; and a significant bloc of CROM deputies took seats in Congress.[36]

A turn in the law that applied to state administrative boards accompanied the empowerment of the CROM. Between 1917 and 1924, the Supreme Court, composed of justices educated in nineteenth-century liberal principles, had refused to recognize the authority of the boards of conciliation and arbitration to decide matters like law courts. Specifically, it had held that board decisions were merely advisory; labor boards—as administrative, not judicial—bodies, were legally incapable of enforcing their decisions (although they might and did try to do so). Until 1924 employers had been able to petition federal judges and ultimately the Supreme Court fairly successfully to prevent the implementation of board awards, pursuant to the *amparo* action. The result had been the undermining of the boards, the claims of unions, and the new labor law, as businesses justified on legal grounds their refusal to recognize Article 123 or state labor legislation.[37] Although the Court's case law had evolved, since its early opinions in 1918–1919, to accommodate the reality of board decision making, it was only in early 1924 that it reversed earlier precedents and doctrine (*jurisprudencia*) so as to acknowledge the boards in effect as tribunals. As of 1924, the Court held that the decisions of the boards were binding on the parties before them. To reach this ruling, the Court reinterpreted the relevant provisions of Article 123 and reasoned that, in order for the boards to be able to resolve labor disputes effectively, their decisions had to be comparable to those of law courts. No longer would their decisions be disregarded so easily. A system of labor justice was thereby constitutionally and legally ratified.[38]

More than other labor organizations, the CROM benefited from the turn in the Supreme Court's law and its recognition of the boards as de facto tribunals. The confederation's leaders' espousal of "multiple action" certainly disposed them to act further through the now legitimized boards when it was convenient to do so; they realized the tactical advantages of participating as decision makers on them. And it was partly through state and local boards and the SICT that the CROM jockeyed for more influence in the labor movement. Independent unions found themselves at odds not only with employers, but also with the CROM and the government, including sometimes the boards. Employers, however, still endeavored to avoid enforcement of awards by continuing to file *amparo* actions before federal judges; delaying a board order could render it, in practical terms, meaningless. Labor law as applied by the boards remained a patchwork limited by state jurisdictions. The administration of labor justice amounted to distinct state entities—state labor boards, the federal judiciary, and the executive power—interacting with rival unions and employers. And individual workers seeking justice did not always fare well in this system.

Administrative boards of conciliation and arbitration nonetheless were becoming the principal institution for resolving labor disputes, whether these were individual claims for accident compensation, wrongful discharge and back pay, or collective conflicts, which often prompted the involvement of other state officials. But the limitation of their jurisdiction to state boundaries and the absence of a corresponding, national board to address industrial relations transcending these boundaries posed legal and practical challenges for the nation's political leadership. The SICT, in 1926–1927, attempted to compensate for the absence of federal jurisdiction in labor matters by issuing circulars to governors, asserting the federal ministry's power to regulate the nationally strategic industries of railways, petroleum, and mining.[39] Meanwhile, Morones, as SICT minister, over two years, 1925–1927, negotiated with textile employers to reach an industrywide collective contract with the federal government and CROM unions. The contract or convention was more comprehensive than what Madero's administration had concluded in 1912 and contemplated factory commissions, then district and regional committees, and finally the SICT ministry resolving labor conflicts.[40] Indeed, after 1924, Morones, as SICT minister, was arbitrating or mediating strikes with national implications. This approach, however, was unconstitutional.

Parallel to its recognition of the legality of board decisions in early 1924, the Supreme Court reaffirmed repeatedly its reading of Article 123 that required all employment disputes to be resolved by labor boards. The SICT's interventions in major labor conflicts ran aground, in part, because of this case law. The problem was dramatically encountered when an independent, militant confederation of rail workers, the Confederación de Transportes y Comunicaciones (Confederation of Transport and Communication Workers, CTC) led a general strike on the railroads in early 1927, against the predominantly state-owned company—which the SICT (Morones) declared illegal. As the strike waned, the CTC filed an *amparo* action against the SICT and President Calles, arguing that the SICT lacked the constitutional authority to declare the strike illegal (and that, accordingly, its members had a right of reinstatement). The Supreme Court agreed and held that only labor boards could make such declarations, and in a case such as this one, implicating the national economy, it had to be a federal board.[41]

President Calles had anticipated such a critical ruling, decreeing the establishment of the federal labor board (Junta Federal de Conciliación y Arbitraje) in September 1927.[42] Precipitously, the new tribunal prepared to hear the dispute between the CTC and company's management. Its composition was stacked against the CTC, of course: except one, representatives were either drawn from management or the CROM (whose railroad affiliates had been trying to displace the CTC's members before the strike and during the strike had operated as strikebreakers). In December, the federal board issued a final decision. While predictable (the award went against the CTC), it was still astounding, and augured a trend for how labor boards would determine the lawfulness of strikes thereafter. For the federal board held not only that the strike had been illicit, as Article 123 defined this term (because of the violence committed by an alleged majority of the strikers)—but actually that the strike had never happened! That is, for a strike to be recognized as having occurred, a majority of the relevant firm's workers must have engaged in the stoppage. In this case, the board found explicitly, as a fact, that only a minority of the workforce had walked out, hence that they had abandoned their employment (and, accordingly, were not entitled to reinstatement).[43]

The CTC immediately filed an *amparo* action against the board's award. In May 1929, the Supreme Court ruled against the CTC, upholding the federal board's discretionary power to make factual evaluations: in this case, its factual determination that workers had abandoned their employment.[44] Perhaps it was disingenuous: its earlier, 1927, opinion had recognized explicitly the existence of the strike, while the federal board had found its nonexistence only by applying a mixed legal-factual standard, which was then evolving among other boards and labor lawyers. But the Court's ruling was also mostly consistent with its case law and ongoing dialectic with labor boards, that is, conceding their authority to decide employment-related disputes. The Court was surely thereby avoiding further contestation with the federal board and the executive power behind it. Ironically, by 1929, that power had become overtly hostile to the CROM.

Political events since 1927 changed the overall balance of power between the CROM and federal government. Obregón's successful reelection bid for the presidency in 1928 and his assassination in July resulted in the CROM's loss of political influence: many of Obregón's followers imputed the assassination to the confederation, and Calles tried to appease them partly by withdrawing his support for it. Morones resigned from his cabinet ministry, as other CROM leaders did from their governmental positions. The federal board continued to operate, but not so clearly captive of the CROM. Meanwhile, the interim president, Emilio Portes Gil, an obregonista and avowed enemy of the CROM, after the Court's 1929 ruling against the CTC, agreed to reinstate in a staggered manner many of the strikers.

The Enactment of the Federal Labor Law of 1931

If the federal labor board with its extensive authority to regulate strikes in strategic economic sectors was a fait accompli by 1929, its constitutionality was doubtful. The Supreme Court, for one, remained ambivalent about its origins.[45] By 1930, the momentum for comprehensive, federal labor legislation was clear. Already at the time of Obregón's assassination, almost all interested actors (much of organized labor, including the CROM; most large employers, except Monterrey's capitalists; and national political elites) favored the federalization of labor law. These same interests, nonetheless, differed over what should be encompassed in any legislation. While many industrialists wished to see federal law that would preempt local laws and pro-union labor boards in such states as Veracruz, others, including Monterrey's industrialists, were warier of the potential for intrusive or pro-union legal provisions. The decline in the CROM's influence in the federal government and the ensuing weakening of the labor movement as the economic crisis worsened, in 1930–1931, probably contributed to employers' disposition to accept national legislation. But the need to legitimize the federal labor board under the constitution by amending the latter so as to enable Congress to pass authorizing legislation also must have been consequential in the calculations of governing circles favoring such law.

In 1929, President Portes Gil succeeded in maneuvering through Congress the constitutional amendments necessary for the federalization of labor law. He had to compromise, and the result was the establishment of separate jurisdictions for labor boards. Although all labor boards would apply the same labor law (assuming passage of a federal labor code), the federal labor board's jurisdiction covered only a few, strategic economic sectors; state labor boards would continue to preside over all others. At the time, the federal labor board's jurisdiction was limited to railways and other federal-concession transportation, hydrocarbon industries, mining, and maritime activities. Since 1929, other economic sectors have been included within the federal board's jurisdiction, but state labor boards have continued to function.[46] In 1929–1930, however, Portes Gil's willingness to compromise was insufficient to broker a comprehensive federal labor statute during his brief tenure as interim president. His administration's attempt to have the same Congress vote for a labor code failed:

major capitalists in the country, in the northern city of Monterrey, and further to the north, in the United States, opposed his particular bill as too radical. Among other propositions, it had included an all-encompassing system of factory commissions and labor boards.[47]

The next president, Pascual Ortiz Rubio, indubitably the weakest since 1917, signed federal labor legislation, in August 1931, in the midst of the Great Depression. He had the backing of Calles, now the maximum political boss of the country—and the support or grudging toleration of major businesses and unions, including a much weakened CROM. Neither capital nor labor was completely satisfied with the statute, despite provisions among its hundreds of articles for both. To avoid a repetition of what had happened to Portes Gil's bill, leading politicians ran this one through the federal legislature on what might be called today a fast track (notwithstanding some substantial disagreements between business and union leaders and the addition of a few pro-union articles by congressmen). Labor legislation finally had been federalized comprehensively, thereby among other things legitimating the administrative adjudication of labor disputes under the executive power of the federal government in nationally important economic sectors. One can compare this outcome with analogous (yet quite distinct) developments in other American countries, such as that of Argentina (as seen in Chapter 8) or the United States (Chapter 2).

The federal labor law (Ley Federal del Trabajo, LFT), consisting of 685 articles (besides several transitional ones), reflected prevalent notions about social legislation.[48] The statute also largely reaffirmed the existing contours and scope of the boards' decision-making power in the two sections or titles dedicated, respectively, to labor authorities in general (Title 8) and to procedures before the boards (Title 9). The LFT detailed the dual jurisdictions for labor justice: an administrative law system independent of the judiciary composed of municipal boards under state-level boards (*juntas centrales de conciliación y arbitraje*) and of federal jurisdiction conciliation boards under the federal board of conciliation and arbitration, which had specific units (*juntas especiales*) for each of the distinct federal jurisdiction economic activities.[49] Administrative labor boards, organized within the executive branch of government (whether state or federal), were to be the key instruments for the adjudication of both individual and collective conflicts arising out of industrial relations, as, in fact, they already were. Importantly, they were made responsible for determining the lawfulness of strikes and business *paros* (both lockouts and production cutbacks with resulting layoffs); the receipt of collective contracts, until which they were not legally operative; and, in state-jurisdiction economic sectors, the registration of unions (for federal-jurisdiction industries, the SICT, and later, the ministry of labor were so designated).[50] Conciliation and arbitration boards would be, as they already had become, essential components of the state's institutionalization of industrial relations.[51] And, under the LFT, they would have broad discretion in reaching their determinations, as the Supreme Court had already acknowledged.

Conclusion

The structure of these tripartite, administrative state bodies in the framework of the LFT almost ensured that the state would dominate industrial relations. The deciding vote on boards continued to be that of the government representative. Because the state boards or federal labor ministry approved the registration of unions (and, in practice, could review their internal affairs), while the federal and state boards, in effect, ratified collective contracts, in practice they facilitated the co-optation of union leaders disposed to collaborate with government officials. Under the LFT, officially recognized unions could insist on a collective contract from the employer, and the contract could stipulate the closed shop (*claúsula de exclusión*). These were, as Kevin Middlebrook has termed them, "legal subsidies" afforded by the state, which strengthened the hand of union leaders even when they lacked rank-and-file support.[52] A union leadership thus would be able to secure a collective contract through administrative and legal leverage (regardless of its power at the worksite or in the labor market) and control rank and file members through contract stipulations requiring management to hire only union members and fire any workers excluded from membership, like dissidents struggling for internal union democracy. Within this statutory framework, a board's disposition whether to allow workers' complaints or support a union leadership, or an employer's interest, would prove crucial. A state-favored union could regularly rely on a sympathetic labor board representative, because of the procedures to nominate labor and employer board members, in addition to the government representative.[53]

The LFT and its elaboration of the system of labor boards, however, did not altogether determine the enduring features of industrial relations in Mexico. As noted, perhaps unlike Brazil's Consolidated Labor Laws of 1943, the LFT was not inherently corporatist. The contemporary nature of labor relations, characterized not only by extensive state regulation but also by the absence of union democracy and even corruption, is at least partly the result of events occurring after 1931. To be sure, the form of state regulation—through the labor boards in large part—is outlined by the LFT. Likewise, the rights of workers vis-á-vis employers (and the parameters of these rights) are set out in the statute. But the legislation did not settle the actual balance of power among labor, capital, and the state; nor did it prescribe the outcomes of future board determinations (indeed, board decisions have varied over time).[54] The nature of the labor movement changed substantially from 1931 through the late 1940s, as did the policies and underlying ideologies of the federal government. And the critical junctures for labor, between 1934–1938 and 1948–1951, while involving administrative board decision making, were actually determined politically and even extralegally apart from the boards.[55]

Both labor and capital denounced the LFT as it was being enacted. To some extent, their respective, bleak predictions were realized. Soon after the LFT went into effect, employers were petitioning labor authorities, including administrative boards, to adjust existing collective contracts so as to allow management to cut back production (and lay off workers) or reduce benefits and wages, or both. Boards accommodated.[56] Strikes also occurred, and as the economy rebounded from depression, more strikes occurred between 1933–1935, as workers began to form independent, industrial unions. The union movement achieved an unparalleled degree of social justice for workers in the period 1934–1938. This was mostly because of the popular-front alliance with President Lázaro Cárdenas (1934–1940) and organized labor's political and social struggles—although the boards were indeed an element of the period's politics, most famously reflected in the federal board's decision in favor of petroleum workers that led to Cárdenas's nationalization of the oil industry in 1938.[57] Likewise, the cementing of an iniquitous industrial relations system, which occurred between 1948 and 1951, was more the result of government manipulation of rivalries among the leaderships of the major industrial unions. Even though LFT provisions requiring union registration and allowing for the closed shop facilitated the eventual government subordination of unions, this was not carried out by the direct application of a corporatist legal structure. President Miguel Alemán (1946–1952) and his secretary of labor certainly utilized the authority of the labor ministry to intervene in the internal affairs of the unions and favor one leadership faction over another—as well as the state's authority to prosecute militant labor leaders on trumped-up criminal charges—in what came to be known as *the charrazos* (so-named for one of the railroad union leaders backed by the government, because of his fondness for *charrería*, or Mexican rodeos). But the *charrazos* that effectively ensured organized labor's subordination to the state as it pursued more pro-business policies to foment further industralization were really pseudo-legal.[58] That is, the government-supported union officers made references to union bylaws, while the government's actions had a rhetorical veneer of legality, but neither government officials nor *charros* truly adhered to legal norms. And the labor boards were not primary determinants of this process.

Rather, to reiterate, administrative boards have constituted the central element of the system of labor justice, which has evolved apart from the judiciary since 1906. Their legal underpinnings were ratified in the LFT and, since then, as they did before, the boards have depended on the executive power (the president of the federal labor board is appointed by the president of the republic).[59] Many of the creators of the labor justice system certainly were influenced by the intellectual currents associated with reformist doctrines of social legislation then circulating in the Atlantic world and Australia and New Zealand, but they were also reacting to social and industrial turmoil in Mexico. To cite two examples, Vicente Lombardo Toledano, one of the first professors of *derecho industrial* (literally, industrial law), wrote his book on labor law, *La libertad sindical*, in 1926, at the behest of the International Labour Organization.[60] Significantly, he was also a major CROM leader and, later, an advocate of the popular front strategy during the 1930s, when he was a founding member and first general secretary of the Confederation of Mexican Workers (Confederación de Trabajadores de México, CTM), which became the country's most powerful labor federation. Mario de la Cueva, also a preeminent and influential labor law scholar, studied social legislation in Weimar Germany and subsequently served as president of the federal labor board.[61] Article 123's provisions about the boards reflect a similar combination of transnational influences and domestic, revolutionary politics. Since 1917, and more so since 1931, conciliation and arbitration boards have continued to resolve almost all labor disputes brought to their attention (while major collective conflicts also tend still to receive the president's attention, as they did in the last decade of Díaz's regime). This is not very different from Macías's vision that he shared with the constitutional congress in 1916. But the boards have not created the system itself, although board members are obviously its accomplices or agents.

Whether or not they affirm justice, the institutional capacity of the boards to decide cases since the 1920s and 1930s is impressive. The few scholars who have studied the decisions of the boards, which remain difficult to access, have considered thousands of cases.[62] The most complete study to date analyzes data of the federal board's decisions between the 1930s and the early 1990s.[63] The conclusions, put simply, are that federal boards have been instrumental in limiting strikes in federal jurisdiction industries (the first ruling of the federal labor board against the CTC, in 1927, has proven a definitional precedent) while individual cases have not been similarly subject to political influences or governmental control.[64] Yet cases brought by individual workers (normally with counsel) have faced long delays (on average, 3.1 years, in one sample).[65] Such delays favor employers and lead workers to compromise their claims.[66] The reality of board adjudication is hardly what one might have hoped would be realized, considering Article 123, or the labor movements of the revolutionary decades (largely defeated or compromised in the late 1940s). Nor is the administrative system clearly better than the judicial one, although it is not obviously worse.[67] Their tripartite character and broad discretion to decide what is just frequently produces capricious or arbitrary outcomes. It is a point that the left-leaning, public intellectual Narciso Bassols already underscored in the 1920s and again in 1930.[68] At the same time, the boards of conciliation and arbitration are an extensive, institutionalized form of resolving disputes between capital and labor, able to channel most forms of individual and collective conflict occurring in connection with the employment relationship, and they are a significant part of Mexico's postrevolutionary political order.[69]

Notes

1. See Suarez-Potts, *Making of Law*, ch. 3; Gutiérrez Álvarez, *Experiencias contrastadas*.

2. *El Imparcial*, January 8, 1907.

3. See the Conclusion and Chapter 9 of this book in connection with corporatism in the Americas and in Brazil in particular. Corporatism is clearly a widely applied term, which thereby loses some of its precision. On why one labor scholar of Mexican industrial relations foregoes applying the term to Mexico, see Middlebrook, *Paradox of Revolution*, n. 82, 341–342.

4. Suarez-Potts, *Making of Law*, ch. 4.

5. Ibid., 105; see, generally, ch. 4.

6. See, e.g., *El Imparcial*, July 2, 1907, "Peligros de las Huelgas. El Contrato de Trabajo Debe Reposar en los Intereses de Obreros y Patrones."

7. Suarez-Potts, *Making of Law*, 84.

8. See Walker, "Porfirian Labor Politics."

9. See Limantour-Corral correspondence, April, 8 and 30, 1907, in Archivo de Limantour.

10. Suarez-Potts, *Making of Law*, 94.

11. See, generally, Baker, *Judicial Review*, for a detailed explanation of the amparo action.

12. Suarez-Potts, *Making of Law*, ch. 2.

13. Ibid.

14. Ibid., ch. 5, on which this and the next paragraph are partly based.

15. See Knight, *Mexican Revolution*, on which this and later paragraphs describing the revolution rely.

16. Suarez-Potts, *Making of Law*, ch. 5.

17. Ibid.

18. De la Cueva, *Derecho mexicano del trabajo*, 98–105.

19. See Suarez-Potts, *Making of Law*, ch. 5, and citations therein, on which this and the following paragraphs are partly based.

20. See Rouaix, *Génesis*; Bensusán Areous, *El modelo*, Part 1.

21. See ¶¶XX and XXI of Article 123, in Constitución Política.

22. See Rocha et al., *La competencia*, 42–43, quoting Victoria, whose statement is ambiguous on the lawmaking capabilities that labor tribunals should have and emphatic on delegating to the states the authority to pass labor legislation.

23. This is a long-standing position among Mexican constitutional scholars, e.g., Trueba Urbina, *Mexican Constitution of 1917*.

24. Múgica obtained a compromise on this point, and a transitional Article 11 was added, stipulating that in the absence of implementing legislation Article 123 rights were still effective. But it is not so clear that Article 11 had much effect. Cf. Bensusán Areous, *El modelo*, 86; and Suarez-Potts, *Making of Law*, ch. 6.

25. Suarez-Potts, *Making of Law*, 137–139.

26. See Malpica, "Las Juntas de Conciliación."

27. See Clark, *Organized Labor*, and Snodgrass, *Deference and Defiance*, 133, citing Gruening, *Mexico and Its Heritage*.

28. See Snodgrass, *Deference and Defiance*, ch. 5. Unlike those of such states as Puebla, records of Nuevo León's labor boards are intact, accessible to the researcher, and have been utilized ably by Snodgrass.

29. García Díaz, *Textiles del Valle*.

30. Collado Herrera, *Empresarios y políticos*.

31. Joseph, *Revolution from Without*.

32. See Carr, *El movimiento obrero*.

33. Ibid.

34. See generally Bensusán Areous, *El modelo*.

35. Carr, *El movimiento obrero*.

36. Ibid.

37. See Suarez-Potts, "Mexican Supreme Court and the Juntas," for a more detailed account of the evolution of the Supreme Court's rulings and doctrine concerning the decision making of the boards. The reversal of case law in 1924 was decided by mostly new justices who had recently assumed their positions on the high court bench. The ascendance of the CROM was notable, too.

38. Ibid.

39. Suarez-Potts, *Making of Law*, 226–227.

40. Bortz, "Genesis of the Mexican Labor Relations System."

41. See Confederación de Transportes y Comunicaciones, October 4, 1927, and Suarez-Potts, "Railroad Strike."

42. Ibid. This and the next paragraphs rely on "Railroad Strike."

43. Confederación de Transportes y Comunicaciones contra Ferrocarriles Nacionales de México [Junta Federal Opinion], December 8, 1927.

44. Confederación de Transportes y Comunicaciones, May 30, 1929.

45. See, e.g., Cía. Industrial de Orizaba, S.A., May 19, 1930, cited in Suarez-Potts, *Making of Law*, 208.

46. See Middlebrook, *Paradox of Revolution*, 54–55, and, generally, ch. 2.

47. *Proyecto de Código*; see also Suarez-Potts, *Making of Law*, ch. 8.

48. See generally Ley Federal del Trabajo; De la Cueva, *El nuevo derecho*.

49. Ibid., Title 8. See also Middlebrook, *Paradox of Revolution*, 60, on which this paragraph is partly based, for a more detailed summary.

50. The department of labor was raised to a cabinet level ministry in 1940, the Secretaría de Trabajo y Previsión Social or Ministry of Labor and Social Welfare; see ibid., 45.

51. Ibid., 61. In addition to board matters briefly mentioned here, they were also charged with enforcement of workplace conditions, minimum wage issues, and other legal requirements related to collective contracts.

52. Ibid., 95–98. This discussion is indebted to Middlebrook's analysis, which also considers analogous financial and political subsidies.

53. See Bensusán Areous, *El modelo*, 214, regarding the functional organization of the boards, including members' elections to them.

54. See Snodgrass, *Deference and Defiance*, ch. 5–7, and Middlebrook, *Paradox of Revolution*, ch. 5, regarding variations in board determinations between the 1930s and 1990s.

55. See Bensusán Areous, *El modelo*, 213–233, and Middlebrook, *Paradox of Revolution*, ch. 4, on which this and the next paragraph draw.

56. Suarez-Potts, *Making of Law*, 250–251; Bensusán Areous, *El modelo*, 209; Clark, *Organized Labor*, 228.

57. See León and Marván, *En el cardenismo*; Snodgrass, *Deference and Defiance*, ch. 7, describes how federal and state boards were crucially involved in labor politics in Monterrey.

58. The charrazos are narrated in detail by Basurto, *Del avilacamachismo al alemanismo,* and Middlebrook, *Paradox of Revolution*.

59. See De la Cueva, *El nuevo derecho*. Subsequent amendments to the federal labor law in 1970 and in 2012, or to Article 123, while not negligible, have not substantially modified the structure of the labor boards. But the February 24, 2017 Constitutional Amendments to Article 123 and 107 should transform the existing system of labor justice. They direct, over the next year, the replacement of the boards of conciliation and arbitration with new law tribunals, which will be situated in the federal and state judicial branches of government; new procedures for the registration of unions and collective contracts, among other points, are also mandated. At the time of this writing, however, the extent to which implementing legislation will carry out effectively these constitutional reforms remains to be seen; see *La Jornada*, May 13, 2017, "Dilemas de una histórica reforma laboral."

60. See Lombardo Toledano, *La libertad sindical*.

61. De la Cueva, *Derecho mexicano del trabajo*; Middlebrook, *Paradox of Revolution*, 398, n. 87.

62. Meyers, *Mexican Industrial Relations*, 19, observed that in 1976, about 10,000 individual cases were filed with the federal labor board; Middlebrook, *Paradox of Revolution*, 185, notes boards resolved on average 12,240 cases p.a. between 1939 and 1963.

63. Ibid., ch. 5.

64. Ibid., 205–208; see, generally, ch. 5 for a more detailed and nuanced assessment.

65. Ibid., 199.

66. Ibid., 198–201.

67. See Oñate, "Administración de justicia."

68. Bassols, "Qué son, por fin, las Juntas?"

69. *La Jornada.*

Bibliography

ARCHIVES, PERIODICALS, AND SERIALS

Archivo de José Yves Limantour, Fondo CDLIV, Microfilm Roll 42. Centro de Estudios de Historia de México, Carso Foundation, Mexico City.

Confederación de Transportes y Comunicaciones contra Ferrocarriles Nacionales de México [Junta Federal Opinion] December 8, 1927, in Expediente 1, Caja 1, Ramo de la Junta Federal de Conciliación y Arbitraje. Archivo General de la Nación, Mexico City.

Confederación de Transportes y Comunicaciones, October 4, 1927, *Semanario Judicial de la Federación*, 5th época, vol. 21, p. 944.

Confederación de Transportes y Comunicaciones, May 30, 1929, *Semanario Judicial de la Federación*, 5th época, vol. 26, p. 892.

El Imparcial.

La Jornada.

ARTICLES AND BOOKS

Baker, Richard D. *Judicial Review in Mexico: A Study of the Amparo Suit.* Austin: University of Texas Press, 1971.

Bassols, Narciso. "Qué son, por fin, las Juntas de Conciliación y Arbitraje?" *Revista General de Derecho y Jurisprudencia* 1 (1930): 185–211.

Basurto, Jorge. *Del avilacamachismo al alemanismo (1940–1952).* Vol. 11 of *La clase obrera en la historia de México*, ed. Pablo González Casanova. Mexico City: Siglo Veintiuno Editores, 1984.

Bensusán Areous, Graciela. *El modelo mexicano de regulación laboral.* Mexico City: UAM-Xochimilco, Fundación Friedrich Ebert, FLACSO, Plaza Valdés, S.A. de C.V., 2000.

Bortz, Jeffrey. "The Genesis of the Mexican Labor Relations System: Federal Labor Policy and the Textile Industry, 1925–1940." *The Americas* 52, 1 (July 1995): 43–69.

Carr, Barry. *El movimiento obrero y la política en México, 1910–1929.* Mexico City: Ediciones Era, S.A., 1981.

Clark, Marjorie Ruth. *Organized Labor in Mexico.* Chapel Hill: University of North Carolina Press, 1934.

Collado Herrera, María del Carmen. *Empresarios y políticos, entre la restauración y la revolución, 1920–1924.* Mexico City: INEHRM, 1996.

De la Cueva, Mario. *Derecho mexicano del trabajo.* Mexico City: Librería de Porrúa Hnos. y Cía., 1938.

———. *El nuevo derecho mexicano del trabajo.* 6th ed. Vol. 2. Mexico City: Editorial Porrúa, 1991.

García Díaz, Bernardo. *Textiles del Valle de Orizaba (1880–1925): Cinco ensayos de historia sindical y social.* Xalapa, Mexico: Universidad Veracruzana, 1990.

Gutiérrez Álvarez, Coralia. *Experiencias contrastadas. Industrialización y conflictos en los textiles del centro-oriente de México, 1884–1917.* Mexico: El Colegio de México and Instituto de Ciencias Sociales y Humanidades/BUAP, 2000.

Joseph, Gilbert. *Revolution from without: Yucatán, Mexico, and the United States, 1880–1924.* Durham, N.C.: Duke University Press, 1994.

Knight, Alan. *The Mexican Revolution.* 2 vols. Lincoln: University of Nebraska Press, 1990.

León, Samuel, and Ignacio Marván. *En el cardenismo (1934–1940).* 2d ed. Vol. 10 of *La clase obrera en la historia de México*, ed. Pablo González Casanova. Mexico City: Siglo Veintiuno Editores, 1999.

Lombardo Toledano, Vicente. *La libertad sindical.* Mexico City: Universidad Obrera Mexicana [1926], 1974.

Malpica Uribe, David. "Las Juntas de Conciliación y Arbitraje en Puebla 1931–1940." In *Memorias del encuentro sobre historia del movimiento obrero.* Vol. 2, ed. Centro de Investigaciones Históricas del Movimiento Obrero. 127–147. Puebla: Universidad Autónoma de Puebla, 1981.

Mexico, Secretaría de Gobernación. *Constitución Política de los Estados Unidos Mexicanos.* Edición Oficial. Mexico City: Imprenta de la Secretaría de Gobernación, 1917.

Mexico, Secretaría de Industria, Comercio y Trabajo. *Ley Federal del Trabajo.* Mexico City: Talleres Gráficos de la Nación, 1931.

Meyers, Frederic. *Mexican Industrial Relations from the Perspective of the Labor Court.* Los Angeles: Institute of Industrial Relations, University of California, 1979.

Middlebrook, Kevin J. *Paradox of Revolution: Labor, the State, and Authoritarianism in Mexico.* Baltimore: Johns Hopkins University, 1995.

Oñate, Santiago. "Administración de justicia." In *El derecho obrero*, ed. Graciela Bensusán Areous. Vol. 4 of *El obrero mexicano*, ed. Pablo González Casanova, Samuel León, and Ignacio Marván Laborde. Mexico City: Siglo Veintiuno Editores, 1985.

Proyecto de Código Federal de Trabajo para los Estados Unidos Mexicanos que somete el C. Lic. Emilio Portes Gil, Presidente de la Republica, al H. Congreso de la Unión. Mexico City: SICT, 1929.

Rocha Bandala, Juan Francisco, and José Fernando Franco. *La competencia en materia laboral: Evolución.* Mexico City: Editorial Cárdenas, 1975.

Rouaix, Pastor. *Génesis de los artículos 27 y 123 de la Constitución Política de 1917.* 2d ed. Mexico City: INEHRM, 1959.

Snodgrass, Michael. *Deference and Defiance in Monterrey: Workers, Paternalism, and Revolution in Mexico, 1890–1950.* Cambridge: Cambridge University Press, 1989.

Suarez-Potts, William. "The Mexican Supreme Court and the Juntas de Conciliación y Arbitraje, 1917–1924: The Judicialisation of Labour Relations after the Revolution." *Journal of Latin American Studies* 41, 4 (November 2009): 723–755.

———. "The Railroad Strike of 1927: Labor and Law after the Mexican Revolution." *Labor History* 52, 4 (November 2011): 399–416.

———. *The Making of Law: The Supreme Court and Labor Legislation in Mexico, 1875–1931.* Stanford, Calif.: Stanford University Press, 2012.

Trueba Urbina, Alberto. *The Mexican Constitution of 1917 Is Reflected in the Peace Treaty of Versailles of 1919.* New York: n.p., 1974.

Walker, David. "Porfirian Labor Politics: Working Class Organizations in Mexico City and Porfirio Díaz, 1876–1902." *The Americas* 37, 3 (January 1981): 257–289.

PART II

Costa Rica, Colombia, and the Andean Countries

CHAPTER 5

Labor Justice in Costa Rica, 1821–2016

RONNY J. VIALES-HURTADO

DAVID DÍAZ-ARIAS

C osta Rica experienced tremendous sociopolitical transformations from 1940 to 1943 resulting in the construction of the most important social reform in the history of this country. During those years, the first populist movement in the country's history mobilized thousands of people supporting it. As happened in countries like Argentina, Brazil, Mexico, Venezuela, Colombia, and Nicaragua, populism in Costa Rica embraced and propelled workers' unionist activities. Labor laws and institutions were the result of that movement but also of a complex process of social inclusion and political battles that had appeared since the turn of the twentieth century.

This chapter focuses on the development of labor laws and justice in Costa Rica. Our objective is to introduce the Costa Rican labor legislation and its institutions built during the course of this country's history and to delve further into workers' organizations and their struggles for labor rights during the 1940s. Special emphasis is given to the populist movement that shaped the Labor Code of 1943 and the political confrontation that drove the country to the Civil War in 1948, as well as its consequences for unions and workers. Finally, we go on to briefly examine the Costa Rican contemporary situation with regard to labor justice.

Leaving aside the democracy-at-birth myths created by several generations of politicians, intellectuals, and teachers, Costa Rica had successfully constructed a representative political system by the first decades of the twentieth century. It is true that minority groups (such as blacks from the Caribbean region) and women did not have political rights under that system, but liberal politicians and intellectuals were able to invent a national discourse that included most of the population in the imagined community known as Costa Rican nation. Costa Rica was more inclusive in social terms if compared with other Central American countries. Yet, unlike what many Costa Rica's historians commonly recognize, in comparative terms Costa Rica followed the international paths to the labor legislation. Indeed, the rise of labor law in Costa Rica is very close to what happened in countries like Argentina, Chile, Brazil, and Uruguay. By the 1940s, Costa Ricans were strongly integrated as an imagined community. In that sense, the populist regime that came to power in the 1940s did not integrate the working class into the nation, as they were already incorporated. Rather, it elaborated a discourse that consisted in giving a social content to the notion of nation in a similar way to what Peronism did in Argentina and what Getulismo did in Brazil.

After a brief analysis of the nineteenth century, this chapter focuses on the rise of some specific labor laws and tribunals during the 1920s and 1930s, also analyzing several labor courts' rulings and their legal consequences. Special emphasis is given to the populist movement that shaped the Labor Code of 1943 and the political confrontation that drove the country to the Civil War in 1948, as well as its consequences for unions and workers. Finally, we go on to examine Costa Rican contemporary labor justice.

As occurred in other countries, in Costa Rica the institutionalization of labor laws appeared during the early-to-middle twentieth century. During the nineteenth century, Costa Rica established a number of *inclusive political institutions*, that is, institutions that "broadly distributed power in society" and constrained its "arbitrary exercise."[1] Inclusive institutions such as open elections, public education, and constitutional protection of free association and free press created the legal framework that regulated labor relations until approval of the Labor Code in 1943. Then, although several 1948 Civil War victors wanted to undercut labor legislation, the legitimacy of social institutions created during the 1920s–1940s and the social transformation they brought about guaranteed that there was no reversal. The 1940s had created the institutional framework that would protect Costa Rican labor legislation from the 1950s up to 2015. Now, we believe that these institutions are under attack in a new context—neoliberalism—and that the future of the recognition of labor rights depends on the defense of the welfare state constructed in the early twentieth century.

Labor Justice in Nineteenth-Century Costa Rica

Costa Rica gained its independence from Spain in 1821. Between 1824 and 1835, it was part of the Federal Republic of Central America, which disappeared in 1839 as a result of economic and political problems. At that time, Costa Rica had experienced a period of some political stability and had engaged in two brief civil wars in 1823 and 1835. Due to its political stability, Costa Rica was able to create political institutions that were strengthened in spite of the occurrence of some political unrest. By the end of the 1830s, politician Braulio Carrillo produced a political and legal reform that reinforced some political institutions and the national army. By the end of the 1830s, some entrepreneurs began planting and exporting coffee, which became the most important product for the Costa Rican economy after the 1840s. Coffee production allowed an elite to take control of political power and develop political institutions to consolidate a modern state. Costa Rica was officially declared a republic in 1848 during the administration of President José María Castro Madriz.[2]

During those years, private law defined labor relations in the country. Employment was considered by private law as an arrangement between two equal parties in which employers would hire workers to do specific jobs. In that sense, labor contracts did not include social protection for workers.[3] Between 1821 and 1841 (during the early years of the coffee economy expansion), however, specific legislation did begin to regulate worker registration (that is, employers had to provide lists of their workers to the state), wages, payment methods, labor inspections, and workplace health conditions. Laws like the *Ordenanzas de Minería* (May 20, 1830) and *Orden No. 4* (January 27, 1841), for example, regulated night working hours in sugar mills.[4]

In 1841, the Carrillo administration issued the *Código General*—the first Civil Code of Costa Rica. This code regulated private activities for servants, laborers, muleteers, and foremen while it defined labor agreements as legal instruments in a time of agrarian expansion. On July 20, 1849, two years after Costa Rica became a republic, a reform to the code required the specification of the duration of the contract, workdays, and "fair" wages in every labor agreement.[5] It was illegal for an employer to recruit workers without stipulating the duration of the contract. The agreements defined the penalties in case of failure to observe the terms.

Juan Rafael Mora (in power during 1849–1859) fortified the standing army and concentrated power in the president's hands. Particularly, he consolidated the coffee economy and the privatization of land. Several communities lost their lands and peasants experienced proletarianization, thus becoming part of a growing agrarian working class.[6] Some discussions on vagrancy and the need to guarantee some workers' rights started to appear. By the end of the nineteenth century, the banana enclave established in the Caribbean Coast also promoted public debate about labor rights inside transnational enterprises like the United Fruit Company and Costa Rica's workers. In 1893, Bishop Bernardo Augusto Thiel published his pastoral letter on the fair wage, which was a consequence of Pope Leo XIII's encyclical *Rerum Novarum* and a local attempt to claim for the regulation of labor conditions.

Part of the labor problems was the absence of real labor courts. In general, during the nineteenth century the police were responsible for the solution of labor issues.[7] But public discussions on labor conditions appeared more commonly in the early twentieth century due to a combination of factors, which will be addressed later. On October 15, 1901, *Ley No. 15* ruled on salesclerk and sailor wages in case of employers' bankruptcy.[8] On August 10, 1902, *Ley No. 81* stated the conditions in which working debts should be paid in the cases of unskilled laborers and servants—something done in other parts of Latin America to confront the usual debt peonage in agrarian areas. This law required that any public or private labor contract explicitly indicate the existence of any cash advances. It also established that employers could request police assistance in cases when laborers or servants abandoned their work without a just cause. In those cases, the police were admonished to listen to both laborers and employers before issuing a decision.[9]

Ley No. 81 also defined the minimum wage for laborers and servants. Employers could retain as much as a third part of the wages in order for workers to pay their debts, but employers were forced to pay the full salary if a worker became sick or had another certified reason to demand his entire wage.[10] Laborers had to work in order to pay their debts, but failure to do so led them to the risk of fines or even twenty-five days of imprisonment. If they could pay or work, they were forgiven.[11] According to the law, workers were not to work in unhealthy places; if workers became ill they were not obliged to return to work in the same place. However, if they had received income advances, they were in debt until they paid back their employers. Employers were required to hand out receipts to the workers in order to certify their debts and payments.[12]

Labor rights on health conditions and labor accidents were not discussed in nineteenth-century Costa Rica. The Civil Code of 1888 established that employers were not held liable in case of workplace accidents (*culpa-aquiliana* or quasi delict); workers needed to prove the employers' fault in order to claim liability. In 1902, an amendment to the Civil Code established the contractual fault. In this new legal context, employers had to prove their innocence in order to avoid liability for accidents.[13] In 1907, the labor movement began a struggle for a law on work-related accidents, opening a new age in the development of the nation's labor laws.[14]

Labor Justice and Legislation Changes, 1907–1928

Costa Rican society experienced tremendous changes leading to social mobilization at the dawn of the twentieth century. Transformed into a coffee producer and export country since the 1830s, Costa Rica was ruled by the elite that took control of political power and developed political institutions to consolidate a modern state. In 1870, a coup d'état gave the power to a new political class. Although authoritarian in character, the two decades of rule by Tomás Guardia and his successors, Próspero Fernández (1882–1885) and Bernardo Soto (1885–1889), produced the expansion of the public administration and gave rise to a group of politicians and intellectuals who had a clear reform plan. Known as *El Olimpo*—the Olympians—their goal was to modernize the state and build a secular society. They brought about political, legal, and educational reforms known in Costa Rican history as the 1884 Liberal Reforms. They also confronted the Catholic Church's influence on subaltern classes by disseminating scientific and secular visions of life and nature among them. Additionally, the Olympians enacted new civil and criminal codes, opened new police and administrative posts throughout the country, and created the civil registry of births, deaths, and marriages. A centralized, free, primary educational system was created and made compulsory for children of subaltern classes. Divorce was approved. Suffrage expanded during the 1880s, allowing adult males to vote. Costa Rican liberal politicians also focused on policies promoting public education and health. Democracy became sturdier. During the first half of the twentieth century, Costa Rica approved direct secret voting and almost every single man was able to vote—women gained suffrage in 1949. This democracy also permitted the participation of new political parties such as the Communist Party, founded in 1931.[15]

Economic changes yielded an urban working class composed of small producers and artisans. After 1880, urban workers began to organize by creating journals and labor societies. Led by national intellectuals such as Joaquín García Monge, Omar Dengo, and Carmen Lyra, workers founded the *Centro de Estudios Sociales Germinal* (CEG) in 1912. The CEG was a center where intellectuals taught social sciences and organized conferences, lectures, and labor meetings. The CEG intellectuals and urban workers organized the first celebration of May 1 in 1913, as well as the foundation of the *Confederación General de Trabajadores* (Workers General Confederation, CGT) that same year.[16] Toward the end of the 1920s, new groups resumed the legacy left by these early organizations. In 1929, the *Unión General de Trabajadores* (UGT) was created with the purpose of mobilizing workers and the unemployed.[17] During the 1930s, a group of urban workers participated in the creation of the Communist Party of Costa Rica (PCCR).[18]

The organized workers' first political initiatives, simultaneous to similar moves across the industrializing world, impacted the Congress's agenda on labor law. In 1907 Costa Rica's Congress began to discuss the *Ley sobre Accidentes del Trabajo* (Law on Work-Related Accidents).[19] This bill proposed that every "accident that occurred to laborers, employees, settlers, and peasants during working hours in factories, workshops, transportation, mines, and rural farms involved a compensation." This compensation "was a responsibility of every boss or property owner no matter the cause of the work accident except when the victim would have intentionally caused the accident or if he/she was drunk."[20] The bill would have also covered medicines, doctor visits, and compensation during disability.[21] However, this draft law was never debated and was subsequently filed.

In 1913, Congressman Alberto Vargas Calvo presented a new bill aimed at protecting workers. His proposal included a wide array of causes to categorize work accidents and defined regional particularities for classifying workers.[22] The project appointed the Secretariat of Development (*Secretaría de Fomento*) as responsible for implementing the law and it also included a recommendation for creating a Technical Board (*Junta Técnica*) that should "inform the Secretariat of every aspect related to labor accidents."[23] In the analysis of this project, a commission highlighted the need to define labor justice in Costa Rica.[24] Congressmen proposed including a new insurance law "in order to make it easier for employers to carry out their duties and economic responsibilities, arising out of the social legislation."[25] Nonetheless, this project did not reach Congress's agenda and was not approved. In 1915, congressmen reviewed yet another labor accident bill, which was also dropped.[26] Why did those projects fail in Congress? Basically, they failed because of the historical context: in the early twentieth century, the country was experiencing economic problems due to a crisis in the coffee sector; Alfredo Gonzalez Flores's progressive administration (1914–1917) was replaced by a dictatorship in 1917, inaugurating a period of repression and military rule until 1919.

The 1920s, however, inaugurated a reformist period. New political parties such as the *Partido Reformista* advocated for workers' rights and social reforms. Although the *reformistas* did not win any election, they did receive many workers' support, their democratic demands echoed in newspapers, and their ideas motivated other politicians' actions. In 1924, liberal politician and President Ricardo Jiménez Oreamuno issued the *Ley de Accidentes del Trabajo* and created the National Insurance Bank (*Banco Nacional de Seguros*).[27] This bank "played a pivotal role in the determination and issuance of indemnifications. Enterprises whose workers were protected were required to insure their workers with the bank."[28]

The new law also created the *Tribunal Superior de Arbitraje* (Superior Arbitration Tribunal) to solve employer-worker issues in terms of compensations and fines once the bank received the appeals. This tribunal—the first antecedent of arbitral justice in the country—was composed of a lawyer (*letrado*) and two manufacturers (*industriales*) and had the final voice on appeals and payments.[29]

Other important labor legislation advances occurred in the 1920s. Since the 1910s, labor organizations grew, allowing workers to demand social reforms, including an eight-hour workday.[30] In February 1920, organized workers went on strike to put pressure on Congress to pass such a law.[31] On December 9, 1920, the state finally decreed the eight-hour workday.[32] Other reforms that appeared in the following years were also motivated by the new political context: on July 2, 1928 the state created the *Secretaría de Estado en los Despachos de Trabajo y Previsión Social* (Secretariat of Labor and Social Welfare), and on November 22, 1933, Congress passed the law on the minimum wage.[33] After the great banana worker strike in 1934, the state established the Banana Plantations Working Conditions Regulations (*Reglamentación de las condiciones de trabajo en las explotaciones de banano*) (December 10, 1934), and three years later the state ruled on the right of hospitalization for banana workers.[34]

Toward the Institutionalization of Labor Justice, 1928–1940

The Secretariat of Labor and Social Welfare was created to draw up a Labor Code that included legislation on labor contracts, labor insurance, labor association, procedures of arbitration and conciliation, the control of every labor law, and the organization of an Institute for Social Studies.[35] The *Secretaría* received and solved labor disputes during the following years. It was part of the executive branch and dictated solutions for labor injuries based on the *Ley de Accidentes del Trabajo* once cases had been evaluated in local police courts, or by the *Tribunal Superior de Arbitraje*. In that sense, the Secretariat was the final and indisputable institution to render justice concerning labor accidents, thus changing hierarchies with regard to the law of 1924. Some cases clearly evidence the work carried out by the ministry.

In October 1928, the *Secretaría* solved the case of the Northern Railway Company worker, Nicolás Martínez, who suffered an accident in 1927. Martínez claimed to have suffered a hand injury while working for the company. During the arbitration hearing, the company's physician argued that Martínez's lesion could not have been caused by his work. The ministry requested Dr. Carlos Pupo's opinion—from the *Banco Nacional de Seguros*—who gave an opinion that Martínez's accident was the real cause of his hand injury and disability. The *Secretaría* considered the evidence and ruled in favor of Martínez, arguing that the company had to pay him a lifetime allowance.[36]

Martínez's case is important since it reveals the actions the Secretariat of Labor could carry out against foreign companies like the Northern Railway. Likewise, in 1929 the Secretariat demanded that the United Fruit Company pay compensation to worker John Cunningham during his recuperation after an accident, a salary for five years, and the payment of fees for medical attention and medicines.[37] The *Secretaría* made a similar decision in the cases of José Próspero Arancibia who suffered an accident as an employee of *Empresa del Ferrocarril al Pacífico*,[38] William Nelson who was injured while working for the Costa Rica Cocoa Company,[39] and Salvador Paniagua who suffered an arm fracture while working for the government of Costa Rica.[40]

The Secretariat also solved problems involving workers and local businessmen. In November 1928 it considered the case of worker Pío Araya against sugar mill proprietor Abraham Matamoros. In its analysis of Araya's injury, the *Secretaría* recognized Matamoros's mill as "an important enterprise" and insisted that every employer was responsible for his workers' labor security regardless of whether workers carried out their jobs incorrectly, so causing the injury. Although the *Secretaría* also considered Araya's responsibility for having put himself in danger, it concluded that only the employer was obliged to pay.[41] The *Secretaría* also dictated justice in the case of worker Francisco Madrigal González who died in a labor accident while working for Barbará & Neurohr Ltda. In this case, the *Secretaría* demanded that the company pay Madrigal González's wife and children a pension.[42] The *Secretaría* also favored Juan Demetrio Araya, who worked for the powerful coffee planter Julio Sánchez Lépiz. Araya lost a hand while handling a machine at Sánchez Lépiz's coffee mill in San Francisco de Heredia. Sánchez Lépiz argued that the worker was an irresponsible person for trying to fix the machine himself. However, the *Secretaría* considered Araya was helping his boss and "believed to be doing his job correctly." Therefore, the Secretariat of Labor ordered Sánchez Lépiz to pay Araya a lifelong pension.[43] The way in which the

Secretaría solved work disputes was fundamental and should be highlighted since in most cases it benefited workers against employers, regardless of whether they were transnational enterprises, local businessmen, or local *caciques*.[44]

In other cases, workers obtained justice but not exactly as expected. In those instances, the problem was to determine who was the worker's boss—the person responsible for paying him—and the correct amount the worker should receive due to his injury. Let us consider the case of Lesmes Chavarría, who worked in Hacienda Mojica, Guanacaste, owned by U.S. citizen George Wilson Russell. The *Secretaría* examined Chavarría's case in March 1929 and determined that he was not Wilson's employee at the time he suffered the accident. Rather, Chavarría had been hired by a second party, Mercedes Rodríguez, to whom Wilson had contracted the job, during the time in which Chavarría suffered the injury. The *Secretaría* held Rodríguez responsible for Chavarría's health and released Wilson.[45] In another case, the ministry ruled in favor of a worker but, based on the law, recalculated the payment the Northern Railway Co. should disburse its employee, thus reducing the initial amount ordered by the *Tribunal de Arbitraje*.[46] In compliance with the Law, the Secretariat of Labor also refused to admit cases of workers when their claims were filed more than a year after suffering the injury,[47] when they were not at their workplace when the accident occurred,[48] or when they carried out a job they were not appointed to do.[49] In general, in the documented cases, the *Secretaría* ruled in favor of employees during its first years of work (see Table 5.1).

In 1932, the government created the *Oficina Técnica del Trabajo* (Technical Labor Office) within the *Secretaría* of Labor in order to better regulate conflicts between employers and employees.[50] This new office complemented the work carried out before by the aforementioned conciliatory tribunals and represented another space for dialogue in labor conflicts. Essentially, it took care of working conflicts not involving accidents. In 1934, the government formed an Employers and Workers Council to collaborate with the office in its efforts. This council was another instance to help workers and did not compete with the legal power of the Tribunal de Arbitraje. This council was composed of three employer representatives and three worker representatives;

Table 5.1. Decisions by the Secretariat of Labor of Costa Rica in Cases of Work-Related Accidents, 1928–1931

Year	Number of Cases	In Favor of Workers	In Favor of Employers
1928	3	3	0
1929	21	19	2
1930	10	9	1
1931	21	21	0

Source: Created by the authors with data from República de Costa Rica, *Colección de Leyes y Decretos*, 1928–1931.
Note: Not all the cases solved by the Secretariat of Labor were published in this collection of documents. Nevertheless, this table shows the changing pattern of activity in solving labor struggles.

Table 5.2. Number of Labor Cases Solved in Costa Rica, 1937–1940

Year	Tribunal Superior de Arbitraje	Oficina Técnica del Trabajo
1937	4332	Nd*
1938	4583	Nd*
1939	6840	712
1940	7976	619

Source: Created by the authors with data from República de Costa Rica, *Memorias de Gobernación y Policía, 1937–1940.*
*Nd = No data available.

the state did not include a representative.[51] The office appears to have gained prestige among the working class as an instrument to confront employers.[52]

While analyzing the cases resolved by the *Oficina Técnica del Trabajo* during 1935–1942, historian Carlos Hernández identified the main complaints filed by workers before that office: labor exploitation, control of hours of work, wage allegations, reorganization of wage commissions, and minimum wage claims.[53]

The influence the new institutions for labor issues had in employer-worker disputes is evident, despite the incomplete data. As mentioned before, more and more workers relied on tribunals to demand labor justice (Table 5.2). Indeed, the *Oficina* dedicated its efforts to solving work-related issues such as wages. The *Oficina* relied on police officers, particularly in rural areas, to administer labor justice. In the Caribbean region, police officers were in charge of social control but they also worked denouncing labor problems. In 1939, however, Alberto Durán Rocha, who was in charge of the *Oficina*, announced that police officers in the banana region would be withdrawn, since the state could not afford the expense.[54] In cases of injuries, the *Tribunal Superior de Arbitraje* evaluated the evidence and resolved the issue—most of the time for the benefit of the workers.

Populism, Unionism, and the Labor Code, 1940–1943

In 1940, Rafael Ángel Calderón Guardia won the presidential elections in Costa Rica on a program of so-called "social reform." Calderón was a renowned physician coming from the Costa Rican elite who had studied in Belgium, so he was familiar with social Catholicism. As a philanthropist, he had political pretensions that drove him to make social changes. During his presidential term, he tried to transform himself into a populist leader who could combine politics, social reforms, and unionism without losing power.[55] In this effort, Calderón received the uncommon dual support of the Catholic Church and the Communist Party of Costa Rica (PCCR, founded in 1931). Early on, the PCCR understood the political meaning of the social reform. Therefore, communists tried to publicly appear as defenders of any social transformation favorable to the working class, just as they sought to become part of such a process. The

Catholic Church leaders also understood the importance of this reform in its effort to obtain social justice. In this specific framework, Catholics and Communists forged an alliance to pass the social law. The union organization and the systematic Communists' support allowed Calderón to gain certain control of the social forces and combine it with his concept of social justice and political leadership. Thus, while the government, the PCCR, and the Catholic Church were spreading a populist discourse around Calderón and his social reform, the Communists were also strongly organizing their unions—trade unions were not important before the 1940s—and workers to back the president's social and World War II policies (actions against possible fifth-column activities since Costa Rica declared war on Germany in December 1941).

The constitution of a powerful trade union activity took place along with the social reform. Because of the PCCR's insistence on organizing the working class, in May 1942 several labor leaders organized the *Comité Sindical de Enlace* (Union Coordinating Committee, CSE), a leading group composed of representatives from several labor organizations. Rodolfo Guzmán, representative of the *Sindicato Nacional del Calzado* (National Shoemaker Union), was elected president of the CSE. The objectives of the CSE were: "a) Unifying and coordinating the actions of every single workers organization in the general and national struggles. b) Immediate simplification of the acts of solidarity of every single workers organization with each other while backing the Government's efforts to support the labor movement. c) Strengthening the union movement of the Costa Rican workers. d) Laying the foundations for the creation of the *Confederación de Trabajadores de Costa Rica* (Costa Rican Workers Confederation)."[56]

By the end of May 1942, as part of the CSE goals, the communist journal *Trabajo* reported on the fortification and organization of several labor unions. Thus, on May 25, leaders of the shoemaker, tailor, and baker unions in Heredia decided to create a local CSE cell. Their first decision was to back Calderón Guardia's social legislation. Three days later, the metalworkers formed a union while the *Sindicato Nacional del Calzado* reorganized its representation in Turrialba, a village in the province of Cartago.[57] On June 1, Rodolfo Guzmán gave a lecture explaining why workers had to mobilize to back the social reform.[58]

The so-called social reform included a public health program, social guarantees, and a labor code. In 1940, in his inaugural speech Calderón Guardia stated that, during his administration, important changes would take place in the public health system, such as a reorganization of the *Secretaría de Salubridad Pública* (Ministry of Public Health), the enactment of a law concerning public welfare, the consolidation of rural offices dedicated to public hygiene, and the provision of medical care for all Costa Ricans.[59] To bring about these transformations, Calderón Guardia sent his friend Dr. Guillermo Padilla to study the Chilean social security system, as it was considered one of the most sophisticated at that time.[60] The result was the presentation before Congress of a social security project in July 1941. This bill "called for compulsory mass protection against the risk of illness, premature disability, old age, death and maternity insurance."[61] Congress passed the bill in November 1941, after some important changes to the institutional framework in which the project would be inserted, as well as after some modifications regarding the characteristics of the population to be covered by the plan. Thus, the project prompted the creation of the *Caja Costarricense de Seguro Social* (CCSS) to administer the public health program, but Congress decided to monitor the CCSS by controlling it through a board of representatives from the Treasury, the National Bank, and the Insurance Bank, all of which were recognized liberal institutions. Moreover, Congress set 300 colones (US$54.00 at the 1941 rate of exchange) as the *salario tope* (wage limit) for private and public workers who would be covered by the plan. Finally, Congress decided that the coverage "was to be extended on a regional basis to those sectors of the wage-earning population where its implementation would be easier."[62]

The second part of Calderón Guardia's term (1942–1944) brought forth another series of reforms, including the amendments to the constitution, known as Social Guarantees, and a Labor Code. In his presidential address of May 1942, Calderón Guardia announced that he would send a draft bill of Social Guarantees to Congress. This reform aimed to elevate to constitutional status various labor laws already enacted but not implemented by most employers. It included the right to employment, the minimum wage limit, the legal right to form unions, the right to strike, the right to health and work insurance, and the establishment of a tribunal to litigate work-related issues (*tribunales de trabajo*).[63] This reform was approved in June 1943.[64] Almost simultaneously, in April 1943, the Labor Code was submitted to the Congress and ratified in August 1943.[65]

As of May 16, 1942, *Trabajo* published telegrams from peasants and urban workers to Calderón Guardia informing him of their support for the social reform. Such telegrams proved that the workers were strongly identified with the reform.[66] Moreover, on May 26, members of the *Consejo Nacional de la Unión Campesina* (National Council of the Peasants' Alliance) visited President Calderón Guardia to show their approval of the Social Guarantees bill.[67] This evidenced the peasants' interest in the transformation associated with the reform—but they were not alone. In mid-June, a group of construction workers attended a meeting of the CSE in Heredia to ask for help in forming a union. According to the CSE, the workers explained that they needed a union "to face the cost of living and to support the Social Guarantees."[68] To express the heterogeneity of workers who identified themselves with the reform, the CSE organized a meeting on June 21. The location chosen for the activity was the Teatro Raventós. The purpose of the meeting was to reveal the popular classes' support of the social reform.[69] The activity was a success. *Trabajo* estimated that five thousand persons attended. Calderón Guardia was present and addressed the workers, explaining that the idea of a social reform arose from his work as a physician, thus replicating the populist rhetoric on his image as a *caudillo*. Other union leaders addressed the crowd, and communist leader Manuel Mora (deputy and secretary of the PCCR) closed the meeting by encouraging the workers to fight for the social transformation promoted by the new social laws.[70]

On October 18, 1942, the CSE organized the *Segunda Conferencia Nacional Sindical* (Second National Union Conference). Sixty-four unions attended the conference and arrived at two major decisions. First, they agreed to renounce their right to strike for the duration of the World War. Workers called for a new *Tribunal de Arbitraje*, consisting of a union representative, an employer delegate, and a government official, to solve any collective or individual labor disputes that arose, so that strikes would be avoided. Second, they decided to make the CSE the leading organization of the labor movement.[71] In a move that illustrates the strong connection between Calderón Guardia's administration, the CSE, and other unions, the government responded to the unions' initiative by creating the *Comisión Nacional de Arbitraje* (National Arbitration Commission, CNA) in December 1942.[72] As the *Segunda Conferencia Nacional Sindical* proposed, the CNA was composed of three members and had jurisdiction over labor contracts, work hours, workplace safety and hygiene, dismissals, and the regulation of apprentices.[73] The CNA took the place of the *Tribunal Superior de Arbitraje*.

The accent on a class struggle discourse gave unions the chance to confront employers and shop and factory owners, by contextualizing their demands for higher wages as part of the same struggle for the social legislation. In February 1943, the labor union of the banana industry in Limón mailed a letter to President Calderón Guardia requesting his help for a wage increase.[74] The same month, several labor organizations agreed to launch a campaign to defend the Social Guarantees, a plan the CSE carried out with the unions in March.[75] This link between two fronts—the social legislation and the struggle for higher wages—allowed the CSE and the unions to confront employers and demand the government's intervention with regard to those who did not increase salaries. Some employers denounced the combination of unionism, social demands, and the government populists' discourse as the "danger of absurd unionism."[76]

By February 1943, fifty-nine unions were affiliated to the CSE. Urban workers such as shoemakers, bakers, and carpenters organized most of those unions (forty-nine), but it is clear that peasants were also promoting unionism, especially in Siquirres and Heredia. Calderón Guardia was also receiving credit as a mediator between workers and employers and—more importantly—as a social reformer. Considered the source of social transformation, crowds of people would travel with *el Doctor* (Calderón Guardia's nickname) to the places he would visit. On March 28, 1943, Calderón Guardia visited Turrialba, invited by workers and the PCCR.[77] Hundreds of people attended the meeting, which *el Doctor* employed to portray the social reform as the result of his medical practice. Moreover, Calderón Guardia warned the crowd about "blind and selfish capitalists" who wanted to thwart the social legislation. According to *Trabajo*, the crowd then shouted: "Doctor, it does not matter, the *pueblo's* fist will back your social policies." Moreover, *Trabajo* added a comment: "[P]eople of Turrialba, as all of the Costa Rican people, identified themselves with Mr. President's work and are willing to defend it no matter what."[78] In the same edition, *Trabajo* published Manuel

Mora's article declaring PCCR's support toward the Government and warning about an uncertain future. Mora argued that Costa Rica was moving toward "an exacerbating age that will lead to bloodshed and, likewise, to a government of force."[79] Mora's admonition about a possible social clash was in response to the opposition's attacks on the government. In addition, Mora's rhetorical strategy encouraged social mobilization. The message was quite simple: if people did not mobilize, the government would not be able to defend the social reform against its adversaries.

The enactment of the Labor Code in August 1943 reinforced the alliance between the administration and the organized workers. Among several dispositions, the Labor Code established a Labor Ministry, made collective bargaining mandatory in disputes between labor and management, guaranteed the right of workers to organize, afforded protection against arbitrary dismissal, and created labor courts.[80] Certainly, as had occurred with other legislative initiatives, unions and workers decided to mobilize to support the Labor Code against its possible adversaries. They organized rallies in all the provinces to defend the code several days after its approval. The creation of the *Confederación de Trabajadores de Costa Rica* (CTCR) gave a way for workers and Calderón Guardia to strengthen bonds of unity.[81]

Some historians claim that the Labor Code negatively affected some labor unions. In the case of the shoemakers' union, for example, Víctor H. Acuña insists that the Labor Code limited its association by eliminating unionism as a mandatory requisite—it was now an option and not an imposition.[82] Yet, unionism definitely gained strength during the 1940s.

The implementation of the Labor Code involved an agenda to bring about other changes. According to historian Eugene D. Miller, between 1943 and 1955 the Labor Code achieved over 60 reforms. Miller indicates that "some of the changes were of a procedural nature; however, the most important of them were in three general areas: agrarian labor, general working conditions, and the expansion of the state bureaucracy."[83] Miller asserts that a major area of reform was "the expansion of the authority of the Ministry of Labor and its agents." Reforms included

> the reduction of worker and employer representation on salary commissions (1944), the expansion of the number and authority of labor judges (1946, 1947, and 1951), the institution of cooling-off procedures (1946), the increase in the coercive power of the ministry to punish violations of labor laws, and the shifting of responsibility to denounce violations from local political officers to centrally appointed Ministry of Labor officials.[84]

Miller's interpretation points out the growing authority of the state with regard to labor justice. After the Civil War of 1948, he points out:

> The Labor Ministry's labor inspectors received a sharp expansion in their responsibilities and authorities. In 1949 the Inspector General of Labor was authorized to intervene in all labor conflicts "to restore harmony between workers and employers."

The ministry itself was empowered to respond to any abnormal social condition. Labor judges (who now could be women) were authorized to act in an official capacity in any part of the country, and appeals outside the labor courts to the country's highest court, the *Sala de Casación*, were sharply restricted. Finally the Ministry of Labor received the right to monitor union contacts with international labor organizations.[85]

This intervention of the state, we believe, had started in the early twentieth century and, as Miller suggests, was consolidated after 1943, especially after the Civil War of 1948.

Civil War of 1948

In March-April of 1948, Costa Rica experienced a civil war produced by the social crisis that began in 1940 and the political confrontation created by Calderón's attempts to preserve power. The Civil War of 1948 confronted the government of Teodoro Picado (a follower of Calderón) and its old allies (the Communist Party) against a plural political opposition. This revolution was divided into four stages. The first stage (March 12–23) involved battles between revolutionaries and pro-government troops. The second stage (March 24–April 6) included attempts at peace negotiations during the continuation of hostilities. The third stage (April 7–13) was marked by the revolts' unexpected attempts to take over two important cities: Cartago and Limón. The fourth stage (April 14–20) brought the implementation of peace by agreements between revolutionaries and government authorities. The agreements included Teodoro Picado's resignation and the installation of a Junta de facto to rule the country for sixteen months.[86] The war was won by José Figueres, an entrepreneur who opposed the government since 1942. Some historians claim Figueres to be a representative of the interests of a middle bourgeoisie and an emerging middle class—although new studies suggest that Figueres first acted following personal interests.[87] Figueres became a very important political leader after the war and created the *Junta Fundadora de la Segunda República* or Junta, for short.[88]

The Civil War of 1948 put an end to the union rivalry when the victors moved to outlaw the CTCR and the communist unions. The Catholic Church had formed the *Confederación Costarricense de Trabajadores "Rerum Novarum"* (CCTRN), a Catholic labor confederation led by Father Benjamín Núñez, whose goal was "to purge Costa Rica of communism."[89] During 1944–1948, the CTCR and the CCTRN had disputed labor unionism.[90] After the Civil War, Núñez—now labor ministry of the Junta—and others saw the opportunity to dismantle communist unionism. On June 2, 1948, Junta investigators formally charged that the CTCR had actively participated in support of *Calderonismo*. Junta members conceived the CTCR as dangerous for the new status quo,[91] and their view coincided with that of Father Núñez. As Minister of Labor of the Junta, he went before the labor courts (created by the Labor Code) in June 1949, to request the dissolution of the CTCR. Núñez held that the CTCR had violated article 280 of the Labor Code, which prohibited union involvement in politics.[92] Communist lawyer Jaime Cerdas mounted the legal defense of the CTCR, which asserted that there was no written evidence to implicate the CTCR. Furthermore, Cerdas held that race, religion, or political creed were not barriers to be part of the CTCR. From that point of view, any relationship between the *Partido Vanguardia Popular* (PVP, the new name for the PCCR after 1943) and the CTCR had been a consequence of free will, not an imposition of the confederation's structure.[93] However, most unions decided not to fight what they believed was a clear correlation: the CTCR had indeed politically backed Calderón Guardia's and Picado's governments (1940–1948).[94]

In fact, the outcome of the Civil War had strongly affected unions: the PVP was outlawed, the communist leaders were often in jail and persecuted, many union members were killed during battles and others fled the country to avoid reprisals. The CCTRN also created public pressure, demanding the prompt dissolution of the CTCR. From the Ministry of Labor, Father Núñez schemed to destroy the CTCR by dissolving its affiliate unions before the labor courts decided the CTCR case. The urban unions, such as that of the shoemakers, tried to challenge repression by declaring themselves independent of the CTCR. Some union leaders and communists, such as shoemakers Víctor Sierra and Juan Rafael Morales, successfully fought to keep various urban unions functioning after 1949.[95] The peasants' unions, however, were not spared. In July 1949, the Ministry of Labor outlawed the peasants' unions of Cartago, Heredia, San José, and Alajuela. Union activity in the countryside disappeared.[96] On April 21, 1950, the First Labor Court ordered the dissolution of the CTCR. Cerdas appealed the decision before the Supreme Court, which reopened the case but in the end confirmed the verdict.[97]

Once the CTCR was dissolved, the CCTRN remained as the sole confederation of workers. However, the CCTRN was unable to increase its power over union activities. On the contrary, as James Backer documented, the CCTRN paved the way to its own disintegration since the early 1950s. In 1950–1951, a great number of CCTRN leaders abandoned it to form part of the *Partido Liberación Nacional* (PLN). This move created a lack of leadership within the confederation, which experienced a crisis within its structure. In 1950, the crisis gained force when the CCTRN organized a national conference to examine its ideology. By this time, two cultural attachés of the Argentinean Embassy in San José were strongly advocating for the CCTRN to change its affiliation from the *Confederación Interamericana de Trabajadores* (CIT) to the *Agrupación de Trabajadores Latinoamericanos Sindicalistas* (ATLAS). The ATLAS was the Peronist regional union confederation. CCTRN members were divided with regard to the Argentinean influence in their union movement. Then, at the CCTRN national conference, the majority of its members agreed to expel those who had identified themselves with Peronism. About 1,500 union members left the CCTRN and founded the *Confederación Nacional de Trabajadores* (CNT) under the influence of the ATLAS. However, when Perón was overthrown in Argentina, the CNT disappeared in Costa Rica. Meanwhile, other unions had abandoned the CCTRN. Finally, in 1951, upon the death of Archbishop Víctor Sanabria, the conservative wing of the Costa Rica's Catholic Church gained power. The new Archbishop was not interested in union struggles, which weakened the relationship between the Catholic Church and the unionist movement.[98]

From the 1950s to the 1970s, the social policies of the PLN, and the paternalistic state that it fostered, contributed to the growth of the public sector and attendant labor unions, especially after 1954—PLN governments were in office from 1953–1958, 1962–1964, 1970–1978. Nevertheless, the majority of these labor unions identified with the PLN and the trend toward the reduction of overt labor battles continued until 1965. From that point on, the labor union movement grew and the public sector unions became stronger throughout the 1970s. By the end of the twentieth century, private sector unions had practically disappeared. In inverse proportion, anticommunist mutual aid associations that were markedly antiunion flourished in the private sector. Consequently, public sector unions have become the most visible and vocal defenders of workers' rights. Today, the union movement is almost exclusively made up of public sector workers, while private sector labor has neither strength nor influence. We would argue that the Civil War of 1948 determined the future of union activity in Costa Rica, despite the fact that the Labor Law continues in effect.[99]

The Constitution of Labor Tribunals

The Labor Code created and organized labor courts in Costa Rica. It established that when pertaining to work issues, justice would be administered by the following tribunals: the Labor Courts, the Conciliation and Arbitration Courts, the Superior Court of Labor, and the Appeal Chamber of the Supreme Court of Justice.[100] The code also created labor tribunals in every judicial district (*circuitos*).

Article 393 of the Labor Code set forth that all labor courts were functionally dependent on the Supreme Court of Justice. They were presided over by a professional judge appointed by the *Corte Plena* (a superior organ of the judicial power with mainly administrative functions) for a four-year period according to article 401. On the other hand, according to Article 404, the Conciliation and Arbitration Courts were intended to maintain a "fair balance between the different production factors, with harmonization of the rights of capital and those of labor."[101] The judge presided in his capacity as state representative, while two other representatives, one for the employers and another for the workers, also took part in the process.

According to Article 405 of the Labor Code, the Superior Court of Labor had its seat in the capital city and jurisdiction throughout the Republic. It was composed of a superior labor judge representing the state and two other representatives, one for the employers and another for the workers, all appointed for a four-year term. Its fundamental role, as provided in Article 406, was to review the decisions rendered by the labor judges or the Courts of Arbitration when an appeal or consultation was appropriate. Jurisdiction conflicts between common courts of law and labor courts were settled by the Appeal Chamber.

Meanwhile, article 109 of the *Ley Orgánica del Poder Judicial* (Organic Law of the Judicial System) lays down the responsibilities of the labor courts as follows: to judge all individual or collective judicial conflicts, all economic and social conflicts, all conflicts related to the enforcement of the social security law, all cases of impeachment arising from the enforcement of the law on occupational hazards, and other issues related to the labor law.

Labor Justice after the 1950s and Its Reforms during 1966–2015

After 1950, Costa Rica made some gradual but important advances in the labor justice system. In 1966, the government created the *Tribunal de Trabajo de Menor Cuantía* (Small Claims Labor Tribunal) in San José. In 2007, the judicial system created similar courts in Alajuela, Heredia, Cartago, Limón, and Puntarenas.[102] Today, although labor tribunals exist, some courts are authorized to judge both labor and civil issues (mixed courts).[103] In 2009, Costa Rica had 115 labor judges working in 15 labor courts (in 2005 there were only 7), 83 mixed labor courts, and 112 judicial officers entitled to solve labor conflicts throughout the country. The *Ley No. 7338* (May 5, 1993) indicates the requirements for appointing labor judges. Candidates must be licensed lawyers (a requisite already established in the Labor Code since 1943) and trained in labor justice at the *Escuela Judicial*. That same year, the Second Tribunal of the Supreme Court evaluated 1,349 cases, of which 1,124 were labor lawsuits.[104] Although some advances have been made regarding labor justice, Costa Rica requires more labor inspectors to guarantee an adequate control by the Minister of Labor. In 2009, there were 102 labor inspectors working in 31 offices (Table 5.3).

Today, within the justice system there are three levels of courts that deal with labor cases: small claims, major claims, and the Supreme Court of Justice. With respect to small labor claims, there are two instances (except in San José which has only one). With respect to major labor claims, there are three instances: one that supervises the small claims and hears major claims, another that hears appeals, and a third (the Superior Labor Courts) that provides a second level of appeal. The Second Chamber of Appeals of the Supreme Court of Justice hears appeals of major labor claims, and in 2013 the constitutional Chamber of the Supreme Court (*Sala Constitucional de Costa Rica*) heard 487 labor cases and ruled that 139 decisions were unconstitutional.[105] Labor judges have recently resisted reforms made by the government (workday changes), with the effect of limiting outsourcing practices.[106]

In Costa Rica, trade unions' immunity (the protection of their members from legal action in civil law) appeared, thanks to *Voto 5000–93*—a Supreme Court decision—announced in 1993 and endorsed by union leaders. This occurred before the Labor

Table 5.3. Conflict Resolution Mechanisms According to the Labor Code (1943) and Other Legislation, 1943–2011

Mechanism	Legislation	Coverage
1. Conciliation and arbitration courts as alternative conflict resolution mechanisms	Labor Code of 1943	Labor courts (Tribunales de Trabajo) work as conciliation and arbitration instances in its first stage. They resolve individual and collective conflicts applicable to the private sector.
2. Center for Conciliation of the Judicial System	Labor Code of 1943	Individual labor conflicts not included. Applicable to the private sector.
3. Direct Settlement	Labor Code of 1943	Direct dialogue between parties. Restricts the actions of unions and the importance of collective agreements. Implementation within companies (weak). Union affiliation: less than 5% (2008). Few companies allow collective agreements. Boards or committees of permanent workers.
4. Arbitration/Mediation	Ley de Resolución Alterna de Conflictos y Promoción de la Paz Social (January 14, 1998)	New private centers are created, but few labor processes are carried out. Two conciliation institutions in the *Ministerio de Trabajo y Seguridad Social: Oficina de Asuntos Gremiales y Conciliación Administrativa* and the *Centro de Resolución Alterna de Conflictos.*

Source: Created by the authors using data from Calvo, "La Justicia Laboral en Costa Rica," 113–114.

Code was amended to include Chapter 3 in its Title V: "On the protection of the right to unionize."

In contemporary Costa Rica, labor justice played an important role in the organization of labor relations and the constitution of strong public sector unions. Andrew Schrank and Michael Piore have pointed out: "The Costa Rican labor ministry has not only limited the extent of informality and unemployment but has simultaneously endowed workers with de facto bargaining power and thereby forced the 'upward equalization' of wages and working conditions in the informal and low wage formal sectors."[107] But some transformations are taking place; Schrank and Piore argue:

By the late 1990s, however, the labor ministry found itself confronted by three interrelated challenges. First, Costa Rican employers began to decry the "burdensome" nature of their country's labor regulations and to make a concerted effort to amend or avoid their reach. Second, Costa Rica's trading partners began to ask whether the country's regulations were burdensome or protective enough and to demand the adoption of *more* safeguards and *stricter* enforcement. And, finally, Costa Rican planning authorities (the *Ministerio de Planificación*, or MIDEPLAN) declared the country's regulatory apparatus hidebound and inefficient and began to call for thoroughgoing administrative reform.[108]

After 1948, union power became stronger in public institutions rather than in the private sector. This means that private unions in Costa Rica practically did not experience any growth, which led to constrained negotiations for better labor conditions between private employees and their employers. Instead, *asociaciones solidaristas* (solidarity associations) flourished in the private sector. Unlike unions, these associations generally maintain cordial relations with employers and allow employees to save funds for practical purposes.[109]

In 2015, public sector unions remained as strong political protagonists, but neoliberal politicians accused them of receiving special benefits that must come to an end. Moreover, Costa Rican labor legislation must face the fact of an increasing number of informal employees whose labor rights are usually violated by informal employers. In that respect, after almost two centuries of labor legislation, some Costa Rican workers must still fight for their labor rights.

The current discussion addresses the question on a reform to the *Código Procesal Laboral* (Procedural Labor Code) in order to solve some problems concerning collective rights presented in the Labor Code of 1943. On December 9, 2015, Congress approved the *Ley de Reforma Procesal Laboral*, a procedural reform that reduces the waiting time for labor judgments from five to ten years, to two years. Now, judgments will include "orality" in several stages of the trials. Moreover, the reform allows specific unions to fight for other worker rights while it establishes that labor judges have up to three days to declare a strike illegal.[110]

Conclusions

Since its independence, Costa Rica has created a number of institutions aimed at intervening in labor relations. Yet, we believe it is a mistake to conceive these institutions only as forms of power and control over workers. In fact, legal institutions endorsed the construction of social and labor legislation that would eventually benefit workers, particularly after the 1930s. In consequence, during the nineteenth century, labor legislation and the institutions responsible for administering labor justice appeared as part of the construction of the state. Labor and salary agreements became a part of the labor relations regulated by civil courtrooms. In the early twentieth century, workers organized and fought for better conditions, encouraging the discussion of new labor legislation in Congress. During the 1920s, the state created two important institutions that would define labor justice during the 1930s: the *Banco de Seguros* and the *Oficina del Trabajo*. Both institutions stood up for workers in their legal struggles against employers when it came to labor accidents and pensions. In the 1940s, the developing social movement coincided with the emergence of a populist government that sought to rally workers' support in order to bring about Costa Rica's most important social reform. This reform included a Labor Code, which has ruled labor relations in Costa Rica to this day. The power of these social institutions is clearly proven by their continuity, despite the intent of a group of victors of the Civil War of 1948 to abolish them. These institutions and the Labor Code endured through the 1950s and into the twenty-first century in Costa Rica, remaining as an essential piece of the labor and social justice of this society. Yet, some changes have taken place during the last thirty years. Several of the fundamental institutions that shaped Costa Rica's social inclusion policies are under attack by a new neoliberal political order. In this framework, labor relations are undergoing changes in view of some employers' requests for law reforms that could affect work schedules, salary agreements, working hours, union rights, and others. But one thing is certain: new social struggles will appear in the near future to confront those imminent changes.

Notes

1. We take the term *inclusive institutions* from Acemoglu and Robinson, *Why Nations Fail.*
2. See Díaz, *Construcción de un estado moderno*, 12–34.
3. This is discussed in Chapter 1 of this book.
4. Le Franc, *Regulación laboral en Costa Rica.*
5. Ibid., 102–103.
6. Díaz, *La era de la centralización.*
7. Communication with Costa Rican historian Adriana Sánchez, November 19, 2014.
8. De la Cruz, *Las luchas sociales en Costa Rica*, 134.
9. Administración González Víquez, *Manual para la Policía Judicial*, 83.
10. Ibid., 83–84.
11. Ibid., 84.
12. Ibid.
13. Villalobos, *Alfredo González Flores*, 22.
14. De la Cruz, *Las luchas sociales en Costa Rica*, 134.
15. For a summary of all these changes, see Palmer and Molina, *Costa Rica Reader*, and Molina and Palmer, *History of Costa Rica.*
16. Oliva, *Artesanos y obreros costarricenses*, 184–185; De la Cruz de Lemos, *Los Mártires de Chicago*, 74–88.
17. Botey and Cisneros, *La crisis de 1929*, 113.
18. De la Cruz, *Las luchas sociales en Costa Rica*, 247; Botey and Cisneros, *La crisis de 1929*, 129–130.
19. Monge Alfaro, *Nuestra historia y los seguros*, 98.
20. Quoted by ibid., 100–101.
21. Ibid., 102.
22. Ibid., 111–113.
23. Ibid., 114.
24. Ibid., 104–108.
25. Ibid., 110.
26. Ibid., 124–128.
27. Ibid., 278–520.
28. Miller, *A Holy Alliance?* 69.

29. Ibid., 78.

30. Acuña Ortega, *Los orígenes de la clase.*

31. De la Cruz, *Las luchas sociales en Costa Rica*, 107–108.

32. Ibid., 108.

33. Campos, "Aspectos jurídico-laborales," 4.

34. Umaña, *Legislación laboral costarricense*, 3.

35. República de Costa Rica. *Colección de Leyes y Decretos*, San José: Imprenta Nacional, Decr. 33, 1928, 1–2.

36. *Colección de Leyes y Decretos*, Decr. 7, 1928, 254–257.

37. *Colección de Leyes y Decretos*, Decr. 45, 1929, 295–296.

38. *Colección de Leyes y Decretos*, Decr. 59, 1929, 379–380.

39. *Colección de Leyes y Decretos*, Decr. 20, 1930, 187–188.

40. *Colección de Leyes y Decretos*, Decr. 27, 1930, 28–29.

41. *Colección de Leyes y Decretos*, Decr. 8, 1928, 327–328.

42. *Colección de Leyes y Decretos*, Decr. 1, 1929, 44–45.

43. *Colección de Leyes y Decretos*, Decr. 2, 1929, 47–48.

44. Other cases involving similar protagonists and solutions: *Colección de Leyes y Decretos*, Decr. 33, 1929, 115–116; *Colección de Leyes y Decretos*, Decr. 60, 1929, 380–382; *Colección de Leyes y Decretos*, Decr. 64, 1929, 429–430; *Colección de Leyes y Decretos*, Decr. 66, 1929, 453; *Colección de Leyes y Decretos*, Decr. 3, 1930, 38; *Colección de Leyes y Decretos*, Decr. 24, 1930, 260; *Colección de Leyes y Decretos*, Decr. 34, 1930, 59; *Colección de Leyes y Decretos*, Decr. 35, 1930, 60; *Colección de Leyes y Decretos*, Decr. 30, 1930, 31–32.

45. *Colección de Leyes y Decretos*, Decr. 29, 1929, 111–114.

46. *Colección de Leyes y Decretos*, Decr. 5, 1929, 67–69.

47. See. for example, *Colección de Leyes y Decretos*, Decr. 23, 1929, 246.

48. *Colección de Leyes y Decretos*, Decr. 36, 1929, 245.

49. *Colección de Leyes y Decretos*, Decr. 17, 1930, 146–148.

50. *Colección de Leyes y Decretos*, Decr. 14, 1932.

51. *Colección de Leyes y Decretos*, Decr. 55, 1934.

52. Hernández Rodríguez, "Trabajadores, empresarios y Estado," especially 66–72.

53. Ibid., 69.

54. República de Costa Rica, *Memoria de Gobernación y Policía, 1939*. San José: Imprenta Nacional, 1940, 16.

55. Díaz, *Crisis social y memorias en lucha.*

56. *Trabajo (Journal of the Communist Party of Costa Rica)*, May 23, 1942, 2.

57. *Trabajo*, May 30, 1942, 2.

58. Ibid., 1.

59. Calderón Guardia, Rafael Ángel, "Mensaje inaugural del Dr. Don Rafael Ángel Calderón Guardia, presidente de la República, al Congreso Constitucional." In *Mensajes Presidenciales 1940–1958*, ed. Carlos Meléndez, 9–22. San José: Imprenta Nacional, 1990.

60. Rosenberg, *Las luchas por el seguro*, 57.

61. Rosenberg, "Social Reform in Costa Rica," 286.

62. Ibid., 286–288; Rosenberg, *Las luchas por el seguro social en Costa Rica*, 58–65.

63. Botey Sobrado, "Las Garantías Sociales," 202.

64. In this way, Costa Rica became part of the social constitutionalism movement inaugurated by the Mexican constitution of 1917 and the German constitution of 1919; see Chapter 2 of this book.

65. De la Cruz de Lemos, "El Código de Trabajo," 255–260.

66. *Trabajo*, May 16, 1942, 1; *Trabajo*, May 30, 1942, 2; *Trabajo*, May 30, 1942, 2.

67. *Trabajo*, May 23, 1942, 1 and 4; *Trabajo*, May 30, 1942, 1 and 4.

68. *Trabajo*, June 20, 1942, 2.

69. Ibid., 1.

70. *Trabajo*, June 27, 1942, 1, 3–4.

71. *Trabajo*, October 24, 1942, 2 and 4.

72. *Colección de Leyes y Decretos*, Decr. 37, December 24m 1942.

73. LaWare, "From Christian Populism to Social Democracy," 87.

74. *Trabajo*, February 20, 1943, 2.

75. Ibid.; *Trabajo*, March 13, 1943, 2.

76. *La Tribuna*, February 6, 1943; LaWare, "From Christian Populism to Social Democracy," 90.

77. *Trabajo*, March 27, 1943, 1; *Trabajo*, April 3, 1943, 1 and 4.

78. *Trabajo*, April 3, 1943, 4.

79. Ibid., 3–4.

80. Bell, *Crisis in Costa Rica*, 31. In this way, Costa Rica (like Brazil in the same year) became part of other Latin American countries that approved labor codes. See the Introduction and Chapter 1 of this book.

81. *Trabajo*, October 9, 1943, 1 and 4.

82. Acuña Ortega, *Conflicto y Reforma en Costa Rica*, 24.

83. Miller, *A Holy Alliance*, 99.

84. Ibid., 99–100.

85. Ibid., 100.

86. López, *Los cuarenta días de 1948*.

87. For a discussion on Figueres's political and personal interests, see Díaz, *Crisis social y memorias en lucha*.

88. Bell, *Crisis in Costa Rica*, 142–152.

89. Núñez, *Benjamín*, 54–59.

90. All the references about this confrontation are in Molina, *Anticomunismo reformista*.

91. Junta Fundadora de la Segunda República, *Actas 1948–1949*. San José: Centro de Investigaciones Históricas (Biblioteca Carlos Meléndez), Universidad de Costa Rica, s/d,23.

92. Backer, *La Iglesia y el sindicalismo*, 128; Aguilar, *Clase trabajadora y organización*, 73; Miller, "Labour and the War-Time Alliance," 538.

93. Miller, "Labour and the War-Time Alliance," 539.

94. Aguilar, *Clase trabajadora y organización*, 76.

95. Morales Alfaro, "Autobiografía," 177–235.

96. Aguilar, *Clase trabajadora y organización*, 73–77.

97. Archivo Judicial de Costa Rica, "Disolución de la CTCR y organizaciones afiliadas: Benjamín Núñez en su capacidad de Ministro de Trabajo y Bienestar Social vs. Confederación de Trabajadores de Costa Rica," Remesa 467, Estante 186, Archivo 416, Sección 5.

98. Backer, *La Iglesia y el sindicalismo*, 128–136.

99. Aguilar, *Clase trabajadora y organización*.

100. http://www.ilo.org/dyn/natlex/docs/WEBTEXT/44102/65002/s95cri02.htm#t6c2 (accessed March 3, 2016).

101. http://www.ilo.org/dyn/natlex/docs/WEBTEXT/44102/65002/s95cri02.htm#t6c2 (accessed March 3, 2016).

102. Calvo, "La Justicia Laboral en Costa Rica," 97.

103. Ibid., 98.

104. Ibid., 103–105.

105. Briones, "Diversos temas," 107.

106. Weller, "Retos y respuestas," 24.

107. Schrank and Piore, *Norms, Regulations, and Labour Standards*, 24.

108. Ibid., 24–25. According to Schranl and Piore, the MIDEPLAN and the labor ministry attempted "to professionalize the already reasonably competent inspectorate by: (1) treating inspectors as skilled professionals with a wide span of authority rather than cogs in a bureaucratic machine; (2) offering inspectors new incentives including better salaries, improved career prospects, and performance bonuses; and (3) making every effort to ensure that the inspectors would be up to the task by adopting more restrictive recruitment criteria, frequent training exercises, and incentives for continuing education. Nevertheless, the results have been ambiguous at best. While public officials have been able to adopt 'stroke of the pen' reforms like decentralization, planning, and human resource upgrading, and have thereby produced what appear to be modest gains in the efficiency of the inspection process, they have been unable to alter the behavior of their street level bureaucrats or their private sector interlocutors in meaningful ways. Inspectors continue to pursue a largely prosecutorial approach to their jobs. Proactive inspections, though numerous, are determined with the accessibility of the target rather than the likelihood or nature of the transgression in mind. Inspections tend to be concentrated in and around the capital of San José. And efforts to bolster tripartite negotiation have foundered on the shoals of suspicion and indifference."

109. Bensusán, *La efectividad de la legislación*, 1.

110. *La Nación*, December 10, 2015.

Bibliography

Acemoglu, Daron, and James A. Robinson. *Why Nations Fail: The Origins of Power, Prosperity, and Property*. London: Profile, 2012.

Acuña Ortega, Víctor Hugo. *Los orígenes de la clase obrera en Costa Rica: las huelgas de 1920 por la jornada de ocho horas*. San José: CENAP-CEPAS, 1986.

———. *Conflicto y Reforma en Costa Rica: 1940–1949*. San José: Universidad Estatal a Distancia, 1992.

Administración González Víquez. *Manual para la Policía Judicial. Compilación arreglada de orden del señor Ministro de Policía Lic. don Alfredo Volio*. San José: Tipografía Nacional, 1910.

Aguilar, Marielos. *Clase trabajadora y organización sindical en Costa Rica 1943–1971*. San José: Editorial Porvenir, 1989.

Backer, James. *La Iglesia y el sindicalismo en Costa Rica.* San José: Editorial Costa Rica, 1974.

Bell, John Patrick. *Crisis in Costa Rica: The Revolution of 1948.* Austin: University of Texas Press, 1971.

Bensusán, Graciela. *La efectividad de la legislación laboral en América Latina.* Ginebra: Instituto Internacional de Estudios Laborales/OIT, 2007.

Botey, Ana María, and Rodolfo Cisneros. *La crisis de 1929 y la fundación del Partido Comunista de Costa Rica.* San José: Editorial Costa Rica, 1984.

Botey Sobrado, Ana María. "Las Garantías Sociales: su significado histórico." In *El significado de la legislación social de los cuarenta en Costa Rica.* Ed. Jorge Mario Salazar. 185–214. San José: Ministerio de Educación Pública, 1993.

Briones, Erick. "Diversos temas de inconstitucionalidad laboral." *Revista de Ciencias Jurídicas* 133 (Jan.–Apr. 2014): 103–162.

Calvo, Esteban. "La Justicia Laboral en Costa Rica." In *La Justicia Laboral en América Central, Panamá y República Dominicana,* ed. Adolfo Ciudad. 95–147. San José: OIT, 2011.

Campos, Carlos María. "Aspectos jurídico-laborales de la actividad agropecuaria de Costa Rica." *Reforma Agraria* 3 (1962): 1–63.

De la Cruz, Vladimir. *Las luchas sociales en Costa Rica: 1870–1930.* San José: Editorial de la Universidad de Costa Rica, 1980.

De la Cruz de Lemos, Vladimir. *Los Mártires de Chicago y el 1° de mayo de 1913.* San José: Editorial Costa Rica, 1985.

———. "El Código de Trabajo: despliegue y consolidación del Estado social de derecho." In *El significado de la legislación social de los cuarenta en Costa Rica.* Ed. Jorge Mario Salazar. 215–266. San José: Ministerio de Educación Pública, 1993.

Díaz Arias, David. *Construcción de un estado moderno. Política, Estado e identidad nacional en Costa Rica, 1821–1914.* San José: Editorial de la Universidad de Costa Rica, 2005.

———. *Crisis social y memorias en lucha: guerra civil en Costa Rica, 1940–1948.* San José: Editorial de la Universidad de Costa Rica, 2015a.

———. *La era de la centralización: estado, sociedad e institucionalidad en Costa Rica, 1848–1870.* San José: Editorial de la Universidad de Costa Rica, 2015b.

Hernández Rodríguez, Carlos. "Trabajadores, empresarios y Estado: la dinámica de clases y los límites institucionales del conflicto. 1900–1943." *Revista de Historia* 27 (Jan.–June 1993): 51–86.

LaWare, David Craig. *From Christian Populism to Social Democracy: Workers, Populists, and the State in Costa Rica 1940–1956.* PhD diss., University of Texas at Austin, 1996.

Le Franc, Inés. *Regulación laboral en Costa Rica de 1821 a 1841.* Tesis de Licenciatura en Derecho, Universidad de Costa Rica, 1987.

López, Juan Diego. *Los cuarenta días de 1948: la Guerra Civil en Costa Rica.* San José: Editorial Costa Rica, 1998.

Marín, Juan José. "Balance y perspectivas para una historia social de los movimientos sociales en Costa Rica, 1990–2012." In *Musa obrera: historia, balances y desafíos de la clase trabajadora en el centenario del 1 de mayo en Costa Rica, 1913–2013.* Ed. Juan José Marín and Mario Torres. 167–238. San José: Centro de Investigaciones Históricas de América Central, 2015.

Miller, Eugene D. "Labour and the War-Time Alliance in Costa Rica 1943–1948." *Journal of Latin American Studies* 25: 3 (Oct. 1993): 515–541.

———. *A Holy Alliance? The Church and the Left in Costa Rica, 1932–1948*. Armonk, N.Y.: M. E. Sharpe, 1996.

Molina Jiménez, Iván. *Anticomunismo reformista. Competencia electoral y cuestión social en Costa Rica (1931–1948)*. San José: Editorial Costa Rica, 2007.

———. *Revolucionar el pasado. La historiografía costarricense del siglo XIX al XXI*. San José: Editorial de la Universidad Estatal a Distancia, 2012.

Molina Jiménez, Iván, and Steven Palmer. *The History of Costa Rica: Brief, Up-to-Date and Illustrated*. San José: Editorial de la Universidad de Costa Rica, 1998.

Molina Jiménez, Iván, Francisco Enríquez Solano, and José Manuel Cerdas Albertazzi, eds. *Entre dos siglos: la investigación histórica costarricense 1992–2002*. Alajuela: Museo Histórico Cultural Juan Santamaría, 2003.

Monge Alfaro, Carlos. *Nuestra historia y los seguros*. San José: Editorial Costa Rica, 1974.

Morales Alfaro, Juan Rafael. "Autobiografía." *Revista de Historia* 27 (Jan.–June 1993): 177–235.

Núñez, Santiago. *Benjamín: siempre y ante todo sacerdote*. Heredia: Editorial de la Universidad Nacional, 2000.

Oliva, Mario. *Artesanos y obreros costarricenses, 1880–1914*. San José: Editorial de la Universidad Estatal a Distancia, 2006.

Palmer, Steven, and Iván Molina. *The Costa Rica Reader*. Durham, N.C.: Duke University Press, 2004.

Rosenberg, Mark. "Social Reform in Costa Rica: Social Security and the Presidency of Rafael Angel Calderón." *Hispanic American Historical Review* 61:2 (May 1981): 278–296.

———. *Las luchas por el seguro social en Costa Rica*. San José: Editorial Costa Rica, 1983.

Samper, Mario, ed. *Revista de Historia* "Special Issue," 1996.

Schrank, Andrew, and Michael Piore. *Norms, Regulations, and Labour Standards in Central America*. Mexico City: CEPAL, 2007.

Umaña, Verny. *Legislación laboral costarricense*. San José: EUNED, 1991.

Villalobos, Bernardo. *Alfredo González Flores. Políticas de Seguros y de Banca. 1910–1917*. San José: ECR, 1981.

Villasmil, Umberto. *La incidencia de la OIT en el momento fundacional del derecho de trabajo latinoamericano: unas notas introductorias*, Documento de Trabajo 33, Ginebra: OIT, 2011.

Weller, Jürgen, "Retos y respuestas: Las políticas laborales y del mercado de trabajo en Costa Rica, Panamá y Uruguay." In *Serie Macroeconomía y Desarrollo* 90. Chile: CEPAL, 2009.

CHAPTER 6

Origins of Labor Rights and Justice in Colombia, 1850–1950

VICTOR M. URIBE-URAN WITH GERMÁN PALACIO

Introduction

Works addressing the history of Colombian labor rights and justice during the period covered in this chapter are limited in number and depth. Contemporary technical juridical manuals and legal compilations, quite useful as historical sources, are certainly available.[1] Other than these, the one text that pays greater attention to historical legal aspects is an insightful book written from a Marxist perspective. Its authors suggest that the labor legislation enacted during some of the decades covered in this study was mainly the result of the implacable "logic of capital," directed at crippling the labor movement and maximizing capitalist productivity.[2] However, they do not pause over the emergence, nature, and meaning of labor justice, and neither do they discuss the *labor jurisdiction* (a separate specialized court system) as such.[3] After all, the labor one was just an expression of bourgeois justice in general and, thus, at the service of capitalist accumulation. An additional study combining historical insights with technical legal analysis pays closer attention to the vicissitudes of unionization-related laws than labor courts and justice.[4] Another work examines historical aspects briefly and mainly as background information for a sociological discussion concerning the operation of labor justice in recent decades.[5] One more touches on a period closer to that under examination here but does not focus at all on the transition from civil to labor justice, an aspect addressed in this essay.[6] Therefore, this chapter is a preliminary attempt to fill a historiographical gap on the circumstances behind the emergence of a specialized system of labor courts and procedures. As the introduction of this book suggests, like the rest of the chapters this one strives to connect labor history and legal history. It offers, in particular, a general "archeological" overview of a labor justice in Colombia, looking at its connections to labor conflicts and related state reforms and policies. While the chapter highlights the overall historical meaning of this new legal and judicial specialty, the actual operation of labor justice is beyond the essay's scope and would require further studies.

Modern labor justice started to surface in Colombia between about 1923 and 1936. The first major step was the creation of an *Oficina General del Trabajo* (Law 83 of 1923) during the period of the Conservative government presided over by modernizing military, engineer, and politician Pedro Nel Ospina Vásquez (1922–1926), rancher and coffee entrepreneur, professor of mining and its promoter, and advocate of railroads and aviation in the country. The second significant step, over a decade later, was the creation of Labor Inspections (Decree 666 of 1936 and Law 12 of 1936). Inspections surfaced during a liberal, progressive, and moderately populist government, presided over by banker, export merchant, journalist, and President Ospina Vásquez's former minister of the treasury, Alfonso López Pumarejo (1934–1938). The two institutions in question, the Oficina General del Trabajo and Labor Inspections, and also the creation of a Ministry of Labor in 1938 under López Pumarejo, were the culmination of a series of norms issued from about 1915 to 1929, a period of Conservative party rule and intense labor agitation.

Some of the institutions listed were indeed preceded or accompanied by legal measures during the 1910s and 1920s aimed mainly at regulating escalating work accidents, waves of strikes, and collective labor conflicts. The measures also addressed workers' critical social conditions (pensions, hygienic housing, and life insurance), especially in sectors strategic to Colombia's integration into the world economy at the time, including the petroleum and transportation industries. However, the labor jurisdiction per se and the system of "expert functionaries" referenced by this volume's introduction, emerged just in 1944, under López Pumarejo's second administration (1942–1945). It was then that the establishment of specialized labor courts, and a procedure separate from the one observed in civil courts, took place.[7]

The tight historical summary of labor justice just offered, however, leaves out an important part of the story. Unlike other contributions to this volume, this chapter actually holds that the remote antecedents of labor law and justice date back to the nineteenth century and seem linked not necessarily to labor struggles but rather, in the last instance, to civil wars and general political crises. One could even venture the hypothesis that, whether directly or indirectly, this modality of justice derived from the mixing of practices and institutions found in the military and merchant *fuero* (special jurisdiction or "immunity"), sprinkled with elements from canon law.[8] Furthermore, labor justice had connections and affinities with "police" regulations, because hygiene and morality (two of the police's key concerns, alongside security) were central reasons behind the state's proactive involvement in the regulation of labor relations and spaces.

It must be remembered that in the ecclesiastical realm, from very early on (since medieval times), there emerged specialized courts of justice separate from ordinary civil courts and run by clergymen. In Spanish America, since at least the sixteenth century, the mercantile and military realms also featured specialized justice tribunals (*consulados* and *consejos de guerra*) that observed summary and oral procedures under judges belonging to the same occupational group as the plaintiffs and defendants. The arbitration of disputes was also central to merchant courts.[9] Therefore, it is fair to say that once the density of people working in the same agrarian or industrial establishments grew, and their conflicts with employers over excessive workdays, uncompensated workplace accidents, low salaries, and poor housing and hygienic conditions became more widespread and acute, government elites made use of relatively familiar mechanisms—namely, special courts and swift procedures—to restore social peace. This was even more so as the elites were faced with workers' growing anarchist, syndicalist, and socialist ideas. Especially in a context of renewed "corporatism," the dominant groups relied on familiar remedies available to tackle the conflicts of sectors under *fuero* on account of their affiliation to specific guilds or occupational groups. The elites' approach was reinforced by their growing conviction that it was indispensable to address, as a priority and with utmost care, the "social question" giving rise to revolutionary movements around the world, conflicts that during the 1910s had special visibility in places such as Russia and Mexico.

We shall offer some tentative findings concerning three distinctive periods in Colombian history: 1850–1910, 1910–1930, and 1930–1950.

Wars, Patriotic Rewards, Political Crises, and "Labor" Rights between 1850 and 1910

Similar to the experience of other countries in the region, the earliest social and legal expressions of a "labor" type in Colombia occurred in the realm of both (patriotic) state service and artisanal work. In both instances, as stated earlier, civil war and political crises were decisive catalysts. For instance, shortly after the end of the Wars of Independence in New Granada, during the 1820s, several military patriots or, in the case of those who died during the conflict, their relatives (especially mothers, widows, and orphaned children) petitioned the new republican government to grant them life pensions in compensation for their services to the fatherland.[10] Later petitions by craftsmen were of a somewhat different nature.

During the mid–nineteenth century, exceeding the expectations of the newly formed Liberal Party, which tried to organize, educate, and co-opt them to support its electoral needs and reformist agenda, artisans developed a certain working-class consciousness, became organized as an occupational group, and demanded the betterment of their economic conditions. In 1854 they even supported a coup d'etat that brought to power an army general (José María Melo) whom they understood to be their best ally against the mistreatment they felt victims of at the hands of ruling elites, both Liberals and Conservatives alike. In their effort to implement "scientific" policies resulting from the lessons of liberal political economy, such elites, and also their middle-class intellectual followers, were committed to defend at any cost free trade reforms which, craftsmen rightfully feared, could lead to the ruin of small artisanal industries and workshops. At the time, artisans came to embrace, as an alternative, "communist ideas," which were actually a mixture of utopian socialism and Christian doctrines.[11]

None of the above—neither demands from patriots or their relatives nor those from artisans—gave rise to legislation favoring in "abstract" and general terms deserving patriotic state servants or artisans as a whole in view of their economic vulnerability. The state's response was rather the granting of individual pensions or benefits in recognition of specific (individual) patriotic services[12] or, in the case of artisans, only refusal to abandon free-trade measures or to introduce social or economic protectionism. Furthermore, many artisans who supported the coup by General Melo were killed, jailed and, later, exiled to Panamá.[13] Thereafter, except for short-lived protests, artisans lost political protagonism, which they only regained early in the twentieth century in alliance with the growing working class.[14]

The laws enacted around the 1880s to address labor issues did not really follow social or labor protests but obeyed other considerations, especially patriotic and charitable concerns. At the end of the nineteenth century, several norms—for instance, Laws 14 of 1882, 58 of 1886 and 149 of 1896—summarized all previous measures concerning rewards and pensions to which members of the army were entitled. The laws targeted in particular those who on account of their adherence to independence in the period 1810–1827, suffered confiscations of their properties, imprisonment, exile, or death. The norms covered as well their offspring or minor grandchildren or those who were living under poverty.[15] As can be inferred, this legislation mixed in patriotic criteria with ideas derived from Christian charity toward those who were vulnerable due to their young age or poor economic situation.[16] It must be noticed that the processing of such benefits continued to be piecemeal rather than general. Although around the 1880s a gradual transition to general measures started to take place, the granting of retirement pensions was carried out through individualized laws, closely monitored by reward commissions (*comisiones de recompensas*) established inside the national congress and aimed at favoring specific individuals rather than a certain occupational category or group of people (say, "workers").[17]

Among the various laws that hinted at a transition toward policies "rewarding" not individuals but an abstract group of workers as a whole, a very emblematic one was Law 58 of November 11, 1886. This was part of the symbolic measures enacted by a conservative government that had just defeated its rivals during a civil war. The law's title suggests the type of changes taking place regarding retirement pensions: "Law to Establish General Rules on the Award of Benefits and Retirement Pensions"

(*Por la cual se Fijan Reglas Generales Sobre Concesiones de Pensiones y Jubilaciones*). Such law occurred at the outset of an era that came to be known in Colombia as the *regeneration* (*regeneración*), part and parcel of a long period of Conservative hegemony (1886–1930) in the country. The period's regimes were contrary to any liberal, much less revolutionary, measures. Instead, in order to move forward in the forging of a "nation," patriotic and Catholic ideals inspired them. This law, for instance, established that "any pension from the national treasury is by nature a reward for longstanding and major services to the fatherland" (art. 5) by the pensioner or his grandfather, father, son, or husband—gender distinctions being quite clear in it. Besides patriotic criteria, the text of the law also embodied charitable concerns, for the law provided that in several instances the right to a pension was related mainly to the disability or poverty of the claimant as a result of such services.[18]

Article 11 of the law under consideration extended the right to a retirement (or disability) pension to a broader category of people beyond veterans (or patriotic heroes). It benefited all "civil employees who had served in judicial or political jobs for at least twenty years" as long as, because of their service, they had become "disabled" and lacked any other means of subsistence or reached the age of sixty.[19] Even more significant was the fact that the law recognized the same benefit for those working in public education (*empleados en la instrucción pública*), which was deemed to include private teachers (*magisterio privado*). These norms clearly inaugurated a new historical moment involving not just public servants but even a symbolic portion of private workers in recognition, most likely, of their valuable contribution to the education of the nation's future citizens.[20]

The aforementioned norm was meaningful not only from the standpoint of the history of substantive proto-labor law but also in terms of the history, albeit incipient, of labor justice. It contained elements of specialized labor law procedure, except they corresponded to "administrative" justice rather than labor justice as such. For the issuing of pensions, the law established a procedure, not before any (civil) judicial authorities but before Congress itself, observing evidentiary rules different from those applicable in particular to civil procedures. Contrary to what would become a dominant characteristic of labor law during the 1930s and 1940s, such norms emphasized that written documents prevailed over oral testimony.[21] One must notice that at the time there was not yet a special "jurisdiction" for the resolution of disputes over pensions or the filing and processing of any other labor claims. These were all for the most part issues within administrative law (a fluid but identifiable specialized legal field at the time) or, otherwise, were understood to be civil law matters.

At the beginning of the twentieth century, additional new laws granted general benefits to certain clusters of workers, quite similar to those that would later become typical examples of advantages awarded to laboring groups in view of their perceived vulnerability as a social sector and, even more so, danger as a political force. It is not surprising that many of them did not spring from an ordinary legislature but originated in an extraordinary constitutional assembly (*Asamblea Nacional Constituyente y Legisla-tiva*) called to address a major political crisis. The assembly was called by a government that, although Conservative, made an effort to promote "national reconciliation" (*concordia nacional*) after a financially crippling and administratively destructive civil war known as the Thousand Days War (*Guerra de los Mil Días*) unfolding between 1899 and 1901.[22] The laws also came on the heels of the recent and highly traumatic loss of the province of Panamá by Colombia in 1904. Seeing his administration blocked by a congress controlled by an extreme faction of his own political party, entrepreneurial Conservative President Rafael Reyes (1904–1909)—explorer and colonizer of the frontier, agrarian entrepreneur, promoter of the production and exportation of bananas, exporter of quinine from the Amazon region, military hero of civil wars during the 1880s and 1890s, and former diplomatic representative—decided to close the legislature in 1904 ahead of schedule, declared a state of siege, and called a constitutional convention.[23]

The same year, progressive leaders of the Liberal party led by Liberal lawyer, law professor, congressman, journalist, and army general Rafael Uribe Uribe, a former rebel during the civil wars of 1895 and the Thousand Days War, started to promote debates around labor issues, including the monitoring of the hygienic conditions of workshops (*vigilancia sobre las condiciones higiénicas de los talleres*).[24] However, the main priority of the Reyes administration did not seem to have been common workers after all but more politically influential employees—namely, high-ranking judges removed from the Supreme Court whom, along with other members of the judicial branch, the regime appears to have wished to mollify. Another priority of the regime may have been to lower public expenditures in general by increasing the age to receive certain retirement pensions. The Assembly thus issued, among others, Law 29 of April 2, 1905, establishing a lifelong pension for certain justices of the Supreme Court (those whom President Reyes had not recently confirmed to remain in their jobs) who had reached the age of 60, regardless of their years of service to the state.[25] This law also ratified the award of lifelong pensions to "civil employees" who had performed some unspecified public duties (*destinos públicos*), most likely as educators of the nation's offspring, as long as they had served for thirty, rather than just twenty, years and had reached the age of sixty. Soon thereafter, however, another statute from the same Assembly, Law 12 of 1907, modified some aspects of the 1905 law. Generalizing the benefits awarded in 1905, the new law granted a lifelong retirement pension to all justices in the Supreme Court and appeals courts (*Tribunales Superiores de Justicia*) and to district and circuit judges (*Jueces Superiores y de Circuito*) who had served during a fairly generous fifteen-year period and reached the age—less generous than the one established in previous norms—of sixty five.[26]

State employees, only this time judges rather than members of the army, again tended to be the ones who (except for teachers in the private sectors who had been exceptionally included as pension beneficiaries in the 1886 law discussed above) led the way and pioneered what, years later, would become generalized labor benefits for all workers. None of the judicial disputes emerging around civil or military pensions for public employees, though, were at the time filed before a specialized body of courts. They continued to be under the care of civil judges, whether district (*Superiores*) or circuit ones (*de Circuito*). These justice officials remained in charge of litigation derived from contracts of any type. Further, labor relations were understood to spring from contracts involving the "provision of services" (*prestación de servicios*), then an entirely civil law matter. Therefore, in the absence of a notion of "labor contract," the conceptual articulation of a labor law field and ideology had not yet taken place explicitly in Colombia either. This would occur incipiently shortly thereafter, in particular during the decades of 1910 and 1920 when, as Chapter 1 of this volume notes, an international network of policy reformers and a "climate of ideas" favorable to labor law, and social legislation more generally, came to be in place. Besides, the presence of a working class became visible in Colombia and other countries of the region at the time, not only due to its relative size but also to its considerable activism and pugnacity.

(Administrative) Labor Law with Civil Justice, 1910–1930

In the 1910s, Colombia continued to be a predominantly agrarian country (75 percent of the economically active population belonged to the agrarian sector) and industrial production sprang largely from artisanal workshops of, among others, shoemakers, tailors, typographers, jewelers, blacksmiths, and foundrymen. Still, there already were numerous groups of wage workers (*por cuenta ajena*). Several worked in the transportation industries (railroads, river boats, and docks), trade, extractive industries (oil, in particular) and in manufacturing. For instance, there were wage earners in activities involving the processing of coffee, tobacco (cigarettes), chocolate, and other food; beverage making (especially beer); and textiles.[27] Many more worked in agroindustries, especially banana plantations operated by the United Fruit Company in the northern province of Magdalena.[28] Several of the workers in these economic sectors experienced growing confrontations with their employers during the 1910s and 1920s.

In 1918, for instance, there were strikes in the port cities of Barranquilla and Cartagena and also on the docks and railroads of nearby Santa Marta. That same year, there were also protests by the banana workers under the United Fruit Company. In 1919 major labor mobilization took place on the docks by workers linked to United Fruit, in the Girardot and Cundinamarca railroad, and in the riverine enterprises along the Magdalena River, in the city of Girardot. In 1920, textile workers in the city of Bello, Antioquia, and those of the railroads of La Dorada also took to the streets to demand better wages and improved working conditions.[29] Whether as a direct result of such confrontations or as a product of a paternalistic and politically profitable attitude, the opposition Liberal Party led the initiative to issuing a series of norms favorable to workers. Gradually, a corpus of laws concerning labor issues was put in place.[30]

Some representative examples include Laws 57 of 1915 (Ley Uribe), 46 of 1918, and 32 of 1922, respectively addressing accidents in the workplace, "hygienic housing for the proletarian class," and life insurance, all of which became the responsibility of the employers. The list must also include Decree 2, 1918, and Laws 78 of 1919, and 21 of 1920, which regulated strikes and other labor conflicts. Finally, it is equally important to mention Law 83 of 1923 creating the General Labor Office (Oficina General del Trabajo). All of these norms started to characterize "labor" as an activity deserving special attention from and protection by the state (and also by the Church, an institution closely allied with the Conservative regimes under which the norms in question were enacted). It must be noticed that the first group of norms came into existence, not surprisingly, just around the time of the Mexican and the Russian Revolutions of the 1910s. It is reasonable to infer that these two watershed events considerably influenced the imaginations of the elites and Colombia's historical process. However, undoubtedly there were internal factors of perhaps greater significance.

For instance, the 1915 law on workplace accidents was a tribute to the memory of General Rafael Uribe Uribe. Uribe Uribe, for a while the sole Liberal representative in Congress alongside sixty Conservatives and, later, leading member of the Liberal minority in the Reyes government's Constituent Assembly, promoted social ideas and progressive agrarian and labor policies. Having supported small landholdings and advocated in favor of increasing working wages, among other things, made him gain significant political presence and the widespread support of peasant and working-class groups. In the early twentieth century, Uribe Uribe developed a proposal on "state socialism," which was really a modernized version of liberalism, favorable to state intervention. His ideology included the promotion of the eight-hour workday, the regulation of safety in factories, and the requirement of insurance to protect workers in case of accidents in the workplace. He also advocated restrictions to the work of children and women.[31] However, the Conservative majority controlling congress and the state apparatus implemented few of these ideas.

Nevertheless, after Uribe Uribe's brutal murder in October 1914, Congress enacted a workplace accident law bearing his name. On one hand, a matter of posthumous homage, it was also an indication that several groups within the Conservative party, still the majority in Congress, accepted that providing benefits to the working classes was necessary to placate them. In doing so, they anticipated the logic of the German Catholic politician who, a few years later in 1918, suggested the need to promote social reforms and carry to its ultimate consequences Pope Leo XIII's labor encyclical so as to avoid that "tomorrow, hungry and naked multitudes [could impose on us] the codification of fear."[32]

It could be argued that similar objectives surrounded the enactment of a decree and several laws regulating strikes and other labor conflicts in 1918, 1919, and 1920, only they apparently also resulted directly from intensified labor struggles at the time.[33] For instance, Decree 2 of 1918, issued under state of siege, sought to neutralize labor protests, including even a riot in Cartagena where groups of disgruntled workers had looted some of the city's shops; there were also riots, looting, and destruction of telegraph lines in the neighboring port city of Santa Marta. In 1919, major labor protests also took place in the port cities of Girardot and La Dorada along the Magdalena River, in the country's interior, where railroad workers took to the streets over appalling labor conditions. The protests led by Bogota's tailors in 1919, resulting in several deaths, were another expression of growing unrest on the part of local workers, this time independent artisans alienated over the importation of foreign goods they felt entitled to produce locally in order to make a living.

Even the pro-American government of Conservative Marco Fidel Suarez, a grammarian and literary figure, former senator and Minister of Public Instruction and Foreign Relations, responded to several of these conflicts. Law 78, issued in November 1919, recognized that strikes were a legitimate form of protest, which could not thus be considered a criminal expression, as had heretofore been the case. This was a major victory for Colombian workers and came to symbolize as well the idea, being embraced globally at the time, that social justice, including fair treatment for workers and attention to their demands, was indispensable for the achievement of universal and lasting peace. It must be remembered, as Chapter 1 suggests, that as part of the Treaty of Versailles, which put an end to WW I, the International Labor Organization (ILO) was created early in 1919 precisely to promote permanent peace through the advancement of social justice at a global level. In addition to aligning with worldly concerns over social justice, the Colombian government was also obviously interested in mollifying and depoliticizing labor protests facing the country.

At the same time that it appeared to accept their demands, however, the 1919 law ordered that workers restrict strikes exclusively to demands concerning wages and hygienic conditions and required that work stoppages have an absolutely peaceful nature. When Congress discussed the reasons behind the law in question it stated clearly that the legislation was geared to "reducing the duration of strikes" to what was "naturally" indispensable, so as to avoid that any "foreign aspects be mixed in with this phenomenon."[34] This was probably a way to allude to the possible involvement, unacceptable to the ruling elites, of political organizations such as the Socialist Party, created early in 1919 after the first Workers' Congress held in Colombia that year. This political party participated actively in the organization and mobilization of workers in different regions of the country, which the government considered inconvenient and dangerous.[35] Negotiating labor disputes was deemed acceptable, but engaging in allegedly revolutionary agitation certainly was not.

To appease what otherwise would be protests with potentially more serious political consequences, the law provided for the first time that workers had the right to collective bargaining and also prescribed the organization of arbitration boards or tribunals. The latter were a means known and available for quite a long time in the realm of *ius mercatorium* or commercial law. They had recently been introduced in some regions of Mexico, probably an example considered worth following.[36] This mechanism would soon become a central component of labor justice in Colombia and other regions of the world. The following year, weakening the use of strikes as political leverage, another law came to require the issuing of advance notice prior to the declaration of any strike and, as in the Mexican, Argentine, and Chilean cases, established a mandatory conciliation effort intended to eliminate the pressure resulting from, and risks attached to, abrupt strikes. However, unlike the Mexican or Chilean but similar to their Argentine counterparts, conciliation committees in Colombia were ad hoc rather than permanent administrative bodies of the state and thus less susceptible to be turned into political instruments of specific partisan or social groups. They were presided over by a third party designated on a case-by-case basis by both employer and workers by mutual agreement. The expectation was to promote direct agreements that could, as much as possible, make strikes avoidable and unnecessary.[37] All of these laws had an important impact in fostering the settlement of numerous labor conflicts through direct agreements after very short-lived strikes, a particularly beneficial situation in economically strategic sectors such as railroad transportation and the transportation enterprises along the Magdalena River. Workers seemingly started to be successfully demobilized through the new state policies and became compelled to enter into agile negotiations, thus avoiding, as was intended, any disruption to the activities of capitalist entrepreneurs and the country's economy, which greatly pleased a regime increasingly concerned over and afraid of labor agitation.[38]

Space limitations preclude us from discussing further these norms and their context in more detail. For now it shall suffice to emphasize that they introduced special procedures (arbitration, in particular) to solve labor disputes, procedures that later, during the 1940s, would become central mechanisms of labor justice as such. It is worth mentioning as well, at least briefly, the law that modernizing Conservative President Pedro Nel Ospina signed in November 1923, establishing the General Labor Office (*Oficina General del Trabajo*), quite similar to the Department of Labor created over a decade earlier (1908) in Chile and a couple of years later (1926) in Bolivia, as discussed in Chapters 10 and 7 of this volume, respectively. This institution, whose main purpose was to develop regular inspections of industries and other workplaces, seems to have obeyed the ruling elites' conviction on the need to reduce social and labor conflicts. Following the logic and procedures typical of "policing" (meaning the protection of "security, morality, and public hygiene"), the General Labor Office assumed quasi-judicial functions. This aspect reflects the deeper lineage or "archeology" of labor justice.

It must be observed that this was not the first time an initiative to "inspect" workplaces to preempt potentially greater conflicts took place in Colombia. A constitutional reform (*Acto Legislativo No. 1*), passed in 1918, had established the basis for the inspection of said spaces.[39] For instance, that same year in the city of Medellin, Antioquia, cradle of Colombia's industrialization, an Office of Factory Inspections

(*Oficina de Inspección de Fábricas*) was put in place, which was also known as Factory Police (*Policia de Fábricas*), a pioneering experience in the country. Its mission was to conduct inspections as a means to monitor the observation of moral, safe, and hygienic practices in all of the city's workplaces with more than ten workers.[40] This institution was particularly focused on preempting the work of children under ten years of age, ensuring that any workers under fifteen, and women, did not work more than eight hours a day and that pregnant women were asked to perform just "gentle" work. It also had to ensure that workers were not fined excessively, that families of workers who suffered any accidents be allowed to retrieve their belongings, and so forth. This office actually performed inspections of local breweries, textile mills, shoemaking factories, and mills processing grains. Inspectors produced detailed reports about their visits that, due to the lack of a specialized labor justice to file them before and process them, resulted mainly in police or administrative sanctions.[41]

According to the 1923 law creating the General Labor Office, the main objective of this entity was to "ensure compliance with laws aimed at fomenting *social action*, improving the condition of the working classes, and promoting their development and prosperity" [emphasis added]. This same office had the mission of drafting a legal codification titled Code of Labor (*Código del Trabajo*), intended to regulate in a comprehensive manner the activities of the laboring classes and their conflicts.[42] In the meantime, the Office would be in charge of surveilling and studying all matters that

> are related to the conflicts between workers and capitalists over wages; individual and collective insurances; housing for workers (*obreros*); the application of norms concerning hygiene and health in factories and industrial and commercial enterprises; work accidents; female and child labor; the civic education of the proletarian classes; minimum wages; technical training; and, for the combat of vagrancy, syphilis, alcoholism, tuberculosis and other diseases impacting primarily the proletariat.[43]

This enormously telling list of issues foretold most of the themes to be addressed not only by the newly created institution but also by an entire field of law in the making and on its way to reaching symbolic maturity through the production of a specialized codification—namely, labor law. The list also made apparent the active involvement of the central state in the relations between workers and capitalists, which even included the entrance of state officials inside of the factories, workshops, and other collective workplaces, through regular administrative inspections. All of this, in any event, as in the Medellin experience, still continued to be restricted to police and administrative regulations and litigation before civil magistrates, with observance of the usual procedures ordinarily followed in civil or commercial conflicts (over, say, sales, loans, or, in this case, the "lease of labor services"). It would be during the 1930s that special labor procedures, oral and summary, came into place even before a specialized labor justice surfaced a decade later, in the mid-1940s. However, before considering such developments it is critical to notice that neither the regulation of strikes, nor man-datory conciliations or regular inspections to workplaces sufficed to entirely mollify workers, reduce their frustration, or lessen their labor protests or the political agitation that typically accompanied these. It is no wonder that experts on the subject refer to the years 1924–1929 as the period of "spontaneous strikes."[44]

A good proportion of the labor mobilization and protest, including the three biggest strikes of the 1920s, occurred in oil and banana enclaves under the control of American companies. In October 1924, for instance, about three thousand workers of the Tropi-cal Oil Company, organized under the "Sociedad Obrera de Barrancabermeja" took to the streets. In the process, they destroyed the company's plant and the railroad tracks, blocking the use of all of the company's vehicles. They even took temporary control over the port city, north of the Magdalena River, where the dramatic events occurred. The movement faced violent repression and officially there was at least one fatality. The company fired hundreds of workers and had them expelled from the city. Never-theless, this did not preempt another strike from happening a couple of years later, in 1927, during which at least two more workers died and many suffered imprisonment or exile, as the entire country was placed under a "state of siege." Between October and November 1928, banana workers employed by the United Fruit Company declared another strike, with an even more tragic outcome. The army's intervention to put down the movement is said to have caused between 60 and 2,000 deaths, depending upon the version.[45] This so-called "massacre of the banana fields" was immortal-ized in Gabriel Garcia Marquez's *One Hundred Years of Solitude*. The incident caused a heated parliamentary debate in September 1929, led by the prestigious Liberal lawyer and congressman Jorge Eliecer Gaitan, who by then had already become one of the most visible spokesmen on behalf of the labor movement.[46] Several more popular protests, the crisis of 1929, and the party's internal division led to the collapse of the Conservative regime in 1930. Liberals, now the government party, would soon lead the production of a new series of labor laws, including the ones giving origin to the labor "jurisdiction" as such.

The Birth of Corporatist Labor Justice and Procedures, 1930–1950

The ascent of Liberalism brought about a new labor climate, and relations between the Colombian government and workers experienced positive changes, at least dur-ing the early years. For instance, labor organizations and protests fell under more clear regulation, later true institutions, during the beginning of the administration of Liberal lawyer, journalist, former Minister of the Treasury, and former diplomat Enrique Olaya Herrera. Early on during his term in office, Olaya Herrera signed Law 83, 1931. This was not truly the result of immediate identifiable labor struggles but, rather, appears to have been a state initiative to channel institutionally future labor organizations and protests establishing precise parameters for their development.

Even though the law prohibited labor organizations' participation in politics, under threat of their dissolution, workers now had an explicit right to organize unions and demand sanctions against those who obstructed their creation or hindered the affiliation of workers to them. The favorable interpretation and application of the new statute by the government had a major impact, which can be measured statistically. During the decade following the law, six times more unions were chartered than during the three decades prior to it. Many such unions were organized even under the aegis of the government's Office of Labor and in its very building, and several more surfaced inside of the public service sector. It is also meaningful that three strikes that took place in 1931 did not turn violent at all.[47] It was apparent that the Liberal Party was determined to court the labor movement and win its support. The civil character of the processing of labor disputes, however, did not change during the early years of the law's implementation.

The Judicial Code issued that same year of 1931 provided that all contractual disputes, including labor ones, would be processed before civil judges and following the rules ordinarily applied to civil proceedings. During the middle of the decade, a first specialized procedure surfaced, designed specifically to address labor conflicts, but civil judges remained in charge. Law 10, 1934, and Decree 652, 1935, both signed by Olaya Herrera's successor, Liberal Alfonso López Pumarejo, put in place the first statute for "particular workers." These norms entrusted municipal civil judges with the resolution of conflicts between employers and workers through oral hearings, which was emblematic of the attempt to solve cases in a summary manner. Still, the government continued to approach labor disputes as derived from a contract among equals and, rather than favoring them, even exhibited suspicion toward workers.

Early in 1936, for instance, some labor conflicts elicited serious concern on the part of the government. In a letter sent to the Governor of Antioquia, concerning a protracted strike in the El Rosellón Textile Mill, in the city of Envigado, neighboring Medellin, the Minister of Government (Interior), Alberto Lleras Camargo, argued that it was indispensable to "build a national front against communist agitation."[48] In part to contain the alleged communist threat, the government undertook additional social reforms, even amid fierce opposition from both the Conservative Party and the Catholic Church.[49] Workers, of course, sided with the government and marched massively to support the social reforms under consideration. Even Communist Party leaders, following the strategy of a Popular Front against fascism approved in the Seventh Comintern (Communist International), spoke in favor of the constitutional reform being promoted by President López.[50] Through the appointment of Liberal lawyer Jorge Eliecer Gaitán, widely admired by the masses, as mayor of the city of Bogotá, President López probably tried to shore up popular support for his government. With the lower classes behind his administration, the López reform was eventually approved in August 1936.

The Colombian constitutional amendment of 1936 echoed worldwide debates around "social" issues, even the "social function" of private property, an idea drawn from French solidarism in the legal field, an aspect discussed in Chapter 1.[51] The reform actually provided that labor itself was a social obligation and deserved the state's special protection. Furthermore, it conferred constitutional status to freedom of association and the right to strike, except in activities linked to "public services." Through it, two important institutions were also established: the Department of Labor and the Social Protection Savings Bank (*Caja de Prevision Social*).[52]

The social and labor reforms promoted by the Liberals did not stop there. Law 96, 1938, enacted by the moderate government of lawyer, journalist, former minister, and diplomat Eduardo Santos, gave birth to the Ministry of Labor, Hygiene, and Social Protection.[53] An additional constitutional reform (*Acto Legislativo 1*), enacted under Santos, ordered the establishment of a "special labor jurisdiction" (*jurisdicción especial del trabajo*).[54]

Finally, in the mid-1940s, as part of a broader series of labor reforms, labor justice became detached from civil law (*jurisdicion ordinaria*) and acquired independent institutional status. Emergency Decree 2350, issued under a state of siege in September 30, 1944, during Alfonso López Pumarejo's second administration, built upon legislative initiatives discussed over the previous six years in Congress. According to the decree, these initiatives had received approval from legislative commissions, organized workers, and capitalists ("economic groups, industrialists, agriculturalists, big and small entrepreneurs"). The statute addressed collective bargaining and trade unions, and it paved the ground for the future relegalization of strikes.[55] However, its purpose was actually to eliminate the causes behind unnecessary "clashes" between workers and employers, promoting the "pacific resolution of conflicts," and thus diminishing the "grave danger" labor conflicts were said to represent to public order.

The López government argued that the new legislation was not only a means of restoring social peace but also a response to "international obligations" under which the country could not delay any longer the "modernization of labor statutes." President López claimed as well that, given that the country was at war (having declared belligerency against Germany in November 1943), it was indispensable to strengthen the cooperation between salaried workers and employers, ensuring equitable compensation for the former and the reduction of any juridical insecurity for the latter.[56] Besides determining that it was to be a permanent rather than an emergency institution, following this cooperative (corporatist) spirit, the decree also put together the organic structure of the new labor jurisdiction. By design, similar to, among others, the cases of Chile and Brazil examined in this volume, it was to be composed of representatives from all parties critical to labor disputes—labor, capital, and the state.

The new specialized labor justice was to be made up of Municipal Labor Tribunals (Courts) in charge of processing disputes in the first instance; Seccional Labor Tribunals, above the municipal ones, charged with hearing appeals and processing a few cases in a single instance; and the Supreme Labor Tribunal, as the highest court of appeals (*órgano de casación*). Reflecting the government's apparent populist leanings, each tribunal was to be composed of a representative from the laboring groups, one drawn from employers, and one more, who presided over it, from the state. Only those on the Supreme Labor Tribunal had to be law graduates. Proceedings, which up until then had been under civil ("ordinary") courts, now came under the new tripartite tribunals. The mentioned decree established also the basic principles guiding procedural labor law thereafter, which continue to be in place up until the present: orality, complementarity, conciliation, publicity, propinquity, and the equitable evaluation of evidence, among others.[57]

President López argued that, despite opposition from many journalists and political leaders to the use of the executive's emergency powers to regulate labor issues, which they deemed unrelated to the maintenance of public order, the new labor jurisdiction and all of its principles were actually indispensable to avoid the unleashing of "unprecedented social agitation, a wave of strikes, and disorder" should the country return to normalcy. He also acknowledged that, once the state of siege came to an end, his provisional emergency legislation had to be followed up by an act of Congress, ratifying or modifying it.[58] That is precisely what, taking advantage of the Liberal majority in Congress, the government accomplished shortly thereafter.

Less than five months later, very likely before the full implementation of the recent emergency norms on labor justice, President López Pumarejo signed Law 6 of February 19, 1945 (known as *Ley General del Trabajo*) declaring the permanent character of the labor jurisdiction. Although article 67 of the new norm reiterated the basic principles of labor procedure (orality, conciliation, and so forth), the law nevertheless proceeded to reorganize labor courts in a significant manner. Instead of the tripartite ones established the year before, at the municipal level the new law created Labor Courts (*Juzgados del Trabajo*) presided over by an individual magistrate. Appointed by the Sectional Labor Courts, the magistrate's job was to decide some labor conflicts in a single instance and many others in the first instance, depending upon the value of the plaintiff's claims. At the regional level, the law left in place the Sectional Labor Tribunals (*Tribunales Seccionales del Trabajo*) that would be composed of three representatives selected (by the Supreme Court of Labor) from lists forwarded separately by the government and by workers' and employers' associations. These tribunals were exclusively in charge of hearing appeals. Finally, as an appeals court in the last instance, there was a Supreme Court of Labor, whose three members were designated by the House of Representatives on the basis of three lists forwarded by the president, each one made up of three candidates. In turn, the president's lists of candidates resulted from rosters proposed respectively by workers, employers, and the government itself.

Although promoted by a Liberal regime, the structure of all of these judicial institutions ultimately embodied not just a populist approach to the labor question but also corporatist ideals.[59] Interest groups, rather than individuals, were the focus of the state's efforts to form a sort of organic community capable of coordinating labor and capital for the neutralization of social conflict and the promotion of collective harmony. Much less populist in orientation than the previous norm was the fact that, in the new one, none of the labor judges, whether at the municipal, regional, or national level, could be a layperson. They all had to be professional lawyers, ideally experts in labor law.[60]

To ensure that the norm would be implemented, the president was given a five-month deadline (until July 20, 1945) to organize the new system of courts, provide a budget for it, and establish the precise procedure the new courts were to observe.[61] Shortly thereafter, forty-eight labor courts, fifteen labor tribunals, and the Supreme Court of Labor were put in place throughout the country.[62] Further research would be necessary to ascertain the actual operation and impact of the new organs. It is clear, in any case, that a labor jurisdiction came into existence in the mid-1940s thanks to the Colombian Liberal Party's corporatist push to articulate capital and labor in an effort to channel and reduce social conflict on a more permanent basis.[63] The fact that in the next few years a Code of Labor Procedure was put in place, this time by a Conservative administration, is indicative that the labor jurisdiction came to stay.[64]

Conclusion

The passing of constitutional and legal norms (both procedural and substantive) and the creation of related institutions—social institutions, in general, and labor institutions, in particular—presented peculiar characteristics in Colombia. Some of this was the result of the strategy of Conservative and Liberal elites intent on reducing actual or future social conflicts, which it was feared could easily worsen. Before the norms were adopted there were actually intense labor struggles, in particular some related to a strategic geographical axis linked to the transportation, both in and out of the country, of commercial goods, including mineral products, raw materials, and agrarian foodstuffs—the Magdalena River. Several more were labor conflicts also related to another vital means of transportation, railroads. Other labor disputes were linked to the extraction of oil by American companies, such as Tropical Oil, and to the construction of public works in the 1920s, a period of intense influx of foreign capital, rightly known as the "dance of millions." Acute conflicts in the textile industry came to aggravate the situation during the 1920s and 1930s, as did the struggles of agrarian workers around the same years, especially those working for the multinational banana producer, United Fruit Company, in the Magdalena region.

This chapter, however, acknowledges the impact of some international factors that contributed to the eventual emergence of special labor procedures and a specialized labor justice and jurisdiction in Colombia during a particular moment in the country's history. Despite the various national idiosyncrasies observable in Colombia or in other countries of the region, as Chapter 1 clearly established, the construction of a labor/social institutionality in Latin America and elsewhere occurred during a far-from-coincidental period: approximately between 1920 and 1950. Besides the nature of capitalist development at a global level, three of the international factors that most contributed to the growth of labor law and labor justice include reformist European ideologies, even Catholic Social Doctrine, socialist ideas from the mid-to-late nineteenth century, and the French solidarist ideology in the legal realm; watershed sociopolitical events such as the Mexican and Soviet Revolutions; and, finally, the creation in 1919 of the ILO, an institution with a truly global reach and impact.

In this internal and external context, like the rest of those in the region, the Colombian state gradually developed a specialized set of labor institutions derived in part from elements of military justice, commercial law *(ius mercatorum)*, ecclesiastical law, and police regulations. Labor justice was also the offspring of ordinary civil justice, which had dominated ideologically the judiciary throughout the liberal nineteenth century and continued to prevail until the 1930s. During this decade, Colombia's Liberal party put an end to the forty-year (1886–1930) hegemony of the Conservatives. Revitalized by a new social vision about the mission of the state, Liberals modified their classical *laissez faire* ideology, "embraced" the cause of the working class and, apparently inspired by corporatist models prevalent in other countries of the region, promoted labor legislation aimed at neutralizing communist threats regarded as imminent. Some of this legislation involved the creation of a specialized and summary labor jurisdiction, projected as more responsive to the needs of the laboring classes through agile, oral, public, equitable, and no-cost procedures. The study of the actual operation of this jurisdiction during its early years awaits further research.

Notes

The authors thank Universidad Nacional de Colombia's Ms. Natalia Soto González for her research assistance. Also professor Mauricio Archila, Frank Luce, and the editors, Palacio and Fink, for their valuable comments and suggestions.

1. For some valuable legal manuals and compilations see, in particular, Sánchez, *Manual teórico y práctico*; Herrstandt, *Tratado de derecho social colombiano*; Vives Echeverría, *Derecho procesal del trabajo*; González Charry, *Doctrinas y leyes del trabajo*; Zubiría y Consuegra, *Derecho colombiano del trabajo* and *El derecho del trabajo*. All published in the mid-1940s and 1950s.

2. Rojas and Moncayo, *Luchas obreras y política laboral*. For important case studies on the history of Colombia's labor movement, labor struggles, and working-class culture, respectively, see Urrutia, *Historia del sindicalismo colombiano*; Pecaut, *Sindicalismo y política en Colombia*; and, Archila, *Cultura e identidad obrera*. For a comparative perspective, see Bergquist, *Labor in Latin America*.

3. Notice that this chapter distinguishes *justice* from *jurisdiction*. The former concerns the resolution of labor disputes, whether this is done by judges who, at the same time, address other types of conflicts, civil and commercial, for example. The latter presupposes a specialized body of judges with exclusive competency over labor disputes.

4. Silva Romero, *Flujos y reflujos*, ch. 1–3.

5. Rodríguez, "La justicia laboral."

6. Nemogá, "Contexto social y político," 1, 215–259.

7. Vives Echeverría, *Derecho procesal del trabajo*.

8. Most recently, those associated with the Catholic social doctrine found most especially in Pope Leo XIII's 1891 encyclical *Rerum Novarum* on the rights and duties of capital and labor.

9. Mitchell, *Essay on the Early History*, 22–38. The concept of "fuero," rooted in colonial times, included special legal regimes not only for specific localities, regions, or geographical entities (kingdoms), but also for specific corporations—in particular, the army and the clergy. This concept became central to the labor realm as time went on, especially to refer to legal protections for trade union leaders in view of their vulnerability.

10. In other regions of Spanish America, antecedents can be found even in late colonial times. See Chandler, *Social Assistance and Bureaucratic Politics*.

11. Sowell, *Early Colombian Labor Movement*; Gutiérrez Sanín, *Curso y discurso del movimiento plebeyo*. A good example of socialist (and communist) ideas can be found in the newspaper *El Alacrán*, published by two Newgranadan intellectuals.

12. In 1843, a law created an association for the mutual benefit of the military and their families, modeled after colonial mutual aid institutions. See the June 9, 1843, law reestablishing the Monte Pío Militar.

13. Gaviria Liévano, *El liberalismo y la insurrección de los artesanos*.

14. References to an artisanal riot in Bucaramanga in 1883 against German merchants and the destruction of public lamps in Bogotá in 1893 as a protest against the government can be found in Archila, *Cultura e identidad obrera*, 89–90.

15. Antecedents of several of these norms can be found in the *Código Militar*, Law 35 of May 1881.

16. The protection of people considered vulnerable as a result of illness, age, or social condition dates back to classic antiquity and came to be an integral part of canon law since medieval times. See Helmholz, *Spirit of Classical Canon*, ch. 5, esp. 122, 126.

17. Examples of individual concessions at the end of the century can be found in Law 11 of 1884 that, in its only article, granted a pension to the granddaughters of lawyer Crisanto Valenzuela, the "hero" sacrificed during independence. Besides their grandfather's services, a justification behind the pension was that the three of them were living under extreme poverty. See also Law 14 of June 11, 1884, granting a pension to an old man, Antonio Gómez Tobón, a republican soldier who fought in 1819 and, as a sergeant, was forced to retire in 1826 due to disability. Finally, an additional example can be found in Law 16 of July 2, 1884, awarding a pension to the minor grandchildren of republican colonel José Concha, who fought for independence.

18. Article 5, Law 58, 1886.

19. Article 11, Law 58, 1886.

20. Article 13, Law 58, 1886. This law also mentioned a curious category of pensions for cloistered nuns ("monjas enclaustradas") a subject worthy of further research. See article 24.

21. Articles 7 to 9, Law 58, 1846. See Vives Echeverría, *Derecho procesal del trabajo*; González Charry, *Doctrinas y leyes del trabajo*.

22. On the One Thousand Days War, see Bergquist, *Coffee and Conflict in Colombia*.

23. It was composed of 27 representatives designated by the departmental government councils or the juntas in their stead, three per each of the nine departments. One-third were members of the Liberal Party. The gathering was originally expected to be in place for thirty days but ended up operating four separate periods between 1905 and 1909, instead of the

national legislature. A good summary of this period's politics can be found in Henderson, *Modernization in Colombia*, ch. 3.

24. Uribe Uribe referred to this subject in a famous speech on "State Socialism" ("Socialismo de Estado") that he gave in Bogotá's Teatro Municipal in October 1904. For a full text of the speech, see http://cruzadasur.blogspot.com/2012/01/socialismo-de-estado.html (accessed on December 7, 2015).

25. Article 1, Law 6, 1905.

26. Article 3, Law 12, 1907.

27. Poveda Ramos, "Historia de la Industria en Colombia," 98.

28. See Bucheli, *Bananas and Business*.

29. Independent artisans also experienced similar conflicts. Bogotá's tailors, for instance, staged massive protests against the importation of military uniforms in 1919. They were repressed; between 4 and 10 people were killed and no less that 17 suffered injuries. There were shoemaker strikes in Medellin and Bucaramanga in 1920 and strikes of tailors, shoemakers, and bricklayers in Manizales that same year. See Rojas and Moncayo, *Luchas obreras y política laboral*, 38; Archila, *Cultura e identidad obrera*, 211.

30. This is the interpretation advanced by one of the most authoritative experts on the subject. See Archila, *Cultura e identidad obrera*, 131.

31. Uribe Uribe, *Escritos Políticos*, 130, 190–192; Morales Benítez comp., *El Pensamiento social de Rafael Uribe Uribe*.

32. Saenz Rovner, *La ofensiva empresarial*, 135. Leo XIII's famous encyclical *Rerum Novarum* virtually summarized all of Catholic social doctrine's main proposals in favor of workers.

33. See Decree 2, 1918, on the "regulation of strikes" and Laws 78, 1919, "on strikes and labor conflicts" and 21, 1920, on "labor conflicts."

34. *Leyes expedidas por el Congreso Nacional en su Legislatura del año de 1919*, 130.

35. Urrutia, *Historia del sindicalismo colombiano*, 97–98.

36. Since 1916 in various regions of Mexico there came into existence the Juntas de Conciliación y Arbitraje to settle labor disputes. See de Buen Lozano, "El nacimiento del derecho del trabajo," 38; Avella Gómez, "Las instituciones laborales en Colombia," 24; Suarez-Potts, *The Making of Law*.

37. See Law 21, 1920.

38. On the efficacy of the new institutions see Rojas and Moncayo, *Luchas obreras y política laboral*, 46.

39. The norm provided that "state authorities shall inspect industries and professions regarding morality, safety and public health." ("*Las autoridades inspeccionarán las industrias y profesiones en lo relativo a la moralidad, la seguridad y la salubridad públicas*"). Acto Legislativo No. 1, 1918. See also Molina, "La Inspección de Trabajo en Colombia," 65–92.

40. It was created through Ordenanza No. 25, 1918. See García Londoño, *Niños trabajadores y vida cotidiana*, 20. See also Restrepo Ochoa, "La Asamblea Departamental de Antioquia," 443; Archila, *Cultura e identidad obrera*, 131.

41. Restrepo Ochoa, "La Asamblea Departamental de Antioquia," 445–448.

42. In 1926, under the dictatorship of Miguel Primo de Rivera, Spain enacted a similar code. See the Real Decreto, August 23, 1926. Cited in de Buen Lozano, "El nacimiento del derecho del trabajo," 36.

43. See Law 83, November 1923, article 2.

44. Urrutia, *Historia del sindicalismo colombiano*, Chapter VII. For full statistics on the labor conflicts of the period 1919–1929, see Archila, *Cultura e identidad obrera*, 223, 227.

45. According to various sources, the number of dead was either 60, 100, 400, 800, 1000, 1500 or 2000. See the various studies cited by Bucheli, *Bananas and Business*, 132.

46. Urrutia, *Historia del sindicalismo colombiano*, 129–131. See also Rojas and Moncayo, *Luchas obreras y política laboral*, 54–56.

47. Between 1909 and 1931, 126 trade unions were recognized, all of which had been created under the mechanisms provided for civil associations. Between 1931 and 1941, about 659 more were established and legalized. See Urrutia, *Historia del sindicalismo colombiano*, 76, 137.

48. See part of the text in "Colombia y el Mundo, 1936," *Credencial Historia*, 207 (Marzo, 2007).

49. In March, Conservatives and the clergy claimed that the social reforms to the country's constitution proposed by the Liberals represented a true "revolutionary upheaval as inopportune as it was disgraceful." They assured that if the reform project was taken out of the political scene, "as if by magic the civic life of the country would be normalized and tranquility, safety, and trust restored." "Colombia y el Mundo, 1936," *Credencial Historia*, 207 (Marzo 2007).

50. Urrutia, *Historia del sindicalismo colombiano*, 142–143.

51. Mirow, "Origins of the Social Function."

52. Tirado Mejía, *Aspectos políticos del gobierno* .

53. Decree 996, 1938, developed the new law.

54. See the only article that constituted Acto Legislativo 1, September 19, 1940.

55. On July 10, 1944, López had faced a coup attempt after which he prohibited strikes and ordered the mandatory arbitration of labor conflicts. See Decree 1744, 1944.

56. See "Circular del Presidente López sobre el Decreto que regula las relaciones de patronos y trabajaores y establece la jurisdicción especial del trabajo," *Diario Oficial*, No. 25659, October 3, 1944, 17; and Decree 2350, 1944, *considerandos*.

57. See, in particular, article 37, Decree 2350, 1944.

58. See "Circular del Presidente López," 17.

59. *Populism* is broadly understood here as a political movement alleged to embody the interests of ordinary people, workers in particular.

60. See article 64, Law 6, 1945.

61. See articles 66 and 67, Law 6, 1945.

62. See articles 2 and 3, Law 26, 1946, and art. 4, inciso 2, Decree 2158, 1948.

63. See González Charry, *Doctrinas y leyes del trabajo*, 364–381.

64. Decree 2158, June 24, 1948; Law 90, 1948.

Bibliography

PRIMARY SOURCES—CONTEMPORARY LAWS AND DECREES

Jurisdiccion del Trabajo. Organización y procedimiento. Bogotá: Imprenta Nacional, 1948.

Leyes expedidas por el Congreso Nacional en su Legislatura del año de 1919. Bogotá: Imprenta Nacional, 1920.

Morales Benítez, Otto, comp. *El Pensamiento social de Rafael Uribe Uribe.* Bogotá: Biblioteca del Ministerio del Tabajo, 1960.

Uribe Uribe, Rafael. *Escritos Políticos.* Bogotá: Editorial Populibro, 1977.

SECONDARY SOURCES

Archila, Mauricio. *Cultura e identidad obrera. Colombia, 1910–1945*. Bogotá: CINEP, 1992.

Avella Gómez, Mauricio. "Las instituciones laborales en Colombia. Contexto histórico de sus antecedentes y principales desarrollos hasta 1990." *Borradores de Economía*, Banco de la República, 613 (2010): 1–87.

Bergquist, Charles. *Coffee and Conflict in Colombia, 1886–1910*. Durham, N.C.: Duke University Press, 1978.

——. *Labor in Latin America: Comparative Essays on Chile, Argentina, Venezuela and Colombia*. Stanford, Calif.: Stanford University Press, 1986.

Bucheli, Marcelo. *Bananas and Business. The United Fruit Company in Colombia, 1899–2000*. New York: New York University Press, 2005.

Buen Lozano, Néstor de. "El nacimiento del derecho del trabajo." In *Instituciones del derecho del trabajo y de la seguridad social*. Néstor de Buen Lozano and Emilio Morgado Valenzuela, Coords. 27–46. México: Academia Iberoamericana del Derecho del Trabajo y de la Seguridad Social-UNAM, 1997.

Chandler, D. S. *Social Assistance and Bureaucratic Politics: The Montepios of Colonial Mexico, 1767–1821*. Albuquerque: University of New Mexico Press, 1991.

"Colombia y el Mundo, 1936." *Credencial Historia*, 207 (Marzo 2007).

García Londoño, Carlos Edward. *Niños trabajadores y vida cotidiana en Medellín, 1900–1930*. Medellín: Universidad de Antioquia, 1999.

García Villegas, Mauricio, and Boaventura de Souza Santos, eds. *Caleidoscopio de las Justicias en Colombia*. 2 vols. Bogotá: Colciencias-ICANH-Universidad de Coimbra-Universidad de los Andes, 2004.

Gaviria Liévano, Enrique. *El liberalismo y la insurrección de los artesanos contra el librecambio*. Bogotá: Universidad de Bogotá Jorge Tadeo Lozano, 2002.

González Charry, Guillermo. *Doctrinas y leyes del trabajo: jurisprudencia del H. Tribunal Supremo del Trabajo correspondiente a los años 1947, 1948 y 1949 y junio inclusive de 1950. Organización judicial del trabajo, código sustantivo del trabajo y código de procedimiento en los juicios de trabajo*. Bogotá: Universidad Nacional de Colombia, 1950.

Gutiérrez Sanín, Francisco. *Curso y discurso del movimiento plebeyo (1849–1854)*. Bogotá: IEPRI-El Ancora Editores, 1995.

Helmholz, R. H. *The Spirit of Classical Canon Law*. Athens: Georgia University Press, 2010.

Henderson, James D. *Modernization in Colombia: The Laureano Gómez Years, 1889–1965*. Gainesville: University Press of Florida, 2001.

Herrstandt, Ernesto. *Tratado de derecho social colombiano. Comentarios. Código sustantivo y procedimental del trabajo. Jurisprudencia del Tribunal Supremo del Trabajo*. Bogotá: Editorial Kelly, 1951.

Mirow, Matthew. "Origins of the Social Function of Property in Chile." *Fordham Law Review* 80 (2011): 1183–1217.

Mitchell, William. *An Essay on the Early History of the Law Merchant: Being the York Prize Essay for the Year 1903*. Cambridge: Cambridge University Press, 1904.

Molina, Carlos Ernesto. "La Inspección de Trabajo en Colombia." *Revista Lationoamericana de Derecho Social* 6 (Jan.–June 2008): 65–92.

Nemogá, Gabriel Ricardo. "Contexto social y político de las transformaciones institucionales de la administración de justicia en Colombia." In *Caleidoscopio de las Justicias en Colombia*, ed. García Villegas and de Souza Santos, vol. 1. 215–259.

Pecaut, Daniel. *Sindicalismo y política en Colombia*. Bogotá: Editorial La Carreta, 1978.

Poveda Ramos, Gabriel. "Historia de la industria en Colombia." *Revista ANDI* 11 (1970): 1–98.

Restrepo Ochoa, Alejandro. "La Asamblea Departamental de Antioquia y la aprobación de tres policias. Aspectos del Constitucionalismo social antioqueño, 1912–1927." *C&P*, Bucaramanga (Jan.–Dec., 2013): 428–450.

Rodríguez, César. "La justicia laboral." In *Caleidoscopio de las Justicias en Colombia*, ed. García Villegas and de Souza Santos, vol. 2. 615–682.

Rojas, Fernando, and Víctor Manuel Moncayo. *Luchas obreras y política laboral en Colombia*. Bogotá: La Carreta, 1978.

Saenz Rovner, Eduardo. *La ofensiva empresarial. Industriales, políticos y violencia en los años 40 en Colombia.* Bogotá: Tercer Mundo Editores, 1992.

Sánchez, Jorge Enrique. *Manual teórico y práctico del derecho del trabajo colombiano*. Bogotá: Ediciones Lex, 1946.

Silva Romero, Marcel. *Flujos y reflujos. Proyección de un siglo de derecho laboral colectivo colombiano*. 3rd edition. Bogotá: Universidad Nacional de Colombia, 2005.

Sowell, David. *The Early Colombian Labor Movement: Artisans and Politics in Bogota, 1832–1919.* Philadelphia: Temple University Press, 1992.

Suarez-Potts, William. *The Making of Law: The Supreme Court and Labor Legislation in Mexico, 1875–1931.* Stanford, Calif.: Stanford University Press, 2012.

Tirado Mejía, Alvaro. *Aspectos políticos del primer gobierno de Alfonso López Pumarejo, 1934–1938.* Bogotá: Procultura, 1981.

Urrutia, Miguel. *Historia del sindicalismo colombiano. Historia del sindicalismo en una sociedad con abundancia de mano de obra.* 3rd edition. Bogotá: La Carreta, 1978.

Vives Echeverría, José Ignacio. *Derecho Procesal del Trabajo*. Medellín, Universidad de Antioquia, 1950.

Zubiría y Consuegra, Roberto de. *Derecho colombiano del trabajo. Leyes, doctrinas, contratos colectivos, decretos-leyes.* Bogotá: Librería Siglo XX, 1944.

———. *El derecho del trabajo ante la jurisprudencia y la medicina industrial. Código sustantivo y procesal del trabajo y disposiciones legales que los complementan.* Bogotá: Empresa Nacional de Publicaciones, 1956.

CHAPTER 7

Inclusions and Exclusions

From Labor Legislation in the Andean Nations to the Formation of Labor Courts in Bolivia (1900–1952)

ROSSANA BARRAGÁN ROMANO

Introduction

Bolivia, Ecuador, and Peru were marked historically by the magnitude of the indigenous population (between 70 and 90 percent) during the first half of the twentieth century. In these countries where mining and other traditionally "advanced" industrial sectors were relatively small, many lived in indigenous communities and on haciendas (private estates) under specific labor relationships described by various degrees of servitude. The question is whether the indigenous were considered workers or not.[1] The issue is crucial given that the answer would determine the jurisdiction and sphere of operation of the Labor Courts. It is important then to consider, first, the emergence of the social question for each country in the first half of the twentieth century. In Peru the changes are seen as the result of state-centered reforms, while in Ecuador they seem to have been related to the pressure of popular movements. In Bolivia, the introduction of legal changes took place later, although the existence of peasant and indigenous movements was important throughout the century.

Peru would represent, according to Paulo Drinot, a top-down process through which a racialized and patriarchal state was formed with an industrial and civilizing project. In this way, the notion of worker was created with the exclusion of indigenous peoples. The author showed that factory and industrial workers, identified as the agents of progress and civilization, were associated with people of mixed race or European heritage, while indigenous people were characterized as bad workers and as an obstacle to progress. As such, there was a need to redeem them by "de-indianizing" them.[2] During this period, the "Indians" (or Native Peoples, called in contemporary times Indigenous Population or Indigenous People) were at the center of attention of some intellectuals of different ideological positions. The work of School of Arts and Crafts Director Alayza Paz Soldán on *The Indian Problem in Peru* (1928) considered Indians as the source of national setback and weakness, proposing the need for their civilization through education, transport, and industrial work. The so-called "Indian problem" also existed for José Carlos Mariátegui, one of the most important socialist thinkers of the twentieth century, although he proposed other solutions centered on land rights. It was also present in Víctor Raúl Haya de la Torre's founding of the APRA (American Popular Revolutionary Alliance) in 1925; he considered that indigenous people had potential but had to undergo an economic, social, and technological transformation.[3]

In Ecuador, on the other hand, the labor reforms allowed a "revolution in stages," according to Valeria Coronel.[4] The period between 1925 and 1945 was marked by conflicts and negotiations that involved shifting alliances between different groups pressuring for state reforms, particularly for social rights.[5] The expansion of the popular constituency of the different political parties, particularly since 1925, should be understood, therefore, not as the result of the decision of their leaders to seduce the masses with reforms but rather as an inverse process resulting from social conflict.[6] The intervention of leftists coming from the middle classes was also fundamental in the legal transformation of the state, according to Coronel.[7] Finally, it was also significant that the dialogue arose between groups in rural and urban areas, as well as among different regions.

The case of Bolivia is different because the reforms seem in general quite lukewarm and implemented much later than in the other countries. Here, there was a very important movement of indigenous community members who defended their lands inch by inch from the end of the nineteenth century. Laura Gotkowitz called this process "the revolution before the revolution,"[8] a process that nevertheless had no great effect on legislation. My explanation is that the great achievement of the indigenous people in this period was just that: containing the status quo of state power that sought to transform the agrarian structure since at least 1864, to the detriment of communal property. At the same time, the organization of mine workers took place, expanding progressively during the first decades of the twentieth century. Here, as in the case of Peru, there was also dissociation between the industrial workers and the rural Indians.

The differences among the three countries could be attributed not only to the peculiarities of each of them but also to the approach and perspectives of the scholars. More in-depth research is certainly necessary in order to understand the convergences and divergences between Peru, Ecuador, and Bolivia. Beyond the direction of the changes in the first half of the twentieth century, from the top-down or the bottom-up as established by the scholars, this article assumes that the inclusion/exclusion of indigenous people in the category of workers defined by the social laws, by the labor codes and by the labor courts, was a constant dynamic, subject to a broader or narrower definition. This dynamic is precisely the focus of this chapter. The first part of this essay reconstructs the context in which the labor laws were enacted around the "social question" deploying the cases of Perú, Ecuador, and Bolivia (in this order) and the initial experiences in the administration of labor conflicts in the first two countries. Bolivia did not have this earliest experience of managing these labor conflicts until very late. The second part analyzes the tension between the expansion and reduction of the state sphere based precisely on the dynamic of inclusion/exclusion of the indigenous people in labor codification. This codification is part of the judicial-legal renovation resulting from the enactment of new constitutions marked by a different concept of the role of the state in society. The codes outlined the universe to which the new rights of labor would be applied, a universe that could be expanded or restricted. Here we analyze the codes of Ecuador and Bolivia because Perú did not enact one in the same period. Finally, the third part focuses on the case of Bolivia, from the conflicts administered by the Labor Inspection Offices to the emergence and creation of the Labor Courts.

The Rhythm of Changes

Between the end of the nineteenth century and the crisis of the 1930s, the Andean countries experienced important changes. The rise of export industries and growth of cities brought a concentration of workers. In political terms, artisan and worker organizations grew while the ideas of anarchism, socialism, Marxism, communism, and indigenism gained ground. Intellectuals contributed to the ideation of their countries by participating in politics and in the debates of the era. In this context, classical liberalism lost ground and the state began to take on another role, as is thoroughly described in Chapter 1 of this book. "Social Constitutionalism" emphasized the role of the state in the welfare of its citizens,[9] while the concept of a "Labor State" (Drinot) underscored this new role: regulating and protecting workers but also creating the conditions for the industrialization project that would bring civilization and progress. The state's sphere of action grew noticeably,[10] which brought continuous changes in its very structure and in the relations established with society.

This economic, political and social process will first be sketched for each country, where new constitutions were adopted: in Peru in 1920, in Ecuador in 1928, and in Bolivia in 1938, revealing the different political and social rhythms that are also explicit in the social legislation adopted in this period. In all of them, the state assumed the responsibility for the protection of indigenous people by issuing special laws, creating also Labor Inspection Offices and Conciliation and Arbitration Tribunals.

These changes, occurring at a different pace in each of the three countries, are clear in the established new social laws, adopted between 1900 and 1928 (Table 7.1). Peru became the forerunner, while in Bolivia the laws appeared later and were frequently and initially applicable only to certain groups of workers. In Peru, as early as 1904, a professor from the University of San Marcos (Jose María Manzanilla) presented

Table 7.1. Social Laws, 1900–1928, in Bolivia, Ecuador, and Peru

TOPIC	Date	Peru	Ecuador	Bolivia
Work accidents	1911 and 1913	X		
	1921 and 1927–28		X	
	1924 and 1925			X
Limiting work hours of women and children, establishing its conditions	1918, 1921	X		
	1928		X	
Savings and social insurance	1924, 1925, 1926			X
	1926	X	X	
8 hours daily work	1916, 1928		X	
	1919	X		
	1924, 1925			X
Minimum wage of Indians, personal work	1916	X		

Scheme based on a detailed table, using OITe, *Legislación Social de América Latina*, Vol. I, II. Ginebra, 1929.

several bills in Parliament on job-related accidents, hours of work, weekly rest periods, obligatory time off, child and women's labor, contracts, conciliation and arbitration.[11] In the case of job-related accidents, Peru issued some laws as early as 1911, while Ecuador did so in 1921 and Bolivia in 1924. A similar situation occurred with regard to women's labor and child labor: Peru issued laws in 1918; Ecuador did so nearly ten years later. In terms of the eight-hour workday, Ecuador was first (1916), while in Bolivia (1924) it was applied to very limited groups and its extension would take much more time.

The initial experiences in administering social and labor cases linked to all these early changes appears particularly important in Peru and Ecuador where people of the left occupied new posts and state functions. These spaces then became the arena of political and social struggle, particularly important in Ecuador.

Let us summarize the process of change in each country, beginning with the case of Peru. Here, export production—basically sugar and cotton—was clustered on the coast, while minerals were principally located in the Andean mountains. Between 1914 and 1930, there were about 50,000 operators in the mining and sugar industries. The growth of industry also brought increasing power to urban workers. Lima grew from 172,927 inhabitants in 1908 to 223,807 in 1920 (30 percent more) and 376,097 in 1931.[12] Particularly important were bakers, influenced by anarchism, textile workers, and port workers.[13] Anarcho-syndicalism and the organization of the Local Workers' Federation of Lima in 1918 explain the success of the great strike and general movement of 1919, demanding an eight-hour workday and improved conditions.[14]

That same year, the so-called "Aristocratic Republic" (1899–1919) would end with a coup d'état, giving way to the "New Fatherland" (*Patria Nueva*), the eleven-year rule of Augusto Leguía, which would last until 1930. In this period, a new constitution was adopted in 1920 in which national, individual, and social rights would have a significant role. The state assumed its new role of legislating industrial labor (Art. 47) and intermediating in conflicts between capital and labor, creating the Conciliation and Arbitration Tribunals (Art. 48 and 49). The state also established the necessary public assistance, social welfare, savings and health services (Art. 55 and 56). Finally, it assumed functions of "protecting" the "indigenous race" by issuing special laws for its development and culture, recognizing at the same time indigenous communities (Art. 58).

Thus a new social contract began. As Drinot points out,[15] Leguía provoked contradictory interpretations. He has been considered a liberal, a conservative, a defender of the poor, a populist, and a statesman who subordinated his country to imperialist domination. For some, he was a modernizing force; for others, despite the coup d'état, he was the man who allowed for the country's democratization. There are those who highlighted the role he had in putting an end to the oligarchic state by building a new one, developing at the same time the state's institutionalization in the name of the people. His commitment to social justice has also been emphasized, with a parallel drawn to Peronism, as well as his importance for the emergence of the middle and lower classes.

In this period, the "indigenous question" in Peru was very much present. In 1904, one of the greatest anarchist thinkers, Manuel González Prada, published the essay "Our Indians" ("*Nuestros indios*"), proposing that it was an economic and social issue (not attributable to the inferiority of the race, as was frequently asserted in the nineteenth century). The great Marxist thinker José Carlos Mariátegui, influenced by Gonzalez Prada, insisted in 1927 that the Indian issue was a land problem that required the elimination of the feudal system, which was predominant in the rural areas. In 1929, he proposed that the race dispute in Latin America was not ethnic but rather economic and sociopolitical.[16] Mariátegui's writings were essential for Peru's social analysis but also for all Andean countries because he identified the oppressed class as Indian, rather than just proletarian.[17]

In Peru, Drinot underlined the distinction between workers and "Indians," with different sets of rules that would become apparent in the creation of a Labor Section[18] and an Indigenous Affairs Section as two separate entities.[19] The Labor Section was led by intellectuals like Erasmo Roca, a lawyer and writer for the anarchist newspaper *La Protesta*; the socialist Hildebrando Castro Pozo, head of the Indigenous Affairs Section and author of indigenous communities studies; and Haya de la Torre.[20]

In the new Tribunals, claimants and defendants were summoned for conciliation meetings and the chief of the Labor Section would rule on the dispute. If there was disagreement, an Arbitration Tribunal assumed the case, formed by arbitrators representing each of the sides involved, while the Judiciary designated a third member for a final ruling.[21] The Labor Section was a success, both in terms of the number of social organizations that asked to be recognized by the state and by a significant number of disputes mediated between 1920 and 1922. These conflicts ranged from sugar workers from the plantations in northern Peru to workers in the London and Pacific oil companies and hacienda workers. However, indigenous people and women were largely absent.[22]

Despite the temporary success of the Labor Section, it lost importance due to a certain repudiation on the part of employers because of the ineffectiveness of mediations and agreements and because of a less favorable policy that removed from their posts well-known leftists like Roca or Castro Pozo. At the same time, and in response to protests and movements between 1918 and 1921, the elites generated oppositional discourses and policies oriented to persecute and exile those considered to have dangerous labor militancy, including intellectuals. They also encouraged the creation of other parallel labor organizations, and the idea of the redemption of Indians emerged. Later on in 1930, with the fall of the Leguía regime, the Labor Sections were reorganized and several progressive people were designated once again to occupy those posts.[23] Regional Labor Inspection Offices were also created in the principal cities. Despite a more negative perception of the Labor Section, many workers continued to bring in their disputes, throughout the 1930s.[24] Under the Law of April 12, 1930, Labor Courts were introduced in Lima and Callao to deal with claims related to workplace accidents, and years later offices were established for the pro bono defense of laborers in such claims.[25] There was also a tendency to create special jurisdictions for indigenous people.[26] The 1931 strike, called by the CGTP (*Confederación General de Trabajadores del Perú*) and controlled by the Peruvian Communist Party, culminated however in the lifting of civil liberties by decree. Nevertheless in 1935 the Ministry of Public Health, Labor and Social Welfare was created, and in 1936 the attributes of each of its four sections—Sanitation, Labor, Social Welfare and Indigenous Affairs—were established. At the time, Moisés Poblete Troncoso, a specialist in labor in Latin America and at the ILO, recommended the creation of a Ministry of Indigenous Affairs.[27]

In the case of Ecuador, export production consisted mainly of cacao, which was controlled by an oligarchy and a bourgeoisie on the country's coast. There, the Liberal Revolution (1895–1912) gave greater influence to the state, which recovered many of its powers from the church. The liberal radical *caudillo* Eloy Alfaro confronted conservatives and the Catholic Church (source of the common saying, "Lord save us from the Indian Alfaro," or, "*del indio Alfaro líbranos señor*"), expressing the interests of regional oligarchies, although research has shown that his government was also based on small and medium-sized agricultural landowners, indigenous people, and a rising workers' movement.[28]

In 1920 there was a crisis related to World War I (1914–1918) that caused a contraction in the European market for cacao, which was worsened by the appearance of plagues on Ecuadorean plantations. On November 15, 1922, there was an important workers' strike in Guayaquil where hundreds of people were killed. Some believed this was the end of the liberal state. The *Revolución Juliana* of 1925 marked a new direction, as did Leguía in Peru, giving the state a central role. The members of the military involved in the revolution have been called reformists, messianic, and providential, assuming that they represented the people.[29] The protagonists of the *Revolución Juliana* sought "equality for all and protection for the proletarian."[30] No less important was the emergence of the Ecuadorian Socialist Party in March 1926.

In the new constitution of 1929, the Constitutional Assembly introduced a series of "basic rights." The state had to protect the "worker and peasant," legislating according to "the principles of social justice . . . ensuring for all, a minimum of well being, compatible with human dignity" (paragraph 18 of Art. 151). As in Peru, Conciliation and Arbitration Tribunals were created for the resolution of conflicts (paragraph 24 of Art. 151). The constitution also proclaimed the main social and labor rights, such as labor contracts, freedom of association, weekly rest periods, maximum hours of work, and regulations of labor for women and children. The state committed to safeguarding these rights, becoming also the protector of the "indigenous race," particularly in terms of education and economic conditions (Art. 167).

In Ecuador, although the difference between workers and indigenous people existed, as in Peru, a distinct political dynamic developed. The junta of the *Revolución Juliana* (beginning in 1925) assumed not only social welfare as a state responsibility but also played a role in land litigation. With the concept of "workers" within the legal discourse, the collective organization of recognized entities, such as agricultural associations, unions, or cooperatives, was promoted to represent different social sectors as interlocutors with the state. In 1925 the Ministry of Social Welfare and Labor was created, converting labor into a foundational category of rights,[31] and in 1926 the post of Inspector General of Labor was inaugurated.[32] It was precisely within this ministry that the socialist and leftist movement had a key role because through it were channeled the demands of peasants and other laborers.[33] For Coronel, the fact that land was no longer considered as mere merchandise allowed indigenous communities to confront hacienda owners in the highlands and large landowners on the coast.[34]

The dynamic of the Labor Section, and the different resolutions adopted, caused a conservative backlash between 1931 and 1934. The new liberal minister of the *Ministerio de Prevención Social y Trabajo* (MPST) wanted to emphasize the role of social welfare and sanitation, diminishing that of land arbitration. The labor and rural inspectors were eliminated and there was also an effort to diminish the reception of judicial cases.[35] Nevertheless, during this period, the most common conflicts were between haciendas and indigenous communities, between *huasipungueros* (indigenous people who received a parcel of land on a hacienda in exchange for their labor) and communities, and between neighboring peasants. Cases of water and land dispossession were also frequent, and the ministry resolved many cases through processes of partition and adjudication of land.[36] At the same time, the number of associations, unions, and cooperatives grew steadily. In this process, there was a reinforcement of ties with parties of national reach, alliances between workers and peasants, and the creation of peasants' assemblies at a regional and national level.[37] Organizations increased among peasants and among workers, giving rise to the creation of popular fronts like the one that emerged in Guayaquil in 1934 when thousands of workers from 30 organizations came together to fight against speculation. The ministry continued to be important and was also influenced by its own history of relationships with organizations and movements.[38] In response to this dynamic between organizations, unions, and the state bureaucracy, the liberal elite sought greater control, the Labor Ministry was restructured, and a large part of its staff was fired. Socialist Miguel Angel Zambrana continued nevertheless in his post and was commissioned to review labor legislation and prepare the Labor Code. To appreciate the magnitude of the work carried out by the ministry, between October 1935 and August 1937, they processed 2,148 trials and ruled on about 20,000 oral complaints through negotiations that involved the ministry. Under these circumstances, the more conservative groups sought to depoliticize relations with the organizations. During the presidential term of Federico Paez (1935–1937), the 1929 constitution was abolished and the 1906 constitution reinstated. Unions were persecuted and disbanded but later on reemerged with state support.[39] Thus, a new corporatist project was proposed from the top down after reorganizing the ministry and purging most of the socialists.[40]

In Bolivia, entry into the twentieth century was marked by the advent of the Liberal Party, the end of the civil war, and the switch of the political capital from Sucre to La Paz, thanks to the massive indigenous peoples' support, whose main concern was the defense of their lands from being transformed in large haciendas. In 1920 liberalism lost its hegemony: the Republican Party, led by Bautista Saavedra, emerged and had the support of various groups, including indigenous people, because party leaders had provided advice to the important network of *caciques apoderados* (indigenous leaders) in 1916–1917, particularly to the principal indigenous leader Santos Marka Tola. This network emerged as the legal representation for the communities of five of the nine departments, from 1895 until the Chaco War (1932–1933), establishing their aim of protecting their lands, which were threatened by the expansion of the hacienda. It was during this period that the first social laws came about, and here, as in the case of Peru, a split was made early on between workers on the one hand and indigenous people on the other. In October 1920, for example, the Institute of Social Reform was created to come up with proposals for "labor and indigenous legislation" (Supreme Decree October 7, 1920).[41] Despite the "social" commitment of Saavedra's regime, his government took violent action in the rural area of Jesús de Machaca in 1921 and in the Uncía mines in 1923. In the department of Potosí, Oruro, and Chuquisaca, there was also an "epidemic of conspiracies and uprisings" from 1924 to 1927, culminating in a great insurrection—in which about 12,000 indigenous villagers participated—that gave rise to an alliance with socialist sectors.[42]

The comparisons among Peru, Ecuador, and Bolivia show important changes from 1900 to 1930, although the adoption of social laws mainly applied to mine and urban workers. This meant that Indians were in general excluded from these laws. However, the Ministry of Labor in Ecuador became involved in indigenous conflicts, among them land issues. In consequence, in this sense Indians were included in the labor policies, reducing the distinction between "workers" and "Indians" as different groups.

In any case, it is important to underline that in the three Andean countries labor conflicts began to be considered as a special sphere giving place to Conciliation and Arbitration Tribunals, mentioned in the Constitutions of Peru (1920), Ecuador (1929), and Bolivia (Special Tribunals in 1938). In Peru, in 1930, the Law established the first Labor Judges in Lima and Callao while, in the rest of the country, labor conflicts were still heard by the normal judges. However, a decade later, in 1941, Labor Tribunals were established in the entire country.[43] Ecuador seems to be similar to Bolivia: an articulation between the Labor sections of the Ministry of Labor and the spheres of the Judiciary System. There were Labor Inspectors and Labor Commissioners who were in charge of labor conflicts. Their rulings could be appealed to the regular Courts of Justice and to the Supreme Court of Justice.[44]

Between the Expansion and the Restriction of the State's Sphere of Action

The inclusion or exclusion of Indians in the world of workers expanded or restricted the state's sphere of action. This dynamic was present in the descriptions of workers and in the Labor Codes discussed and enacted in the Andean countries. While the Ecuadorian Code had a broad description of workers, implying a wider sphere of action of the state, in the Bolivian Code there was a restricted definition of labor.

Let us start with the diverse and broad world of labor depicted for Peru, because it will allow us to imagine the magnitude of the constant tension of inclusion/exclusion of indigenous peoples in the laws in all three countries. The authoritative treatment of the subject derives from Moisés Poblete Troncoso. His work was the result of the ILO Labor Conference held in Santiago de Chile in 1936, due to the demand of the Peruvian delegate[45] to carry out a study on "indigenous workers" in order to "determine a future continental action for the protection of aboriginal races."[46] The ILO Director Harold Butler assigned this task to Poblete, who received the full support of the Peruvian Minister of Labor and the Office of Labor, Social Welfare and Indigenous Affairs. The author was no doubt familiar with the contributions about the Indians of well-known intellectuals of the time like José Carlos Mariátegui, Hildebrando Castro Pozo, Julio C. Tello, and Luis E. Valcárcel. Additionally, he had the opportunity to hear several presentations and to receive twelve committees of indigenous people who arrived from different parts of Peru.[47]

Poblete presented his lengthy and interesting report in 1938, in which he first asked himself about "the subject" of his investigation, that is to say the Indian, as characterized by his/her economic situation and education. He proposed, on the one hand, that Indians made up the majority of the poor population, "producing little and consuming less," without participating actively in the national mainstream, becoming practically an "almost negative element in the national economy." Thus it was necessary to raise their standard of living, "incorporating the Indian into civilization, and the economic and social structure, making him into an efficient element of progress." Aside from being poor, indigenous people were illiterate or had a very low level of formal education, and resistant to letting go of "their customs and traditions." His calculation of the indigenous population varied according to the breadth of the definition: for some it was barely half a million, while others said it was three-fourths of the Peruvian population. With the most expansive definitions, "secondary types" were included—people of mixed race, such as mestizos born of whites and Indians or the result of other mixes.[48] An estimate of the total population of Peru in 1920 was 5.5 million inhabitants, of which 1,776,000 were classified as Indians, 2,941,500 of mixed race, 610,500 white, 110,000 yellow and 111,000 of "color" meaning mainly black people.[49]

Yet the most interesting part of Poblete's report is the description of the indigenous presence in practically all imaginable jobs. It is thus a definition of the worker that includes the indigenous people in cities, mines, and agriculture. He affirmed that indigenous people in the cities "were part of the workers" in factories; others were craftsmen, domestic servants, and workers in health and sanitation services. He also said that Indians worked in oil fields and in copper, silver, gold, and other mines.[50] Finally, in the rural area they worked in indigenous communities, but also on haciendas. At the time, there were about 2,000 indigenous communities around the country, although it is unknown exactly what their population was or how many hectares they controlled and cultivated. These communities had been recognized in the 1920 constitution and by 1933[51] their lands were indivisible and nontransferable.

He also sustained that more than two-thirds of the laborers working on large agricultural holdings of sugar cane, cotton, coffee, tobacco, and coca were indigenous. The total number of workers between 1919 and 1928 was calculated between 11,000 and 16,000 in rice production,[52] 26,000 and 30,000 in sugar production, and 32,000 and 40,000 in cotton.[53] There were also indigenous workers on large estates and haciendas under a system of sharecropping (rented land in exchange for goods, labor, or a mixture) who were called *colonos* and *yanaconas* that the author identifies with *enganche* or debt bondage workers in sugar cane, cotton, and rice plantations. The author also confirms that in many regions the truck system persisted,[54] that is, payment via vouchers and tokens that forced workers to buy at company stores.

On mining labor, Poblete wrote that there were 22,000 to 28,000 workers,[55] 90 percent were indigenous and the system of debt bondage was frequently used,[56] despite being prohibited in principle. The author also mentioned that all the regulations for hiring labor in the Civil Code—approved in 1936—were very general without any formalities and guarantees; contracts of indeterminate time were the norm, which according to him gave rise to all sorts of abuses,[57] although there was an eight-hour workday set specifically for the mines.[58] Finally, he showed that there was still forced and unpaid servitude among indigenous people, such as for various services in the master's house, mail service,[59] and public works (bridges, roads, and so forth).

Poblete's vision could be applied to Bolivia or to Ecuador: the labor world was very diverse and heterogeneous, and any legislation would have to take into account whether it sought to include all jobs in the various economic sectors and geographic regions. The Andean countries faced this situation in different ways. The three states sought to regroup legislation together, but only Ecuador and Bolivia enacted a Labor Code. Nevertheless, Ecuador opted for a broader labor jurisdiction, taking into account the previous experience it had with the Labor Ministry in dealing with workers from both the urban and rural areas. Bolivia would restrict its sphere of influence to the urban area and to laborers in the narrow sense of the word.

Thus, when Ecuador experienced another period of openness under the alliance between the military and the popular movement during the presidential administration of Enríquez Gallo (1937–1938), the socialists returned to the Labor Ministry and introduced various changes. In July 1938, various services rendered by the indigenous communities for the haciendas were abolished.[60] Another series of measures was also important, including the Cooperatives Law, the law of tenancy and affordable homes, primary and secondary education, salary protection, legal statutes for indigenous communities, and the review of mining concessions. The cases presented to the ministry grew again in different regions and in more than the 40 cases presented, land was the principal reason of contention.[61]

In this context, the Ecuadorian Labor Code was presented to the Constitutional Assembly of 1938.[62] An initial version had been elaborated by Miguel Ángel Zambrano, head of the legal department at the Social Welfare Ministry with the collaboration of other socialists such as César Carrera Andrade, Luis Geraldo Gallegos, and Juan Genaro Jaramillo.[63] As Icaza has shown, a large part of the press reacted negatively, associating the code with communism and the dictatorship of the proletariat. Opponents criticized the code as being a copy of the Mexican Labor Law of 1931, pointing out its nonapplicability to the conditions of the country.[64] This code, unlike the one approved in Bolivia, was much broader and was applied to all *workers*, a term that included employees and laborers alike. As such, it addressed peasant laborers, also known as peons, day laborers, *huasipungueros* of the land estates, piece-rate workers (by unit of work), and *yanaperos* or casual workers (for a specific number of days).[65]

The code received backlash as did other social gains, and the most difficult situation occurred after the resignation of Enríquez Gallo when a liberal-socialist alliance gave the presidency to Liberal Party Director Aurelio Mosquera. The new president did not implement the constitution approved by the Constitutional Assembly and began governing via a civilian dictatorship. Abandoning the 1938 constitution meant abandoning the precepts that forced the state to directly exploit the subterranean wealth and to subdivide large estates into small properties and agricultural cooperatives, and it meant forgetting the "social function" of property and the state protection for laborers and small peasant producers, in terms of the maximum workday, the cost of living, increase in salaries, social security paid by employers, and the protection of union organization.[66] In other words, it was a setback for the workers.

Under these circumstances, in the legislature two sides confronted each other: the socialists, who called for the approval and publication of the code, and the conservatives and liberals. Finally in October of 1938, the code was approved.[67] The dispute gave rise to the formation of the Committee for the Defense of the Labor Code, whose objective was to disseminate the norm among workers. A short time later, the Union of Workers of Pichincha called a general strike for the enforcement of the Labor Code.[68] In other words, the danger that it would remain unapplied brought about its defense. One manifesto from the railway workers of Durán said that "the monied and powerful class" saw the Labor Code as a threat and that despite the fact that a liberal constitution had existed for more than 100 years, until the passage of the Labor Code "the boss was judge and jury" as in countries where slavery existed:

> With the Labor Code, the employer must leave his comfortable featherbed to appear before a judge. This and the cruel exploitation that could victimize the working class have been the reasons that the monied few planned to secure via blackmail and other vile methods . . . the disappearance of . . . the modest legislation of the Labor Code.[69]

However, the ILO representative in Quito, Víctor Gabriel Garcés, former minister of Social Welfare, underlined that it was a copy of the Mexican Labor Law (attempting to delegitimize it) and that it was forcing social payments to be made exclusively by employers.[70] A short time later, in 1940, the government desired to invite an ILO specialist to advise and revise the code, generating immediately "suspicions" among workers, particularly in Guayaquil. The ILO representative himself had to intervene and did so by "depoliticizing the case." For Garcés, it was a merely technical and a specialist matter.[71]

In Bolivia, after the Chaco war with Paraguay, which took place between 1932 and 1935, the social tensions deepened and changes accelerated. The conflict triggered a period of demonstrations, organization of civil society, debates, and reflections, engendering the great reforms of the mid–twentieth century (the National Revolution, with the nationalization of mines and the agrarian reform).

Both the Chaco war and the postwar period pushed a wave of expansion in labor rights. During the war, a series of decrees were issued on salaries: how they should be paid, and the amounts to insure, for example, for transportation from the highlands to the faraway battlefields. After the war, the injured and maimed demanded recognition of various kinds, with all of the legitimacy garnered by having fought for the nation. The Legion of Veterans thus became a fundamental actor in this period.

The result of the war was the ascent of those who called themselves "Military Socialists" (*Militares Socialistas*) in 1936, who held the presidency after a great workers' strike led by Waldo Alvarez, director of the Graphic Union of the Workers' Labor Federation, with a series of demands for veterans and their families, principally salary increases and freedom to associate. Alvarez was then named Labor Minister, seeking in this way political participation for unions. The number of unions increased and, despite attempts to control them, the two principal federations, the Local Workers' Federation (FOL) and the Workers' Labor Federation (FOT) created the Socialist Confederation of Workers of Bolivia.[72] In 1936 there was also a change from the Ministry of Public Instruction and Agriculture to the Ministry of Education and Indigenous Affairs, which synthesized the view and policies that had been emphasized toward the indigenous population. President Germán Busch (1937–1939), one of the main leaders of the Military Socialists, felt that if indigenous people constituted 70 percent of the population, this was the most serious problem the nation had to face. That same year took place the First Inter-American Congress of Indianists.[73]

One of the most important events of this period was the 1938 Constitutional Convention, which came in response to the crisis unleashed by the Chaco War and was also one of its achievements. It expressed the desires for change and the need to redirect political destiny. For the first time, representatives of tendencies deemed "socialist"—perhaps more precisely nonliberal—were present in Congress: laborers' representatives, young people's representatives, representatives of different urban economic sectors, and representatives from Santa Cruz and Beni. It was also crucial because it gave greater importance to the role of the state, and because the debates generated—although not always materializing in immediate constitutional and political changes—the outline, the environment, and the path by which Bolivia would move forward over the next fifty years. There we find the seeds of the 1952 revolution; its future leaders; the presence and voice of the laborers who for the first time entered the legislature; the discussion "about the indigenous people" and "about women," and thus their "absence"; and finally the creation of the ninth department (Pando) in the country.

In this context, the Labor Code was enacted in May 1939 by Busch, which established in its first article that the law determined the rights and obligations of labor "with the exception of agriculture," which should be the object of another law.[74] There was thus a clear focus of the code on the urban area, which restricted its range of action enormously. Therefore, between 70 and 80 percent of the population remained outside the jurisdiction of the Labor Code, implying also a split between the policies toward urban and proletarian workers, on the one hand, and toward the rural and indigenous population, on the other. Nevertheless, more open and inclusive options existed. In doing this research, I found that there were three versions of the Labor Code: the 1935 version by Roberto Zapata, the version by Alberto Mendoza López (although it was not his but rather a bill created under his direction), and the one enacted in 1938.

Roberto Zapata worked for the Social Reform Institute in 1920,[75] created to produce legislative bills on labor and indigenous issues (Supreme Decree October 7, 1920), and was also Director General of Labor during the 1930s. His proposal for the labor code included the rural area and allows us to see how labor and workers were thought about and defined.[76] The labor of workers, defined as *manual labor*—as opposed to professional work[77]—included seven categories of workers: mine workers, industrial and public workers, sharecroppers or peons in haciendas in the rural areas, professionals, home-based workers, independent craftsmen, and domestic workers.[78] This was the broad definition of workers. But in the same code, there was also a narrow definition. It specified that when referring only to "workers," this meant solely those working in mines and industries.[79] Under the broad definition, the sharecropping system on haciendas was recognized and legislated. It was defined as "the assignation of lands and parcels to a community or to individual indigenous people obliged to work a number of days during the week in the owner's land providing also services to the hacienda's house."[80] It is also important to emphasize that "domestic service" was included (Title Four) and legislated in this code.

The other version of the code was elaborated between December 1936 and January 1937 by various members of "the Convention of Labor Employers" led by Dr. Alberto Mendoza López, Director General of Labor; by the Labor Inspectors of the different geographic departments, principally the ones with mining resources; by the Labor Ministry; by the Inspector General; and by representatives of the Workers' Insurance and Savings Fund.[81] This document reveals that the commission that created this code had in its possession more than a dozen drafts. The final proposal was the result of "consultation not only with the dictates of the International Labor Office" but also with the outcomes of various International Conferences, considering the customs of the country and assuming the jurisprudence established by the Supreme Court of Justice, which established "the true basis of Bolivian Social Law."[82]

The Bill regulated the "relations between Capital and Workers" although the word *worker* goes practically unmentioned.[83] It speaks more of employers and employees in five groups of industries: extraction, manufacturing, transport, trade, and agriculture.[84] The preferred term was that of *laborer* (*obrero*), defined as "any person who works physically on projects, in enterprises or industries as a paid employee . . . by virtue of a verbal or written contract."[85] There was a clear distinction between a worker and an employee, the latter defined as one in whose work "intellectual effort predominates over physical effort."[86]

This code was sent to the ILO in Geneva. The correspondence allows us to see that the ILO representatives divided up the analysis of the code by specialty and sent the Bolivian government their comments.[87] In 1939, when Bolivia approved its code, the ILO office suggested carrying out a reading and careful analysis to evaluate the technical advice given.[88] It was surely a great surprise when, after a first reading, a certain M. Nieduszinski wrote that the code was totally different: the previous one had 614 articles and the one enacted included just 121 articles, confirming that some of the recommendations made did not appear at all in the code, particularly those referring to minimum wage, paid vacation, or labor jurisdiction, as well as specifying that it did not apply to agricultural workers.[89] Although we do not know exactly what happened and what were the reasons for enacting a new version, it is fundamental to note that in the end, although following the general guidelines of the ILO, the country made its own decision. Not including the rural area was without a doubt less problematic for the government, given the struggles that had existed for the past fifty years and were still unresolved.

From Work-Related Accidents to the Labor Courts in Bolivia

An initial step toward the emergence of the Labor Courts in Bolivia was the creation of the Department of Labor under the auspices of the Ministry of Industry (Law of March 18, 1926). It was formed by a Director, two District [Labor] sub-Directors (with residence in the departments of Oruro and the Uncía mine, with its jurisdiction extended to the Departments of Oruro and Potosí, respectively), two Trip Inspectors, and a Medical Adviser. The responsibilities of this department were to solve any issue at work, such as accidents in mines, working conditions, and all problems of labor contracts and salary disputes between employers and laborers; to make visits to the mines and industrial establishments; to keep statistics on living expenses; and to formulate reforms on social issues (Art. 3).[90]

One of the main concerns of the Department of Labor was work-related accidents and diseases, covered by the Law of January 19, 1924. Based on this, the department personnel had to supervise safety and protection measures for workers. Companies had to compensate people who had accidents and if they did not do so, the Department of Labor could assume representation of the victim, carrying out a proactive trial or debt collection process in order to achieve severance payment on their behalf. It is important to emphasize that procedures were already outlined for cases of work-related accidents, constituting the basis for the subsequent development of labor cases. A short-term administrative procedure was established and when there was no agreement reached, evidence had to be received within eight days. The District Chiefs gave their rulings and they could be appealed before the Department Chief in La Paz, whose decision in turn could be impugned before the Supreme Court of Justice. A year later, the government installed four Labor Districts with their seats in the main mining regions, with jurisdiction over two or more departments (states) each. The geographic scope of this system of labor justice widened notoriously, from the mines in Oruro and Potosí to all the departments of Bolivia (Chart 7.1). The labor issues ruled on by the Directors of the Labor Districts could be revised by the General Director of Labor, and requests for abrogation and nullity could go then to the District Courts of Justice (juridical level in each of the capitals of the departments or states) or to the Supreme Court of Justice.[91]

Chart 7.1. The Labor Administration and the District Headquarters for the Administration of Labor Justice Courts in Bolivia in 1927

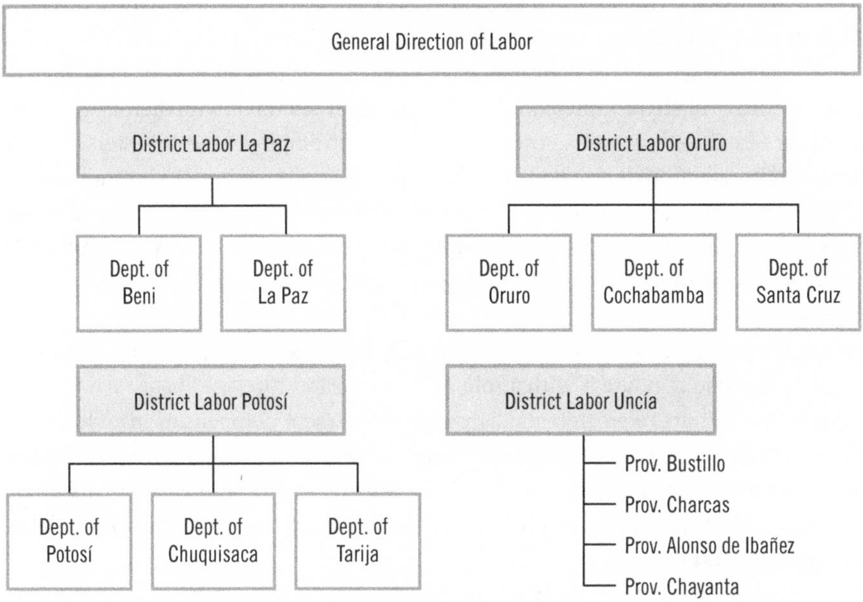

Scheme based on Law of February 12, 1927, in Arduz Eguía, 1941, 77–78.

I managed to find a group of appeal files from this period (116 in total from 1926–1927) in the Supreme Court of Justice in Sucre: 76 out of the 116, or 65 percent, were about compensation related to work accidents in various mines, particularly those belonging to the "King of Tin," Simón Patiño (Patiño Mines Enterprises).[92] However, a ruling in favor of the worker was given to only 11 workers, which is undoubtedly extremely low. In large part, the rulings were in favor of nullifying the demand or declaring it inadmissible or unfounded.

A decade later, in 1936, the Ministry of Labor and Social Welfare was created with the mission of "organization of the labor and wellbeing of the working classes," which were considered "determining factors of socioeconomic progress." It is fundamental to point out that its creation was considered a triumph for workers and received the support of the Socialist Left Bloc in which radicals like Aguirre Gainsborg (founder of POR or the Revolutionary Workers' Party in 1934) and Angélica Azcui were members. Within the ministry and with the counseling of intellectuals, obligatory unionization was promoted.[93] At that time, the ministry had two areas, the Labor Area with eight departments and the Welfare Area with four departments.[94]

Within the Labor Area, the Department of Legal Affairs analyzed legal labor issues, centralized labor contracts created with the intervention of Labor Judges, ruled on files about the creation of unions and the acquisition of legal personality, compiled the decisions of the Supreme Court on trials carried out in the Departments of Labor, centralized agreements and resolutions in the Conciliation Commission and Arbitral Tribunals, and had control and oversight of the Departments of Labor, responding to complaints presented against them as well.[95]

The Department of Inspection received various faculties, including some quasi-judicial: to establish the Conciliation and Arbitration Tribunals with their own norms and procedures and to resolve controversies between employers and workers that fell under its jurisdiction. It also had an important role in all work-related complaints.[96]

The Department of Labor Prosecution took charge of the defense of the working classes. They represented and advised workers who so requested, they promoted conciliation, heard complaints from workers, and presented the necessary appeals for their defense.[97]

The Department of Peasant Labor not only had to study this specific economic activity but also regulate it with a role of "defense and tutelage" (*defensa y tuición*). Among its attributes were the establishment of contracts, compensation for losses in harvests and accidents, establishment of agricultural cooperatives, oversight over the effectiveness of personal services that did not fall under agricultural labor, "supervising and protecting communal properties," studying and proposing the foundations of the Rural Code.[98]

The Social Welfare Area had the "function of protecting the working classes": prevention of accidents, risks, and illnesses. Its Department of Social Protection had to, "through State action, make up for the absence of planning of the working people," that is, to foresee and guarantee their future, eliminating the "causes of their moral and social degradation," regulating social securities and savings.[99]

In 1939 (following the Labor Code analyzed in the previous section), Bolivia enacted new Labor Law that was key to the widening of workers' rights. However, the law established clearly, in its first article, that the rural area was not included because it would receive its own rules. The administration of conflicts that were until then assumed by the Ministry of Labor, particularly in the first instances, were now labeled as the Labor Judiciary (*Judicatura del Trabajo*) under the Judicial Power (Chart 7.2). The Executive Power still had a role because the government named the Judges of the National Labor Court of Justice.

The old headquarters of the District (*Jefaturas de Distrito*) received the new denomination of Labor Courts (*Juzgados del Trabajo*).[100] The National Labor Court replaced the General Direction of the Labor Office, arguing that it was necessary to substitute that "single-person institution" (*institución unipersonal*) with a court and trained personnel,[101] that is, a president and two judges, all lawyers,[102] who had to rule on appeals from the courts of first instance.

Unfortunately, there is no study to date on labor trials in Bolivia, possibly because the archives are not easily accessible and because many have been destroyed. In any case, I managed to synthesize in Table 5 the labor cases that were heard by the Supreme

Chart 7.2. The Labor Judiciary in Bolivia in 1940

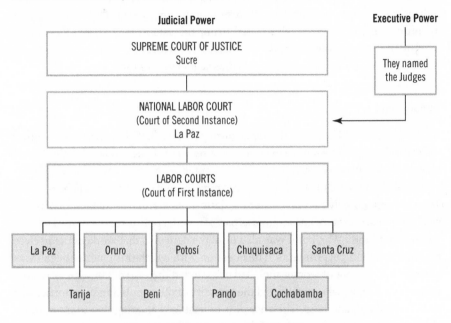

Scheme based on Decree Law of March 2, 1940, in Arduz Eguía, 1941, 409–410.

Court of Justice on appeal, which represent about 15 percent of all cases. Of the total labor cases, more than 95 percent were for compensation relating to work accidents and even deaths. Finally, almost all the appeals were declared unfounded or inadmissible, which means that the Supreme Court was upholding the legal decisions of the lower courts. These statistics coming from the Supreme Court revealed a small labor universe associated in large part with the mines and other urban enterprises.

The table also shows a higher percentage in 1942 and a drastic decrease in 1952, which should be attributed to the Revolution of the Revolutionary Nationalist Movement that led a far-reaching transformation. The Agrarian Reform of 1953 appeared

Table 7.2. Cases Heard by the Supreme Court of Justice, 1939–1954

Summary	1939	1940	1941	1942	1952	1953	1954
Total cases settled	1385	1174	1151	1300	104	726	1021
Labor cases	227	64	175	430	12	128	139
%	16.39	5.45	15.20	33.08	11.54	17.63	13.61
Compensation	224	62	171	425	11	120	106

Table created based on information from the Judicial Gazettes of the Supreme Court of Justice. My thanks to Alfredo Ballerstaedt for his collaboration.

then as the measure for the rural world, putting an end not only to the loss of land of indigenous communities but also to its restoration, a long-lasting problem for almost a century (since 1864). It also eliminated an unpaid system of indigenous labor practiced by large land-states (*latifundios*) owners. The old dream of 1938 to have a special Rural Code was transformed into a very drastic measure in 1953.

Conclusions

As shown in other chapters of this book, during the first half of the twentieth century the countries of Latin America experienced a series of changes related to the "social question." This was expressed in the implementation of social constitutionalism or in the development of the Labor State, meaning the end of the classical liberal state. This was undoubtedly a wave of labor regulations, rights, and protection that nation states began to introduce and assume as part of broader policies that emerged following the First World War, but it was also from the demands that workers themselves placed upon their governments. The question with which this chapter began was whether the concept of worker included or excluded the workers in rural areas and indigenous people, who constituted the majority of the population in countries like Bolivia, Ecuador, and Peru. The answer is crucial in evaluating the extent of those changes and the sphere of action of the Labor Courts.

The review of social laws, codes, and labor courts shows that we cannot reach a categorical answer, but rather we find a tension and dynamic of inclusion/exclusion. At certain points, the indigenous people may be included, while at others excluded; but even more frequent is their differentiation.

The social legislation of the first decades of the twentieth century was designed, for example, fundamentally for workers in the classic sense: urban laborers, given that the measures taken had to do with work-related accidents in industrial places, with work hours, and with the regulation of the presence of women and children in those environments. The constitutions, on the other hand, were much more inclusive, specifying the state's role as protector of the indigenous population's rights. Labor acquired a visibility it did not previously have and this was expressed in the creation of specific institutional instances. Ecuador was absolutely a pioneer, since it created in 1925 the Ministry of Social Welfare and Labor. This country shows also a social and political dynamic in which rural workers and urban workers were more involved and included. In the case of Peru and Bolivia, there was a duality: different departments of labor and of Indigenous Affairs.

The new role of the state in the Andean countries was then present in the new constitutions adopted (1920 in Peru, 1929 in Ecuador, 1938 in Bolivia). This explains the role to mediate labor conflicts in the new ministries created. The Conciliation and Arbitration Tribunals were included in the constitutions, and these were important before the creation of the Labor Courts. The Ministry of Labor had, in the three countries, a role of mediation of conflicts. In all three countries, special spheres of justice for labor issues were implemented after 1930. In Peru, Labor Tribunals were put in place in 1941. In Bolivia and Ecuador, there was an articulation between the Ministry of Labor, within the executive power, and the development of labor courts within the judicial power.

The tension between the inclusion and exclusion of the indigenous population was present much more clearly in the labor codes. In principle, the codes were broad and inclusive. The labor code of Ecuador differentiated the employee from the laborer, including in the latter category both agricultural laborers and nonagricultural ones. In Peru, the rural area was also included, which should have covered a large part of indigenous labor, but in this case the drafts were never enacted. In Bolivia, previous drafts included the situation of the rural area although it was excluded from the Labor Code and from the Labor Law that were finally enacted, indicating in both cases future measures and a Rural Code.

Finally, the sphere of action of the Labor Courts in Bolivia was much more restricted, due to the emphasis placed on work-related accidents and social security issues, including basically workers laboring in mining companies and in some other urban enterprises. Outside of these reduced urban and industrial spheres, a broad group of workers were marginalized from labor courts practically until 1950. Nevertheless, that does not mean that they were absent from the halls of justice. Since land was a key resource around which different types of labor relations were established, the Law of Agrarian Reform in Bolivia not only ended a long process of land struggle, but also started another long phase of litigation with even more radical results than the law that was initially issued.[103]

In any case, the comparisons among these three Andean countries are still a major challenge for future research and historical analysis.

Notes

1. The interrogation also emerges from the knowledge we have of Bolivia, where "worker" by antonomasia is the factory worker or the wage-earning and proletarian miner. Also, as shown by Drinot (in *Allure of Labor*) in Peru, the "Indian" was set in opposition to the industrial worker, with the consideration that the former would be redeemed by industry.

2. Ibid., 33, 37, 39, 49.

3. Ibid., 44–48.

4. Coronel, "Revolution in Stages"; See also Coronel, "Orígenes de una democracia corporativa."

5. Coronel, "Revolution in Stages," X.

6. Ibid., 770.

7. Becker, *Indians and Leftists*.

8. Gotkowitz, *Revolution for Our Rights*.

9. Klein, "'Social Constitutionalism' in Latin America," 258.

10. Drinot, *Allure of Labor*, 7, 9, 31.

11. Klaren, *Nación y Sociedad*, 266.

12. Contreras, *Historia del Perú contemporáneo*, 178, 201.

13. Sulmont, *El movimiento obrero en el Perú*, 78.

14. Ibid., 81–82, 84–85.

15. Drinot, "Introducción."

16. Chang, "José Carlos Mariátegui," 103, 108–110, 114.

17. Bethell, "Political and Social Ideas in Latin America." *Cambridge History of Latin America*.

18. The Labor Section was created in Peru in 1919 within the Direction of Fomento of the Ministry of Fomento or Development. Poblete, *Condiciones de vida y trabajo*, 158.

19. The Indigenous Section was created in 1921 (Decreto Supremo 12 de Septiembre de 1921) in the Ministerio de Fomento. See Poblete, *Condiciones de Vida*, 1938, 163.

20. Drinot, *Allure of Labor*, 64, 66, 68.

21. Arts. 7 to 13 of the Decreto Supremo de 6 de Marzo de 1920. See also Decreto de 27 de Marzo de 1920, Decreto de 9 de Abril de 1920 and Decreto del 14 de Septiembre 1920. Poblete, *Condiciones de vida y trabajo*, 131. In 1931 Labor Inspections were created in industrial areas (Decreto Ley de 17 de Junio de 1931). See also Ley de 23 de Marzo de 1936 (ibid., 136).

22. Drinot, *Allure of Labor*, 71, 78–81.

23. Ibid., 99, 105, 109.

24. Ibid., 114–116.

25. Decreto de 10 de Julio de 1935; Poblete, *Condiciones de vida y trabajo*, 165.

26. Poblete, *Condiciones de vida y trabajo*, 165.

27. Ibid., 132, 163–164. See, about Poblete, Yañez Andrade, "La OIT y la red sudamericana."

28. Ayala, *Resumen de Historia del Ecuador*, 88–89.

29. Paz y Miño, *La Revolución Juliana en el Ecuador*, 29, 32.

30. Cueva, "El Ecuador de 1925 a 1960," 91.

31. Coronel, "Revolution in Stages," 757–758, 787.

32. Ibid., 760.

33. Ibid., 772.

34. Ibid., 813, 851.

35. Ibid., 829.

36. Ibid., 863.

37. Ibid., 872.

38. Ibid., 902.

39. Ibid., 918.

40. Ibid., 914.

41. The Decree established that the Institute had to be integrated by two representatives of the Universities of La Paz, Sucre, Cochabamba, Potosí, Santa Cruz, and Tarija and by representatives of workers associations, one for each capital of the department. Decreto Supremo 7 de Octubre de 1920.

42. Bethell, *Historia de América Latina*, 212.

43. Ley 6871, March 2, 1930, and Ley 9483, December 31, 1941. See Leguía Gutiérrez, "La jurisdicción laboral peruana."

44. See Administración Justicia del Trabajo, in Código del Trabajo del Ecuador: Archive OIT, Ministerio de Previsión Social y Trabajo. Departamento Jurídico, Código del Trabajo,

1938. Code: 3HG (866) A32c and Ministerio de Previsión Social y Trabajo. *Código del Trabajo.* Quito: Talleres Gráficos Nacionales, 1954.

45. Mr. Edgardo Rebagliati, Director of the Labor Department of Peru.

46. Poblete, *Condiciones de vida y trabajo*, 1.

47. Ibid., 4.

48. Ibid., 11–12.

49. Ibid., 9.

50. Ibid., 46.

51. Ibid., 55–56.

52. Ibid., 70–71.

53. Ibid., 66–67, 70–71, and subsequent pages.

54. Ibid., 78–79, 84.

55. Ibid., 105.

56. Ibid., 137, 139.

57. Ibid., 91.

58. Ibid., 122.

59. Ibid., 93.

60. Coronel, "Revolution in Stages," 942.

61. Ibid., 931–933.

62. Icaza, *Historia del Movimiento Obrero Ecuatoriano*, 39.

63. Ayala Mora, *Nueva Historia del Ecuador*, 130.

64. Icaza, *Historia del Movimiento Obrero Ecuatoriano*, 41–43. See also Zambrano, *Breve Historia del Código.*

65. Arts. 241, 242, and subsequent pages of the Code of 1938 and of the Code of 1950. Icaza wrote that the code reduced his scope to urban workers marginalizing rural workers, peasants, and indians; Icaza, *Historia del Movimiento Obrero Ecuatoriano*, 47. Nevertheless, as we have seen, they were included in the code and in comparison to the Bolivian code, the Ecuadorian code is wider in its scope.

66. Ibid., 67.

67. Ibid., 45.

68. Ibid., 47.

69. Manifiesto . . . por la democracia y de América, por la libertad del Ecuador, debe respetarse el actual Código del Trabajo. Eloy Alfaro, Imprenta Tribuna Libre, Septiembre 21, 1939. In Icaza, *Historia del Movimiento Obrero Ecuatoriano*, 48.

70. Archive OIT/ILO Correspondencia Ecuador, 1938.

71. Article in a newspaper. Víctor Gabriel Garcés expone sus opiniones acerca de la revisión del Código de Trabajo. *El Comercio*, Quito 1ero. de Abril de 1940. Archive OIT/ILO. LE 231 Código del Trabajo Ecuador.

72. Gotkowitz, *Revolution for Our Rights*, 112–113.

73. Ibid., 114, n. 71.

74. The Law will establish "rights and duties for labor issues with exception of the rural labor that will receive a special treatment."

75. This could be an influence coming from Madrid where there was an important Institute with the same name.

76. Roberto Zapata, Proyecto de Código de Trabajo, 1935. Archivo OIT/ILO LE 302.

77. Ibid., Art. 1 Disposiciones Generales, hereafter, DG.

78. Ibid., Art. 2 DG.

79. Ibid., Art. 3 DG.

80. Ibid., Art. 108, Second Part, Title 2.

81. OIT/ILO LE 302. Código del Trabajo. Proyecto de Código. Alberto Mendoza. 1935. See back cover.

82. See Presentación in ibid.

83. Archive OIT/ILO LE 302/1. Código del Trabajo. Proyecto de Código. Alberto Mendoza. 1935. The first part of his code had the title "About workers, employers and trade-unions."

84. Ibid., Arts. 1, 3.

85. Ibid., Art. 12.

86. Ibid. Art. 287.

87. Archive OIT/ILO, LE 302.

88. Archive OIT/ILO LE 302—Lettre en français, 19–10–1939, Tixier.

89. Ibid., 25.10.39.

90. Portal Jurídico Libre de Bolivia (LEXIVOX), Law of March 18, 1926. See also Pérez Patón, *Bases del Derecho Procesal del Trabajo*, 911–913; Arduz Eguía, *Legislación Boliviana del Trabajo*, 64.

91. Pérez Patón, *Bases del Derecho Procesal del Trabajo*, 911–913.

92. This percentage could be higher because other cases are also related to compensation although we do not know if they were due to labor accidents.

93. Stefanoni, "Los inconformistas del Centenario."

94. Decreto del 28 de Noviembre de 1938, in Arduz Eguía, *Legislación Boliviana del Trabajo*, 259, and subsequent pages.

95. Cap. III, Art. 6, Arduz Eguía, *Legislación Boliviana del Trabajo y de la Previsión Social*, 262–263.

96. Art. 10, 11 Cap. III, ibid., 266–268.

97. Art. 11, Inciso h, ibid., 274–275.

98. Art. 20, ibid., 273–274.

99. Capítulo V, ibid., 277.

100. Art. 2, Decreto Ley del 2 de Marzo de 1940, that became the Ley el 8 de Octubre de 1941, Pérez Patón, *Bases del Derecho Procesal del Trabajo*, 913.

101. Considerandos y Art. 1 del Decreto Ley del 2 de Marzo de 1940, in Arduz Eguía, *Legislación Boliviana del Trabajo*, 409–410.

102. Art. 3., ibid.

103. Soliz, "Fields of Revolution."

Bibliography

Arduz Eguía, Gastón. *Legislación Boliviana del Trabajo y de la Previsión Social*. La Paz: Imprenta Eléctrica, 1941.

Ayala Mora, Enrique. *Nueva Historia del Ecuador. Vol. 10*. Época Republicana IV. Quito: Corporación Editora Nacional, 1984.

———. *Resumen de Historia del Ecuador*. Quito: Corporación Editora Nacional, 1993.

Barcelli, Agustín. *Medio siglo de luchas sindicales revolucionarias en Bolivia*. La Paz: Editorial del Estado, 1956.

Becker, Marc. *Indians and Leftists in the Making of Ecuador's Modern Indigenous Movements*. Durham, N.C.: Duke University Press, 2008.

Bethell, Leslie. *Historia de América Latina. Política y sociedad desde 1930*. Barcelona: Ed. Crítica, 1997.

———. "Bolivia since 1930," 509–584; Chapter DOI: http://dx.doi.org/10.1017/CHOL97805 21266529.010 (accessed May 10, 2017).

———. "Political and Social ideas in Latin America, 1870–1930," 367–442; Chapter DOI: http://dx.doi.org/10.1017/CHOL9780521232258.01 (accessed May 10, 2017).

———. In *The Cambridge History of Latin America*. Cambridge: Cambridge University Press. Online version: 2015. Book DOI: http://dx.doi.org/10.1017/CHOL9780521232258 (accessed April 23, 2015).

Castro Gomes, Angela de y Teixeira Da Silva Fernando. *A Justica do Trabalho e sua historia*. Brazil: Editora Unicamp, 2013.

Centro Interamericano de Administración del Trabajo. *Colección de anteproyectos y proyectos de Código del Trabajo del Perú*. 1934. Lima: CIAT, 1981.

———. *Colección de anteproyectos y proyectos de Código del Trabajo del Perú*. 1950. Lima: CIAT, 1981.

Chang Rodriguez, Eugenio. "José Carlos Mariátegui y la polémica del Indigenismo." *América sin nombre* 13–14 (2009): 103–112, 114.

Contreras, Manuel y Cueto, Marcos. *Historia del Perú contemporáneo*. Lima: Red para el Desarrollo de las ciencias sociales en el Perú, 1999.

Coronel, Valeria. "Orígenes de una democracia corporativa: estrategias para la ciudadanización del campesinado indígena, partidos políticos y reforma territorial en Ecuador (1925–1944)." In Eduardo Kingman, *Historia Social Urbana: Espacios y Flujos*. Quito: FLACSO, 2009, 323–364: https://www.flacso.edu.ec/biblio/shared/biblio_view.php?bibid=110276& tab=opac (accessed April 14, 2017).

———. "A Revolution in Stages: Subaltern Politics, Nation-State Formation, and the Origins of Social Rights in Ecuador, 1834–1943." PhD diss., New York University, 2011.

Cueva, Agustín. "El Ecuador de 1925 a 1960." In E. Ayala Mora, ed. *Nueva Historia del Ecuador*. Quito: Corporación Editora Nacional, 1983.

Drinot, Paulo. "Introducción: La Patria Nueva de Leguía a través del siglo XX." n.d.

———. *The Allure of Labor: Workers, Race and the Making of the Peruvian State*. Durham, N.C.: Duke University Press, 2011.

Fink, Leon, ed. *Workers across the Americas. The Transnational Turn in Labor History*. Oxford: Oxford University Press, 2011.

French, John. "Another World History Is Possible. Reflections on the Translocal, Transnational, and Global." In L. Fink, ed. *Workers across the Americas. The Transnational Turn in Labor History*. Oxford: Oxford University Press, 2011.

Gotkowitz, Laura. *A Revolution for Our Rights. Indigenous Struggles for Land and Justice in Bolivia, 1880–1952*. Durham, N.C.: Duke University Press, 2008.

Herrera Fabián y Herrera, Patricio, coords. *América Latina y la Organización Internacional del Trabajo. Redes, cooperación técnica e institucionalidad social, 1919–1950*. Michoacán: Instituto de Investigaciones Históricas, 2013.

Icaza, Patricio. *Historia del Movimiento Obrero Ecuatoriano. De la influencia de la táctica del frente popular a las luchas del FUT*. Segunda Parte. Quito: CEDIME, Ciudad, 1991.

Klaren, Peter. *Nación y Sociedad en la Historia del Perú*. Lima: Instituto de Estudios Peruanos, 2008.

Klein, Herbert. "'Social Constitutionalism' in Latin America: The Bolivian Experience." *The Americas* 22, 3 (1966): 258–276.

Leguía Gutiérrez, Joaquín. "La jurisdicción laboral peruana, su competencia y sus órganos" (without any additional information: https://dialnet.unirioja.es/descarga/articulo/2495278.pdf (accessed April 14, 2017).

Organización Internacional del Trabajo. *Legislación Social de América Latina*, Vol. I, II. Ginebra: OIT, 1928–1929.

Paz y Mino, Cepeda. *La Revolución Juliana en el Ecuador (1925–1931)*. Quito: Ministerio Coordinador de Política Económica, 2013.

Pérez Patón, Roberto. *Bases del derecho Procesal del trabajo*. La Paz: Juventud, 1957.

Poblete, Moisés. "La legislation sociale dans L'Amérique Latine." *Revue Internationale du Travail* 17, 1–2 (1928): 51–67, and 204–230.

——. *Condiciones de vida y trabajo de la población indígena del Perú*. Oficina Internacional del Trabajo. Estudios y Documentos. Serie B. Condiciones económicas y sociales No. 28, 1938.

Soliz, Carmen. "Fields of Revolution: Agrarian Reform and Rural State Formation in Bolivia, 1936–1971." PhD diss., New York University, 2014.

Stefanoni, Pablo. "Los inconformistas del Centenario, Intelectuales, socialismo y nación en una Bolivia en crisis (1925–1939)." Tesis Doctoral, Universidad de Buenos Aires, 2014.

Sulmont, Denis. *El movimiento obrero en el Perú, 1900–1956*. Lima: Pontificia Universidad Católica del Perú, 1975.

Tilly, Charles. "How to Detect, Describe, and Explain Repertoires of Contention." *Working Paper Series*. New York, 150, 1–42, 1992.

Yañez Andrade, Juan Carlos "La OIT y la red sudamericana de corresponsales. El caso de Moisés Poblete, 1922–1946." In Herrera y Herrera González, coords. *América Latina y la Organización Internacional del Trabajo. Redes, cooperación técnica e institucionalidad social, 1919–1950*. Michoacán: Instituto de Investigaciones Históricas, 2013.

Ycaza, Patricio. *Historia del movimiento obrero ecuatoriano. De la influencia de la táctica del frente popular a las luchas del FUT*. Segunda Parte. Quito: CEDIME, 1991.

Zambrano, Miguel Angel. *Breve Historia del Código del Trabajo Ecuatoriano*. Quito: Casa de la Cultura Ecuatoriana, 1963.

PART III

Argentina, Brazil, and Chile

CHAPTER 8

The Rise of Labor Courts in Argentina

JUAN MANUEL PALACIO

Labor courts appeared in Argentina on a precise date. On November 30, 1944, the military government, which had come to power the year before, issued a decree establishing the Labor Courts of the city of Buenos Aires. Two years later, in March 1947, the government of the recently inaugurated president, Juan Domingo Perón, transformed the decree into national law.

Such concrete dates, at first glance, tell us little about the rise of labor law in Argentina—but they are significant signs of broader trends. The military coup that came to power in June 1943 (known as the June Revolution) put an end to a period known as the "infamous decade," which had likewise begun with a military coup in 1930. In response to the fraudulent elections and corruption that had permeated politics during the 1930s, the new military government, led by a group of young nationalist officers, took office on a platform of national regeneration and justified their revolution under a banner of anticorruption and legitimate elections. The leaders of the 1943 coup proposed that their ascendance would mark the dawn of a new era for Argentina. To embark on this project, they situated their policies in opposition to the standing principles of liberalism, free trade, and export-based economic growth; instead, they advocated industrialization guided by an interventionist state. They also proposed a new social and economic strategy, grounded in a broader aim for economic independence.

An important component of the program proposed by these officials was a social agenda that sought to address problems that had arisen during the 1930s and had been hastened by the mass migration of rural workers to large cities (principally Buenos Aires). The platform advocated incorporating social sectors that had been previously marginalized, expanding rights, and improving the living and working conditions of

Argentina's laborers. This new concern for the working classes and those lacking legal protections was particularly pronounced among one of those officials: Colonel Juan Domingo Perón. Perón was also the leader who best articulated a long-term strategy for the June Revolution, envisioning its expansion under the project for a "New Argentina."

Perón chose to take the role of Secretary of Labor (head of the *Secretaría de Trabajo y Previsión*, henceforth STP) in order to propel his social and labor policies into action. It was an office he created months after the revolution, built on the grounds of the old Labor Department (*Departamento Nacional de Trabajo*). It was also from this post that he launched his meteoric rise to the presidency, which began only months after the revolution. Perón converted the office into a political juggernaut that absorbed other state offices and centralized almost all of social policy during the military government's rule.

The creation of the Labor Courts by decree was just one chapter in a larger strategy of social and labor intervention. Perón, however, gave the initiative importance, recognizing that it was a key mechanism by which labor legislation, and any action on behalf of the workers, would be advanced. Thus, Perón proposed that the creation of the new courts would serve as a milestone in Argentine history, generating a true "before and after." He was not mistaken. Until the establishment of these specialized tribunals, the few pieces of labor legislation that were on the books had largely been debilitated by poor execution, a lack of enforcement, and the complicity of civil courts, which often proved resistant to enforcing social legislation. Perón's efforts to create the new courts and back them with a new legal framework and state oversight reflected a will to enforce policy, but it also put the labor courts in the crossfires of vehement debate.

The first section of this chapter examines the ways in which labor law had already developed in Argentina in the decades leading up to 1943. It shows that legal scholars and practitioners debated the creation of a specific branch of the judiciary dedicated exclusively to labor conflicts; it traces how international innovations on the subject made an impact by inspiring national scholarship and jump-starting a slowly forming consensus around "new law" (or *nuevo derecho*, as it came to be called in legal circles), which would inevitably make a broader impact. Then, the section examines the extent to which labor justice predated the Labor Courts in Argentina, which is to say, the forms in which the judicial system resolved labor conflicts before a separate judiciary branch was created.

The second part of the chapter focuses on the short-term changes that took place from the start of the June Revolution through Perón's first two presidencies. It examines concrete and decisive ways that the government enacted social legislation, as well as its efforts to create bureaucratic institutions to ensure that the legal framework would be enforced. Among these new measures was the decree that founded the labor tribunals. The section describes the various methods that the state, via the

STP, intervened in labor issues and, in particular, its efforts to step in to arbitrate labor conflicts. It also examines its endeavors to inaugurate labor tribunals throughout the country, a process that began with the 1944 decree but continued for the duration of the 1940s.

Finally, the third section analyzes the contentious debate that emerged around Peronist efforts to empower his Labor Courts. It examines the reactions that developed over the course of implementation of the new judicial structure, particularly among business owners, landowners, political opponents, and the provincial elites. Finally, it examines the more paradoxical controversy that arose from the judicial establishment.

Labor Law before Peronism

Although it is true that from its outset, Peronism began to fulfill workers' aspirations in a manner that was previously unimagined even by legislators and legal scholars (through labor laws, regulatory bodies, and the labor courts themselves), it is also true that there was already a rich precedent for these projects both in Argentina and in the world. This was true of both the content of labor laws and doctrines and the institutions built and empowered during this period. Comparative law also predated Perón, as did comparable experiences in the broader Western world. Too, there existed a camp of internationally engaged labor reformers—*laboralistas*—who were active in the local judicial field. A review of Argentina's congressional history also highlights a number of labor laws and efforts to write labor codes, as well as early endeavors to build labor courts. There also existed labor jurisprudence, although it did not come out of a "labor" tribunal. These antecedents counter a narrative that had previously imagined Perón as the forefather of social justice (and, specifically of labor law) in Argentina, and they serve to enrich a growing historiography that has "unmasked" and contextualized the supposed innovations of Peronism.[1]

In effect, in 1943, Argentina possessed an inventory of protective labor laws that were not numerous or necessarily respected or applied, but which nonetheless constituted a milestone set of pioneering labor laws.[2] These initial steps toward a cohesive labor legal structure also reflected a growing crescendo of calls for social legislation—calls that were not isolated to Argentina but had extended over a large sector of the Western world during the twentieth century. These laws also echoed a debate over social legislation that slowly began gaining ground in the liberal legal world at the end of the nineteenth century, and which was described in the first chapter of this volume. However, beyond their links to a broader climate of international ideas, Argentine laws were the result of at least two other combined processes: social unrest and organized labor's efforts to improve terms of work; and the work of congressmen, primarily socialists but also conservative and liberal reformers, who brought social legislation to the parliamentary agenda. Thus, it is no coincidence that Argentina's first labor laws were enacted in the first two decades of the century, at a time of considerable social unrest. Nor was it happenstance that the proposals were written by the first socialist to be seated in the National Congress (Alfredo Palacios), or that the renowned liberal reformist, Joaquín V. González, championed the first congressional campaign to create a labor code (one of the first in Latin America) in 1904.

Politicians like González or Palacios also spoke openly of a phenomenon that was key to this process: the rise of a generation of legal scholars who came from diverse political, social, and professional positions and had begun to develop the study of social law and propose modifications to the legal *corpus*. In time, these scholars became the true pioneers of labor law in Argentina. One must also recognize a longer list of key contributors: José Nicolás Matienzo, the first director of the Labor Department in 1907; Juan Bialet Massé, the author of an exhaustive study on the working classes at the beginning of the twentieth century and a key participant in Gonzalez's project; Alejandro Unsain and Carlos Saavedra Lamas, each an author of proposed labor codes during the 1920s and the 1930s; and Leónidas Anastasi, legislator and national representative to the International Labour Organization (ILO) during the 1920s and founder of the prestigious legal journal *La Ley* in 1935, among others. Beyond parliamentary action, these pioneers and their disciples formed the nucleus of Argentina's first *laboralistas* and would develop a multifaceted course of action that would impact university education, as well as a diverse array of other institutions. They created what could be called a veritable academic field around the subject of labor law in Argentina.

The university became the epicenter of this movement and the oldest universities in the country, the Universities of Buenos Aires, Córdoba, La Plata, and Litoral, located in the city of Santa Fe, became the most important centers for innovation. These institutions began offering labor law courses at their law schools, and the field gained prominence at the turn of the century. A similar pattern took hold in each locale. First, specialized courses emerged as offshoots of other legal curricula offerings, like economics or industrial law. In 1906, Juan Bialet Massé began teaching Agriculture and Industrial Law at the University of Córdoba—the oldest in the country; in 1919 he changed the course's name to Labor and Industrial Law. In 1915, the University of Buenos Aires offered a course in Industrial Law within the Economic Sciences School, taught by Alfredo Palacios; in 1919, it also offered *Legislación Industrial y Obrera* in the school of Law and Social Sciences (*Facultad de Derecho y Ciencias Sociales*), taught by Carlos Saavedra Lamas. In Santa Fe, the University of Litoral created its Labor Law course in 1921, as a part of its School of Legal and Social Sciences. For its own part, the University of La Plata—founded in 1906 by the author of the first labor code, Joaquín V. González—created the Industrial and Labor Law program in 1920 as part of the School of Legal and Social Sciences and selected Leónidas Anastasi as its director. Alfredo Palacios's rise as dean of that school two years later would bring new weight to the trend toward "new law" in the curriculum.[3] He brought in Alejandro Unsain as an adjunct professor and began to require that all law students take a course on labor law called, Labor Legislation.[4]

Beyond these courses, a number of new research seminars focused on specific labor law topics and formulated a sort of parallel activity to teaching. Together, these seminars, courses, and departments created a launching point for professional and academic research as well as doctoral dissertations that studied the world of labor. These projects contributed to the intellectual formation of the most important labor scholars of twentieth-century Argentina: Armando Spinelli, Manuel Pinto, and Juan Ramírez Gronda in La Plata; Mariano Tissembaum in Santa Fe; Saavedra Lamas and Unsain in Buenos Aires; Dardo Rietti, Telasco Castellanos, and Luis Despontin, in Córdoba.

Along with courses and seminars, these men also developed specialized institutions. Thus, the University of Cordoba created the *Instituto del Derecho del Trabajo* in 1929 and named Dardo Rietti as its chair; the University of La Plata created an institution by the same name in 1937, under Anastasi. At the University of the Litoral, Mariano Tissembaum—Professor of the Labor Law course—became chair of a similar institution the following year.

These institutes, seminars, and departments were responsible for an array of new activity that spread ideas about the practices of *nuevo derecho* throughout the academic world, slowly forming a curriculum, educating future labor law professionals, printing specialized journals, and circulating information and news published not just in Argentina but in the larger universe of labor law. These institutions also became incubators for new legal projects and government proposals later enacted by Congress. These legislative efforts relied on the collaboration of labor scholars, many of them also politicians, congressmen and active statesmen.

Beyond the university, a major part of the formation of the field of labor law in Argentina was the gradual institution of spaces, including journals and conferences, for pointed academic discussion on the subject. Further examination shows that work related to labor studies increased in these older and preexisting spaces over time. Articles on the subject began to appear in university law journals, and scholars organized roundtables at law conferences or other professional meetings. These preliminary efforts were typically followed by the founding of new publications and meetings that were solely dedicated to the subject of labor law.

A review of the indices of these journals illustrates that in the decades before 1943, articles and bibliographies that discussed labor law in Argentina and abroad appeared gradually. Over time, questions regarding labor began to take a more prominent position, and with each passing year, they appeared to become a subject of greater concern in the pages of prominent publications. In addition to publishing articles by local and international specialists on labor law, there was also a growing presence of book reviews and commentary on laws that were appearing in Argentina as well as the rest of the region and world.

The most significant marker in this realm was the creation of the first journal specializing in labor law in Argentina: *Derecho del Trabajo. Revista crítica mensual de jurisprudencia, doctrina y legislación* (known simply as *Derecho del Trabajo*), which published its first issue at the beginning of 1941. Under the leadership of Anastasi and the direction of Mario Deveali (a prominent Italian scholar of law who migrated to Argentina in 1939), the journal included many of the major *laboralistas* on its advisory board, including Alejandro Unsain, Manuel Pinto, and Mariano Tissenbaum. The journal contained a section on doctrine (*doctrina*) with contributions from renowned national and international legal scholars; a section on jurisprudence with notes and commentaries on decisions from Argentina and abroad; information on new legislation, which also included legislation being passed in other countries; and bibliographical reviews with commentary on books and articles from both Argentina and the field at large. *Derecho del Trabajo* was a critical forum in which Argentina's labor law history was debated, and in which global labor news was commented upon; its pages became a space in which scholars supplemented and discussed all major developments in the field as they occurred (e.g., the passing of new laws, the creation of new courts, relevant court rulings) and, as such, the journal offers a relatively complete narration of this history.

Another fundamental component in the construction of the academic field of labor law in Argentina was local scholars' participation in broader international networks related to social law. Such participation came in many forms but primarily was made possible through the movement of people, bibliographies, publications, projects, news, and diplomatic and political contacts. Scientific and professional conferences, including the Pan American conferences and bilateral diplomatic talks, further greased the wheels of change and encouraged improved circulation of information. Likewise, as has been noted, local readings of foreign legislation and treaties (as well as jurisprudence) published in journals or used as cases for study in curricula or at research institutes, also became part of a network of information.

An early expression of these international trends can be found in the creation of the International Labour Organization (ILO) as part of the League of Nations in 1919. The ILO's first International Labour Conference was held in Washington, D.C., that same year and was of considerable importance to the group of Argentine academics who closely followed international labor law. Argentina sent Leónidas Anastasi and Alejandro Unsain as delegates. Both men worked closely with international labor specialists and became acquainted with the diverse and distinctive ways that labor law had developed in an array of national contexts. From this point on, Argentina continued to send representatives to successive meetings; the declarations advanced at the conferences were, in turn, debated in academic circles and later ratified by Congress.

As was the case for other Latin American countries, the process of consolidating the field of labor law in Argentina had a significant international dimension, and while the process of adopting "new law" was different in each national context, it is impossible to understand national labor laws without taking into account the broader international context in which they were conceived. Indeed, Argentina's *laboralistas* grounded their work in both their local and international experiences. The principal architects of this field saw themselves as members of an international fraternity of scholars that shared in a common challenge. Even if the development of labor law was uniquely suited to each country, the field was rooted (both programmatically and theoretically) in international assembly and debate.[5]

Labor Justice before the Labor Courts

By 1943, labor law had strong academic and legal roots in Argentina. It had likewise acquired strong precedents in the courthouse. There were preexisting methods for resolving labor conflicts in the justice system. As Line Schjolden's doctoral dissertation has shown,[6] in Argentina there was "labor justice before the Labor Courts." The origins of labor justice can be traced to trial judges who applied the law to labor conflicts and, in so doing, generated labor jurisprudence that filled a significant lacuna in Argentina's legal corpus, a gap that became all the more notable as the twentieth century advanced.

Who were these judges? Until the installment of a specific branch of law, labor conflicts were directed into civil courts, which were considered to be the expected place for adjudication of work-based conflicts. In ascending order, conflicts, in accordance to their importance, could be presented before a Justice of the Peace for minor cases (in particular if the money at stake did not exceed modest sums) and then would continue eventually to a court of first instance; from there, in the case of appeal, to courts of appeal; and in exceptional cases, to the Supreme Courts. In rural areas, it was common for labor conflicts to be heard first by a Justice of the Peace.

The other possible institutional arena for labor conflict hearings was outside the civil court. In this case, it fell to administrative authorities who resolved conflicts through "conciliation and arbitration," which, as the phrase suggests, tried to resolve conflicts through settlement between the parties, submitting them, in some cases, to peer or expert reviews. These conciliation boards followed the principle of corporate representation and had a tripartite representation that included a workers' representative, a representative from industry, and a state authority. While these "courts" were extrajudicial, and not binding in the event of a lawsuit before the civil courts, they played a significant role in creating a forum for labor conflict hearings prior to the creation of a separate court system.

State agencies like the Administration of National Railways, the National Commission of Transportation, or the National Agrarian Council were the first to make use of these boards to arbitrate conflict. The most well-known boards were those created within the Department of Labor (DNT) in 1912. These boards (known as *Consejos de Trabajo*) were organized ad hoc in the event of labor conflicts and made use of tripartite representation to reconcile or arbitrate between the parties. The historiography tells us little about the reach and actions of the DNT and the different provincial labor departments, although it does show that its territorial presence was relatively limited (outside the cities and in rural regions it was virtually absent) and that its actions were limited to mediation of collective conflicts.[7]

The Establishment of Labor Courts

In his initial position in the military government of 1943, Perón fed off of this climate of ideas and built upon these antecedents. To design a comprehensive intervention that could impact diverse arenas of labor law and social policy simultaneously, he relied on the knowledge accumulated by labor scholars. The most known and studied field of intervention was social legislation, which touched on a number of norms that included the de facto government's first decrees, laws later passed by Congress,[8] and a myriad of decrees and administrative resolutions that came from diverse structures of control (like the STP) and which together formed a dense web of regulations. Recounting all of the Peronist regulations is practically impossible, but it suffices to say that while the half-century prior to the rise of Perón generated a handful of labor laws that can be listed relatively easily, Peronism exhibited a level of legal production that had never been seen before. Both the quantity of dictated rules and the quality of their content were unprecedented.[9] Peronism regulated aspects of labor law that had never been touched or fully considered,[10] whether for a lack of previous legislation or for a lack of application or execution. This was particularly true for rural areas, a space that was largely left untouched by state regulation until the middle of the twentieth century. The regulation of rural areas had been left, consequently, to rather unpredictable local powers and officials.

The second terrain of intervention, also well known (although less studied), is bureaucratic reform. These reforms concerned the creation of ad hoc state offices that, on the one hand, organized and prioritized state interventions in labor matters, and on the other hand, sought to ensure a more efficient and professional administration of social policy.[11] The most decisive feat in this arena was the transformation of the old DNT into the *Secretaría de Trabajo y Previsión* (STP) in November 1943 (as president, Perón would turn the STP into the Ministry of Labor).

This was not a simple matter of changing names. The creation of the STP generated a new hierarchy and enhanced the possibility of state interventions in the field of social policy. It operated with new personnel, a new budget, and new functions, with the specific aim of improving the quality and effectiveness of state intervention. Only a few days after its founding, the new office was bursting with feverish activity. It was not only tasked with enforcing regulations but also with taking control of interventions that extended across a much larger territory: the STP would eventually extend its supervision of applied labor laws to all parts of the country, demonstrating its capacity to undertake inspections, receive reports, impose infractions and declare closures throughout the national territory.

The third method of intervention—also the method that most directly relates to the subject of this essay and is least studied in the historiography—focused on the judiciary and also had its origins in the STP. In effect, following its establishment by decree, the STP absorbed all existing provincial labor departments, and from that moment on, these local departments became regional entities (*delegaciones regionales*) under the authority of the national office. As the STP took in these local offices, it also absorbed their labor boards—thus centralizing all labor conflict in the nation directly, either by receiving demands or by intervening ex officio.

This formed part of a wider and well-orchestrated plan of state intervention in the judicial sector. The STP ultimately targeted the civil courts and disputed their jurisdiction over contractual and labor conflicts. In effect, Perón did all he could to avoid a scenario in which the existing judiciary might be tasked with enforcing his social legislative program. He remained convinced that, left in the hands of the existing conservative judicial power (which had already proved critical of his program), any legislative advances he made would be immediately undercut in practice. Thus, Perón made extensive use of the administrative tribunals, resizing some and creating new ones where needed. In essence, beyond consolidating the conciliation boards under the domain of the STP, he also maximized this use of mediation and reinforced its application in new laws and decrees, for example, the Peon Statute (*Estatuto del Peón*), the 1947 Law of Rural Labor, or the Rural Tenancy Law of 1948.[12] The latter, for example, created Parity Chambers (*Cámaras Paritarias*), which extracted any disputes between landowners and tenants from the civil courts' jurisdictions. The change spurred a long procession of claims made on the behalf of landowners by their lawyers before different courts, each charging that the law was unconstitutional. Although these claims multiplied over the years, they were almost always unsuccessful.[13]

Finally, STP regional offices did not limit legal action to those claims that came before their boards. The STP launched an extensive campaign to make sure that workers were aware of their legal rights. This campaign was organized all over the country through the regional offices: it encouraged workers to denounce employers that did not comply with the law, and it helped them formulate their demands. These efforts were explicitly outlined in the decree that created the STP. The decree expressed the intention to convert STP offices into forums where workers could access information and aid, stating that "it falls to the State to develop a strong effort to publicize and spread awareness among the Argentine people that no [employer] has the right to evade his social duties."[14]

The culmination of Perón's judicial policy was the creation of the Labor Courts. Decree No. 32347, issued November 1944, began this process by "creating and organizing Labor Courts."[15] However, this mandate really applied only to the judicial system of the city of Buenos Aires, since it was the only site over which the executive power had jurisdiction, according to the existing constitution.

The decree, drafted by a group of legal scholars working at the STP, was the product of extensive and exhaustive research, as can be judged by its warm reception among labor scholars of the time.[16] The courts that it established combined different models in practice. First, unlike other countries in the region, such as Brazil and Mexico, these Labor Courts limited their jurisdiction to individual labor conflicts, leaving collective actions to state institutions (like the STP). Second, they were created as a separate appendage of the judicial branch and, thus, were not encompassed in the executive branch of government (as was the case in Mexico). They were also composed of different levels of tribunals that included the STP Labor Boards (which, as noted, used tripartite representation and were presided over by a state representative), First Instance Judges, and an Appellate Board, divided into three chambers, each with a president and two panel members (*Vocales*). Procedures began in the STP conciliation boards, and if conciliation failed and the case went to trial, the STP continued to act as an auxiliary to the judges by receiving the statement of claim, the response, and the evidence. The decree also created the office of a labor prosecutor (*Ministerio Público del Trabajo*), headed by a general prosecutor (*Procurador General del Trabajo*), with authority to initiate enforcement action.

This new system was enacted when the first judges were selected in June and July of 1945. They consisted of seven members of the Court of Appeal (*camaristas*) and twenty judges of First Instance who were sworn into office at the end of July, in front of the president and other executive officers. As we will see later in this chapter, this event occurred in the midst of political upheaval. The judges began their work from their new office at 1366 Esmeralda Street in Buenos Aires immediately after being sworn in.

The installment of the new labor legal system would not be so easily undertaken, however. The new system pushed up against two important obstacles, both of a constitutional nature. According to the constitution of 1853, the power to apply national labor legislation, like any legislation not explicitly assigned as a federal power, fell to provincial authorities. This presented a basic obstacle to the creation of a nationally centralized state labor policy. In reality, the federal government could pass national laws but their enforcement could be guaranteed only within federal jurisdiction—which was to say, within the Federal Capital of Buenos Aires. Laws could be extended nationally only when sanctioned by provincial authorities. For this reason, the government was only able to create Labor Courts in Buenos Aires in 1944. To see the new labor system applied throughout the nation, Perón would have to wait until each province organized and enforced its own court system.

The second obstacle was more circumstantial, but it was nonetheless a considerable challenge. It stemmed from the character of the regime that had taken power in 1943. Despite its origins as a de facto government that came to power in a coup, the government had obtained the recognition of the Supreme Court, which empowered the executive office to dictate decrees. However, this power was limited to legislation considered to be of "urgent necessity." At least in theory, this wording placed limitations on the government's capacity to reform. In reality, a brief look at the myriad of decrees issued by the government during the period highlights that the court interpreted the idea of "urgent necessity" in the broadest form possible. Yet, even still, this limitation existed and was there to be used, if necessary, against any decree: it was an Achilles heel for a government that looked to generate decisive, centralized reform.

In time, and following considerable changes in the political context, both obstacles would be overcome. The first was resolved with the creation of provincial Labor Courts, something that the Peronist hegemonic power was able to incite in less than a decade. In 1946, the new government approved a decree "inviting the provinces to join the National Government in an agreement to organize labor courts." The signing jurisdictions committed to forming labor tribunals according to the Buenos Aires model.[17] Over the span of only a few years, most of the provinces in Argentina organized labor courts, although the rhythm and degree of acceptance of the decree's recommendations varied, and individualized adjustments to the Buenos Aires model were made.[18]

Perón overcame the second obstacle by enacting federal legislation that legitimated the new courts, giving them the same standing as the civil, commercial, and criminal courts. That is, shortly after taking office, Perón presented a plan to Congress to turn Decree 32347 into a law, which would give the Labor Courts constitutional status equal to that of the other courts. In December 1946, after a lengthy debate, these new courts were created by Law 12948, which was finally promulgated on March 6, 1947.[19] By that time, of course, the Labor Courts had already been operating for almost two years in the city of Buenos Aires, with a considerable level of activity.

Resistance to the New Courts

As was noted, by 1944, there were few people in Argentina who publicly opposed "new law" and the convenience and utility of Labor Courts. Global advances in labor law, the development of scholarship on the subject, and the steps made by the ILO minimized opposition from the political or judicial establishment and generated a broad consensus. Given this, creating the Labor Courts should have been a relatively easy development, as it had been in other countries, where labor law developed along a normalized path of parliamentary debate, academic and editorial commentary, and political discussion. Indeed—as other chapters in this book attest—in most contexts, labor law developed as the logical result of a sequence of measured steps gradually adopted in both the judicial and political arena.

In Argentina, by contrast, the new tribunals embarked on a very different—and far more contentious—path. The establishment of these new courts became a subject of bitter debate and impassioned reactions, culminating in a deeply contentious battle among irreconcilable positions. This clash was not confined to academic or media discussion; it resulted in highly volatile political challenges and an outright legal war that included claims of unconstitutionality and unfavorable decisions by the Supreme Court.

What was behind this unique course of events? Answers can be found by more closely examining the political moment in which these courts were created. The Labor Courts were founded during two of the most tumultuous years for the country, 1945 and 1946, when two polarizing camps of Peronists and anti-Peronists were taking shape. Nothing in Argentina could escape this divided political field. Despite the relative consensus in Argentina and in the world in regards to the necessity of labor courts, in this context, the construction of a new labor legal structure was destined to become the target of political crossfire.

Beyond a general context of ripe political tension, there were also specific aspects of the labor courts that heightened controversy. The project, on the one hand, touched on sensitive terrain for anti-Peronist liberals: it represented a threat to checks and balances, the separation of powers, provincial autonomy, and the integrity of the constitution. On the other hand, the universal application of labor law only strengthened Perón's clout and his ability to mobilize Argentina's working classes. For Perón's opposition, then, the new developments in labor law appeared to perfectly encompass the major threats posed by the new leader.

The most predictable opposition to the labor laws—and, in particular, to the enforcement of this law at the national level—could be found among the business and landowning elite. This group had witnessed the advance of labor legislation at the beginning of the twentieth century and observed as the state developed a more interventionist stance on behalf of the working classes. However, given that their objections to these processes had not been particularly energetic or audible during that era, it is safe to assume that neither undertaking affected them significantly. This was particularly the case in rural areas, where neither the labor legislation nor the supervisory state had any real impact. These privileged sectors were able to comply with the laws or mediate their effects by processing them through civil courts, which had often proved resistant to enforcing labor legislation.

Peronism changed this. The creation of the STP, its structure of controls and labor boards, as well as the new Labor Courts, produced a growing and explicit resistance from these previously quiet sectors. It was a logical response to the challenge that Perón—and by extension, the workers—posed. The Labor Courts and the STP challenged business and landowners' privileged position in the courtroom, a realm in which they had traditionally been the advantaged party. They denounced the enactment of the STP and, in particular, the creation of the conciliation boards that, they argued, reflected an unacceptable threat to separation of powers by empowering the executive branch to interfere in the judicial system. They likewise objected to the boards' antibusiness tendencies, which encumbered judicial impartiality and, they feared, was the beginning of partiality that would take form later in the Labor Courts.

For these opponents, it was not so much the existence of these new courts, but rather their methods, their implicit bias, and their capacity to alter the balance of power in the judicial system that made them an aberration. Likewise, the STP's efforts at raising awareness among workers translated into an incredible rise in demands and a detrimental judicialization of labor relations. Opponents feared that this awareness, coupled with the new ability to turn labor conflicts into judicial suits, would eventually consolidate in these nascent labor courts and that the pro-labor bias of the administration would, in turn, affect court decisions.

Business owners voiced their criticism in two principal arenas: the public forum and the courts (through their lawyers). In the public arena, they organized statements on behalf of their organizations, wrote editorials, and generated columns in press outlets with similar political affinities. They also took to the street, organizing protests.[20] In the courtroom, meanwhile, they organized a defense that systematically questioned the validity of the STP and the constitutionality of the new judicial arenas. It was a logical response to institutions that they regarded as hostile and in "enemy" hands but which also appeared to have a point of weakness. The STP had been, indeed, created by decree and under dubious constitutional validity.

Another contingent of objectors arose from the political arena. Leaders from opposition parties and provincial elites were particularly vocal opponents. For these politicians, it was the fact that the Peronist administration utilized the STP to gain the favor of voters that was most threatening—and this threat appeared all the more salient as the February 1946 elections neared. These opposition groups were well aware of the considerable political might that was being built behind the STP administrative tribunals. They also followed the decisions made in Buenos Aires Labor Courts and the STP regional labor boards closely and saw a type of change that had never been witnessed before in Argentina: the workers, for the first time in a more or less systematic way, were winning lawsuits against their employers. There was little doubt that the new labor tribunals would fortify the working-class loyalty to Peronism, and that this would be only the first step in the movement's political consolidation.

Provincial elites were largely concerned that these events would begin to take hold in their local polities. Previously, when the national government had a less consequential presence in regional affairs, they were largely immune to "foreign" interventions, particularly those that sought to empower rural workers. The STP, by contrast, not only promised to transform workers into tried and true Peronist soldiers but also promised to upend their political loyalties and disentangle provincial strongholds, generating "nationalized" loyalties that linked working-class constituents directly, without intermediary, to the national government and its new leader, Juan Perón.

In this way, despite the fact that they could have expressed their resistance in terms of constitutional objections or as a defense of the federal system, the opposition did not build their arguments around theoretical questions or on legal grounds. Their stance reflected a practical problem: both the administrative boards and the labor courts used political rhetoric and acted in favor of the working classes, and thus built new political ties with those groups. In other words, the advance of these courts could permanently endanger opposition parties' capacity to gain political favor with the working classes; this new and unforeseen concern became particularly significant in the provinces. In effect, the STP and its regional offices not only became a representation of Peronist labor politics in every corner of the country but, as the election approached, they became a key component of Perón's electoral campaign; they would propel Perón's dramatic rise to the presidency. Finally, many provincial politicians (including both Peronist supporters and detractors) saw the regional offices of the STP as little less than an occupying force that was imposed on their territories by the national state. These new offices were intervening in labor relations, rearranging local political loyalties and, moreover, altering bureaucratic boundaries and jurisdictional limits. Their presence and power came into clear conflict with preexisting provincial agencies.[21]

Finally, if mounting opposition among business owners and provincial elites was perhaps understandable given the gamut of interests at stake, then the negative reaction on the part of the judicial establishment appeared more paradoxical, and even more so as their protest became substantially more rigorous and inflexible. As we have seen, in Argentina during the 1940s, labor law was well established and the academic world had largely accepted the idea that further reform was needed. The judicial establishment had more than once even encouraged the formation of Labor Courts. In effect, the autonomy of "new law," based on its own principles and as a branch separate from civil law, was already on the road to becoming fully incorporated in the judicial system.

For substantial sectors of the judiciary, the interventionist advances made by Perón and the STP in the judicial branch changed this course of events. Many took Perón's incendiary speeches against the existing system as a declaration of war and they reacted with firm opposition to these interventions, and, in particular, to the Labor Courts. In waging this political battle, the judiciary found no lack of arguments to counter the imposition of the STP conciliation system and the installment of Labor Courts. They focused their arguments on the constitutional limits of the national executive power, both in the realm of the provinces and in the judiciary, in order to more broadly counter all of Perón's advances.

The first reactions transpired in the wake of the initial decree that announced the creation of the new tribunals. A few months after the decree, the Buenos Aires Bar Association (the *Colegio de Abogados de Buenos Aires*) issued a statement that pronounced that the decree "goes against the principle of separation of powers and violates the provisions of Articles 18, 67, 14 and 27, and 95 of the National Constitution," which provide that "the Executive Power lacks the authority to create courts of law," even more so with these courts which, while distinguishing themselves from tribunals "created by law" "in reality constitute the 'special commissions,' which were permanently prohibited by the drafters of the [1853] Constitution."[22]

The attack, therefore, was multifaceted. On the one hand, they alleged that the government was violating the separation of powers in a double sense (because the creation of courts was within the competence of Congress and not the executive and because by creating these courts the executive was indirectly assuming a judicial function), aggravated by the fact that it was done by a de facto government. On the other hand, they critiqued the idea of installing a "special commission," an idea contrary to constitutional principles, which were based precisely on a critique of the privileges that such "special commissions" (*fueros*) implied (military, ecclesiastic, and so forth). Thus, despite the fact that the labor tribunals were quite different from these more traditional "special" tribunals, the mere notion that such a special *fuero* would be deemed necessary was anathema to liberal beliefs.

The most significant reaction came from the Supreme Court. In a decision issued on July 4, 1945, the Court resolved that it would not swear in the labor judges designated by the executive power, as was established in Decree 32347.[23] It contended that the process was not necessary, given that the courts merely held local jurisdiction (within the city of Buenos Aires), where there were higher courts (civil and commercial) that could carry out this function.[24]

Although this argument was well grounded in a legal framework, in the political context of 1945 it surfaced as a challenge to the military government and it tested the strength of the judicial establishment in the face of executive intervention. The aim of the decision was to ensure that the new tribunals were granted minimal status, or in any case, that they ultimately held less importance than what the military government—and Perón—had envisioned. For Perón, the courts represented the culmination of his social justice program, as well as an important advance in Argentina's legal system. For the court, meanwhile, the ruling insisted that the Labor Courts had limited reach and would remain dependent on civil and commercial courts. In this way, it minimized and devalued the Peronist advance.

The government did not wait to react. A few days after the Court's ruling, it approved another decree that modified Article 142 of Decree 32347 and determined that the new judges would be sworn in before the president.[25] Thus, on July 23, a mere twenty days after the Court's decision and ten days after the new decree, the new labor judges were sworn in during a grand ceremony before President Farrell and Perón, the cabinet, military leaders, and union leadership. The scene was staged to underline a confrontation between a government that served as the defender of workers' rights by founding a precise instrument for their defense, and the "oligarchy," the enemy of the people: in this camp, were the judicial establishment and its grand leader, the Supreme Court.

But the final blow was still to come. On February 1, 1946, only days before the presidential election, the Supreme court issued the last of a series of legal challenges to Perón's projects. The Court declared the STP to be unconstitutional.[26] The court's decision originated in a case in which the inspector of the STP regional office from

Buenos Aires province had issued the "Dock Sud" company a fine for a labor infraction (a violation of the eight-hour workday). The fine was endorsed by a civil court, and the company appealed to the Supreme Court, alleging that the STP had no jurisdiction beyond the City of Buenos Aires. The Supreme Court upheld the appeal, deciding in favor of the company. Not fully satisfied, however, it added a broader indictment of the STP, declaring that its 1943 founding decree, which had converted provincial labor departments into STP regional offices, "had revoked a provincial law, had transformed the provincial agency into a national agency and intruded into the province's jurisdiction regarding questions that were regulated by existing legislation. The decree was a clear violation of the Constitution. Not even the National Congress possessed the power to do this."[27]

The decision was reprinted in *La Nación* the next day, where commentators applauded it over the following days.[28] The *Colegio de Abogados de Buenos Aires* also embraced the decision; a few days later, it announced its support for the Supreme Court and its "defense of the Constitution."[29] In this manner, and as had happened with other interventionist governments of the twentieth century, Peronism would find that overcoming the "federal question" would become its most difficult challenge. The Supreme Court would prove to be its most formidable enemy.[30]

Over the following years, the constitutionality of the labor courts continued to be questioned by diverse sectors, including business owners and their lawyers. Nonetheless, these challenges diminished over time. Their effectiveness lessened when Perón transformed the decree into national law in 1947, and the claims were made virtually obsolete when the Supreme Court finally declared the courts to be constitutional.[31]

Final Reflections

The creation of Argentina's Labor Courts occurred at the crossroads of two coinciding processes. The first process, which took place over a longer period, reflected a slowly growing consensus regarding the necessity of labor reform and the adoption of the principles of "new law," which was visible in the gradual incorporation of social legislation into the legal corpus since the beginning of the twentieth century. The second process, which came to pass over a shorter period of time, is evident in the boom of social and labor legislation that accompanied Peron's rise to power and his first two presidencies. The latter process, often the one emphasized in Peronist narratives, allowed the leader to take on a reputation as the father of labor rights in Argentina.

However, as this chapter has highlighted, reformist labor legislation and debate predated Peronism in Argentina. New legislation and ideas regarding labor law originated in academic circles, where Argentine legal scholars debated insights from international legislation (laws, labor institutions, social constitutionalism) and were prominent players in international forums, where they were in contact with other leading legal scholars and labor reformists. In Argentina, this field developed gradually, spreading with the inauguration of new courses at major universities and the creation of specialized institutes and journals. Many of these legal scholars, moreover, were politicians and congressmen who brought the policies and reforms debated in academic circles (labor codes, specialized tribunals) into the political arena. These men worked to pass labor legislation in Congress.

Peronism, nonetheless, marked a veritable watershed in the history of labor law in Argentina. Beginning with the creation of the STP, the Peronist state marked a period of immense legal productivity that broadened the bureaucratic structure and brought new life to old projects—foremost among them, the Labor Courts.

Thus, the rise of Labor Courts in Argentina figures as part of Perón's broader effort to transform state structures during his first two presidencies. On the one hand, the courts played an important role in centralizing federal state control and nationalizing public policy. On the other hand, the courts were part of a more specific plan to intervene in the judicial system: they would take labor conflicts out of the jurisdiction of the existing judicial branch and grant an expansive role for the executive power. In this way, the Peronist state could ensure that its labor legislation would escape the conservatism of the existing courts—an important epicenter of resistance—and be enforced according to Peronist criteria, in administrative tribunals, in STP conciliation and arbitration boards, and in the labor courts.

The clearest indications of the critical difference that Peronism made in the sphere of labor law (particularly in contrast to previous governments' application of the law), were, precisely, the fiery reactions that his policies inspired among the sectors of Argentine society that were most negatively affected. Business owners, anti-Peronist politicians, and the provincial government elites lashed out against the project, envisioning these new courts and their pro-labor tendencies as a menace to social peace, particularly in the realm of business, and (for some) a threat to their ability to gain political favor among the working classes. Finally, the contentious fight waged by the judicial establishment emerged as a logical reaction to an interventionist Peronist state; they saw these courts as a direct challenge to their interests.

Nonetheless, despite the barrage of sophisticated and powerful tools used against the Labor Courts and, above all, despite the real operation of destruction, negation, and secrecy that the military government that removed Perón in 1955 displayed against any vestige of Peronism that existed in the country, the Labor Courts survived. Indeed, they continue to thrive as a relevant institution in Argentina's contemporary democratic system.

The durability of the Labor Courts is not difficult to understand. As has been noted, when Perón created the STP there was already a consensus in Argentina about the need for labor tribunals. Thus, the resistance that Perón found to the project arose not from an objection to the courts themselves, but from the political context in which they were conceived, the methods by which they were being created and installed, and the rapid action they took in their first years of operation. Perón presented the courts alongside incendiary rhetoric that pitted "worker's" courts against the "oligarchy's" courts, he judicialized labor relations, and he confirmed partisan judges who issued partial and ideology-driven rulings. These were the actions that sounded alarm and rallied detractors. Indeed, detractors were not expressing explicit opposition to the concept of labor law or labor courts, but rather were expressing a strong objection to *Peronist* Labor Courts, specifically. Given this, it comes as little surprise that after 1955, the courts were able to regain the acceptability they once had acquired before the rise of Juan Perón. It was not the idea or the need of that institution what was wrong, but rather the color that Perón had imprinted on it.[32]

Notes

1. For more on this historiography, see Palacio, "El primer peronismo."
2. The law establishing Sunday rest (1905); work-related accidents (1915); domestic labor (1918); industrial security (1921); salary payment (1923); child and women's labor (1924); the eight-hour workday (1929); the establishment of "English Saturday" (1932); maternity protection (1934), among others.
3. That was the expression used by Alfredo Palacios in his 1920 book *El nuevo derecho* to refer to labor laws and the movement that originated labor law in the Western world at the beginning of the twentieth century.
4. Buchbinder, *Historia de las universidades.* For the case of La Plata, see Graciano, *Entre la torre de marfil.* For Córdoba, see Portelli, "Saberes modernos."
5. See Palacio, "Legislación y justicia laboral."
6. Schjolden, *Suing for Justice.*
7. See Lobato and Suriano, *La sociedad del trabajo*; Gaudio and Pilone, "Estado y relaciones laborales"; Korzeniewicz, "Las vísperas del peronismo."
8. When he reached the presidency in 1946, Perón asked Congress to convert all military government decrees regarding labor into national law; these took form in Law 12921, on August 17, 1947. See *Anales de Legislación Argentina* (henceforth *ALA*), 1947, 143–169.
9. Félix Luna calls this the "legal mania" of the June 1943 revolution, which produced more than 20,000 decrees between 1943 and 1946. See Luna, *El 45*, 31.
10. For example, legislation on union membership (1943 and 1945); obligatory vacation time (1945); paid holidays (1944); annual bonuses or *aguinaldo* (1945); minimum wage (1945); professional statutes (various, between 1944 and 1946); employers and professional associations (1952); collective negotiation (1952); and many others.
11. See, among others, Berrotarán, *Del plan a la planificación*; Berrotarán et al., *Sueños de bienestar.*
12. Respectively, Decreto 28169, 18/10/44, *ALA*, 1944, 574–592; Ley 13020, 6/10/47, *ALA*, 1947, 354–357; and Ley 13246, 18/9/48, *ALA*, 1948, 85–106.
13. I have analyzed the workings of these judicial bodies in Palacio, "La justicia peronista."
14. Decreto No. 15074, cit., 459.
15. Decreto No. 32347, 30/11/44, *ALA*, 1945, 4–13.
16. For example, the decree was celebrated in the journal, *Derecho del Trabajo*, which dedicated various articles and editorials to the subject. See *Derecho del Trabajo*, Buenos Aires, La ley, Vol. V, 1945, 49–59.

17. Decreto No. 6717, 13/8/46, *ALA*, 1946, 232–234.

18. The courts were created in the province of Buenos Aires in the year 1947 and, by 1950, there were Labor Courts in Buenos Aires City and in Santiago del Estero, Córdoba, Santa Fe, Buenos Aires, Tucumán, Jujuy, Salta, and Corrientes.

19. Ley No. 12948, 6/3/47, *ALA*, 1947, 203–204.

20. See, for example, Campione, "La Unión Industrial Argentina." Also see Palacio, "El grito en el cielo."

21. For a detailed analysis of these conflicts in Córdoba, see Romanutti, "Discurso político e instituciones."

22. *Revista del Colegio de Abogados de Buenos Aires*, Vol. XXIII, No. 1, 1945, 191–192.

23. Decree 32347 Article 142 established that the first labor judges would need to be sworn in by the Supreme Court.

24. *Jurisprudencia Argentina*, Año 1945, Vol. III, Buenos Aires, 1945, 635–636.

25. Decree No. 15718, 13/7/45, in ALA, 1945, Vol. V, 287.

26. *Fallos de la Corte Suprema de Justicia de la Nación*, Vol. 204, Año 1946, Buenos Aires, Imprenta López, 1946, 23–30.

27. Ibid., 28–29.

28. See *Diario La Nación*, February 3–6, 1946.

29. *Revista del Colegio de Abogados de Buenos Aires*, Vol. XXIV, Boletín Suplemento, February 1946, 26–28.

30. This was the case for the Roosevelt administration. The Supreme Court placed limitations on his ambitious interventionist New Deal. In famed decisions like the Schechter case, the U.S. Supreme Court declared the *National Industrial Recovery Act* (NIRA) unconstitutional because it intended to regulate the economic activity of states, where the federal government had no jurisdiction. In 1947, Perón would call for impeachment of the Supreme Court, which would result in the instatement of pro-Peronist judges.

31. Decision on March 3, 1947, *Fallos*, Vol. 169, 309.

32. After Perón's overthrow in 1955, the military government that followed removed most of the labor judges appointed during Peronist rule replacing them with other judges with no sympathies with Peronism.

Bibliography

Berrotarán, Patricia. *Del plan a la planificación. El Estado durante la época peronista*. Buenos Aires: Imago Mundi, 2003.

Berrotarán, Patricia, Aníbal Jáuregui, and Marcelo Rougier, eds. *Sueños de bienestar en la Nueva Argentina. Las políticas públicas durante el peronismo, 1946–1955*. Buenos Aires: Imago Mundi, 2004.

Buchbinder, Pablo. *Historia de las universidades Argentinas*. Buenos Aires: Sudamericana, 2005.

Campione, Daniel. "La Unión Industrial Argentina ante el ascenso de Perón. Reacciones ante la política económica y social en el período 1943–1946." *Realidad Económica* 145 (Jan.–Feb. 1997): 44–74.

Gaudio, Ricardo, and Jorge Pilone. "Estado y relaciones laborales en el período previo al surgimiento del peronismo, 1935–1943." *Desarrollo Económico* 94 (Jul.–Sept. 1984): 235–273.

Graciano, Osvaldo. *Entre la torre de marfil y el compromiso político. Intelectuales de izquierda en Argentina, 1918–1955*. Bernal: Universidad Nacional de Quilmes, 2008.

Korzeniewicz, Roberto P. "Las vísperas del peronismo. Los conflictos laborales entre 1930 y 1943." *Desarrollo Económico* 131 (Oct.–Dec. 1993): 323–354.

Lobato, Mirta Zaida, and Juan Suriano, eds. *La sociedad del trabajo. Las instituciones laborales en la Argentina (1900–1955).* Buenos Aires: Edhasa, 2013.

Luna, Félix. *El 45. Crónica de un año decisivo.* Buenos Aires: Sudamericana, 1986 [1971].

Palacio, Juan Manuel. "El primer peronismo en la historiografía reciente: nuevas perspectivas de análisis." *Iberoamericana* 39 (Sept. 2010): 255–265.

———. "Legislación y justicia laboral en el populismo clásico latinoamericano: elementos para la construcción de una agenda de investigación comparada." *Mundos do Trabalho* 3:5 (Jan.–June 2011): 245–265.

———. "La justicia peronista: el caso de las cámaras de arrendamientos y aparcerías rurales (1948–1955)." *Anuario IEHS* 26 (2013): 75–99.

———. "El grito en el cielo: La polémica gestación de los tribunales del trabajo en la Argentina." *Estudios Sociales* 48 (2015): 59–90.

Palacios, Alfredo L. *El nuevo derecho.* Buenos Aires: Claridad, 1960 [1920].

Portelli, María Belén. "Saberes modernos para políticas eficaces. El derecho laboral y el estudio del mundo del trabajo. Córdoba, 1906–1930." *Población y Sociedad* 18:2 (2011): 145–185.

Romanutti, Virginia. "Discurso político e instituciones. La Delegación Regional de la Secretaría de Trabajo y Previsión como organizadora de la cuestión social en Córdoba durante el peronismo." Paper presented at "Primer Congreso de estudios sobre el peronismo: la primera década," Mar del Plata, November 6–7, 2008.

Schjolden, Line. *Suing for Justice: Labor and the Courts in Argentina, 1900–1943.* PhD diss., University of California, Berkeley, 2002.

CHAPTER 9

Labor Courts in Brazil

Their Origins, Challenges, and Expansion

ANGELA DE CASTRO GOMES
FERNANDO TEIXEIRA DA SILVA

The Brazilian Labor Courts are an institution that has proved to be a decisive factor in the defense of workers' social rights and, through these, the defense of human rights in Brazil. During the decades in which the institution has been active, although it has undergone modifications, its initial structure is still intact, and it is noteworthy for its endurance compared with its counterparts in other countries. This chapter has two main objectives. First, we provide a broad overview of the process of forming these special courts, underscoring the characteristics that have marked their operation. These characteristics, starting with the fact that the courts focus on individual and collective labor rights, have given them a diminished prestige within the judiciary, which has had real consequences for their institutional power and the careers of their judges. However, these same characteristics have made the Labor Courts well known to, and widely utilized by, workers, who are generally distrustful of public institutions in Brazil. Second, we analyze an apparent paradox. Over the course of the history of Brazil's Labor Courts, they have suffered harsh attacks on many occasions that have limited their powers and even threatened their very existence, although there is no room here for a full description of those onslaughts. However, despite those difficulties—or, perhaps, because of them—this institution has not only survived but gained strength. It has achieved a position of respect within the judicial system, expanded its prerogatives within labor relations, and extended its jurisdiction throughout the country.

This chapter's focus on the Labor Courts necessarily concentrates on the first Getúlio Vargas administration, established after the 1930 Revolution that brought about a period of state interventionism in the economy and society through nationalistic and centralizing policies. The origins and characteristics of the Labor Courts are therefore deeply rooted in the "modern" political-juridical organization of inter-war corporatism that, as an alternative to the liberal and socialist models, sought to "organize the people" through professional associations, particularly employers' and workers' syndicates. This type of organization is still viewed, both erroneously and simplistically, as a mere copy of fascism. Therefore, we show that its makeup is much more complex, harking back to ideas, experiences and influences generated since the early twentieth century in Brazil and other countries. We then go on to analyze the practices and operations of the Labor Courts, particularly: the expansion of their jurisdiction, to the extent that labor law has gone beyond "employment relations" to cover "labor relations"; their expansion into the interior of the country, involving a process of the nationwide democratization of access to the institution. Between the 1940s and the 2010s, the Labor Courts, akin to the gradually spreading judicial function in the Andean countries, have come to encompass not only urban workers and employees from the so-called formal sector of the economy but also rural and domestic workers, public servants, "informal" employees (freelancers, subcontractors, and so forth) and, more recently, slavelike labor. Based on quantitative data, we present charts that make it possible to understand the pace of their expansion over time and space, according to periods characterized by different political situations and the case load in the Labor Courts—that is, the change in the total number of cases filed with that institution.

Labor Courts in the First Half of the Twentieth Century: Organization and Objectives

It is hard to pinpoint exactly when courts specifically focused on labor relations were first discussed in Brazil. However, it could be said that it was during the First Republic (1889–1930) because in 1905, attorney Evaristo de Moraes, who was associated with labor causes and parties, wrote a book in which he referred to the need for the "official organization of a tribunal made up of employers and workers, intended to resolve issues raised regarding wage labor."[1] *Apontamentos de Direito Operário* (Notes on Labor Law) argues in favor of state intervention in labor relations through laws that established "fair conditions for labor contracts." Moraes was not alone as he was accompanied by other attorneys and politicians who stood out for their links with labor activism, which was increasingly organized.

Two years later, after a serious wave of strikes in several Brazilian cities, primarily in defense of the eight-hour day, a decree issued in January 1907 regulated the organization of syndicates and ordered that they should be formed "with the spirit of harmony between employers and workers," and that both sides should be "connected by permanent conciliation and arbitration boards aimed at resolving disputes and disagreements between capital and labor."[2] Subsequently, based on experiences in other countries, the State Department of Labor (*Departamento Estadual do Trabalho*

[DET]), created in 1911 in São Paulo, considered the advantages of institutionalizing conciliation and arbitration bodies, involving government mediation. In 1912, the 4th Brazilian Workers' Congress, organized primarily by the so-called "reformist elements" of the labor movement, issued a manifesto that demanded the creation of a tribunal "with equal representation of employers and workers."[3] This Congress took place in a context of significant worker struggles in São Paulo and, in 1913, there were notable strikes in opposition to the law for deporting foreigners and protesting the increase in the cost of living.

Although these initiatives were not implemented, they demonstrate how, since the 1900s, we find a recurrent and highly meaningful vocabulary for dealing with conflicts—conciliation, arbitration, and mediation. Furthermore, a range of political-legal proposals attests to the existence of debates aimed at finding "solutions" to conflicts, going beyond mere police repression. However, more systematic projects and initiatives for labor regulation were introduced in 1918 when the House of Representatives took the first steps toward developing social legislation. It was a time of intense labor agitation, particularly in the cities of Rio de Janeiro and São Paulo. The 1917 general strike in São Paulo was a labor convulsion of unprecedented dimensions. Some 50,000 workers put down their tools during a four-day period of looting, shooting, and barricades. At the root of the insurrection was worker discontent over exhausting, unhealthy, and dangerous conditions in the factories, and primarily, the high cost of living. The workers won a 20 percent wage increase, a commitment from employers not sack strikers, and a promise by the state government to both free those imprisoned during the melee and to legislate for better living and working conditions. In the aftermath of their victory, a strong associative spirit spread throughout the city, leading to a proliferation of new unions, neighborhood leagues, and labor newspapers. But the euphoria proved short-lived, as an upsurge of arrests, deportations of foreigners, closures of unions, and disrespect for the agreement on the part of the company owners followed. In 1919 and 1920, a new strike wave arose in other cities, with workers presenting similar demands to those of 1917. The São Paulo strikes provoked redoubled reaction among employers in the next few years: continuous repression and the formulation of social and labor laws.

Internationally, there were also concerns about the "labor question." This was because, following the end of World War I, the Treaty of Versailles, to which Brazil was a signatory, in 1919 recommended the recognition of the new social rights that represented postwar society.

In the context of the post–World War I period, Maurício de Lacerda, a congressman for Rio de Janeiro State, submitted a number of bills to regulate labor relations, such as the one that proposed establishing Conciliation Commissions and Arbitration Councils. These bodies represented both employers and workers. The House Constitution and Justice Committee consolidated all of these bills into a substitute bill that recommended a vote on a Labor Code. This proposal was the subject of heated debate and encountered a great deal of resistance inside and outside the House of Representatives in 1918 and 1919. Then the bill creating a Department of Labor (*Departamento Nacional do Trabalho*; DNT) was approved by the House and Senate. The DNT, which was supposed to be part of the Ministry of Agriculture, Industry and Commerce, was to conduct studies and prepare, implement, and enforce measures regarding labor in general, becoming a Labor Ministry in the future. The DNT was also supposed to have the power to settle labor disputes.[4] However, it was never created.

In 1922, the State of São Paulo created Rural Courts to handle conflicts arising from the interpretation and execution of farmworkers' contracts. They were to be presided over by a judge and include two members, one designated by the landowners and the other by the tenant farmers. They also were to be guided by oral procedures and the principles of being gratuitous and swift. We have found no records of their operations but they find mention in lawyers' comments, particularly those involved in the debate on the creation of the Labor Court.[5] Therefore, it is important to note that as far back as the 1920s, the Rural Courts marshalled principles—representation of interests and cost-free justice—that would take concrete form in the post-1930 corporatist principles.

The most important step toward regulating labor relations in Brazil came through the National Labor Council (*Conselho Nacional do Trabalho*; CNT), approved by decree in April 1923.[6] It would effectively become the first institution to engage in conflict conciliation and arbitration along the lines of the future Labor Courts. The first president of the CNT was jurist and professor Augusto Viveiros de Castro, who in 1919 supported the creation of Industrial Boards (*Juntas Industriais*) whose members were elected by employers and workers, presided over by a government representative.[7] In other words, once again, we see a proposal that, while focused on urban workers, also adopted the principle of representation of interests. In fact, the creation of the CNT meant dropping plans for the DNT, which employers had criticized and rejected, especially because its jurisdiction included arbitration of conflicts between capitalists and workers, which at the time fell within the purview of the police. The fact that the CNT was an advisory body that could neither plan social legislation nor handle labor disputes made it more acceptable to the employers, as they were averse to what they considered undue interference by the state, as called for by the DNT.

The CNT was subordinated to the Ministry of Agriculture, Industry and Commerce, being directed by the minister and made up of twelve members appointed by the president of Brazil—eight representing the government, two the employers and two the workers. Like the Conciliation Commissions and Arbitration Councils proposed on the basis of Maurício de Lacerda's bill, the makeup of the CNT included equal representation of interests. In 1928, this agency was reorganized by a decree expanding its powers. It began mediating and adjudicating conflicts between workers and employers, being authorized to establish jurisprudence, for example, within the sphere of job stability and the law on railway workers' holidays and pensions—some of the few labor laws existing in the country, but this legislation was scarcely applied or enforced. The CNT would become one of the most important sites within the employers' sphere of operation. Although they failed to prevent Congress from introducing bills and voting on laws regulating labor relations, the employers influenced their implementation, especially by intervening in the drafting of the regulations, which were within the purview of the CNT.[8]

Considering the workers' movements and demands and the congressional debates, it is not surprising that the social issue became part of the platforms of presidential candidates in 1919 and 1925. Therefore, by the time of the Revolution of 1930, which is commonly believed to have produced Brazilian labor laws, there were already several related institutions, practices, and legal and political debates in place. Getúlio Vargas had done nothing new by addressing the social issue in his presidential campaign. The innovation was how he approached it, by recognizing its existence and accusing previous administrations of not really wanting to tackle it. For Vargas, the social issue was an indicator of Brazil's economic progress and should be recognized and treated politically by the state through the regulation of capital-labor relations.

Vargas lost the election. However, backed by a broad and diverse alliance, he led an armed response that challenged the prevailing political pact and overthrew the incumbent president. The Revolution of 1930 was undoubtedly a milestone in Brazilian history, signaling important political, economic, and social-cultural changes. However, the historiography contests the version built up by those who held power in the post-1930 period, according to which that movement was a true starting point in history. In the case of the social question, laws had already been passed (workplace accidents, protection of child labor, retirement and pensions for railway workers, and so forth), as well as experiments in establishing conflict regulation agencies such as the CNT. Nevertheless, government intervention faced immense employer resistance and lacked the legal instruments that effectively guaranteed its application. Therefore, among the changes brought about in the post-1930 period, one of the most important was the creation of two ministries: Education and Health, and Labor, Industry and Commerce (henceforth, the Ministry of Labor). In both cases, the state was clearly present in matters of "social interest," expressed in the creation of a new bureaucracy that would be responsible for formulating, implementing, and monitoring public policies to address the problems related to those areas. The first Ministry of Labor team, under the command of Minister Lindolfo Collor, included long-standing labor activists such as Evaristo de Moraes, whom we have already mentioned, and Joaquim Pimenta. They are considered by the literature as being chiefly responsible for building the corporatist union structure that was mounted at the time and approved by the 1931 trade union law.

This example illustrates how government intervention in the social question was not a demand necessarily associated with plans for an authoritarian state, as has sometimes been maintained. That intervention embraced the entire range of labor and social security laws, in addition to those focused on union organization that started in 1931. In fact, academic studies have observed that the period between 1931 and the beginning of the *Estado Novo* (New State) in 1937, concentrated the largest number of government policies for the regulation of the labor market. And this happened despite the great uncertainty of the Brazilian political context. Those six years witnessed first a civil war in 1932, a movement led by part of the opposition in São Paulo state against Vargas, demanding a constitutional order for the country. This movement was defeated, but the federal government then convened a Constitutional Assembly in 1933, composed of employers and employees' representatives, as well as political-party representation, whose functioning in the following year took place amid a wave of strikes and leftist radicalization. The new charter provided trade union autonomy and a Labor Courts system, as well as implying the return of the country to the rule of law. However, at least for the labor movement and communists, a real state of siege started in late 1935 when Vargas used an unsuccessful uprising led by the Communist Party to demobilize the working class and the Left by means of extensive repression. In 1937, using the pretext that the communists were planning a conspiracy once again, Vargas set up the *Estado Novo*, an authoritarian regime that lasted until 1945.

That whole series of social laws, initiated before the *Estado Novo*, was driven, ever more clearly, by a corporatist policy; that is, a policy guideline that valued corporations of interest (such as syndicates) and technical agencies (such as the institutes), which gained the status of public institutions to work with the state in their specific fields of expertise. Since they were linked to corporatist principles and ideals that rejected the "class struggle" and defended social harmony, especially regarding labor relations, these new bodies required formal recognition by the state in order to carry out their function. In the case of trade unions, they were organized according to the principle of their occupational category on a territorial basis. In other words, railway workers, bakers, textile workers, and other professions in a given city or municipality were organized in a single union, which became affiliated to the federation of the same category in the state or region, which, in turn, was connected to the National Confederation for that profession. Only trade unions organized along those lines were guaranteed recognition by the state. Therefore, the unions had status as public entities and in return, since 1943, financial contributions were required from all employees in a given profession, whether they were unionized or not. As for employers' syndicates, due to their opposition to government intervention in their associations, an "alternative" model was created: alongside the employers' syndicates, which were in accord with corporatist directives, the original employers' associations continued to function.

Another part of this picture, rounding it out, was the political plan of those who took power in 1930, which included the creation of a Labor Court, conceived as a special tribunal for the adjudication of labor-related matters, intended to handle individual and collective claims and having specific procedures—free of charge, oral, and swift— among other aspects, such as the presence of "class representatives" (*juízes classistas*) alongside judges. As the body that was supposed to ensure compliance with labor and social security laws, highlighting the possibility of negotiating conflicts between employers and employees (*empregadores* and *empregados*), according to the terminology of the time, the Labor Court was linked directly to the Ministry of Labor. That is, from the very start, Brazil's Labor Courts were an integral part of the executive branch, not the judiciary, a crowning measure for the corporatist architecture of the post-1930 State.[9] Although it has precedents in the practices of entities like the CNT, the Labor Court was established by the 1934 constitution but only became operational during the *Estado Novo* (1937–1945), on May 1, 1941. It is no coincidence that that is the date for celebrating work and workers. About the same time, as can be seen in Palacio's chapter in this volume, Péron was creating the labor justice system in Argentina, seeking to establish a watershed between "liberalism" and "statism," as happened in Brazil.

Even after 1930, creating this institution was not a simple matter. It encountered several obstacles, including resistance from employers and opposition from lawyers who were opposed to the idea of a court focused on collective rights. Therefore, we should understand the period between 1931 and 1941 as one of debates about the legitimacy and feasibility of establishing Labor Courts in Brazil, while two institutions were already focusing on conflicts between employers and workers: the Mixed Conciliation Commissions (*Comissões Mistas de Conciliação*) and Conciliation and Arbitration Boards (*Juntas de Conciliação e Arbitragem*), both created by decree in 1932. Despite the difficulties and limitations, they functioned throughout the decade preceding the creation of the Labor Courts, which only occurred in 1941, as we have seen, when the *Estado Novo* dictatorship neutralized most opposition to its policy initiatives.

The Mixed Conciliation Commissions[10] were not adjudicating bodies and their membership included representatives of employees and employers chosen by lot, for which the unions and syndicates presented lists of their recommendations. The president of the body was appointed by the Minister of Labor, and the position was held by "impartial persons" such as judges, members of the Brazilian Bar Association (OAB), and civil servants. Aimed solely at conciliation, as their name indicated, the commissions mediated collective disputes. When an agreement between the parties was reached, it was reduced to writing. Otherwise, the commission proposed arbitration and, when all else failed, the dispute was referred to the Minister of Labor. The Conciliation and Arbitration Boards were administrative, nonjudicial bodies with the authority to rule on individual conflicts, though not to execute their decisions. To do so, prosecutors from the National Department of Labor (*Departamento Nacional do Trabalho*)—an integral part of the Ministry of Labor—were supposed to initiate the enforcement of Board decisions through the regular courts, and only then would they come into effect. The Boards were also made up of two representatives each of employers and employees, taken from a list of twenty recommended names drawn up by the trade unions and employer syndicates, and had a president appointed by the

Minister of Labor or an official representing him.[11] It's worth underscoring that these boards and commissions of conciliation are not a Brazilian singularity as Mexican labor history has shown. Likewise, there are similar institutions in other countries, such as Colombia and Chile.[12]

The prerogatives of the Commissions and Boards, which were considered limited even by their contemporaries, were reduced even further by a lack of funding, which meant that they worked under very difficult conditions. Of course, all this affected their performance and credibility, which can be perceived by the reactions they elicited among employers and workers alike. This statement by Evaristo de Moraes Filho, the son of Evaristo de Moraes, made between 2002 and 2004, is illustrative:[13]

> Collective labor agreements were drawn up by the Mixed Commission: working hours, vacation time, indemnities. . . . The Boards debated notice, dismissal etc . . . Mixed Commissions were only created in two states: Rio de Janeiro and São Paulo. I was the secretary for the two in Rio, even maintaining contact with union leaders [representing workers]. . . . The most radical people paid no attention to them and didn't go there.

The first half of the 1930s in Brazil was a period marked by tremendous political instability and an economic crisis resulting from the crash of the New York Stock Exchange in 1929. To give an idea of the depth of the problems that the country faced, suffice it to say that there was a civil war in 1932. The reconstitutionalization process occupied 1933 and 1934, concluding in the indirect election of Getúlio Vargas to the presidency. The Labor Courts were initiated during the activities of the National Constituent Assembly, whose task was to draft a new constitution for the country. The 1934 constitution established those special courts with a brief paragraph: "the creation of Labor Courts and Conciliation Commissions must always obey the principle of election of members, half by associations representing the employees and half by employers, with a president freely appointed by the Government."[14]

The constitutional language was very terse, perhaps because of the controversy surrounding the issue, especially about whether the new institution was judicial. In the end, it was not organized as part of the judiciary but within the executive branch and was structured with equal representation. It included several innovations, which is why the new Labor Minister, Agamenon Magalhães, formed a committee to draft a blueprint for organizing the new courts. However, it seems that the burden was placed exclusively on the department's Technical Consultant, Oliveira Vianna, a major supporter of the Labor Courts during the Constituent Assembly.[15]

Until 1937, when a coup created the *Estado Novo*, there was serious opposition to Oliveira Vianna's draft bill, particularly with regard to two points: judges who represented the parties (employers and employees), justified on the basis of the corporatist logic of representation of interests, which was already being practiced by the boards and commissions after 1930; and the normative power of the Labor Courts, that is, the power to create rules to regulate labor relations (wages and working conditions) as a result of collective bargaining. It is not surprising therefore that Vargas would eventually establish the Labor Courts through Decree-Law no. 1,237 in 1939, at a time when there was no legislative power and political centralization was strong, so much so that the state governors were appointed by Vargas. Oliveira Vianna's draft bill prevailed, largely intact, in the Decree-Law, the promulgation of which was announced during the First of May celebrations in 1939. In a counterfactual exercise, one can imagine that if the constitutional order had been maintained, parliamentary debates and the interplay of political might have resulted in Labor Courts that were very different from those that were actually introduced.[16]

According to the 1939 decree, the Conciliation and Arbitration Boards were maintained, presided over by a Bachelor of Laws appointed by the president, thereby giving rise to the labor judiciary. As for the Mixed Conciliation Commissions, we have not found any record of their fate, but it is likely that they ceased to exist because they did not function in practice. Their duties were absorbed by the Labor Courts in the 1940s. The Regional Labor Councils (*Conselhos Regionais do Trabalho*) were the next instance in the area of individual disputes and they conciliated and arbitrated collective controversies from one or more states within the Brazilian federation. Representatives were appointed by the federations of employees and employers and appointed by the president. The highest appellate body was the National Labor Council, also with representation from both sides, initially four of both employees and employers, chosen by the Ministry of Labor.

The system known as Labor Justice (*Justiça do Trabalho*) was created on May 1, 1941, two years before the Consolidated Labor Laws (*Consolidação das Leis do Trabalho*) of 1943. The CLT, as it is called, systematizes the labor laws that were already extant in the country, giving them a new organic structure and strength, including symbolic power. This is because the CLT has become the statute that embodies the very idea of labor rights, as well as the link between Brazilian workers and the state. Although its jurisdiction initially included just urban workers, excluding almost all those working in rural occupations (the vast majority of workers in the country in the 1940s), the CLT has indisputable importance for all "categories" of workers who wanted to be included among those who enjoy the rights guaranteed "by law." It was precisely because of the CLT that the Labor Courts underwent the first changes by altering their makeup. But the most important change would come only with the 1946 constitution, when the National Labor Council became the Superior Labor Court (*Tribunal Superior de Trabalho* [*TST*]). It was then that the Labor Courts ceased to be administrative and subordinate to the executive branch and became a special and independent arm of the judiciary. Between 1946 and the twenty-first century, the most important changes were the elimination of judges who were class representatives in 1999 and the limitation of the judges' normative power in 2004.

The Labor Courts were created to conciliate and arbitrate labor disputes through the legal regulation of individual and collective bargaining. Corporatist directives required an institution of that nature, which included the presence of the state and representatives of employees and employers. That institution was central to the great project of "organizing society" and would maintain basically the same structure for several decades. Its essential characteristics can be enumerated as follows: equal representation; the principles of orality and cost-free conciliation; mandatory arbitration of disputes, and normative power.

It is worth noting that the decree-law that created the Labor Courts was linked to a larger project that took the form of the 1937 constitution. That document consolidated authoritarianism and corporatism as guidelines for a policy of "social peace" and economic development in Brazil. It was that constitution, moreover, which created the position of Attorney General for Labor and the Regional Labor Prosecutor's Offices, which were supposed to work together with the Regional Councils—the Regional Labor Court as of 1946. Prosecutors were responsible for ensuring compliance with labor law, representing "the weak and less sufficient," and working with the judges to strengthen social justice.[17]

For a long time, the 1937 constitution was derided as a mere copy of its authoritarian European counterparts. Along the same lines, for decades politicians and academics viewed the CLT as a reproduction of Italian fascist legislation: similar to the *Carta del lavoro*. These are two misunderstandings that have been confronted and dismantled by the latest studies, whose results point out the special features of those documents, paying attention to the selective and creative interpretations that Brazilian politicians and intellectuals used in the process of appropriating the international literature, whether it dealt with the law, aesthetics, science, education, or any other subject.

Oliveira Vianna, the most prominent intellectual involved in the assembly of the corporatist organization project in Brazil, provides suggestive clues about the circulation of political and legal ideas in that country. He recognized the "inclination toward fascism" among several "technicians" in charge of developing union and labor legislation, who read "the Italian treatises on Social Law and Corporate Law" in "copious abundance," highlighting "the entire luminous galaxy of jurists of Mussolini's corporatism."[18] However, it seems more accurate to say they were inspired by—rather than copying—the Italian legal model, because everywhere in the world, intellectuals often keep a close eye on international debates in order to use those ideas in their own way.[19]

With respect to the Brazilian Labor Courts, it should be noted briefly that the structure and operations of the fascist *Magistratura del Lavoro* were very different.[20] That system abolished class representation in the courts; conciliation was done almost exclusively by fascist unions; a minuscule proportion of individual disputes were resolved by court decisions; collective bargaining agreements were rarely handled by the *Magistratura del Lavoro*, since the party and the executive were involved in such disputes.[21] Many other differences could be cited, but suffice it to say that the Italian corporatist model was appropriated, modified, and adapted to a different national and historical context.[22]

The writings of Oliveira Vianna contain several references to other international experiences, including the French solidarism that marked his intellectual output.[23] During the debates regarding the plans for the Labor Courts' organization, which took place in 1935, he rejected accusations of fascist influences in the document. At the time, he sided with the principles of constitutional law in the United States, where the Supreme Court recognized the constitutionality of delegating regulatory powers, referring to the agencies of the New Deal.[24]

Extending the comparison, we find in the Weimar Republic a German model for judicial organization that is like the one in Brazil, but with the major difference that the unions were independent from the state and could act directly in the workplace. Indeed, the Weimar Labor Courts[25] had a tripartite composition, and their legal proceedings showed several similarities to their Brazilian counterpart: the parties presented their arguments; the representatives of each party sat in the audience; and an agreement between the litigants was initially attempted, but the judge had the initiative and the power to structure the process and ultimately have more say in the outcome. In organizational terms, the lower labor courts were independent of the regular courts and functioned as special courts, although as in Brazil the judges were career magistrates. An even clearer similarity with Brazil was the makeup and election of the members of the lower and higher courts, both represented by a judge and representatives of both parties involved, the latter chosen from a list of candidates drawn up by labor unions and employers' organizations. The structure of the Weimar Labor Courts also included local and regional courts (which served as courts of appeal, like the regional courts in Brazil), culminating in the Federal Labor Court. Such similarities are certainly not mere coincidences, especially as we know that several Brazilian jurists were familiar with that German institution.

Finally, it may be argued that the normative power of the Brazilian Labor Courts originated from compulsory state arbitration introduced in the early twentieth century in Australia and New Zealand. This model was well known to jurists in Brazil, even before the 1930s.[26] In the opinion of jurists Orlando Gomes and Elson Gottschalk, "compulsory arbitration of collective disputes did not originate, as erroneously supposed, from the the *'magistratura del lavoro'* of Italian fascism; [compulsory arbitration] was practiced as far back as 1904 in Australia and New Zealand, through the industrial courts, which were both administrative and judicial in nature because they dictated arbitral awards, with effective judgments."[27] For an overview of the "Australian road" as an available model also in United States at the beginning of the twentieth century, Leon Fink sets up a compelling approach in his chapter that can establish a dialogue with our analysis.

In short, when we carefully observe the footnotes of several works by jurists, we find numerous references to legislation and labor courts in other countries, with abundant and scholarly references to works published in several foreign languages. Therefore, we can say that the organization of the Labor Courts in Brazil resulted from multiple influences. This was due to a broader international repertoire of similar examples known to Brazilian lawmakers and jurists. We should also point out that many features of the Brazilian Labor Courts were already an integral part of similar institutions established in this country since at least the 1920s. Such experiences have given rise to practices, doctrines, and jurisprudence that influenced the creation of the labor court system in the 1930s and '40s. Finally, as its framers wished it, the corporatist union model survived Vargas's *Estado Novo* dictatorship, which was overthrown in late 1945. The Labor Courts were expanded and consolidated from that time forward.

The Labor Courts, the CLT, and the Expansion of Workers' Rights

The 1946 Constitutional Assembly did not make any major changes in the field of labor rights. It basically introduced two important modifications: the right to strike, denied by the 1937 constitution, was recognized, and the Labor Courts became part of the judicial branch, maintaining its procedural characteristics and normative powers. As a result of this new situation, despite strict legal limitations, in the 1950s and early '60s strikes could be used as an instrument of pressure, not only on employers but on the Labor Courts themselves.

It should be explained that, in practice, compulsory arbitration of disputes and the normative power of the labour Courts were not incompatible with strike action. On the contrary, the urban labor movement grew stronger in the 1950s. In the midst of rising prices during the second Vargas administration (1951–1954), in March 1953, the so-called "Strike of the 300 Thousand" took place in São Paulo. For twenty-seven days, workers from textile, metal, glass, printing, and other industries paralyzed production. Despite winning a wage increase of only 23 percent (37 percent less than demanded) the movement was successful, as union membership grew, new leaders emerged from factory councils, union boards opposing the strike were marginalized, and the Pact for Inter-Union Unity was created, which embraced around one hundred unions. This strike was a mark of the future challenges of the working class. Likewise, rural workers began to use strikes and the labor tribunals to fight for the application and expansion of existing rights.

In other words, it was a strategic decade for the organization of workers, including new occupational categories among those with access to labor rights. Therefore, the 1950s was a time when the "social problem" of rural workers ceased to be a secondary matter, growing into an explosive issue in the early 1960s. The organizational capacity and pressure of those workers in the arenas of law and justice came into the forefront. Suffice it to say that, by 1960, there were only five state-sanctioned rural unions, but by 1963 that number had skyrocketed to over 400! In some areas, the demands of rural workers even surpassed those of their urban counterparts.[28]

For years, the CLT was the fundamental document that guided the provision of labor and social security rights, as well as regulating the trade union model. As we have seen, the CLT did not include rural workers due to pressure from landowners and did not recognize them as an occupational category with rights to organize unions and have access to labor and social security legislation. Although they were in the absolute majority in Brazil until the 1950s, and certainly for that very reason, rural workers continued to be excluded from the labor rights agenda. However, as of that decade, activist associations were organized, such as the Peasant Leagues (*Ligas Camponesas*), although they were not recognized by the state. Despite all these difficulties, they were granted some rights within the sphere of the regular courts themselves. This is because, even after the creation of the Labor Courts, there were virtually no Conciliation and Arbitration Boards (*Juntas de Conciliação e Julgamento*) —the initial stage of handling labor disputes—outside major cities. Therefore, for a long time, throughout most of Brazil, labor disputes came under the jurisdiction of judges presiding over so-called regular courts. Although many of those judges considered the claims of rural workers to be legitimate, possibly giving them favorable rulings,[29] the regular courts took much longer to judge these disputes, since they also dealt with other types of claims and did not focus specifically on labor relations. At any rate, not only did employees who were not covered by the CLT achieve existing rights but even rural workers (tenant farmers, sharecroppers, and so forth) won some victories in the struggle for labor rights.

However, rural workers' access to labor rights would increase only during the administration of President João Goulart, when the Statute of the Rural Worker (*Estatuto do Trabalhador Rural* [ETR]) came into effect amid a widespread campaign for basic reforms, particularly land reform.[30] In July 1963, the ETR gave rural workers all existing rights pertaining to urban employees, recognizing the demands of labor. The landowners' response was violent and swift.[31] Even so, the ETR had highly positive impacts in the area of trade union organization in the countryside, although not as great in relation to the effective achievement of labor rights. One reason for this was the lack of a specific provision of budgetary resources to cover this new flood of demands for benefits. Even when the ETR was in effect, rural, self-employed, and domestic workers continued to encounter many obstacles to obtaining full access to labor and social security rights in Brazil.

The civilian-military coup of 1964 that overthrew President João Goulart and introduced another dictatorship in Brazil prevented all kinds of social reforms from being implemented, particularly land reform. Upon taking power, the government intervened in trade unions, deposed leaders, arrested militants (some were tortured to death), and set in motion a process of rigid control over the labor movement. Organized rural workers were also violently repressed, and the ETR lost strength. The next initiative to focus on rural workers would be taken only during the Médici administration (1969–1974): the Rural Assistance Fund (*Fundo de Assistência Rural* [Funrural]), in 1971, which provided social security coverage for that category of workers. The Funrural was more effective because it established an institution, administration, and source of funds that were separate from the National Social Security Institute (*Instituto Nacional de Previdência Social* [INPS]), the agency that covered all other workers. Furthermore, the Funrural created a strategy for obtaining resources that did not impose direct contributions on workers or landowners, which explains the weaker opposition from the latter, especially during an authoritarian regime. Even so, in the same political context, in 1972 and 1973, they were included in the pension benefits allowed to domestic workers and the self-employed, who were then able to sign onto the INPS. Although rural workers were no longer the majority in the country, they had tremendous weight in numbers. The same was true with domestic servants, primarily women.

In the 1970s, thousands of labor and social security rights claims were filed, especially by rural workers who had been organizing for two decades. According to the statutory provisions in effect since 1971, such claims were retroactive. This was crucial in the case of applications for retirement and pensions for rural workers, which had never before been incorporated into the labor rights agenda. As a strategic response, rural landowners began employing huge numbers of casual workers who were not covered by the law, taking full advantage of this legal loophole. Practiced by major companies formed with government subsidies, as well as traditional farms, the effects of the employers' actions were devastating, intensifying the system of exploitation of rural labor. Thus, while Brazilian agriculture modernized through the establishment of agribusiness, the latest technology and productivity growth—largely for export—, new ways of exploiting rural workers emerged.

These ways were expressed, in particular, in the emergence of workers called boia-fria: a worker recruited on a daily basis without any formal employment contract, with payment linked to the fulfillment of production targets that were so exhausting that they were sometimes worked to death.[32] This phenomenon was linked to the international development of a modern and sophisticated practice of using forms of slavelike labor, marked less by limiting freedom of movement than the inhuman conditions in which workers are required to conduct their activities. Since the early 1970s, due to political and social developments brought about by the civilian-military dictatorship, many of the known practices of exploitation of rural workers have taken on new meanings. They are no longer associated with the "backwardness" of agriculture or any public policies leading to agrarian reform, as occurred between the late 1950s and early 1960. Their increasing use has come to be associated with the establishment of government rural modernization programs involving the promotion of existing farms and the creation of large farms in areas that might or might not be new.

Ending the dictatorship in Brazil was a slow process. Between 1979, when the Amnesty Law was passed, and 1988, when a new constitution was approved, the country continued to experience hard times from the standpoint of labor rights. However, it witnessed a new movement of unionized workers, especially in the states of São Paulo and Rio de Janeiro. The 1988 constitution enshrined a new level of citizenship rights, expanding political rights, protecting civil rights, and ensuring social rights. Without fundamentally affecting the CLT, it redefined the powers of the Public Prosecutor's Office (*Ministério Público*—MP) and thus the Labor Prosecutor's Office (*Ministério Público do Trabalho*—MPT). As a branch of the MP, the MPT took on the role of protecting collective and individual rights and had the power to initiate "class action suits" in case of breaches of labor laws. Thus, the MPT started to work with the Labor Courts to control and repress practices that subjected workers to "modern slavery," among other things.

With regard to the Labor Courts, in the 1990s they suffered several onslaughts, even proposals for their elimination, as the winds of international neoliberalism were also blowing in Brazil. Nevertheless, on the whole, the institution was strengthened. This was because, first, Constitutional Amendment no. 24 of December 9, 1999, eliminated the class representatives who had taken part in the Labor Courts by appointment of workers' and employers' unions since the institution had been established. Among other reasons, this had been a major problem for achieving greater recognition of the Labor Courts, particularly within the judiciary itself, which considered them "minor" due to the content of their cases, "simplified" procedural rites, and tripartite composition. Second, in December 2004, Congress approved Constitutional Amendment no. 45, which ended the so-called Judicial Reform that had been underway since 1992. This amendment introduced a fundamental change, since it expanded the Labor Courts' jurisdiction to include "labor relations" as a whole, instead of "employment relations." To give an idea of the magnitude of this change, the article brings into the jurisdiction of the Labor Court not only employed workers (de facto and de jure, in accordance with the actual conditions in which they work) but a very different category of workers providing services "in a non-subordinated manner" as occasional service providers, even the so-called underemployed.

The Labor Courts and Their Expansion

The history of the Labor Courts has been marked by onslaughts on that institution, and there were times when its very existence was jeopardized. However, this is also a story of empowerment, which suggests reflections on the courts' importance and performance over time. Recent studies of proceedings handled in the Labor Courts, albeit partial studies that do not allow for generalizations, have produced some findings.[33] The first is that many of these cases concluded in an agreement—in other words, the Labor Courts exercised their power of conciliation between the parties. Although agreements can often mean losses for workers, they also bring immediate gains, including symbolic ones. Therefore, it is very difficult, if not impossible, to assess this type of outcome. Another finding is that it is also impossible to consider the Labor Courts as an institution that, in theory, protects workers through its decisions, or as a *locus* in which the employers have guaranteed advantages. In many of the decisions studied, it was found that there could be several kinds of advantages for both workers and business owners. Furthermore, there is a wide range of decisions in which the two parties are contemplated in different aspects of the ruling.

Thus, even if one cannot say from the decisions in labor claims that the Labor Courts are a form of justice that favors the workers—which, in theory, would negate a dimension of justice, that of an arena of conflict with a level playing field—one can argue that their existence has been and remains an unequivocal protection of labor rights, which has been decisive for workers' struggles. That is the point: there are laws on labor rights and there are courts to protect and supervise them. In this sense, there is no doubt that the Labor Courts have been positive for workers, even when workers' activities have been curtailed, as happened during the civilian-military dictatorship from 1964 to 1985. So we should not confuse the effects of the political and legal presence of that institution in the market and in labor relations with the adjudication of labor suits, because there are numerous variables to be considered when analyzing the results.

It is against this backdrop that this chapter examines the expansion of the Labor Courts since the 1940s. For this purpose it is worth clarifying how the Conciliation and Arbitration Boards were created, along with the necessary creation of the positions of judges of first instance and bureaucrats. During the *Estado Novo*, as there was no legislative power and the Labor Courts were part of the executive branch, the creation of new boards was decided directly by Vargas and his Labor Minister. After 1946, when the Labor Courts became part of the judiciary, the constitution required that the creation of boards be made through a bill to be submitted by a congressman to the legislature, which should vote on it and then submit it for the executive branch's approval or veto. Therefore, it is clear that a sensitive political negotiation process had to be carried out in order for a bill to be successful. This is because, between 1946 and 1988, the Labor Courts did not have administrative and financial autonomy to submit their requests. The 1988 constitution changed that by allowing the Labor Courts the initiative to submit bills to the legislature to create boards, justifying their need and the existence of funding. Currently, this is done through the Superior Council of the Labor Courts, which, with the approval of the National Council of Justice, sends the requests to Congress, which passes them on to the president. In other words, since 1988, the institution has become more independent and gained more power to manage its own growth, which is an important variable in understanding its expansion since that time.

Figure 9.1 shows the increasing quantitative change in Conciliation and Arbitration Boards (JCJs). They are the best parameter for our analysis, since, as bodies of first instance, they handle a vast number of labor claims.

In 1941, the year the Labor Courts were established, there were 35 JCJs in operation. By the end of the *Estado Novo* in 1945, that number had grown slightly. The country was in a "state of war," which entailed the loss of rights for those who were considered

Figure 9.1. Expansion of Conciliation and Arbitration Boards (1934–2013)

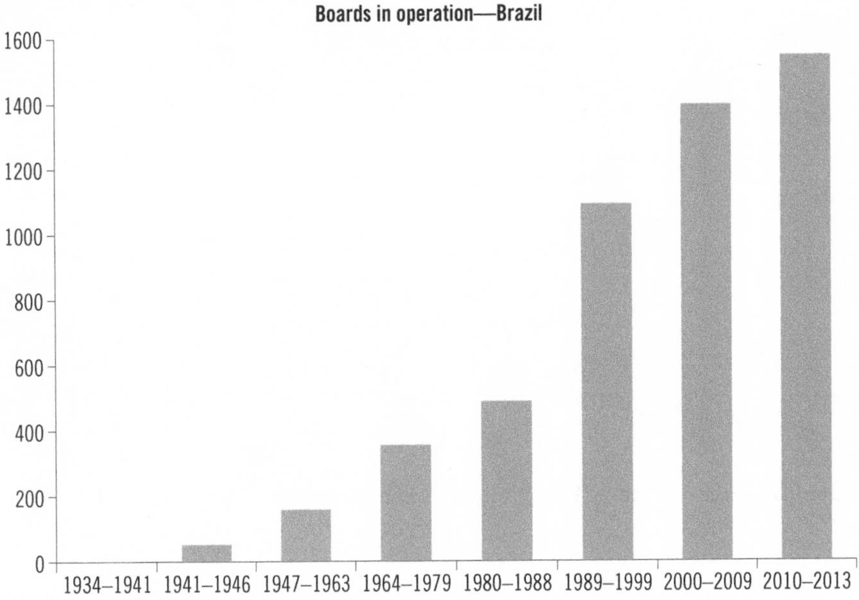

Boards in operation—Brazil

Source: Tribunal Superior do Trabalho, http://www.tst.jus.br/instaladas-e-nao-instaladas.

"soldiers of production." It was a period of the legal increase in working hours; postponement of, or compensation for, vacation time; prohibition of job mobility; and authorization for women and children to work at night. Moreover, workers who wanted to file claims in the Labor Courts through the JCJs were supposed to leave work without pay during the litigation, no matter how long it took. Even under those circumstances, although we do not know how many cases were initiated by employers, the fact is that thousands of workers went to the Labor Courts between 1941 and 1945, reaching an annual average of 29,000 individual disputes.

In 1946 alone, the year the Labor Courts became a special branch of the judiciary, we find the first (and small) peak of growth with the creation of nine JCJs. Following the end of the Vargas dictatorship and the extraordinary rise of the labor and trade union movement in the immediate postwar period, workers expressed their pent-up dissatisfaction through strikes, support for left-wing parties and politicians, and mass claims in the JCJs. This becomes evident when we observe the number of cases handled during that period (Figure 9.2). In 1944, the JCJs reported receiving 36,000 complaints. By 1945, that number had risen to 46,000, and in 1946 it jumped to 62,000. The gap—still not very broad—between the number of claims received (145,000) and judged (130,000) between 1941 to 1945 also helps explain that initial growth spurt. The effect of the expansion of the JCJs in 1946 became clear the following year, when

Figure 9.2. Number of Cases for Conciliation and Arbitration Boards (1941–2013)

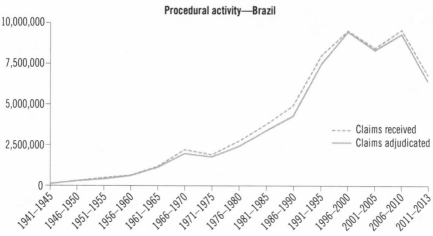

Source: Tribunal Superior do Trabalho, Varas do Trabalho, http://www.tst.jus.br/varas-do-trabalho2

the number of cases adjudicated was 7,000 higher than the claims received. These results clearly suggest the concern of the Labor Courts with judicial efficiency in the initial years of their operations and consolidation, enabling the pace of trials to keep up with the demand.[34]

Between 1947 and 1963, a period that covers most of the democratic era (from 1945 to 1964) between the *Estado Novo* and the civilian-military dictatorships, we see marginal growth of the JCJs until 1956. Conversely, the increase in litigation (suits) accelerated rapidly, reaching an average of 85,200 new cases per year (58 percent more than in 1946), while the average number of cases adjudicated was 77,000. Although the difference between the number of cases received and judged was small, there was a "pent-up demand" that seems to have justified the creation of 17 JCJs in 1957 (second stage of growth), which, along with 1958, was a year that showed visible procedural efficiency (268,000 judgments and 246,000 new cases registered). Between 1959 and 1963 we see a rapid expansion in labor claims (178,000 per year) and a third leap in the expansion of the JCJs. Of the 79 units created during that period, 47 were established in 1962 and 1963, during the João Goulart admin-istration. That is, this occurred in the context of radical political polarization, the mobilization of the labor movement, and the highest rate of strikes ever seen in the country. These two years saw an average of 232,000 cases received by the JCJs. The demand for the Labor Courts' services was so great that despite the creation of so many boards, the number of judgments reached was always lower than the number of new claims received, to the detriment of procedural efficiency. Although we have not found statistics in this regard, we can attribute the increase in litigation and the number of JCJs to the number of cases filed in the Labor Courts by rural workers, who had been organizing in several ways since the late 1950s. The increased presence of these workers and the radicalization of politics do not seem to be a fortuitous coincidence for understanding the significant increase in claims filed in the first instance of the Labor Courts.

Although we have found some symmetry in the democratic period between greater collective mobilization of workers, the growing number of JCJs, and the demand for their services, this correlation must be qualified. This is because (setting aside the increase in the economically active population (EAP) during that period, a variable that does not fit within the bounds of this study) a reverse hypothesis allows us to understand the data in the context of the civilian-military dictatorship. Repression, intervention in most unions, and the heavy restriction of the normative power of the Labor Courts—to the extent that the courts could no longer arbitrate wage increases, being limited to applying the rates stipulated by the government—were decisive factors that led workers to seek out the Labor Courts via individual disputes. That is, during the dictatorship, the Labor Courts became one of the few—often the only—places where workers could seek, and even find protection of, their rights.

Indeed, as of 1964, we see a veritable explosion in litigation. While the annual average of cases received between 1946 and 1963 was 114,000, during the 21-year dictatorship that figure reached approximately 493,000! Of course, we must take into account not only the growing number of workers eligible to file labor claims, but also the expansion of the Labor Courts throughout the country. When we compare the years that saw the largest number of cases during the democratic period and during the dictatorship, we see that 1,713 cases were filed with the JCJs in 1963, while in 1984 the average was 2,053 (55 percent higher), which reveals the intense judicialization of conflicts during the civilian-military regime. It should be noted that during the dictatorship, 223 new JCJs (10 per year) were established, 108 more than in the democratic period (6 per year). However, almost half of them were created between 1978 and 1981, precisely in the years of the "slow and gradual easing" of the authoritarian regime. That period coincides with the revival of the labor movement and an extraordinary wave of strikes, led by the "new unionism" (*novo sindicalismo*). In 1978, a wildcat strike by metalworkers in an industrial area of São Paulo took the country by surprise. Over the following three years, hundreds of strikes across various sectors of the economy demonstrated strong dissatisfaction with the government, challenged the military regime, demanded greater popular participation and freedom for unions, and put workers at the forefront of the struggle for redemocratization. It was also during those years of social and political unrest that the number of cases jumped from about 500,000 to nearly 800,000 per year!

Therefore, the repression of authoritarian rule helps explain the increased demand for the Labor Courts as one of the few alternatives for rights advocacy. The regime's decision to maintain the corporatist structure, including labor laws and Labor Courts, was a bid for legitimacy. However, their continued existence was subjected to strong control by measures from the executive branch. It is also pertinent to the hypothesis that the process of political opening toward the end of the dictatorship, which had workers as one of its most important vectors, contributed to the race to the courts, putting pressure to increase the number of JCJs. But again, we must consider the challenges involved in procedural efficacy. The period between 1971 and 1974 saw terrible repression and a new peak in the growth of the JCJs (76 in all) after seven years of slow growth, during which time the difference between cases received and adjudicated was 233,000 per year, characterizing a period of clearly unmet demand. That lag increased even further until the mid-1980s, despite another spike in the number of JCJs between 1978 and 1981.

In the context of Brazil's return to democracy, we have found a high rate of new JCJs in nine consecutive years (1986 and 1994), with emphasis on peaks in 1989 and 1993, when the Labor Courts, in fact, achieved nationwide coverage. The first peak (with 93 new JCJs) took place shortly after the promulgation of the 1988 constitution, which, as we have seen, greatly expanded the Labor Courts' powers. The institution became even more open to individual claims and, not surprisingly, there was an increase of 209,000 adjudications between 1988 and 1989. The second peak, in 1993, marks the milestone of 202 new JCJs established, expressing a growing demand for the Labor Courts that continued throughout the 1990s, reaching approximately 2 million cases per year.

It is worth noting that the sharp increase in the number of JCJs between 1986 and 1996, perhaps unparalleled in international experience, occurred in the context of the implementation of neoliberal policies. Since 1995–2003, a small number of JCJs has been established, coinciding with the two terms of President Fernando Henrique Cardoso (1995–2002), during which the labor law was subjected to steady attacks, and there was a real threat that the Labor Courts would be eliminated. After all, that administration's neoliberal agenda included the "flexibility" of labor rights and correlative to that, the primacy of the negotiated over the legislated. However, the case load handled during the Cardoso administration was impressive: only 91,000 more cases received than adjudicated, while in the nine previous years of continuous improvement in the number of JCJs, the difference was 996,000 cases. This discrepancy is not hard to explain, as Cardoso's government benefited from previously created JCJs, especially the 293 installed in 1993 and 1994, precisely when the number of cases heard was higher than that received (a difference of 24,000 cases).

The pace of growth of the JCJs resumed in 2004 and has remained constant ever since, with another significant jump in 2005. In other words, shortly after the approval of Constitutional Amendment No. 45, which gave the Labor Courts jurisdiction to arbitrate "labor relations" and not just "employment relations," there was an even greater increase in individual claims. In the years between 2005 and 2013, the number of cases grew by 214,000 per year compared with the previous decade (1995–2005), to the detriment of procedural efficiency (658,000 more cases received than adjudicated).

Clearly the immense demand for the Labor Courts' services is due in large part to the massive deterioration of working conditions and the "delegitimization of the legal rules by the capitalists."[35] However, the explosion in litigation is also related to greater access to the Labor Courts. This is clearly demonstrated when we observe the growing number of JCJs and their expansion beyond the state capitals, where they continued to be concentrated until the 1970s. In other words, since 1989, although the number of JCJs in large urban centers had grown—keeping pace with their population and economic density—the increase was almost twice greater in the areas that we call the interior (outside state capitals and major cities).

Several factors may have weighed in targeting this expansion toward cities of various sizes, which are distributed throughout the territories of Brazilian states: the inclusion of rural workers in labor and social security rights; the establishment of industrial activities and agribusiness operations outside the South-Southeast region of the country; and the work of the labor judiciary itself, which demands action to guarantee labor rights, not leaving them under the jurisdiction of the ordinary courts. In any case, what we can see in Figure 9.3 is that the Labor Courts have become effectively a nationwide institution, establishing their presence throughout the country's vast territory, although, of course, they could still expand even further.

Figure 9.3. JCJs in Operation—State Capitals vs. Interior

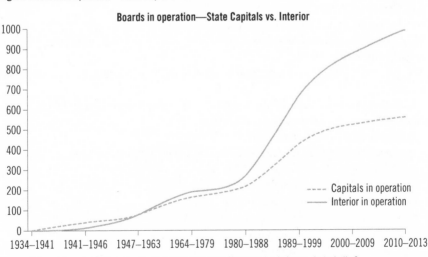

Source: Tribunal Superior do Trabalho, Varas do Trabalho, http://www.tst.jus.br/varas-do-trabalho2.

Conclusion

Over time, public opinion about the judiciary in Brazil has stressed positive aspects of the Labor Courts. The fact is that they are no longer the timid and discredited institution that they were during much of their existence. In fact, in the early decades of the twenty-first century, it was the ordinary courts that sought to approach and appropriate the principles of the labor courts—orality, informality, cost-free justice, and conciliation—in the face of the growing demands and criticisms of Brazilian society, which now require more efficiency, speed and transparency from the judiciary. The present poses new questions to the past now that the Labor Courts are expanding their prerogatives, a difficult but systematic process of democratizing access to legal services. Thus, they have become a guarantee of rights that go beyond the world of work because they are rights that defend the lives and dignity of workers as citizens.

Notes

1. Moraes, *Apontamentos de direito operário*, 19.
2. Decree no. 1,637, January 5, 1907.
3. Chaves, *A trajetória do Departamento Estadual*, 46, and ch. 3.
4. Coleção das Leis do Brasil de 1918. Decree no. 3.550, October 16, 1918, v. I, 168–170.
5. Ferreira, *Princípios de legislação social*, 46–56. Later studies refer to the Rural Courts that were merely supported by Waldemar Ferreira's observations.
6. Coleção das Leis do Brasil de 1923. Decree no. 16.027, April 30, 1923, 368–371.
7. Castro, *A questão social*, 121.
8. Gomes, *Burguesia e trabalho*, particularly ch. 3.
9. The bill also included the creation of another special court, the Electoral Courts, which was done by the Electoral Code of 1932.
10. Decree no. 21.396, May 12, 1932.
11. Decree no. 22.132, November 25, 1932.
12. See the chapters by William Suarez-Potts, Victor Uribe, and Diego Ortúzar and Angela Vergara's chapters in this book.
13. Free translation of an excerpt from Morel, Gomes, and Pessanha, *Sem medo da utopia*, 69–73.
14. Article 122. Constitution of the Republic of the United States of Brazil (July 16, 1934), quoted in Fornazieri, "Os debates parlamentares."
15. Biavaschi, *O Direito do Trabalho*.
16. Fornazieri, "Os debates parlamentares"; Decree no. 1.237, May 2, 1939.
17. Moraes Filho, "Magistrados de pé," 10–11.
18. Vianna, "Razões da originalidade," 278–279.
19. Hall, "Corporativismo e fascismo."
20. Silva, "The Brazilian and Italian Labor Courts."
21. Jocteau, *La magistratura e i conflitti*.
22. Gentile, "O corporativismo fascista."
23. Brescianni, *O charme da ciência*.

24. Vianna, *Problemas de direito*, 48, 57.

25. Wunderlich, *German Labor Courts*.

26. Castro, *A questão social*, 148–163.

27. Gomes and Gottschalk, *Curso de direito*, 924.

28. Welch, *A semente foi plantada*, 282.

29. Linhares and Silva, *Terra prometida*, 161–162.

30. Gomes, *Cidadania e direitos*, 46–60.

31. Ibid.

32. A reference to the packed meals they brought with them, which were cold by the time they came to eat them.

33. Gomes and Silva, *A Justiça do Trabalho*.

34. We must bear in mind that the cases adjudicated were not limited to those filed in the year when the judgement was handed down, since they also include those filed in previous years.

35. Cardoso, "Direito do trabalho."

Bibliography

Arida, Pérsio, Edmar Bacha, and André Resende. "Credit, Interest, and Jurisdictional Uncertainty." In *Inflation Targeting, Debts, and the Brazilian Experience, 1999 to 2003*. Ed. F. Giavazzi, I. Goldfajn, and S. Herrera. Cambridge, Mass.: MIT Press, 2005.

Biavaschi, Magda. *O Direito do Trabalho no Brasil*. São Paulo: LTr, 2007.

Brescianni, Maria S. *O charme da ciência e a sedução da objetividade: Oliveira Vianna entre os intérpretes do Brasil*. São Paulo: Editora Unesp, 2005.

Cardoso, Adalberto. "Direito do trabalho e relações de classe no Brasil contemporâneo." In *A democracia e os três poderes no Brasil*. Ed. Luiz Werneck Vianna. Belo Horizonte: Editora UFMG, 2002.

Castelar, Pinheiro A. "Judiciário, reforma e economia: uma visão dos magistrados, 2002" apud Lopez de Mello, Brisa and Ribeiro, Ivan C. "Os juízes brasileiros favorecem a parte mais fraca?" In Berkeley, *Program in Law & Economics. Latin American and Caribbean Law and Economics Association. Annual Papers*. Berkeley: University of California, 2006.

Castro, Augusto V. de. *A questão social*. Rio de Janeiro: Conselheiro Candido de Oliveira, 1920.

Chaves, Marcelo A. *A trajetória do Departamento Estadual do Trabalho e mediação das relações de trabalho (1911–1937)*. São Paulo: LTr, 2012.

Ferreira, Waldemar. *Princípios de legislação social e de direito judiciário do trabalho*, vol. 1. São Paulo: São Paulo Editora Limitada, 1938.

Fornazieri, Ligia L. "Os debates parlamentares e a situação do Direito do Trabalho no Brasil." Campinas, May 2014 (unpublished).

Gentile, Fabio. "O corporativismo fascista e sua influência na legislação trabalhista brasileira dos anos trinta." Paper presented at the 7º Encontro dos Seminários de Sociologia, Política e História do Programa de Pós-Graduação em Sociologia da Universidade de São Paulo, on November 29, 2012.

Gomes, Angela de C. *Burguesia e trabalho; política e legislação social no Brasil (1917–1937)*. Rio de Janeiro: Editora Campus, 1979.

———. *Cidadania e direitos do trabalho*. Rio de Janeiro: Zahar, 2002.

Gomes, Angela de C., and Fernando T. da Silva, eds. *A Justiça do Trabalho e sua história: os direitos dos trabalhadores no Brasil*. Campinas: Editora da Unicamp, 2013.

Gomes, Orlando, and Elton Gottschalk. *Curso de direito do trabalho*. São Paulo: Forense, 1971.

Grynspan, Mário. "Acesso e recurso à justiça no Brasil: algumas questões." In *Justiça e violência*. Ed. Dulci Pandolfi. Rio de Janeiro: Fundação Getúlio Vargas, 1999.

Hall, Michael. "Corporativismo e fascismo nas origens das leis trabalhistas brasileiras." In *Do corporativismo ao neoliberalismo: Estado e trabalhadores no Brasil e na Inglaterra*. Ed. Angela Araujo. São Paulo: Boitempo, 2002.

Jocteau, Gian C. *La magistratura e i conflitti di lavoro durante il fascismo, 1926–1934*. Milan: Feltrinelli Editore, 1978.

Linhares, Maria Y., and Francisco Carlos T. da Silva. *Terra prometida: uma história da questão agrária no Brasil*. Rio de Janeiro: Campus, 1999.

Moraes, Evaristo de. *Apontamentos de direito operário*. São Paulo: LTr, 1971.

Moraes Filho, Evaristo de. "Magistrados de pé: entrevista com Evaristo de Moraes Filho." *Revista da ANPT*, Silver Jubilee issue, 1979/2004.

Morel, Regina, Angela de C. Gomes, and Elina G. Pessanha, eds. *Sem medo da utopia: Evaristo de Moraes Filho, arquiteto da Sociologia e do Direito do Trabalho no Brasil*. São Paulo: LTr, 2007.

Setti, Paulo. *Merecimento e eficiência: performance de advogados e juízes na Justiça do Trabalho em Campinas*. Campinas: Centro de Memória da Unicamp, 1997.

Silva, Fernando T. da. "The Brazilian and Italian Labor Courts: Comparative Notes." *International Review of Social History* 55 (Dec. 2010).

Vianna, Oliveira. *Problemas de direito corporativo*. Brasília: Câmara dos Deputados, 1983.

———. "Razões da originalidade do sistema sindical brasileiro." In *Ensaios inéditos*. Campinas: Editora da Unicamp, 1991.

Welch, Clifford. *A semente foi plantada: as raízes paulistas do movimento sindical camponês, 1924–1964*. São Paulo: Expressão Popular, 2010.

Wunderlich, Frieda. *German Labor Courts*. Chapel Hill: The University of North Carolina Press, 1946.

CHAPTER 10

Bringing Justice to the Workplace

Labor Courts and Labor Laws in Chile, 1930s–1980s

DIEGO ORTÚZAR

ANGELA VERGARA

> Labor proceeding is born and based
> on the inequality of both parties
> to exert their rights
> —Jacobo Schaulsohn

Introduction

In 1927, Chilean lawyer Óscar Álvarez Andrews published his law thesis on the relationship between working people and the judicial system, paying special attention to the question of work accidents.[1] Álvarez Andrews had worked in the Labor Department as an inspector, where he had gained firsthand experience on the enormous difficulties in enforcing the nation's labor laws. In 1917, he explained, the Labor Department was no more than "eight employees, whose main goal was to collect and submit labor statistics to state authorities, assist injured workers in the best way possible and prepare reports about working conditions." At that time, inspectors did not conduct regular visits and could not provide judicial assistance to workers. One day, Álvarez Andrews recalled, "a humble woman arrived in the Office [The Labor Department]. Her employer had fired her without paying her severance pay." Although the Labor Department had no legal capacity to process the claim, its director, Eugenio Frías, asked Álvarez Andrews to approach the employer and obtain some form of monetary compensation. Like most workplaces at the time, it was a very small shop, located in a dark alley near Santiago's railroad station. After a long and difficult conversation with the employer, they agreed that Álvarez Andrews would come back the following day to collect the money. As arranged, he returned the next day, and as he was entering the building, he heard them saying behind the door, "What! The *rotos*'s lawyer is back."[2] Álvarez Andrews succeeded in collecting the money, and, more importantly, the experience convinced him to become a lawyer and represent the interests of working people.[3]

Álvarez Andrews's account portrays the transformation of Chile's labor relations system and the emergence of a new form of justice. During the first three decades of the twentieth century, Chilean policy makers enacted an impressive system of labor laws to regulate the workplace, institutionalize labor relations, and provide social benefits. Influenced by local political traditions and international intellectual currents, progressive lawmakers conceived labor legislation as a tool to respond to increasing social tensions, rising strike activity, and the radicalization of the labor movement, redefining the meanings and application of the law. From a larger perspective, the enactment of labor laws was part of a deeper transformation of the state and its bureaucracy, bringing together medical, social, legal, and scientific ideas of modernization in what Chilean historian María Angélica Illanes has called the "new social function of the State."[4]

The implementation of this ambitious legal project required a nationwide administrative infrastructure, trained public employees, and a specialized system of courts. Through the Ministry of Labor, the Labor Department, and the Social Security Office, the state attempted to transform the workplace.[5] Labor courts became an important piece of this system. Established in 1927 and more clearly regulated by the Labor Code of 1931, labor courts were concerned with the many legal disputes regarding the enforcement of individual and collective work contracts, the interpretation of labor laws, social security claims, and occupational risks compensations (work accidents and occupational diseases). Initially considered administrative tribunals, in 1955 they became an integral part of the judicial system. Until their dissolution in 1981, they played a relevant role in managing local conflicts between labor and capital, reinforcing the ideas of consensus, mediation, and protection that had inspired early-twentieth-century social legislation.

During the first half of the twentieth century, Chilean policy makers celebrated what they considered an advanced legislative legacy. Moisés Poblete Troncoso, prominent Chilean labor lawyer and expert, exulted in 1949 that "Chile was the first country in Latin America to create special courts to resolve labor conflicts, both collective as well as individual conflicts."[6] To some extent, Poblete Troncoso was correct. Chile, although not necessarily the first one on the continent, was able to create institutions that, over time, protected workers' rights. However, legal cases, documents from the Ministry of Labor and Labor Department, and contemporary accounts included in this chapter also suggest that the Chilean labor-court system suffered from many flaws. Lack of funding and material resources considerably limited the enforcement of the law and the everyday work of the Labor Department and labor courts. Outside larger cities, the presence of labor courts was sparse, and civil courts were usually concerned with labor matters. The heavily bureaucratic and lengthy legal procedures as well as traditional patterns of migration and mobility discouraged workers from filing cases in labor courts. Employers actively opposed the work of labor courts, using political, legal, and social means to harass workers and labor inspectors, contest case resolutions, and evade their legal responsibilities. More importantly, not all Chilean workers had the same opportunities to contest the power of employers; those who were able to confront their employers, as Brian Loveman explains, were also the ones who were able to organize collectively and "acquire the legal tools and knowledge to confront proprietors in judicial and quasijudicial proceedings."[7] The uneven impact of labor courts in Chile also reflects the deep contrasts that existed among different economic sectors and groups of workers as well as the ways in which gender and location (rural/urban) conditioned workers' access to justice.[8]

The chapter is divided into three sections. It starts by placing the history of labor courts into larger debates about the enactment of labor laws in early-twentieth-century Chile, demonstrating how the need to enforce new laws and the unique characteristics of labor legislation eventually required a separate system of justice. Second, it analyzes the formation and structure of labor courts, showing the ways in which Chile set up a comprehensive system of labor courts throughout the 1930s and the many obstacles they faced. By way of conclusion, we reflect on the changes that took place during the second half of the twentieth century, until their formal dissolution by the military dictatorship in 1981. The Chilean labor court system developed during the twentieth century and reflects the larger effort of the state to institutionalize labor relations and resolve work disputes, enforcing a legislation inspired by international ideas of mediation and consensus. This overview of labor courts provides a glimpse into how the system operated in Chile, its accomplishments and limitations, and the ways it became part of the larger state-building process.

From Labor Laws to Labor Courts, 1900–1930

Throughout Latin America, rapid urbanization and the transformation of production raised critical questions about the need to regulate the workplace. The growing activism, radicalization, and visibility of the labor movement challenged countries' political stability, inspiring larger debates about how to incorporate workers, guarantee social peace, and resolve labor conflicts.[9] As Juan Manuel Palacio's introduction to this volume illustrates, this was a transnational debate, and international congresses, the International Labor Organization (ILO) resolutions, and international publications influenced the ways in which locals understood and legislated labor and social issues.[10] Economic and political instability following World War I and during the Great Depression gave a sense of urgency to the question of the state's responsibility to protect the working class and guarantee workers' access to basic social benefits and labor rights, consolidating a transition from private charity to welfare institutions.[11]

In the first decade of the twentieth century, the Chilean state started enacting the first labor laws to regulate working conditions, systematically increasing levels of protection in the following decades.[12] The institutional basis of its labor policy was the Labor Department. Founded in 1907, the department was responsible for the enforcement of labor laws, collection of statistical information on the labor force and working conditions (e.g., salaries, accidents), and generation of proposal for new laws. Its soul was its many and very progressive labor inspectors, who traveled around the country to inspect workplaces, supervise union elections and the formation of labor unions, and educate workers about their new rights. Until 1924, there was little clarity on how labor inspectors and the department could enforce the law and, more importantly, compel employers to comply with the new regulations. In most cases, they attempted to mediate between capital and labor, looking for ways to prevent larger and longer conflicts.[13] One of their most important resources was the work inspection and visit, which allowed them to see firsthand whether employers were complying or not with the law; issue recommendations for improvement; and, when mediation had failed, potentially fine recalcitrant employers.

Without a system of labor courts, the work of labor inspectors remained limited and employers usually evaded their legal responsibilities. The state had enacted new laws, many of which redefined Chile's legal traditions (what came to be known as social rights or *derecho social*), but it had not put in place effective mechanisms to enforce the law, denounce violations of or infringement to the law, or prosecute employers who broke the law. In most cases, police officers and municipal governments were in charge of overseeing enforcement of labor laws, and civil courts were concerned with all legal conflicts and personal disagreements. The early history of work injuries' compensation illustrates the problems in resolving work issues in civil court instances. Since the mid–nineteenth century, Chile had set in place some norms, although limited, to compensate and provide health care for workers who suffered an accident at work.[14] However, because the cases fell under the jurisdiction of civil (and sometimes criminal) courts, workers had to prove an employer's fault, making lawsuits slow, bureaucratic, and expensive.

Unlike the future labor courts, civil courts addressed labor disputes as conflicts among putatively equal individuals, regardless of the real social context of the lawsuit, and focused exclusively on monetary compensation since "work" was considered a "good," and not a social relation.[15] In the case of serious work accidents, criminal investigations were also common, but difficulties finding solid legal evidence to prove employers' criminal responsibility usually led judges to dismiss the cases.[16] The story of Félix Sanderson, a mine worker who died in January 1911 when he fell into a mineshaft in El Salado, Chañaral, illustrates the limits of criminal courts.[17] According to witnesses, Sanderson and other workers were on top of a wooden structure making repairs, when the structure collapsed; he fell down a deep shaft and died. After a short investigation, the judge concluded that it was an accident and there was no responsibility on the part of the mine owner, dismissing the case. A similar case involved the death of Emilio Riquelme, a mine worker at the copper mine of Chuqui-camata in 1916. When he was cleaning its gear, a cart accidentally killed Riquelme, but the criminal court dismissed the case, arguing that it was caused by "a carelessness of the unfortunate worker."[18]

High legal fees and a heavily bureaucratic judicial system discouraged workers from filing a case, and many times employers persuaded them to settle outside the courts and accept some form of compensation.[19] For example, when a mudslide killed 19 workers in 1914 in the copper mine of El Teniente, the U.S.-owned mining company compensated the families of the deceased workers as an act, as it explained in a letter to the local political authority, of "private charity."[20] Unfortunately, most work accidents were never reported or investigated, and workers relied on alternative organizations such as mutual aid societies and labor unions to cover the costs of accidents. In 1916, Chile's first work accident law declared that workers were entitled to economic compensation and medical care in case of work injury. Employers were encouraged, but not forced, to purchase insurance coverage to pay for work accidents' expenses. Although the law made efforts to guarantee work safety, enforce new safety regulations, and establish a system of work compensations for victims and their families, it left disputes in the hands of civil courts. Additionally, intentional accidents or those due to forces of nature were not considered employers' responsibility, providing employers with an easy loophole to evade paying compensation. In reality, injured workers or surviving relatives faced lengthy trials and had to confront powerful insurance companies.[21]

Although civil courts handled numerous work-related cases, progressive legislators, academics, and lawyers started questioning the ability of civil courts to effectively resolve labor conflicts. Baldomero Merino published his law thesis in 1913, examining the characteristics and legal implications of work injury cases. Merino argued that a large number of work accidents were never reported or investigated, and economic compensations were insufficient to fulfill the victim and his family's needs. Throughout the 1910s, Chilean historian Sergio Grez documents, local newspapers published several stories of work accidents and abandoned victims, and workers' organizations started demanding a better system to guarantee protection, especially in the case of work-injury compensations.[22] For many, work accidents became a symbol of an ineffective judicial procedure and the need of a special judicial infrastructure that, as Chilean lawyer Jacobo Schaulsohn recalled, could recognize the inherent "inequality" between capital and labor to "exert their rights."[23]

The movement for social legislation reached a point of critical velocity in 1924, when a group of young military officers exerted pressure on the National Congress to approve a large and overdue package of laws. The laws, later incorporated in the First Labor Code of 1931, created the backbone of the Chilean labor relations system by guaranteeing the right to unionize, bargain collectively, and call a strike. It also set in place a comprehensive system of social protection including social security and health benefits for working families.[24] The laws raised critical questions about legal enforcement and responsibility: How would the state enforce labor laws? How would infractions be sanctioned? Which public and judicial institutions would oversee labor laws? How would the inevitably different interpretations of the law be resolved? How would the law acknowledge the many different local realities and conditions? Historians have extensively studied the political and labor aspects of this process, demonstrating the ways in which the state attempted to use labor laws to co-opt a radicalized labor movement, the complex relationship between workers and the new legal framework, and the larger political impact of this process.[25] The historiography has focused especially on the question of organized labor and larger social and union conflicts, but little is known about the question of labor courts and the ways in which workers navigated, in tandem with the Labor Department and its committed inspectors, this new judicial system.

The initial response to these questions was the creation of the *Juntas de Conciliación y Arbitraje*.[26] Established in 1924 (Law 4056), these boards oversaw both collective conflicts (*conflictos colectivos*) and individual disputes (*litigios*) for blue-collar workers. The law called for the organization of ten permanent boards located throughout the country, but only four were actually formed (all located in larger cities: Iquique, Valparaíso, Santiago, and Concepción). Led by the local labor inspectors, the members of the boards included six elected members (three representatives of the working class and three representatives of employers). Workers' representatives were to be elected by legally recognized labor unions; however, there were only a few labor unions that had achieved the legal requirements at the time. The boards were not synonymous with courts, and they had no power to execute a sentence. In reality, they did not meet on a regular basis, and in most places the responsibility of enforcing labor laws remained in the hands of civil local courts.[27] For example, civil courts were still concerned with work-injury compensations, since employers were responsible to report accidents within a five-day period.[28] Civil courts were also concerned with conflicts and disputes affecting white-collar (*empleados*) employees, limiting the council's jurisdiction to matters affecting blue-collar workers (*obreros*).[29]

Simultaneously with the organization of the boards, the state established housing tribunals. In early-twentieth-century social thought, the question of work was a problem within a larger debate about social welfare and social rights, and medical doctors, lawyers, and policy makers were also concerned with housing conditions, food distribution and cost, pawnshops, and public health. More importantly, safe and affordable housing was a labor demand and an urgent social problem. Following the 1925 renters' strike, Decree Law 261 (Ministry of Social Welfare) looked to limit rent speculation, guarantee basic health and hygiene conditions, and protect the well-being of working families. Fearing the opposition of landlords, the decree created Housing Tribunals (Tribunales de la Vivienda) to determine the "acceptable" standards of rent, supervise buildings to ensure they were habitable (and that repairs were done on time and according to the law), order the demolition of uninhabitable buildings, and protect residents from unlawful evictions. Placed under the jurisdiction of the Ministry of Social Welfare, the tribunals were composed of representatives of the state, residents, and landlords. These tribunals became especially popular, received numerous causes, and ordered the demolition of many buildings considered uninhabitable.[30] Moreover, they influenced the development of labor courts, demonstrating the importance of special courts to guarantee the enforcement of new social rights. The incorporation of housing legal issues into a larger system of labor courts in 1927 further demonstrates the intersections of labor and social rights.

The initial failure of civil courts to solve labor disputes, the difficulties in setting up the arbitration boards, the question of white-collar employees, and the experience of housing tribunals shaped the organization of a comprehensive system of labor courts in the late 1920s. In 1927, the state reorganized the old arbitration boards and formed a two-tier system, bringing together the three institutions that had previously overseen social and labor laws (boards of conciliation and arbitration, boards for white-collar employees, and housing tribunals). The Labor Code of 1931 further regulated the operation of the new labor tribunals, which would be concerned with questions regarding the enforcement of the Labor Code, labor contracts, and social security disputes for both blue-collar workers and white-collar employees. The decree that approved the Labor Code put special emphasis on the need for special procedures to resolve labor disputes, stating that it was convenient to have "a special jurisdiction" and "adequate proceedings" to verify and resolve labor lawsuits.[31]

The two pieces of the system were the *Juzgados del Trabajo* and the *Tribunales de Alzada* (called *Cortes del Trabajo* after 1943). The *Juzgados* were the first resort for all work-related cases and the only option for cases under 1,000 pesos, while the *Tribunales de Alzada* were the final resort for cases over 1,000 pesos. Presided over by a judge, the *Juzgados* were located throughout the country and included one secretary and one or two assistants. The tribunals remained within the executive power and, as a result, the judge was considered an administrative public position and, initially, was not required to have a law degree. The *Tribunales* were initially four and located in major cities (Iquique, Valparaíso, Santiago, and Concepción),[32] and they included three members (a president, a representative of labor—either a blue-collar worker or a white-collar employee depending on the case—and a representative of employers), all of them appointed by the president of the nation.[33] Like the previous *juntas* and housing tribunals, these new institutions were administrative courts, established outside the vertical structure of Chile's judicial system. Additionally, some issues remained outside their jurisdiction, creating some overlaps and confusion. These were the cases of the boards that ruled over cases of classification of white-collar employees and, beginning in 1937, the salary commissions (*Comisiones Mixtas de Sueldos*) that were concerned with cases involving salaries for white-collar employees.

The discussion and design of a new form of justice involved a new generation of lawyers, who trained at the University of Chile (*Universidad de Chile*) and saw in social and labor law a response to the social, economic, and political crisis of the first decades of the twentieth century.[34] They argued that labor tribunals were different from traditional justice administration but responded to a new form of justice and the concept of social rights. Jacobo Schaulsohn, for example, graduated with a law degree from the University of Chile in 1940. Trained as a labor lawyer, he wrote his thesis about labor courts. Like many other new labor lawyers, Schaulsohn believed that labor tribunals had to effectively defend (and protect) workers. If regular courts were organized assuming the "equal conditions of both litigant parts to exert their rights," labor tribunals were organized assuming the profound inequality between employers and employees. In addition, he believed that a system of labor justice played a critical role and had an "enormous collective significance" because it regulated "human work" and had an impact on "social peace."[35] The key principles of labor tribunals, according to Schaulsohn, were (1) to guarantee that workers could actually enjoy their new rights, (2) to protect and guide workers, and (3) to allow the influence of the judge to mediate and resolve.[36] Schaulsohn clearly addressed the limits of civil courts in handling work-related issues, as demonstrated in the cases of work accidents previously described. The workplace was a unique space shaped by unequal power relations, and if labor laws were to ever become a reality, the state—and in this case, the tribunals—had to intervene to rebalance that inherent inequality. Throughout the 1930s, however, the system suffered a host of setbacks.

Labor Tribunals: A View from the 1930s

The system of labor justice came to life in a time of dramatic political, social, and economic instability. Between 1924 and 1938, Chileans experienced social turmoil, unstable governments, and, by 1931, the devastating impact of the Great Depression. Between 1932 and 1938, President Arturo Alessandri carried out draconian economic policies, heavily repressing labor and social movements. In this context, the Labor Department and its recently approved legislation had to adapt to changing politics and cycles of political repression, offering some protection to workers in the midst of economic insecurity. The victory of the Popular Front in 1938, a center-left coalition led by Pedro Aguirre Cerda, and the incorporation of organized labor into the coalition represented both a strong state commitment to workers' rights and the efforts of the labor movement to negotiate with political parties.[37] This shift would also be reflected in an increase in unionization and workers' efforts to organize according to the norms established by the Labor Code. To some extent, this would also create a stronger bond between labor laws, labor courts, and Chilean workers.

During this period, most labor lawsuits focused on very clear workplace grievances: work accidents' compensation, unpaid salaries, layoff, and social security

payments. Labor inspectors were usually responsible for filing a legal action after
their initial mediation had failed, and they translated workers' complaints into the
legal language used by courts. Regular cases (*juicios ordinarios*) had four distinctive
phases: legal action (*demanda*), settlement agreement (*avenimiento*), evidence and
witnesses, and resolution.[38] Although not legally required, the inspector would have
attempted to reach an agreement among the parties, and only when these efforts
had failed would the inspector take the case to the court.[39] All legal actions followed
a very similar structure: names and dates, description of the facts, and legal justification. Work injuries (accidents or occupational diseases) cases followed a different
pattern. Employers were required to report all work injuries within five days after the
accident, and these cases required a medical report that could confirm the injury and
its consequences (disability). Based on medical evidence, witnesses' accounts, and
the confirmed degree of disability, the judge would decide workers' economic compensation. In other words, in order to receive work injury compensation, the case had
to pass through the local labor court. Because of this, work injury proceedings were
very common, and by 1940 they accounted for one-third of the cases addressed by
labor courts.[40] However, if the employer did not report a work injury, which was very
common, the worker or the labor inspector could file a regular legal action.[41]

The legal cases involving work injuries illustrate the many difficulties and obstacles
faced by Chilean workers at the time. Because there were no penalties to employers
who did not report work accidents, many of them simply did not do it, and workers
were forced to file a regular legal case. For example, according to the Labor Department, there were about 20,000 work accidents per year.[42] However, in 1933, the department handled only 1,912 cases in the entire country, 710 of which were resolved by a
labor tribunal.[43] Many employers continued looking to settle cases informally and,
when insured, the insurance companies were ruthless in dealing with workers. Companies manipulated, bribed, and threatened witnesses; distorted medical reports;
and used many other tactics not to pay compensation. A case could last for months
and require additional medical evidence, and the precarious health conditions of the
victims usually discouraged them from continuing with the case, causing them to look
for a fast settlement.[44] In the case of occupational diseases, which were included for
the first time in the 1924 accident law, workers were forced to prove their employers'
responsibility and where they had contracted the disease, which became especially
challenging with chronic diseases such as the many lung complications that affected
mine workers.[45]

The following case shows the difficulties faced by injured workers to get compensation. Andrés Galleguillos, a nitrate worker hospitalized in the northern port
of Iquique, filed a legal case against his employer, Santiago Marinkovic, in 1933. He
claimed to have suffered a work accident in February 1933, and despite the fact that
he was hospitalized and unable to work, he had not received any payments from his
employer. The employer had not reported the accident, and he (Galleguillos) had

decided to take matters to the local labor tribunal. Every labor legal process started with a legal action (either oral or written) filed by the victim, his representative, or a labor inspector. In this regard, Galleguillos directly filed the case at the tribunal. Galleguillos explained in his narrative that after suffering an accident in his workplace, his employers had paid for his medical expenses but not his wages, suggesting some effort of the employer to settle informally. Following the legal action, the employer presented new evidence, arguing that Galleguillos did not suffer a work accident because he was not performing work, but rather he had fallen asleep while drunk and had been affected by a dynamite detonation. The judge summoned both parties and tried to arrive at an agreement. Several witnesses testified, and the judge ruled in December 1933, almost ten months after the accident, that Galleguillos had suffered a "work accident" and that the employer was responsible for compensating the worker.[46]

Doña María Fritz also faced a long and complicated legal road to claim compensation. A widow and mother of four daughters under the age of eighteen, Fritz filed a case in the labor tribunal of Iquique in 1933. She argued that her late husband had died in a work-related accident in January 1933: asphyxia while working for the city electrical company. Based on the work-accident law, she demanded the company provide a life pension for herself (equivalent of 30 percent of his salary) and for each of her four children. The company had insurance, and the case was filed against the insurance company. The insurance company presented new medical certificates that attempted to prove that the victim had died of tuberculosis and not because of the injuries suffered during the accident. The first effort to reach an agreement (*avenimiento*) failed, and the trial continued for a few months with multiple medical testimonies. After a year, the judge ruled in favor of Doña María, but she and her daughters had had no income since the death of her husband.[47]

The lack of an efficient and prompt legal infrastructure and procedures to resolve labor disagreements left many workers unprotected and vulnerable. As in many other parts of the world, this was especially true in the case of work accidents and occupational diseases compensations, since legal and bureaucratic delays had dramatic consequences, given the victim's precarious health condition, the disability, or the economic distress of the family. Workers who suffered an occupational disease had an even more difficult time, since proving that they had contracted the disease at a specific workplace within a limited time frame was, for the most part, impossible.[48] Beginning in the mid-1930s, medical doctors called attention to the need to design a more efficient, compassionate, and humane system of work-injury compensation, one that could effectively protect workers and their families and address the wide range of diseases and accidents that occurred in the workplace.[49] Some cases suggest that workers sometimes settled or accepted employers' offers when available, and a few large companies maintained their own private systems of compensation. For example, in the copper mine of Chuquicamata, following an accident that had left four workers and a supervisor dead, the general manager declared, "the families would be properly assisted, as it is the norm in these cases in this company."[50] The gap between labor and court statistics also suggests that most cases of accidents and occupational disease never reached a tribunal.[51]

Given the enormous power of employers, most of the responsibility fell into the hands of labor inspectors, who were also the ones most familiar with how the system worked, the meaning of the legislation, and the evidence required to file a case. Documents from the Labor Department suggest that workers usually denounced irregularities and abuses at the local labor inspection, and only after efforts to reach an agreement had failed, inspectors recommended filing a legal claim at a labor tribunal. This means that the system heavily relied on the ability of labor inspectors to visit, report, and assist workers. However, the number of labor inspectors was far from sufficient to serve the country. In 1931, the inspection had only 243 employees (including both inspectors and office clerks) to attend people, handle complaints, and conduct regular inspections and visits.[52] Their work was then an "overwhelming task, almost impossible to accomplish."[53] In some cases, male inspectors had difficulties representing women workers' claims; as a report from the Labor Department in Valdivia explained, the department could benefit from hiring more female labor inspectors. This was especially problematic in the case of maternity-leave laws: "Women workers," the report explained, "did not have confidence in labor inspector, to talk about their feelings about maternity."[54] The Labor Department had organized a special women's section in 1926, and the female inspectors paid special attention to the enforcement of maternity leave and day care laws.[55]

With limited personnel and budget, labor inspectors struggled to reach isolated workplaces and maintain regular contact with workers, which at the same time limited the opportunity to represent them in courts. The work of labor inspector, as the Office of Labor understood, was extremely difficult. In 1934, the Minister of Labor explained that inspectors worked in an area where before "had prevailed an atmosphere [in which] outrage and justice had not always been present." He criticized media attacks that portrayed their work as poor or disturbing of "social order."[56] In contrast, according to the editorial page of the Labor Department's magazine (*Revista del Trabajo*), labor inspectors were a sort of "champion of social harmony," which was always under attack, both from the left and the right.[57] To face this, the state attempted to present labor inspectors as "independent" from all political forces, who would embody the spirit of social legislation inspired on scientific ideas. Despite these efforts, both workers and employers complained about the attitudes of labor inspectors. Workers often distrusted labor inspectors, fearing they were siding with employers.[58] In the copper mine of Chuquicamata, for example, the local labor union complained that the inspector looked at their demands with "indifference."[59] Although in most cases this "distrust" was caused by the many obstacles that inspectors faced in enforcing the law, there was also evidence that many inspectors developed friendships and even commercial relations with employers, which jeopardized their capacity to impartially enforce the law.[60]

In the 1930s, there were thirty-one *Juzgados del Trabajo* throughout the entire country, but half of them had no more than one judge, a secretary, and a doorman. The Labor Department's memoir of 1931 pointed out that although the tribunals' responsibilities had increased, their personnel remained the same number and "completely insufficient," and office spaces were "cramped and completely inappropriate for the task."[61] In 1932, a representative of the Ministry of Labor visited the northern province of Atacama and Coquimbo. In his report, he noted that labor tribunals suffered from a shortage of office supplies and personnel. In addition, he noted the enormous difficulty in delivering summons to the parties and the many times they had to use police officers to do so.[62] The number of tribunals was insufficient to cover the needs of the entire country, and the smaller the city, the less likely it was to have a well-staffed court. The distribution clearly responded to demographics and the geographical distribution of the labor force, but it also implied that not all working-class Chileans had the same access to justice, and this was especially evident in the gap between rural and urban workers.[63] If there was no labor tribunal, a civil judge oversaw work-related issues. Most civil courts were overwhelmed with their own caseload, understaffed, and unable to handle labor cases.[64] In La Unión, a small southern city with some industrial activity (timber plants, agribusiness, and breweries), the *Juez de Letras*, the local court that handled all commercial and civil issues also handled labor issues, but, as the *Intendente* explained, "labor cases were poorly attended."[65] Sometimes workers had to travel long distances to file a case, and they couldn't afford to take time or pay the travel expenses.

In addition to material constraints, labor tribunals faced the enormous challenge of confronting powerful employers. Over time, employers developed a series of strategies to undermine the work of labor judges. For example, they moved cases from a labor court to civil court, arguing that it was a civil issue not a work issue (these were the many cases of domestic workers, rural workers, or workers in small shops); in other situations, they directly questioned the work of labor inspectors, accusing them of siding with workers or having radical ideas. In the agricultural valley of Lontué, for example, powerful landowner and Deputy Alejandro Dussaillant launched a campaign to have the local labor inspector fired (Amador Julio Navarro). In his letter to the Minister of Labor, he accused Navarro of hanging out with people who had "bad records" and "subversive ideas." In addition, Dussaillant argued, Navarro had abandoned his work several times and had encouraged a sharecropper to revolt. He went beyond Navarro's behavior, complaining about labor laws, which he described as "premature, too advanced, and unsuitable for our country."[66]

In other instances, employers attempted to interpret the law to their own benefit. To clarify ambiguous cases, the Labor Department maintained a legal office. The *Departamento Jurídico* was in charge of proposing legal reforms and advising courts,

lawyers, and labor inspectors on the meaning and implications of the law. This function was especially important within Chile's legal tradition, which required a clear and
uniform interpretation of the law. Many of these cases were published in the Labor
Department's magazine, *Revista del Trabajo*, as a way to educate judges and workers
and also reflect some of the issues that workers may have faced when filing a legal
claim at a local tribunal. For example, in 1930, the legal office had received an inquiry
regarding a case of work injury compensation: a one-eyed person had suffered a work
accident and lost his only good eye; the employer argued that the worker was entitled
to partial disability (since he lost only one eye), but the Legal Department concluded
that the accident had caused a complete and not a partial disability.[67]

In many cases, workers had to face lengthy legal cases and had little documentation to support their claims. The following case, involving a domestic worker, shows
the difficulties of accessing justice, understating the real work situation, and the difficulties faced by this group of people. Working conditions and agreements were
many times ambiguous and, in the absence of clear laws defining their work conditions, there was often little that labor judges could do. In 1933, Ulda Soto Borcosque,
a young woman from the northern part of the country filed a case in the labor tribunal
of Iquique against her employer, Pedro Mitchel. She argued that she worked and lived
in Mitchel's house as a domestic employee for about eighteen months, but Mitchel
had mistreated her and not paid her the agreed salary of 100 pesos. She presented a
demand for seven thousand pesos. However, Mitchel denied that she worked in the
house, did not recognize the verbal contract, and explained she lived in the house as
a family guest (his wife's niece). Despite the effort of Soto to demonstrate her status
as domestic worker, she had no concrete evidence, and the judge dismissed the case,
arguing that "[f]or a domestic worker to be considered as such, it is necessary to have
worked by reason of a verbal agreement or written contract."[68]

Lengthy and bureaucratic processes affected most workers who attempted to
challenge powerful employers. The case of Pedro González Pizarro and Rosario de
González, a working couple that had been employed by Sánchez in the Mineral del
Inca, Estación Cuba, Provincia de Chañaral, clearly illustrated the bureaucratic difficulties. The couple argued that their employer owed them a total of $1075.00 for two-
month unpaid salaries: $667 pesos to Pedro (a miner) and $408 to Rosario (a cook).
At first, the couple reached out to a local labor inspector at the Estación Cuba, but the
employer had quickly moved the case to the port of Chañaral (about 125 miles away).
The first hearing took place in Chañaral in December 1933; although the employer
recognized the existence of a labor contract between himself and the González couple,
he presented many excuses not to pay. The judge called a new hearing in February
1934 but Sánchez did not show up; before the judge could order a legal seizure of his
assets, he had left the city. The judge had no means to force Sánchez to pay, and at
that point (March 1934), the couple's representative addressed a letter to the labor
judge of Santiago asking for help.[69]

From Consolidation to Downfall, 1940s–1980s

By the late 1940s, labor lawyers started showing an increasing interest in the mean-ing and practice of labor law, which would be reflected in some efforts to improve the system and create more specialized and autonomous courts. In 1933, labor tribunals had been placed under the jurisdiction of the Supreme Court (although they were considered administrative tribunals until 1955). Both the Supreme Court as well as conservative political parties opposed the development of labor courts as autonomous judicial institutions. By placing them within the judicial power, the Supreme Court could exert greater control over labor issues.[70] By 1943, labor judges were required to hold a law degree and the Supreme Court was involved in disciplinary issues affecting the labor tribunals' personnel. This transition ended in 1955, when they transferred completely to the Judicial Power, subject to the regulations of the justice system.[71] The 1955 reform also increased salaries for all magistrates and judges as an effort to make the judicial career more attractive.[72] The increasing focus on labor justice in the late 1940s responded to a larger international concern about labor tribunals and courts. In 1947, the Organization of American States met in Rio de Janeiro, Brazil, and adopted the "InterAmerican Charter of Social Guarantee." In its article 36, the charter specifically refers to the administration of labor justice, agreeing that "every country must have a special jurisdiction for work issues and an adequate proceeding for a fast resolution of conflicts."[73] The problem was brought again to the attention of Latin American governments during the ILO Conference of American States in Montevideo in 1949 that specifically included an item on how countries regulated what it called "the adjustment of labor disputes."[74]

To what extent the labor court system improved during the Cold War Era is still an open question. The large number of cases, an enormous archive still unexplored by Chilean historians, suggests that workers regularly used the courts to resolve labor disputes or, at least, find some recognition of their rights. Despite the overwhelm-ing power and influence of employers, workers and labor inspectors filed a number of cases, struggling, with more or less success, to bring justice to the workplace. In the 1950s, Hernán Oyanguren, a medical doctor who specialized in work-related diseases and who led many public health institutions in the mid–twentieth century, concluded that in the 1950s, there was still a "battle," and the victim usually suffered the economic consequences.[75] However, employers' efforts to curtail the work of the courts had also become a larger labor, political and social issue, reflecting significant political changes in the country.[76]

Most experts argued that the number of labor courts and their personnel were insufficient to meet the growing demand, reflecting both the increase in the size of Chile's workforce as well as the importance of the courts within Chile's labor system. In larger cities, in particular, labor courts were overwhelmed with claims and had become especially inefficient and slow by the 1960s. Most reforms, then, focused on increasing the number of courts, improving funding, and eliminating some of the excessively bureaucratic and lengthy practices. For example, in February 1971, President Salvador Allende introduced a bill that created new courts in Santiago and expanded their personnel. According to congressional records, at the time there were 26 lower labor courts (*Juzgados del Trabajo*) and 3 higher courts (*Tribunales de Alzada*) in the entire country. In the case of the Province of Santiago, where the city population had almost doubled (from 1 to 2 million residents between 1930 and 1970), the number of lower labor courts had been reduced from 6 to 5, overwhelming the work of the remaining courts.[77] The congressional commission agreed on the need to increase the numbers of courts and their personnel, warning that although labor cases had to be processed during a twenty-four–day period, in Santiago, hearings were usually scheduled two or even three months after the claim was filed. The hearings had also become particularly lengthy and it was not unusual to have a labor case extending for "three or four years."[78] Unfortunately, Allende's bill fell by the wayside, delayed by other more pressing reforms and the ongoing political crisis.

The labor system created in 1931 came to an end in the years following the 1973 military coup. The dictatorship led by General Augusto Pinochet heavily repressed the labor movement and initially suspended union elections and the process of collective bargaining. A few days after the coup, on September 21, 1973, the military government created a special tribunal (composed of a labor judge, a labor inspector, and a representative of the armed forces) to resolve disputes regarding layoffs. In doing so, the military argued, the decree would reestablish "labor discipline."[79] By the late 1970s, the military started talking about imposing a new system of labor relations that, according to right-wing ideologue José Piñera, would de-politicize the labor movement and modernize Chile's economy and society.[80] In a larger scheme of privatization and dismantling of the social state and enforcement of neoliberal economic policies, the military undertook a drastic transformation of labor relations and workers' rights. Beginning in 1979, under the name of the "Labor Plan," the military severely limited the right to strike, unionize, and bargain collectively.[81]

As part of this larger effort to transform labor relations, the military also abolished the traditional labor court system, identified as a source of unnecessary conflict and politicization in the workplace.[82] Mónica Madariaga, who served as Minister of Justice between 1977 and 1983, played a central role in the dismantling of labor courts. In March 1981, the military government eliminated labor courts and passed all labor-related cases to regular civil courts. While the new system did not radically change the legal process, it eliminated the labor court and the labor judge as a unique space to handle work disputes.[83] Madariaga also attempted to eliminate, fire, and force to retire all labor court judges and personnel, arguing that they were unprepared to handle cases that did not refer to labor.[84] Not only the courts, but also the "*rotos*'s lawyer" as Álvarez Andrews had called it more than fifty years ago, had become an obstacle to the new authoritarian transformation of the country because, in Madariaga's words, of their now "Marxist tendencies."[85] In the following months, this process of complete "cleansing," as the legal adviser of the Air Force had called it,[86] was softened, and most of the personnel—unless they had clear leftist political tendencies—were reassigned to a civil court.[87] The dictatorship clearly saw labor judges and labor courts as obstacles to the imposition of their neoliberal economic policies. To some extent, the military efforts to dismantle the system suggest its historical importance as a space to negotiate the enforcement of labor laws. Despite its many flaws, the courts had provided an important tool to achieve justice.

On May 1, 1986, the military attempted to palliate the effects of their previous measure and organized the *Tribunales de Letras del Trabajo*.[88] These judicial courts were designed as new instances, completely different from the previous labor courts, to the point that the military government declared that former labor judges would not be admitted since their past actions were "very questionable and there were some bad habits that had to be eliminated."[89] The power and jurisdiction of the new courts were considerably limited and, more importantly in the eyes of the dictatorship, they would eradicate the "problem of class struggle within its jurisdiction."[90] Although the idea of a neutral court has always been present on the minds of legislators, the military reform attempted to reduce legal aid and eliminate what Jacobo Schaulsohn had called an "involved judge." Since the return of democracy in 1990, the labor movement has led a long struggle to reestablish labor rights and reform the legal framework inherited from the dictatorship, including the question of labor courts. In 2003, President Ricardo Lagos proposed to the National Congress the organization of a new system of labor courts, which was approved in May 2005 (Law 20022). In his message, he reflected on the history and importance of these special judicial institutions. "It is worth recalling that in the year 1932, by way of Decree Law No 207, the first labor courts were created in our country. Many years later, in 1981, the specialized labor judiciary was eliminated, and its matters were transferred to civil justice. Although there was a wide consensus that this measure was a big mistake, the reestablishment of a specialized judicature [1986] was insufficient."[91]

Conclusions

The organization of labor courts in Chile in the late 1920s was part of a larger process of political and legal transformation.[92] Designed to resolve individual work disputes between labor and capital, labor courts responded to new ways of looking at the workplace, redefining the role of the law, the court, and the state. As contemporaries clearly understood at the time, labor courts were designed to protect workers, bring justice to a space that had been tainted by abuses and contribute to social peace. However, the history of labor courts described in this chapter is more complex, reflecting the deep social and economic tensions that existed in Chile, as well as the enormous power of employers to obstruct the work of the Labor Department. In reality, not all

Chilean workers were able to access the courts, and when they did, they faced long and bureaucratic delays. The question of work injury compensation (accidents and occupational diseases) clearly shows the limitations of a system that too frequently left injured workers without compensation. In some ways, despite policy makers' strong faith in the power of the law, no labor courts or labor laws could transform the country's traditional power structure. From the 1930s to the late 1960s, labor inspectors and judges faced powerful employers, constraining budgets, and cycles of political repression.[93] Their letters, reports, visits, and testimonies shed light on the larger struggle to bring labor and social justice to the country.

Notes

1. The authors would like to thank Brian Loveman, Frank Luce and the editors of this volume, Leon Fink and Juan Manuel Palacio, for their comments and suggestions. All translations, unless mentioned, are our own.

2. *Roto* is a pejorative word to refer to people of lower class in Chile.

3. Álvarez Andrews, *La asistencia judicial*, 5–6.

4. Illanes, *Cuerpo y sangre de la política*.

5. These administrative units were subject to many changes throughout the twentieth century. At the ministerial level, the question of work was first addressed by the Ministerio de Higiene, Asistencia, y Previsión Social (1924–1927), the Ministerio de Bienestar Social (1927–1932) and, after 1932, the Ministerio del Trabajo. The Oficina del Trabajo was formed in 1907 and, in 1924, it was restructured as the Dirección General del Trabajo. The Caja de Seguro Obrero, founded in 1924, administered social security funds for blue-collar workers and offered medical assistance. It was restructured in 1952 as the Servicio de Seguro Social.

6. Poblete Troncoso, *El derecho del trabajo*, 49.

7. Loveman, *Struggle in the Countryside*, 70.

8. Gender historians have demonstrated the ways in which paternalism and a patriarchal ideology reinforced gender discrimination in the workplace and before the law. As historian Karin Rosemblatt explains, labor inspectors exerted a great degree of paternalism over female workers. Rosemblatt, *Gendered Compromise*.

9. On the labor question in early-twentieth-century Chile, see DeShazo, *Urban Workers*; Grez, "El escarpado camino"; Morris, *Elites, Intellectuals, and Consensus*; Yáñez, *La intervención social*.

10. On the transnational dimensions of this debate, see Rodgers, *Atlantic Crossings*; Herrera and Herrera, *América Latina*.

11. Drinot and Knight, *Great Depression*.

12. Poblete Troncoso and Álvarez Andrews, *Legislación social*.

13. Yáñez, *La intervención social*.

14. Since the mid–nineteenth century, Chilean civil and mining laws provided some protection for workers who suffered a work injury, compelling employers to provide basic medical care and, in some cases, economic compensations. As a result, many civil courts had traditionally handled work accidents. Merino, *Diversas consideraciones*; Gatica, "La responsabilidad del patrón" and "La responsabilidad del patrón (continuación)."

15. Moltedo, "Evolución de la judicatura."

16. The case of Higinia Moyano illustrates how work issues, in this case a work accident, were legally resolved before the organization of labor courts. In 1899, Ms. Moyano filed a case against the national railroad company over the death of her husband, Miguel Angel Molina, a railroad machinist. Molina had died during a dramatic railroad accident: in the middle of a storm, a bridge collapsed taking the train down a river, killing most railroad workers and passengers. The plaintiff argued that the railroad company was responsible for the accident because they were aware of the bad condition of the bridge. In response, the defendant claimed that the accident was "an act of nature that nobody was responsible for," and the civil court dismissed the case for lack of evidence. The case was reopened in 1904, after five years, and the judge ruled that the company was responsible for "evident negligence" because of running a train "when the immediate consequence[s] of a large storm were still present." The court assigned Molina's widow a total of 50 thousand pesos. Jurisprudencia, *Revista de Derecho y Jurisprudencia y Ciencias Sociales* 2 (1904): 47–53.

17. "Sumario por la muerte de Félix Sanderson." Notaría, Conservador de Bienes Raíces, Comercio y Minas; y Archivero Judicial de Chañaral, legajo 3, archivo n° 61, folio N° 2265.

18. "Sumario por muerte de Emilio Riquelme," September 11, 1916. Archivo Nacional Histórico de Chile (hereafter ANHCh), Fondo Judicial de Antofagasta, box 1018, document 27.

19. Merino, *Diversas consideraciones*.

20. Braden Copper Co., June 24, 1914, ANHCh, Intendencia O'Higgins, volume 314.

21. Poblete Troncoso, and Álvarez Andrews, *Legislación social*, 76–132.

22. Grez, "El escarpado camino."

23. Schaulsohn, *De cómo deben tramitarse*, 10.

24. The most emblematic laws approved in 1924 were work contract, social security, work accident, and unionization.

25. Labor historiography for this period is extensive; see, for example: De Shazo, *Urban Workers*; Grez, "El escarpado camino"; Hutchison, *Labors*; Rojas, *La dictadura de Ibáñez*.

26. Historians have studied the role of the juntas as mediators in collective labor conflicts and strikes, but we still know little about their role resolving individual disputes. Grez, "¿Autonomía o escudo protector?" In her study of Chilean Legal Aid Service, Marianne González Le Saux offers an interesting perspective on the role of this institution as mediator between the working class and the state, helping working families to navigate the complexity of social laws and benefits. González Le Saux, "Legal Aid, Social Workers."

27. Neut Latour, *De los tribunales*, 11–13.

28. Poblete Troncoso and Álvarez Andrews, *Legislación social*.

29. The Chilean labor legislation had created two distinctive work categories: blue-collar workers and white-collar employees. The handling of white-collar employees' legal claims experienced many changes between 1924 and 1927. In September 1924, the law declared that the civil courts would address matters concerning white-collar employees; in December 1924, special councils for white-collar employees were formed (Tribunales de Conciliación y Arbitraje). The resolution of conflicts regarding social security remained on the hands of the white-collar social security office (Caja de Retiro de Empleados Particulares). Neut Latour, *De los tribunales*, 13–14.

30. Hidalgo, *La vivienda social en Chile*.

31. Decreto con Fuerza de Ley 178; Chile, *Código del trabajo*, 3.

32. In 1947, the Tribunal in Iquique started closing down.

33. Escribar Mandiola, "La protección del Trabajo"; Chile, *Código del trabajo*.

34. The Law School at the Universidad de Chile became a critical space to discuss legislation. Beginning in 1915, the school offered a concentration in social sciences and economics, with a special focus on labor legislation. Many of the most important lawmakers, like Moisés Poblete Troncoso, taught at the school and trained new lawyers, who became concerned about how the law could be used to advance social justice and resolve social tensions.

35. Schaulsohn, *De cómo deben tramitarse*, 10.

36. Zerega González, *Estudio de la evolución*.

37. For an overview of this period see Loveman, *Chile*. On the relationship between organized labor and the Popular Front, see Pavilack, *Mining for the Nation*.

38. Schaulsohn, *De cómo deben tramitarse*, 37–38.

39. Schaulsohn, *De cómo deben tramitarse*.

40. In 1944, Chilean labor courts received a total of 28,200 legal actions, 10,185 of which were about work injuries. In 1950, they received 42,237 legal actions, 16,998 of which were about work injuries. Work injuries included both accidents and occupational diseases, but because of legal difficulties the number of reported diseases were always low. However, most cases never reached a court. Statistical information can be found in the *Revista del Trabajo* 10 (1933): 32; 1 (1934): 12; 5 (1945): 9–10; 1 (1951): 22; and 5 (1951): 19.

41. Chile, *Código del Trabajo*.

42. Inspección General del Trabajo, "Accidentes."

43. García Oldini, "Exposición."

44. Schaulsohn, *De cómo deben tramitarse*, 74–87, 107.

45. In the 1930s, only 27 percent of Chilean workers were employed by insured employers. The numbers changed little in the following decades, leaving workers more unprotected in case of occupational injury. In 1968, Law 16.744 made insurance compulsory. De Viado, "Reseña."

46. Fallo, Iquique, December 20, 1933. Archivo Nacional de la Administración del Estado (hereafter ARNAD), Dirección General del Trabajo, volume 458.

47. Fallo, Iquique, January 30, 1934. ARNAD, Dirección General del Trabajo, volume 458.

48. Ortúzar, "Legislación y medicina"; Vergara, " Recognition of Silicosis" and "Légiférer sur les maladies professionnelles."

49. Gebauer, "Reeducación."

50. Antofagasta, August 8, 1927. AHNCh, Intendencia de Antofagasta, volume 45.

51. Most cases never reached a court. In 1949, for example, the Department of Labor counted 93,021 work injuries reported to the Labor Department; only 248 referred to occupational diseases. These numbers also demonstrate the gap between accidents registered and accidents addressed by a court. In 1933, for example, there were more than 12 thousand accidents. The Labor Department registered 2,622, and only 710 reached the court. Statistical information can be found in the *Revista del Trabajo* 10 (1933): 32; 1 (1934): 12; 5 (1945): 9–10; 1 (1951): 22; and 5 (1951): 19.

52. According to the 1930 Census, Chile had a population of more than 4.2 million people, and the size of the labor force (economically active population) was more than 1.2 million people. Chile, *X Censo*, 8.

53. Inspección General del Trabajo, "El personal y el presupuesto de la Inspección General del Trabajo en relación con sus servicios," *Revista del Trabajo* 2 (1931): n/p.

54. "Memoria 1933," Santiago, April 12, 1934. ARNAD, Dirección del Trabajo, volume 453.

55. Hutchison, *Labors Appropriate to Their Sex*, 224–230.

56. García Oldini, "Exposición."

57. Rojas, "El Inspector del Trabajo."

58. Most of the time, labor inspectors were highly committed to enforce the legislation and protect workers' rights. But the many obstacles to enforce the legislation led workers to think inspectors had sided with employers. Loveman, *Struggle in the Countryside*, 96.

59. Chuquicamata, September 2, 1937. AHNCh, Intendencia Antofagasta, volume 177.

60. Cury, "O protagonismo popular," 58–70.

61. "Memoria del Departamento Jurídico de la Inspección General del Trabajo correspondiente al año 1931," *Revista del Trabajo* 5–6 (1932): 31.

62. "Informe complementario sobre visita a los servicios de las inspecciones del trabajo de las Provincias de Atacama y Coquimbo," Santiago, January 14, 1933. ARNAD, Dirección del Trabajo, volume 461.

63. Loveman, *Struggle in the Countryside*, 69–112.

64. For an overview of the judicial system in Chile and especially the slow transformation of civil courts, see De Ramón, *La justicia chilena*.

65. "Memoria," Santiago, April 12, 1933. ARNAD, Dirección del Trabajo, volume 453.

66. Alejandro Dussaillant, Santiago, March 2, 1932. ARNAD, Dirección del Trabajo, volume 310.

67. "Absuelve consulta sobre calificación de un accidente del trabajo." *Revista del Trabajo* 6 (1931).

68. Iquique, December 11, 1933. ARNAD, Dirección del Trabajo, volume 458.

69. Angel Isasmendi, Chañaral, March 22, 1934. ARNAD, Dirección del Trabajo, volume 453.

70. See Frühling, *Law in Society*, 129–130.

71. Chile, Ministerio de Justicia, Ley 11,986, article 28, November 19, 1955. In Biblioteca del Congreso Nacional de Chile, online access: http://www.leychile.cl/Navegar?idNorma=26950 (accessed on April 4, 2017).

72. Congreso Nacional, Cámara de Diputados (hereafter CNCD), *Sesión 4.a*, May 31, 1955, 73.

73. Poblete Troncoso, *El derecho del trabajo*, 205.

74. ILO, *Labour Courts*.

75. Oyanguren, "Diagnóstico."

76. In 1941, for example, mine workers from one of the largest copper mines in the country, Potrerillos, announced that the company and its medical doctors arbitrarily "modified the degree of disability of those workers suffering from silicosis." The local union, then, demanded that all medical reports be handled by the recently inaugurated Instituto de Medicina del Trabajo of the Social Security Office (Caja de Seguro Obrero). In "El Instituto de Medicina del Trabajo de la Caja de Seguro Obrero," *Boletín Médico Social de la Caja de Seguro Obligatorio* 89–90 (1941): 717–718.

77. CNCD, *Sesión 18.a*, February 2, 1971, 989.

78. CNCD, *Sesión 22.a*, March 2, 1971, 1499.

79. Ministerio del Trabajo y Previsión Social Decreto Ley (DL) 32, September 21, 1973. The decree was abolished in October 1974 (DL 676).

80. Piñera, *La revolución laboral*.

81. Winn, *Victims of the Chilean Miracle*.

82. Lira and Rojas, *Libertad sindical*, 22.

83. Ministerio de Justicia, Decreto Ley 3648, March 10, 1981.

84. This effort to purge the public administration of radical elements was not new. In 1948, the Law for the Permanent Defense of Democracy banned all members of the Communist Party from serving in public institutions, including labor courts.

85. Junta, *Actas*, April 23, 1981, 14.

86. Junta, *Actas*, April 30, 1981, 4.

87. Ibid.

88. Ministerio de Justicia, Law 18510, May 1, 1986. In Biblioteca del Congreso Nacional de Chile, online access: http://www.leychile.cl/ (accessed April 4, 2017).

89. Junta, *Actas*, March 25, 1986, 32.

90. Member of the Junta, Admiral José Toribio Merino, described the goal of the new courts: "to not step out of what is strictly judicial and get into social issues, because then the courts become, as in the past, real campo de Agramonte (battle grounds)." Junta, *Actas*. March 25, 1986, 16.

91. Biblioteca del Congreso Nacional, "Historia de la ley No 20,022," May 30, 2005. In Biblioteca del Congreso Nacional de Chile, online access: http://www.bcn.cl (accessed on April 4, 2017).

92. It is interesting to note that parallel to the organization of labor courts was the organization of children's courts, which were also based on ideas of protection and the need to develop a different type of justice.

93. The question of inspectors' political affiliation and ideas still needs further research. They probably represent a hybrid mix of old corporativist sectors closer to General Ibáñez, socialists who entered the state during the Popular Front years, and people more influenced by Poblete Troncoso and ILO rhetoric.

Bibliography

Álvarez Andrews, Óscar. *La asistencia judicial.* Santiago: Imprenta Nacional, 1927.

Chile, *Código del Trabajo.* Santiago: Editorial Nascimento, 1932.

Chile, *X Censo de la población. Volumen III: Ocupaciones.* Santiago: Imprenta Universo, 1935.

Cury, Márcia Carolina de Oliveira. "O protagonismo popular: experiências de classe e movimentos sociais na construcao do socialismo chileno (1964–1973)." PhD diss., Campinas, 2013.

De Ramón, Armando. "La justicia chilena entre 1875 y 1924." *Cuadernos de análisis jurídico* 12 (1989).

DeShazo, Peter. *Urban Workers and Labor Unions in Chile, 1902–1927.* Madison: University of Wisconsin Press, 1984.

De Viado, Manuel. "Reseña de la legislación nacional sobre accidentes del trabajo." *Boletín Médico Social de la Caja de Seguro Obligatorio* 70 (1940): 84.

Drinot, Paulo, and Alan Knight, eds. *The Great Depression in Latin America*. Durham, N.C.: Duke University Press, 2015.

Escribar Mandiola, Héctor. "La protección del Trabajo." *Revista del trabajo* 4 (1932): 53–56.

Frühling, Hugo. *Law in Society. Social transformation and the Crisis of Law in Chile: 1830–1970*. PhD diss., Harvard University School of Law, 1984.

García Oldini, Fernando. "Exposición del Ministerio del Trabajo a S. E. el Presidente de la República sobre la labor anual de los organismos del ramo." *Revista del Trabajo* 1 (1934): 12.

Gatica, Tomás. "La responsabilidad del patrón." *Revista del Trabajo* 2 (1931a).

——. "La responsabilidad del patrón (continuación)." *Revista del Trabajo* 3 (1931b).

Gebauer, Teodoro. "Reeducación profesional de inválidos del trabajo." *Revista de Asistencia Social* 4 (1935): 504.

González Le Saux, Marianne. "Legal Aid, Social Workers, and the Redefinition of the Legal Profession in Chile, 1925–1960." *Law and Social Inquiry* 2 (2017): preliminary online version.

Grez, Sergio. "El escarpado camino hacia la legislación social: debates, contradicciones y encrucijadas en el movimiento obrero y popular (Chile—1901–1924)." *Cuadernos de Historia* 21 (2001): 119–182.

——. "¿Autonomía o escudo protector? El movimiento obrero popular y los mecanismos de conciliación y arbitraje." *Historia* 35 (2002): 81–150.

Herrera, Fabián, and Patricio Herrera, eds. *América Latina y la Organización Internacional del Trabajo: redes, cooperación técnica e institucionalidad social*. Michoacán: UMSNH, UN, UFF, 2013.

Hidalgo, Rodrigo. *La vivienda social en Chile y la construcción del espacio urbano en el Santiago del siglo XX*. Santiago de Chile: DIBAM, 2005.

Hutchison, Elizabeth Q. *Labors Appropriate to Their Sex: Gender, Labor, and Politics in Urban Chile, 1900–1930*. Durham, N.C.: Duke University Press, 2001.

Illanes, María Angélica. *Cuerpo y sangre de la política: la construcción histórica de las visitadoras sociales 1887–1940*. Santiago: LOM Ediciones, 2007.

ILO. *Labour Courts in Latin America*. Geneva: ILO, 1949.

Inspección General del Trabajo. "Accidentes del Trabajo." *Revista del Trabajo* 10 (1933): 32.

Junta. *Actas de la Honorable Junta de Gobierno*. Santiago: Junta, 1973–1990.

Lira, Elizabeth, and Hugo Rojas, eds. *Libertad sindical y derechos humanos. Análisis de los informes del Comité de Libertad Sindical de la OIT, 1973–1990*. Santiago: Lom Ediciones, 2009.

Loveman, Brian. *Struggle in the Countryside: Politics and Rural Labor in Chile*. Bloomington: Indiana University Press, 1976.

——. *Chile: The Legacy of Spanish Capitalism*. Oxford: Oxford University Press, 2001.

Merino, Baldomero. *Diversas consideraciones sobre los accidentes del trabajo*. Concepción: Imprenta José Soulodre, 1913.

Moltedo, Claudio. "Evolución de la judicatura especial del trabajo." *Revista de Derecho de la Universidad Católica de Valparaíso* 16 (1995): 235–251.

Morris, James. *Elites, Intellectuals, and Consensus: A Study of the Social Question and Industrial Relations System in Chile*. Ithaca, N.Y.: Cornell University Press, 1966.

Neut Latour, Jorge. *De los tribunales y juicios del trabajo*. Santiago: Editorial Nascimento, 1930.

Ortúzar, Diego. "Legislación y medicina en torno a los accidentes del trabajo en Chile." *Nuevo Mundo Mundos Nuevos*, online journal: *http://nuevomundo.revues.org/66007* (accessed on June 25, 2015).

Oyanguren, Hernán. "Diagnóstico de las enfermedades ocupacionales. Magnitud del problema en Chile." *Revista Médica de Chile* (July 1955): 437.

Pavilack, Jody. *Mining for the Nation: The Politics of Chile's Coal Communities from the Popular Front to the Cold War*. College Park: Pennsylvania State University Press, 2011.

Piñera, José. *La revolución laboral en Chile*. Santiago: Zig-Zag, 1990.

Poblete Troncoso, Moisés. *El derecho del trabajo y la seguridad social en Chile*. Santiago: Editorial Jurídica, 1949.

Poblete Troncoso, Moisés, and Óscar Álvarez Andrews. *Legislación social obrera chilena*. Santiago: Imprenta Santiago, 1924.

Rodgers, Daniel T. *Atlantic Crossings, Social Politics in a Progressive Age*. Cambridge, Mass.: The Belknap Press of Harvard University Press, 1998.

Rojas, Jorge. *La dictadura de Ibáñez y los sindicatos, (1927–1931)*. Santiago: Centro Barros Arana, 1993.

Rojas, Oscar. "El Inspector del trabajo." *Revista del Trabajo* 9 (1934): 1–2.

Rosemblatt, Karin. *Gendered Compromise: Political Cultures and the State in Chile, 1920–1950*. Chapel Hill: University of North Carolina Press, 2000.

Schaulsohn, Jacobo. *De cómo deben tramitarse los juicios del trabajo*. Santiago: Nascimento, 1940.

Vergara, Angela. "The Recognition of Silicosis: Labor Unions and Physicians in the Chilean Copper Industry, 1930s-1960s." *Bulletin of the History of Medicine* 79 (2005): 723–748.

———. "Légiférer sur les maladies professionnelles au Chili." In *Santé et travail à la mine XIXe–XXIe siècle*, ed. Judith Rainhorn. Lille: Presses Universitaires du Septentrion, 2014.

Winn, Peter. *Weavers of the Revolution: The Yarur Workers and Chile's Road to Socialism*. New York: Oxford University Press, 1986.

———, ed. *Victims of the Chilean Miracle: Workers and Neoliberalism in the Pinochet Era, 1973–2002*. Durham, N.C.: Duke University Press, 2004.

Yáñez, Juan Carlos. *La intervención social en Chile, 1907–1932*. Santiago: Ril Editores, 2008.

Zerega González, Daniel. *Estudio de la evolución en Chile de la legislación procesal laboral en su aspecto orgánico*. Santiago: Universidad de Chile, 2009.

Conclusion

The Rise and Consolidation of the Mediatory State

LEON FINK

The side-by-side comparison of systems of "labor justice" across the Americas—especially adding the examples of the United States and Canada to those of their southern neighbors—implicitly resurrects a venerable, if never adequately resolved, problem of political analysis. The "problem," to put it bluntly, concerns the proper relation of the state to labor law, labor movements, and basic worker welfare. As we can quickly appreciate in each national case study exhibited here, the national state—in the form of governmental legislation, the court system (including special labor tribunals), and administrative apparatus—is almost by definition the central player in these systems of dispute resolution. Moreover, as this volume's Introduction points out, there is a roughly common chronology across the hemisphere in the creation of such systems, including a kind of two-stage pattern, first featuring the intellectual formation of "social law" in the first decades of the twentieth century (and drawing on European and even Australasian precedents from the last two decades of the prior century), followed by "activation" of such principles amid the shock and dislocation of the Depression, world war and the pressures of global capitalism in the new century's middle decades.

From a purely formal perspective, the development of labor courts across the Americas testifies to a basic and near-universal aspect of state-building in the twentieth century. Indeed, as early as 1952, Helen L. Clagett's pioneering study of Latin American judicial systems found special labor tribunals to be the norm, not the exception, effectively part of a nation's legal architecture wherever industry had gained an economic foothold alongside agricultural employment.[1] Especially against a common backdrop of strike threats and growing popular unrest, strong governments responded to the economic disruptions of the Great Depression and world war with similar-looking instruments of class conciliation and/or pacification. With a nod to Emily S. Rosenberg's "regulatory state" to describe the instruments of an international economic order arising out of the Depression and World War II, we might speak of a "mediatory state" consolidated in the same period in many different capitals.[2]

Yet, to identify a parallel shaping of new state forms is, of course, not to say that the forms are equivalent, derive from the same stock, were of the same duration, or let alone produced the same or similar effect. What surely will strike any reader of the foregoing studies is the incredible variety and unpredictable trajectory of the "labor justice" arrangements put in place. And, indeed, unlike Rosenberg's international (if U.S.-dominated) institutions, the labor-centered mediatory institutions of the Americas remained under purely national sovereignty as well as open to quick and recurrent legislative modification. To understand the creation as well as the subsequent growth and development of these instruments of labor law requires close attention to national political context, as attempted by each author in this collection.

Still, we might probe for comparison as well as most salient contrasts or distinctions among the national case studies. To begin, we should acknowledge that joining North and South America in a discussion of twentieth-century state making immediately confronts an older intellectual-political divide. In academic as well as popular discourse, government-inflected industrial relations in Latin America regularly summoned the explanatory concept of "corporatism," whereas in the United States and Canada they almost never did. Set against the pluralistic, interest-group model of liberal democracy in the nineteenth-century Anglo-American tradition, the top-down, functional representation of groups associated with corporatism—whether in its oldest form dating to a medieval, feudal system of estates and group rights established in Spain or Portugal; the nineteenth-century Latin American nexus of Church, army, and oligarchy; the "strong" state examples of twentieth-century Latin American republics like Mexico, Brazil, and Argentina—appeared to describe two discreet and incommensurable sociocultural frameworks.

Moreover, beginning in the post–WW II years when international-comparative studies first came into vogue, the comparative impetus in labor studies was determinedly judgmental. In the glow of the postwar "American Century" of relative prosperity, stable and politically moderate labor unions, and Cold War anticommunism, industrial relations experts (mostly but not all Americans) took the Anglo-American model of "free and independent trade unionism" as the preferred standard of measurement. Although "never precisely defined," as Bruce H. Millen summarized in 1963, the model system "[was] primarily, if not exclusively, concerned with the economic function of collective bargaining to win benefits for the worker, [was] not linked with or/and controlled by a government or political party and [had] no Communist connections."[3] For protectors of the Anglo-American model, beyond any explicit danger of communism, which until Castro's Cuba in 1959 never stamped any Latin American territory in its own legal-institutional image, lay the murkier threat of a state-controlled industrial relations system, whether from the Left or the Right.

Throughout the long postwar era, these basic intellectual-political assumptions were officially bolstered by the efforts of the International Confederation of Free Trade Unions (ICFTU), founded in 1949, particularly through its regional office, Organización Regional Interamericana de Trabajadores (ORIT), established in 1951. As ORIT's founding principles declared, it sought "to coordinate the defense of free unions in the face of campaigns tending toward their destruction, the restriction of their rights, the infiltration in union organizations of totalitarian forces or [those] of an anti-labor character, or the submission of free unions to these forces."[4] From such a vantage point, a rather sharp bifurcation of labor law systems seemed to fairly describe historical development in the Americas dating back at least to the beginning of the century. In particular, those countries (or virtually everywhere in the South) which exhibited strong state controls over the labor market and labor actors appeared inferior or less advanced along a curve of modern-day "liberal" development. The distinguished Chilean labor jurist and longtime ILO advocate, Moisés Poblete Troncoso, recognized the inherent tensions between ORIT's collective bargaining vision and the deep structures of the Latin American state. Given the long-standing power of an oligarchy of landowners and businessmen in Latin America, the securing of organizational freedom for trade unions proved inevitably "somewhat retarded." To be sure, Poblete Troncoso argued in 1960 in one of the first synthetic accounts of its kind, the working classes of the continent did make their presence felt in a powerful way by the early to mid–twentieth century. Yet, even when overcoming the opposition of government, the labor forces might fall into the opposite trap, i.e., the equally suffocating embrace of "friendly" governments. Even as they might experience an initial lift from state collaboration—and indeed Poblete Troncoso cites Mexico as a case of a labor movement being "created out of whole cloth by a governing regime'—he warned that there was likely a future price to pay. In such circumstances, labor organizations might fall into the "political arms of the ruling group," lose their independence, and finally suffer reversal when an antilabor government ascends to power.[5] Despite what he called "inordinately strong political currents" affecting Latin American trade-unionism, Poblete Troncoso by 1960 saw signs in Mexico and elsewhere of a move toward "freedom from the dictates of government" and a new stress on "collective bargaining and related activities." If such trends continued, he concluded a bit too optimistically, Latin America might well hope to approach a "measure of maturation commensurate with its counterparts in Western Europe and the United States."[6]

In the intervening years, especially since the end of the post–WW II boom era, the confidence among pro-union commentators of one true path to labor and economic development has faded, even as labor movements themselves have confronted problems more complex and subtle than independence versus absorption by strong states. Particularly in the circumstances of post-1970 disillusionment with a once-size-fits-all development model for the "Third World" and the rise of expansive welfarism (under both Christian Democratic as well as Social Democratic imprimatur) in Europe, what one political scientist calls "disguised corporatism" has made something of a political or at least policy-influencing comeback.[7] From an analytical perspective, abandonment of the bugaboo of corporatism has also made it easier to compare labor regimes north and south, identifying commonalities as well as differences.

As the essays in this volume attest, when it came to labor law, rapid change occurred both north and south in the twentieth century. In Latin America, if democratic and constitutionalist forces never vanquished the old elites or the constant threat of military intervention, fears of popular revolution pushed the holders of political and economic power to accommodate a new "corporate" body within the councils of state in the form of organized workers (i.e., through their state-approved labor unions). One functional result, among others, were the labor courts, which conventionally took a tripartite form, with "corporatist" representation from business, labor, and the state. Even as the Latin American republics were moving to accommodate new group interests, the English-speaking liberal democracies were themselves pushed to recognize the changing dimensions of the marketplace economy to which their laws applied. Industrial capitalism introduced powerful group actors, both as owners and workers, whose conflicts with each other demanded orderly if not consensual resolution. Slowly, mechanisms of conciliation, arbitration, and tripartite "Wagner boards" were also institutionalized, adding a strong "corporatist" element, however temporary, even within the most individual rights–conscious of legal systems.

Clearly, one major spur to hemispheric convergence in the instrumentality of dispute resolution was the world economic crisis of the 1930s. As historian Paulo Drinot notes in a recent, pertinent anthology, the era provoked "political eruptions from the Rio Grande to Tierra del Fuego." Yet, we can likely push out the geographic arms of this drafting compass even further. If, as Drinot notes, the development in Latin America of strong states (with varying versions of labor corporatism) occurred alongside a switch from export-led growth to ISI (import substitution industrialization), so a parallel move to national economic planning also produced the mid-twentieth-century creation of labor courts and institutionalization of collective bargaining in North America.[8] The upward revaluing of such policy initiatives among historians critical of the more recent neoliberal ascendancy is exemplified in Nelson Lichtenstein's influential 1989 essay, "From Corporatism to Collective Bargaining: Organized Labor and the Eclipse of Social Democracy in the Postwar Era."[9]

Even as world economic crisis provided the immediate political stimulus north and south toward accommodation and/or absorption/pacification of labor movements and worker grievances, a transnational intellectual frame for such moves had been established much earlier. Turn-of-the-twentieth-century railway and coal strikes had led enlightened conservatives like Mackenzie King in Canada and Carroll Wright and Mark Hanna in the United States toward embrace of government-mediated conciliation and arbitration plans, if only as a hedge against more radical assertions of power by organized industrial workers. Already by World War I, tripartism had been selectively enacted in Canada's Industrial Disputes Investigation Act and advanced in the United States, individual steps including the Pullman Commission of 1894, the garment workers' 1910 Protocol of Peace, Professor John R. Commons's recommendations for the Commission on Industrial Relations, 1912–1915, and the workings of President Wilson's National War Labor Board, 1917–1918. Still, as a 1949 ILO study of labor courts confirmed, there was no doubt but that the British-derived industrial relations systems in North America leaned more heavily than their southern counterparts on "free collective bargaining," i.e., without government interference, and moved away from that standard of "voluntary agreement" only under compelling, exceptional circumstance.[10] It is telling, in this light, that the same Republican congressional majority that in 1947 passed the restrictive Taft-Hartley Amendments to the National Labor Relations Act, showed little interest in a proposal by two of its members to create a system of separate labor courts.[11]

By way of contrast, Latin American countries reached out earlier and without apparent qualm toward legislative-sanctioned labor tribunals. As in continental Europe, where the French, the Swedes, and the Germans had all established elaborate forms of dispute resolution by the 1920s, Latin American labor courts appeared to spring up within the normative process of state building. Article 123 of the Mexican revolutionary constitution of 1917—mandating tripartite arbitration and conciliation boards—likely set the hemispheric standard for assuaging class conflict through progressive, positive law. The principles of 1917 would be further consolidated in yet another legal breakthrough, the federal labor law (LFT) of 1931. To be sure, things did not work out in Mexico quite as planned. With de facto civil war and governmental instability extending throughout these decades, it was less the law on the books, however protective of worker and trade union rights, than the executive authority of the administrative state that either delivered or withheld "labor justice." With the labor movements of the revolutionary years largely merged by the 1940s into the unchallengeable governing party (renamed the Institutional Revolutionary Party or PRI in 1946), the labor courts, like the unions themselves, as Suarez-Potts summarizes, suffered from constant manipulation of politicians as well as suffocating bureaucratic delay. Rather than ascribed to any deep cultural inheritance, Mexican "corporatism" may better be seen as the product of failed social democracy, a case of a "too-friendly" (in Poblete Troncoso's words) government swallowing up the social movement it had come to serve.

Even the influences shaping the continent's classic "corporatist" regimes of Brazil and Argentina were clearly multiple and hedged with constant contingency. Yes, the rhetoric and example of Mussolini's interwar Italy did capture the fancy of both Presidents Getulio Vargas and Juan Perón. But, in terms of government-labor connections, in each case the foundations were laid earlier and with a more determinedly demo-cratic inspiration. Thus, in Brazil, labor attorney Evaristo de Moraes called for tribunals as early as 1905 and, soon after, the Brazilian Workers' Congress followed suit. When Vargas's post-1930 revolutionary regime established a corporatist Labor Ministry, trade union law, and labor court (the latter not fully operationalized until the Estado Novo dictatorship post-1937), it notably included old labor activists like de Moraes. Moreover, as Chapter 9 documents, the most prominent strategist of the fully fash-ioned Labour Court of 1941 and Consolidated Labor Laws (CLT) of 1943 looked to U.S. constitutional law and Weimar-era Labor Courts in Germany as much as Italy for inspiration.

In the case of the labor courts in Argentina, it seems even more evident that the corporatist "form" was less important than an ongoing social struggle erupting within and outside governmental jurisdiction. Protective labor legislation, based on new theories of "social law" championed by Alfredo Palacios at the University of Buenos Aires in the 1910s created all the intellectual justification that Peron's expansive labor secretary (STP) would need beginning with the military government of 1943. There-after, the "labor judges" and special courts created by Peron would do intense battle with the more conservative rulings of the nation's Supreme Court. As Juan Manuel Palacio makes clear, Argentina's brand of "corporatism" owed less to the governmen-tal forms themselves than a broader, ongoing struggle for control between Peron and oligarchical interests. Precisely because the balance of power remained long in doubt, the trade unions, among other forces in civil society, continued to exercise consider-able political leverage.[12]

Finally, and contrary to the onset of "reforms" forged or abetted by revolution, coups, or other forms of coercion, labor courts came piecemeal to Colombia. Indeed, initial steps toward government regulation of labor markets occurred during the extended electoral hegemony of Conservative regimes (broken only by the tragic rout of the banana workers strike in 1928), while a breakthrough toward far-reaching fac-tory inspections and labor courts occurred through the orderly parliamentary auspices of business reformer and Liberal Party President López Pumarejo. Drawing initial support from Communists as well as Catholic Social Actionists and presided over by a determinedly and self-consciously "liberal" ruling party, Colombia's tripartite tribunals—seemingly as comprehensive in their reach as anywhere else in the hemi-sphere—confirms just how consensual was the acceptance of statist intervention in labor disputes across the non–English-speaking countries.

. . .

While the foregoing essays are strongest in positioning the labor courts as part of the rise and consolidation of what I have called the mediatory state, a process that carries us roughly up through the 1960s, several also conclude by pointing to the more recent unraveling or direct reversal of that same process. As national economic planning has proved more difficult in the face of heightened global market determinants, trade union power has eroded along with related welfarist policy commitments. To be sure, the implications of the global marketplace on national systems of labor justice, like the systems themselves, are likely to vary. The evidence stated earlier, for example, alludes to a concerted attack and subsequent weakening of the labor court mechanism in Costa Rica in the 1990s, while Brazil, to the contrary, experienced ever wider use of the courts as one of the few refuges left for individual worker grievances in the face of weakened labor institutions. The most tragic reversal of labor gains in the post-postwar era likely occurred with the 1973 overthrow of Salvadore Allende's Popular Unity government in Chile and its replacement by the dictatorship of Augusto Pinochet. In a sense, the Chilean coup merely punctuated the demise of Poblete Troncoso's (and the larger ORIT) vision of strong trade unionism and liberal democracy, combined with limited state intervention. Indeed, not only could such a formula not be passed to the South, it was increasingly inoperative in the North as well. As it happens, one prominent victim of the Pinochet coup d'etat was a former general of the Chilean Air Force and economic minister in the Allende government, who was detained and badly tortured before being ultimately exiled to Belgium. General Sergio Poblete Garces was the son of distinguished labor jurist, Poblete Troncoso.[13]

Apart from the contemporary-era drift toward deregulation of labor markets and consequent weakening of labor unions, state-based labor protections, and reach of labor courts, however, the essays in this volume also point to the longer term limits of "labor justice." Many workers, in short, were never "protected" in the first place, particularly among those whose circumstances made it difficult or impossible to organize in powerful collectivities. In the United States, for example, domestics and farmworkers (categories with both gender and strong racial overtones) were initially excluded from the Wagner Act as well as Social Security. Within this volume, Chapter 7 on the Andean nations likely offers the most explicit accounting for those left out of the legal labor regimes in Latin America; in particular, it suggests the vast social territory of indigenous peoples long proved a terra incognita of labor justice claims. Moreover, even if gender, race, and indigenous "rights" claims have, in recent decades, begun to rectify a century or more of legal neglect, the expansion of *informal* labor markets, whether among flower vendors and chewing-gum hawkers on city streets or within the more upscale "sharing economy" of Uber drivers and personal shopping assistants leaves unresolved the question of whether the ranks of social exclusions from national labor laws are growing or diminishing. The law, as our authors all attest, forms but one key element of the hemisphere's larger political history.

Notes

1. Clagett, 81–98. The only Latin American countries without labor courts were Cuba, the Dominican Republic, Haiti, Honduras, Paraguay, and Uruguay.
2. Rosenberg, 13, 190–201.

3. Millen, 5.
4. Poblete Troncoso and Burnett, 142.
5. Ibid., 14, 18, 150.
6. Ibid., 153.
7. Adams, 59.
8. Drinot, 1, 5–6.
9. Lichtenstein, 122–152.
10. ILO, 10, 17.
11. Ibid., 15; Vickery, 548–636.
12. In addition to Chapter 8, the argument here is indebted to Adelman, 19–42.
13. Felices 93 al augilucho General Sergio Poblete: http://www.cctt.cl/correo/index .php?option=com_content&view=article&id=2417:felices-93-al-aguilucho-general-r -sergio-poblete&catid=24&Itemid=60; Sergio Poblete: https://es.wikipedia.org/wiki /Sergio_Poblete (accessed April 4, 2017).

Bibliography

Adams, Paul S. "Corporatism in Latin America and Europe: Origins, Developments, and Challenges in Comparative Perspective." In *Authoritarianism and Corporatism in Latin America—Revisited*, ed. Howard J. Wiarda. 58–87. Gainesville: University Press of Florida, 2004.

Adelman, Jeremy. "Labour Law in Twentieth Century Argentina." In *The Rise and Development of Collective Labour Law, International and Comparative Social History*, ed. Marcel van der Linden and Richard Price. Vol. 6. Berlin: Peter Lang, 2000.

Clagett, Helen L. *Administration of Justice in Latin America.* New York: Oceana Publications, 1952.

Drinot, Paulo. Introduction. In *The Great Depression in Latin America*, ed. Drinot and Alan Knight. Durham, N.C.: Duke University Press, 2014.

International Labour Office (ILO). "Labour Courts in Latin America," *Studies and Reports* No. 13. Geneva: ILO, 1949.

Lichtenstein, Nelson. "From Corporatism to Collective Bargaining: Organized Labor and the Eclipse of Social Democracy in the Postwar Era." In *The Rise and Fall of the New Deal Order, 1930–1980*, ed. Steve Fraser and Gary Gerstle. Princeton, N.J.: Princeton University Press, 1989.

Millen, Bruce H. *The Political Role of Labor in Developing Countries.* Brookings Institution: Washington, D.C., 1963.

Poblete Troncoso, Moisés, and Ben G. Burnett. *The Rise of the Latin American Labor Movement.* New Haven, Conn.: College and University Press, 1960, 142.

Rosenberg, Emily S. *Spreading The American Dream: American Economic and Cultural Expansion, 1890–1945.* New York: Hill And Wang, 1982.

Vickery, Merritt A. "Labor Relations Law: The Ferguson-Smith Bill to Create Labor Courts." *American Bar Association Journal* 33, 6 (1947): 548–636.

Contributors

ROSSANA BARRAGÁN ROMANO is senior researcher at the International Institute of Social History in Amsterdam. Among her most recent articles are "Dynamics of Continuity and Change: Shifts in Labour Relations in the Potosí Mines (1680–1812)," in *International Review of Social History* 61, (December 2016); "Working Silver for the World: Mining Labor and Popular Economy in Colonial Potosi," in *Hispanic American Historical Review* 97 (May 9, 2017) and "La geografía diferencial de los derechos: entre la regulación del trabajo forzado en los países coloniales y la disociación entre trabajadores e indígenas en los Andes (1920–1954)" (2017). She is now writing a book on the role of popular economy in the mining industry in Potosí.

ANGELA DE CASTRO GOMES is professor at the Fluminense Federal University, emerita professor at the Center for Research and Documentation in Contemporary History of Brazil of the Getúlio Vargas Foundation, and a senior national visiting professor at the Federal University of the State of Rio de Janeiro. She is the author of *The Invention of "Trablahismo"* (2005, 3rd ed.); *Bourgeoisie and Work* (2014, 2nd ed.); and with Fernando Teixeira da Silva, *The Labor Justice and Its History* (2013). She has also coordinated projects that resulted in books, including *Rights and Citizenship* (2007, 2 Vol.) and *Looking Inside 1930–1964*, from the Collection Brazil's Nation (2012, Vol. 4).

DAVID DÍAZ-ARIAS is a full professor of history and director of the Center for Central American Historical Studies at the Universidad de Costa Rica. His recent articles and books examine the constitution of populism, social movements, state building, civil war, peace process, and memory battles in Central America during the nineteenth and twentieth centuries. Among his works are *Crisis social y memorias en lucha: guerra civil* *en Costa Rica (1940–1948)* (2015) and "From Radicals to Heroes of the Republic: Anarchism and National Identity in Costa Rica, 1900–1977," in Geoffroy de Laforcade and Kirwin Shaffer, eds., *In Defiance of Boundaries: Anarchism in Latin American History* (2015).

LEON FINK is distinguished professor of history emeritus at the University of Illinois at Chicago and editor of the academic journal *Labor: Studies in Working-Class History*. He is the author or editor of a dozen books, including, most recently, *The Long Gilded Age: American Capitalism and the Promise of a New World Order* (2015).

FRANK LUCE, LLB, PhD, is an associate fellow of the Harriet Tubman Institute, York University, Toronto. He practiced labor law with the trade union movement in Canada and he has published in the area of labor justice and rural workers in Brazil and Angola. He has recently published a series of articles on the relation between Canadian missionaries and liberation movements in Angola, in association with the Tubman Institute's Luso-African Research Group.

DIEGO ORTÚZAR is a PhD student of history at the *École des Hautes Etudes en Sciences Sociales* (EHESS) of Paris. His research focuses on Chile's modern labor and health history and he is the author of the articles "Legislación y medicina en torno a los accidentes del trabajo en Chile, 1900–1940" (2013) and "La política de las enfermedades profesionales: Anquilostomiasis y silicosis en Chile, 1920–1940" (2015).

GERMÁN PALACIO is professor at Universidad Nacional de Colombia. He is a lawyer from Universidad del Rosario, MSc from the Law School at the University of Wisconsin-Madison, and PhD in history from Florida International University, Miami. His published books and articles treat subjects in legal sociology, state formation, globalization, and political ecology.

JUAN MANUEL PALACIO is professor of Latin American history at Universidad de San Martín and Universidad Torcuato Di Tella (Argentina) and a full researcher at the Argentine National Research Council (CONICET). He obtained his PhD at the University of California at Berkeley (2000). A specialist in Argentine and Latin American rural history, his current research focuses on the legal history of Latin America. He has published several articles and books, and edited volumes on those subjects, including *La paz del trigo* (2004), *Justicia, política y derechos en América Latina* (2007), and *Historia de la provincia de Buenos Aires* (2011–2015, 6 volumes).

WILLIAM SUAREZ-POTTS is associate professor of history at Kenyon College. He specializes in legal and labor history and is the author of *The Making of Law: The Supreme Court and Labor Legislation in Mexico, 1875–1931* (Stanford University Press, 2012).

FERNANDO TEIXEIRA DA SILVA is an associate professor at the History Department of Universidade Estadual de Campinas (UNICAMP) and director of the Centro de Pesquisa em História Social da Cultura (CECULT–UNICAMP). He has written articles and books on Brazilian labor history, including *Trabalhadores no tribunal: conflitos e Justiça do Trabalho em São Paulo no contexto do Golpe de 1964* (São Paulo, 2016) and *Operários sem patrões: os trabalhadores da cidade de Santos no entreguerras* (Campinas, 2003). His current research focuses on the comparison between the Brazilian and American labor relations systems.

VICTOR M. URIBE-URAN is a professor of history and law at Florida International University. He is the author, editor, or coeditor of five books including, most recently, *Fatal Love: Spousal Murders, Law and Punishment in the Late Colonial Spanish Atlantic* (Stanford University Press, 2016). Apart from historical work, Dr. Uribe-Uran also works on contemporary legal issues such as judicial reform, the judiciary, and the inter-American legal system.

ANGELA VERGARA is a professor of history at California State University Los Angeles. She obtained her BA in history at the Pontificia Universidad Católica de Chile in Santiago, Chile (1994) and her PhD at the University of California San Diego (2002). Her research focuses on Chile's modern social and labor history. She is the author of *Copper Workers, International Business, and Domestic Politics in Cold War Chile* (2008) and coeditor of *Company Towns in the Americas* (2011) and the special issue of *Radical History Review*, *The Other 9/11: Chile 1973—Memory, Resistance and Democratization* (2016).

RONNY VIALES-HURTADO is full professor of history and director of Graduate Studies in History at the Universidad de Costa Rica. His interests include inequality and poverty studies, economic and environmental history, and social studies of science. Among his recent works are *Historia de las desigualdades sociales en América Central* (San José, 2016), edited with the collaboration of David Díaz-Arias; "Between Matilde and Internet: Computerizing the University of Costa Rica (1968–1993)," in *IEEE Annals of the History of Computing* (2015), with the collaboration of Ana Lucía Calderón and David Chavarría.

Index

LEON FINK is distinguished professor of history emeritus at the University of Illinois at Chicago. His books include *The Long Gilded Age: American Capitalism and the Promise of the New World Order*.

JUAN MANUEL PALACIO is a researcher at the National Research Council of Argentina and author of *La paz del trigo: cultura legal y sociedad local en el desarrollo agropecuario pampeano, 1890–1945*.

THE WORKING CLASS IN AMERICAN HISTORY

Civic Labors: Scholar Activism and Working-Class Studies   *Edited by Dennis Deslippe,*
   Eric Fure-Slocum, and John W. McKerley
Victor Arnautoff and the Politics of Art   *Robert W. Cherny*
Against Labor: How U.S. Employers Organized to Defeat Union Activism
   Edited by Rosemary Feurer and Chad Pearson
Teacher Strike! Public Education and the Making of a New American Political Order
   Jon Shelton
Hillbilly Hellraisers: Federal Power and Populist Defiance in the Ozarks   *J. Blake Perkins*
Sewing the Fabric of Statehood: Garment Unions, American Labor, and the Establishment
   of the State of Israel   *Adam Howard*
Labor and Justice across the America   *Edited by Leon Fink and Juan Manuel Palacio*